THE GARDENER'S GUIDE TO
PROPAGATION

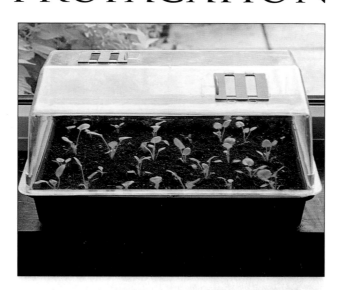

THE GARDENER'S GUIDE TO
PROPAGATION

STEP-BY-STEP INSTRUCTIONS FOR CREATING PLANTS FOR FREE, FROM
PROPAGATING SEEDS AND CUTTINGS TO DIVIDING, LAYERING AND GRAFTING

RICHARD ROSENFELD

PHOTOGRAPHY BY PETER ANDERSON

LORENZ BOOKS

This edition is published by
Lorenz Books
an imprint of Anness Publishing Ltd
Hermes House
88–89 Blackfriars Road
London SE1 8HA
tel. 020 7401 2077; fax 020 7633 9499

www.lorenzbooks.com
www.annesspublishing.com

If you like the images in this book and would
like to investigate using them for publishing,
promotions or advertising, please visit
our website www.practicalpictures.com
for more information.

UK distributor: Book Trade Services;
tel. 0116 2759086;
fax 0116 2759090;
uksales@booktradeservices.com;
exportsales@booktradeservices.com

North American distributor:
National Book Network;
tel. 301 459 3366;
fax 301 429 5746;
www.nbnbooks.com

Australian distributor:
Pan Macmillan Australia;
tel. 1300 135 113;
fax 1300 135 103;
customer.service@macmillan.com.au

New Zealand distributor:
David Bateman Ltd;
tel. (09) 415 7664;
fax (09) 415 8892

Publisher: Joanna Lorenz
Senior Editor: Felicity Forster
Photography Manager and Proofreader:
    Andrew Mikolajski
Photography: Peter Anderson
Illustrator: Liz Pepperell
Designer: Nigel Partridge
Editorial Reader: Penelope Goodare
Proofreading Manager: Lindsay Zamponi
Production Controller: Wendy Lawson

© Anness Publishing Ltd 2011

ETHICAL TRADING POLICY
At Anness Publishing we believe that
business should be conducted in an ethical
and ecologically sustainable way, with
respect for the environment and a proper
regard to the replacement of the natural
resources we employ.

As a publisher, we use a lot of wood pulp
in high-quality paper for printing, and that
wood commonly comes from spruce trees.
We are therefore currently growing more
than 750,000 trees in three Scottish forest
plantations: Berrymoss (130 hectares/
320 acres), West Touxhill (125 hectares/
305 acres) and Deveron Forest (75 hectares/
185 acres). The forests we manage contain
more than 3.5 times the number of trees
employed each year in making paper for
the books we manufacture.

Because of this ongoing ecological
investment programme, you, as our
customer, can have the pleasure and
reassurance of knowing that a tree is
being cultivated on your behalf to naturally
replace the materials used to make the
book you are holding.

Our forestry programme is run in
accordance with the UK Woodland
Assurance Scheme (UKWAS) and will be
certified by the internationally recognized
Forest Stewardship Council (FSC). The
FSC is a non-government organization
dedicated to promoting responsible
management of the world's forests.
Certification ensures forests are managed
in an environmentally sustainable and
socially responsible way. For further
information about this scheme, go to
www.annesspublishing.com/trees.

PUBLISHER'S NOTES
Although the advice and information in
this book are believed to be accurate and
true at the time of going to press, neither
the authors nor the publisher can accept
any legal responsibility or liability for any
errors or omissions that may have been
made, nor for any loss, harm or injury that
comes about from following instructions
in this book.

Great care should be taken if you decide
to include pools, ponds or water features
as part of your garden landscape. Young
children should never be left unsupervised
near water of any depth, and if children are
able to access the garden all pools and
ponds should be fenced and gated to the
recommended specifications.

In the United States, throughout the Sun
Belt states, from Florida, across the Gulf
Coast, southern Texas, southern deserts to
southern California and the coastal regions,
annuals are planted in the autumn, bloom
in the winter and spring, and die at the
beginning of summer.

Contents

Introduction

Propagation is thrilling and easy. When you are new to gardening, propagation might sound highly specialized, but it is exactly what you do every time you sow lettuces and chilli peppers, marigolds and nasturtiums. Anyone can do it. It is the art of creating more through a natural process. But, like everything else in gardening, you need expert tips on what to do and when, what works and what does not.

Most of the techniques in this book are just clever adaptations of what is happening in the wild. We explore everything you might need to know, from making sure you have all the right equipment and understand the nature and requirements of your soil to learning about seed – reproduction, dispersal mechanisms, germination, collection, sowing (indoors and out), and looking out for potential threats. The book then focuses on the other five major areas: cuttings; division; propagating bulbs, tubers and corms; layering; and grafting.

Propagating is especially useful because it will save you a fortune, will help you create larger numbers of favourite plants and, best of all, lets you see nature at work in close up.

LEFT Just a few packets of seed can inject borders with a long-lasting, eye-catching show of summer reds and yellows.

Why propagate?

Once a garden is in full swing, it is a good idea to keep propagating for three very important reasons. First, propagating fills unexpected gaps – and even in the best-planned garden these will occur, often around newly bought plants (especially shrubs) which have not yet reached their full size. Such spaces provide an excellent chance to grow and experiment with colourful annuals. Second, propagating provides replacements for mature plants that are getting tired and ragged, and no longer produce a particularly attractive flower display. Third, it allows you to grow a wide range of annual crops in the vegetable garden. It is important to keep thinking ahead so that you have always got new plants to hand.

ABOVE When propagating your own plants to create a new border or fill gaps, it is vital that you inject plenty of variety – in terms of shapes and colour – to ensure a varied flow with lots of interesting, eye-catching 'highs' and 'lows'.

Filling gaps

Anyone can rearrange a room and get it right the first time. Try that with a garden. Medium-size plants suddenly become very big, casting those behind in shade, colour combinations that sounded thrilling look positively quotidian, while other plants sit and sulk and refuse to look like their press release. Time to act and rearrange, and with new combinations come new gaps and the need for repeat planting so that the best colours echo throughout the garden, leading the eye to new areas.

Once you have got one key plant, it is usually a simple job to create extra numbers from it. At the simplest level, look for one large, plump specimen, and immediately divide it into several more. One perennial could yield three or four plants immediately if you gently tease it apart or use a knife to slice it up, making sure that each new plant has the two basics needed for survival: a good root system to drink and feed and anchor it in the ground, and good top growth for photosynthesis, a self-powering chain reaction using energy from sunlight.

Dividing is what is called vegetative propagation – and that involves every kind of technique

ABOVE Strawberries are one of the easiest plants to propagate because they virtually do all the work for you, sending out runners. Once they have rooted, sever the link and use the young plants to fill any gaps.

LEFT From a spring sowing you can get a vegetable bed that is packed with produce, keeping you going right through summer.

LEFT The greenhouse is the engine room of the garden, where everything begins. Buy the biggest greenhouse you can because once you start growing your own plants, you will always find scores of new varieties to try.

Replacing mature plants

Some plants fire up so much growth that they gradually become congested in the centre and die out. In the wild they have space to expand, with the new growth occurring at the fringes, but, in a beautifully crafted border where everything has to earn its place, who wants a plant with gappy, poor growth in the middle? Again, dividing a plant to use the fresh, new, vigorous outer growth means that you get new plants for elsewhere in the garden, and can replace the old, poorly performing one. Other plants do not just die out in the centre; they die out altogether after a few years. They have a short shelf-life. Others become so big that they need to be thrown out and replaced by a younger version. Being able to propagate means that you will always have a solution to these problems.

except for seed sowing. You are basically creating new, uniform plants from a grown, established plant, using anything from a division to a severed root, leaf or shoot. Shoots are certainly one the easiest ways of growing new plants and plugging gaps. Just nip off new, young, non-flowering shoots that are growing strongly and plant each shoot in a small container. They will soon root, grow and branch out. Why multiple numbers? So that you have got spares in case you have an accident with the first. And why small containers? So that the cuttings do not get waterlogged and rot and die, which is what might happen if they sit and stagnate in a large pot of wet compost. The extent of the young, emerging roots should be commensurate with the size of the container.

Some shoots do not need to be immediately severed from the parent to create a new plant. When they come in contact with soil, they tend to root where they are, which

is why a sucker (spearing out of the ground from part of the parent plant, beneath the soil) can be left to get a good root system before it is then used as a new plant. If the top growth of other plants is bent to the ground and pinned in place, or is left growing when covered in piles of soil, it too will root and can eventually be severed to make a healthy, substantial new plant. All can be used to flesh out a border.

RIGHT A traditional spring-bedding scene with standard roses above rows of tulips. As soon as the latter have faded, they can be dug up and replaced by newly sown summer annuals.

ABOVE Once you have raised your first batch of poppies, collect their seed for next year.

Growing a wider range of crops

If you want a productive kitchen garden, no matter what size, you have got to learn the basics of seed propagation because crops such as beans, carrots, courgettes, cucumbers, leeks, lettuces and tomatoes are all grown from (ideally fresh) packets of seed. All of these annuals grow like a typical flower (see Anatomy of a Plant), producing a good set of feeding roots – which will also stabilize the plant in the ground – and stems or leafy growth. Some flower before they crop (e.g. courgettes and tomatoes), providing us with the tasty, fleshy covering around a batch of seeds, while others (e.g. lettuces) must be eaten before they start to flower. Once a lettuce does this (called 'bolting'), the taste becomes too sharp and bitter.

Sexual reproduction

In general, the best way to get an exact copy of a plant is by vegetative propagation. Some plants do not set viable seed in cool climates (*Stipa gigantea*), many with double flowers

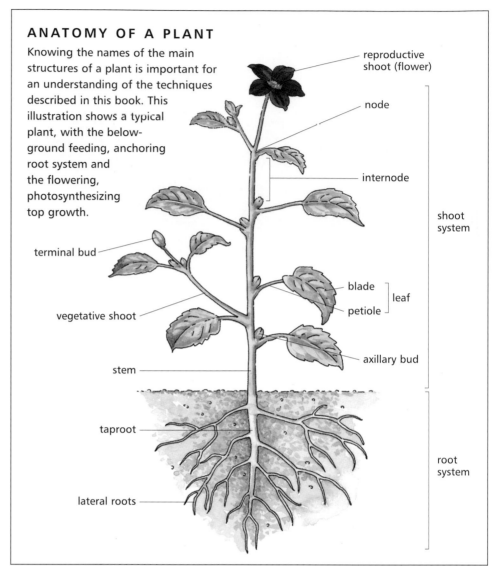

ANATOMY OF A PLANT

Knowing the names of the main structures of a plant is important for an understanding of the techniques described in this book. This illustration shows a typical plant, with the below-ground feeding, anchoring root system and the flowering, photosynthesizing top growth.

reproductive shoot (flower)
node
internode
shoot system
terminal bud
blade
petiole
leaf
vegetative shoot
axillary bud
stem
taproot
root system
lateral roots

ABOVE The species crocus *Crocus tommasinianus* will self-seed freely to produce prodigious sheets of flowers in spring. It naturalizes easily in grass and thrives in light woodland.

ABOVE A very practical cold frame with high light levels for raising young plants. The large shape allows the plants to be spaced out nicely, giving good air circulation.

ABOVE An impressive display of border wallflowers can be easily raised from seed.

tend to be sterile (primroses), some need a separate male and female plant (most hollies), and the seed of most cultivars will not recreate the parent exactly, although there are always some exceptions (including *Borago officinalis* 'Alba', *Lobelia* 'Queen Victoria' and *Viola* 'Bowles Black'). Because seed carries the genetic characteristics of two parents, there is inbuilt variety. That is good news for the plants and for us.

Genetic diversity increases the likelihood of survival when the environment might change, and it might make a species even more successful in its existing environment. You might well find a seedling in the garden that is a new, absolute beauty. Plant breeders are constantly trying to find newer, better plants with more disease resistance, longevity, scent, weather resistance and ease of growing, allied to an attractive shape and a long season of good colour (with excellent yield, taste and storage in the case of crops). They are trying to engineer plants that sell

well. Most plants grown in gardens are basically wild plants that have been modified by humans. Some are modified by nature when a genetic change causes a mutation, a typical example being a shoot with variegated leaves. If a gardener sees a branch with beautifully variegated leaves, they can take a cutting and, with luck, be able to name the new, best-selling cultivar something like 'Now I'm Rich'. Propagation does not just keep the garden alive, it keeps gardening alive with new possibilities.

In this book

This book takes you carefully through each stage of the propagation process, so that no matter what kind of plant you want to raise, you will know what to do and when. Of course, there is no point in propagating unless you can raise the new young plants properly, so a section on knowing your garden soil will ensure that you will be able to get the best possible results. Then come the six key areas: propagating by seed, cuttings, division, propagating underground

storage organs (bulbs, tubers and corms), layering and grafting. The final part of the book is an A–Z directory of plants, with propagating notes and growing tips throughout, to help you choose the best plants for propagating in your garden.

ABOVE A collection of young plants being raised in a large, light, airy polytunnel.

DIY Propagation

Propagating your own plants is a fun, cheap way of packing your garden with everything from shrubs to crops, and you don't need that much equipment. Almost everything is small, cheap or a one-off buy that will last for years. The only big decision is whether you are going to buy a polytunnel or greenhouse, and where you're going to put it. Find specialist brochures and, when you've got a shortlist, check with the manufacturers so that you can inspect the equipment before you buy it. Also, buy the largest polytunnel or greenhouse you've got room for because you can use it for growing a wide range of tender crops that will thrive far better inside than out, and for storing tender plants over winter. And once you're hooked…

Growing your own plants also means understanding your soil, and keeping it in peak condition. Unless you have got perfect loam, there are all kinds of ways of improving the ground so that your plants give a terrific display. Check the notes on the following pages to see how you can improve the structure, giving better aeration and drainage, and upgrade the fertility.

This chapter covers everything you need to do in order to get started, from buying equipment such as secateurs and dibbers, to testing your soil and making your own compost.

LEFT It does not take long for a batch of seedlings to become a major part of the summer garden. Make sure that they are well watered, spaced out and standing in bright, but not scorching, light.

Getting started

You can propagate plants using just a few pots and bags of compost (soil mix), but the moment you start tackling large numbers of different plants, you will need more equipment. All is readily available, and the only major acquisition is a greenhouse or polytunnel.

Secateurs

Choose the bypass or parrot kind that act like a pair of scissors with two sharp blades slicing past each other giving a good, clean cut. Anvil secateurs instead rely on one blade cutting down on to a softer piece of metal, inevitably crushing and damaging the stem in the process. Price is a good indication of quality, but a good pair will last many years, especially if well maintained. Many manufacturers run a repair-and-sharpen service, or sell spare parts. Avoid using secateurs for any purpose other than taking cuttings and pruning, and never use them to cut wire, even if it means a lengthy walk back to the garden shed for wire cutters. Keep them regularly cleaned, oiled and sharpened.

Knives (garden, budding, grafting, scalpel)

Knives give a good, clean cut when taking cuttings, without any chance of damaging the stem tissue, reducing the chances of successful

ABOVE Biodegradable containers

propagation. All need to be regularly sharpened and cleaned. Cut toward yourself for maximum control.

Containers

The range of containers includes plastic seed trays with clear plastic covers or lids, pots (biodegradable and plastic), root trainers, modules and even lengths of guttering. Seed trays are the best option when you are sowing large numbers of a

particular plant, but pricking out tight, congested clumps can be tricky so try to space out the seedlings when sowing. Do not delay pricking out, because you will end up with a mass of intermingling, knotted roots that grow down and then out horizontally, making separation very difficult. Pots are ideal for small numbers of seed, the best option being plastic because it is durable, light and quick to wash clean. Biodegradable pots, made from compressed peat or wood fibre, are ideal for plants that hate root disturbance. When the roots poke out of the sides and bottom, you simply put the pot and the seedling in a bigger container and fill in with compost (soil mix), although biodegradable pots can badly dry out or, conversely, go mouldy if kept too wet. Clay pots are certainly more attractive but are more expensive and

LEFT Plastic and terracotta containers

ABOVE Plastic modules

ABOVE Secateurs

ABOVE Scalpel

ABOVE Root trainers

ABOVE Soil sieve

ABOVE Horticultural sand and grit

cover tiny seed needing good light to germinate. Other alternatives for improved aeration and drainage include coarse horticultural sand or grit.

Soil sieve

Absolutely essential for covering tiny seed with a fine layer of compost (soil mix). A kitchen sieve is fine, separating the chaff from the dust.

Rooting powder

Most cuttings readily produce their own roots at the severed bottom end, ideally just below a node, but

LEFT Dibber

you can dip them in rooting powder (also available as a liquid) to encourage good results. Always tap off any excess.

Dibber

A pointed tool for making holes in compost (soil mix) or soil when sowing seed and inserting seedlings. Pencils or crayons can be used as an alternative.

Labels

All too easily overlooked, but inexpensive, stiff white plastic labels are absolutely invaluable (though the pencil writing eventually fades) for recording what has been sown and when. Always buy more than you need because there is nothing worse than planting up several seed trays and suddenly finding you've none left.

dry out quicker, losing moisture through evaporation via the sides. Root trainers (with hinged compartments) encourage deep roots that are not disturbed, and can be used for getting vegetables such as lettuces and beans off to an early start, growing them under cover for planting out the moment the weather is right, as well as for deep-rooted trees and shrubs. Modules (which are not hinged) also enable you to grow seedlings in separate compartments so that when they are potted on there's no root disturbance.

Drainage material

Seed needs to be grown in aerated, free-draining material, and it is worth adding some light perlite (sterile, inert rock granules). Similar vermiculite holds more water but less air. Both can also be used to just

ABOVE Perlite

ABOVE Vermiculite

ABOVE Rooting powder

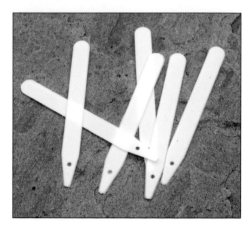

ABOVE Labels

ABOVE An upturned rose spray, arching a fine shower that will not damage young seedlings.

ABOVE The most useful propagators, such as the one shown here, have a range of temperature settings. More limited types are unheated, with a seed tray and a clear plastic lid.

Watering can

The most important prerequisite is the fine rose spray that can be turned face-up so that the spray arches up and then down in fine drops. Do not ruin a good batch of seedlings by sending a heavy bombardment of great big water drops straight down, which will batter and crush the weak stems and disturb the compost. Alternatively, stand small pots or seed trays in a large pan of water so that it soaks up, or use a special sprayer, holding several litres of water, with an adjustable nozzle that gives a fine misting and a good soaking.

Clear plastic bags

Excellent for slipping seed trays or pots inside to create a warm, humid atmosphere when germinating seed. The moment growth appears, promptly remove.

Propagator

Available in various sizes with varying degrees of sophistication (prices vary accordingly), they provide the warmth and humidity necessary to raise large numbers of plants. The temperature is electronically controlled. DIY kinds can be made using soil-warming cable. Always go for a large size.

Cold frame

The intermediate stage between a protected warm environment and life outdoors, where seedlings are hardened off and toughened up, and hardy seeds can be given a winter chilling. The term is a good literal description – a solid, unheated frame or low wall surrounds the plants, while a hinged, transparent lid can be closed or opened according to the weather.

Cloche

A traditional, portable means of protecting seedlings growing out in the open, and warming the soil. Use it to get crops off to an early

ABOVE It is very easy to create your own, very effective DIY propagator using just a pot and a large, clear plastic covering.

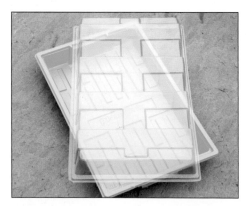

ABOVE Large unheated seed trays with a clear lid are ideal for raising hardy annuals and cuttings that do not need bottom heat.

ABOVE See-through cold frames might not be as strong as those with brick sides, but they let in more light. Stand in a sheltered place.

ABOVE A small cloche can double as a mini cold frame for just a few plants, or be used to cover an early crop until the weather improves.

ABOVE The advantage of a sunny, lean-to greenhouse is that the inside brick wall bounces back heat, ideal for producing grapes and figs.

start. Made from short metal hoops covered with clear plastic or glass. Remove immediately once the weather permits.

Nursery bed

A useful area, space permitting, where young plants can be grown until they are large enough to be planted out in their final position.

Greenhouse

The engine room of the garden, a greenhouse is almost a necessity. You can just about get by without

ABOVE In the kitchen garden, you can use an ornamental bell jar for covering and protecting a young plant in its final position.

one by raising young plants on a sunny windowsill, but there will not be room for many, and it can be a major inconvenience. The best advice is to decide what size greenhouse you need, and then buy one that is even bigger, providing a larger working space. The big choice is between aluminium, brick and wood, and the polytunnel. Aluminium is the easiest to care for with excellent interior light levels. Wood is more attractive, but casts more shade and needs some upkeep unless expensive cedar frames are used. Brick also looks attractive, and solid, but you can lose a lot of light to about waist height. Polytunnels are the most inexpensive option, but they are not that attractive, can be costly to heat (therefore are often used unheated), and might need running repairs to the fabric. In all cases look for internal structures that will provide supports for climbers. Also beware the build-up of pests and diseases, and note the need for good hygiene and summer ventilation, using side and roof vents in the greenhouse with shading, because temperatures inside can

rocket. Heated greenhouses obviously increase your growing options, especially with regard to tender plants, with electric heaters being easier than gas because of the need for ventilation to avoid the build-up of fumes and condensation. Paraffin heaters have several drawbacks (fumes and condensation), and need regular attention, but make a good emergency option. Being able to attach bubble plastic insulation in winter can make a big difference. Finally, stand the greenhouse away from trees and shade.

ABOVE Some containers are available with clear plastic domes that act like a mini-cloche to protect young plants.

Knowing your garden soil

You will never grow good plants unless you can grow them in the kind of soil they need. With new gardens, do check what kind of soil you've got, and if it is completely inappropriate for your crops, start improving it. You can have the best plants in the world, but if they're rooted in poor or the wrong soil, they will be an amazing let-down.

Plants' needs

Most soil was originally rock that has gradually been weathered and ground down over the centuries, and the kind of soil you have in your garden depends on which kind of rock it came from. The soil provides your plants with nutrients, and while it is possible to grow plants without any soil at all (using a technique called hydroponics), you will then have to make sure they're fed. Food is vital. Plant roots also need oxygen, found in the gaps between the soil particles, and water. Surprisingly,

ABOVE Before planting a border, check that you've got the right soil for your plants. Most summer annuals and perennials need free-draining ground, enriched with organic matter.

most root growth takes place in the top 10–15cm (4–6in) of soil, and even the roots of huge, mature trees rarely go deep, with well over 90 per cent well within the top 100cm (40in). They provide stability by

fanning out, also absorbing every bit of rain that soaks through the ground beneath the outer edge of the canopy. That is why few plants perform well beneath a tree because its massive network of near-horizontal roots are feeding on the nutrients in the top layer, quickly absorbing the moisture. It is also worth stressing that soil, as

SOIL PROFILE

The soil beneath trees will not suit all kinds of plants. This is because the extensive spreading root system is mainly found in the top layers, and it quickly absorbs the moisture and nutrients. The added shade from the canopy means that woodland-type plants – e.g. ivy (*Hedera hibernica*) – have the best chance of thriving.

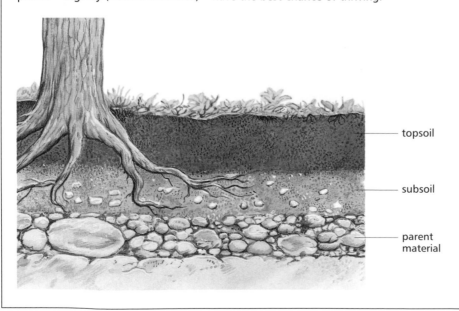

topsoil

subsoil

parent material

ABOVE To get a large crop of tomatoes, start regularly feeding the plant with potassium once the first batch of fruit has set.

ABOVE To create extra fruit-bearing branches on a chilli plant, give it an early feed of nitrogen.

Nutrient deficiencies

- Nitrogen – yellow foliage, especially lower down, accompanied by feeble growth with reduced branching.
- Phosphorus – poor growth with dull yellow leaves.
- Potassium – discoloured leaves that acquire purple, blue or yellow tints with brown blotching, and generally poor performance.
- Calcium – cupped leaf tips while the young leaves turn black.
- Magnesium – mottled yellowing on older leaves between the veins. Typically occurs when plants needing acid (or ericaceous) soil are grown on alkaline soil.
- Sulphur – stiff, erect foliage and new yellow leaves. Also often occurs when acid-loving plants are grown in alkaline soil.

To bolster nitrogen levels, use sulphate of ammonia or pelleted poultry manure, adding sulphate of potash to improve potassium levels, and superphosphate in the case of poor phosphorus levels. Magnesium and sulphur problems are often remedied by growing acid-loving plants in the correct soil, while extra magnesium is provided in the form of Epsom salts or magnesium sulphate.

mentioned, stabilizes plants in the ground, and provides a buffer against adverse temperature changes. When putting new plants in the ground, always firm them in well.

Nutrients

The six main soil nutrients essential for good plant growth are:

- Nitrogen
- Phosphorus
- Potassium
- Calcium
- Magnesium
- Sulphur

with boron, chlorine, copper, iron, manganese, molybdenum, nickel and zinc helping, while some plants also benefit from cobalt, silicon and sodium. The first three on the list are the most important. Nitrogen (called N on packets of fertilizer) promotes soft, leafy growth and determines the amount of growth a plant can make. Nitrogen levels are invariably low at the start of spring because so much has been sluiced out of the ground by winter rain, but bacterial activity

ensures that levels rise by the end of summer. It is very tempting to force feed leafy vegetables with plenty of nitrogen to generate even more growth, but too much soft growth can make them vulnerable to disease. They also need phosphorus (or P), which is vital in generating root growth. The third of the major nutrients is potassium (K), which boosts disease-resistant growth and, crucially, flower and fruit

development, which is why so much is bought each year for crops such as tomato plants to generate bigger fruit. Gardens rarely face any shortage of phosphorus (the possible exception being heavy clay after heavy rain) or potassium (possible exceptions being confined to light, sandy, or chalky soil following heavy winter deluges), but it is worth noting the possible symptoms should such cases arise.

LEFT Pale green or yellowish chlorotic leaves can be caused by mineral deficiencies, especially with excess lime, or poor light.

BELOW Plants are very quick to tell us when they are stressed. This badly neglected plant needs repotting and a good drink.

Fertilizer

Most gardens need only an all-purpose feed (that will last a few weeks) lightly forked into the soil a few weeks before planting. This boosts the plants in all the key areas (i.e. root, stem, leaf and flower growth). The strength of the feed is denoted by an NPK reading. So, 5:8:10 indicates 5 percent nitrogen, 8 of phosphorus and 10 of potassium, making it ideal for fruiting plants, such as tomatoes. 'Growmore' is an inorganic compound fertilizer, its organic counterpart being fish, blood and bone. For a quick nutrient boost, use a liquid form that is watered directly into the soil, where it can be taken up by the plants' roots.

Manure and compost

Also a valuable source of N, P and K, manure must be at least three months old before being used. However, you will not know how much N, P and K are contained, and this depends on the animals involved and their bedding.

RIGHT Worms are an essential part of the garden, helping to churn up a compost heap, while getting in extra oxygen.

IMPROVING THE SOIL

1 When adding organic matter to improve garden soil, use a fork to ensure that the two are thoroughly mixed.

2 When adding non-organic fertilizer to the soil, carefully follow the manufacturer's instructions and apply the correct amount.

3 When putting in new plants, take the opportunity to improve the soil by adding compost to the planting hole.

4 Apply a mulch twice a year, in spring and autumn, to help keep down weeds, keep the soil moist and protect plants' roots.

Well-rotted compost has poor nutrient levels but it is excellent in other ways. It is an incredibly good way of improving the soil structure, making it dark, crumbly and workable, especially where you have an extreme soil (for example, heavy clay or sand or chalk), thereby benefiting soil life, and of improving the water-holding capacity. Aim to add one full bucket to every 1m² (10sq ft).

Compost is also extremely valuable as a mulch. Pile it over the soil about 6cm (2½ in) deep in spring to block out any weeds and lock moisture into the ground, stopping it from quickly evaporating (which is why it is best applied after a night of heavy rain). In time it will break down, thereby also improving the soil. An autumn-winter mulch is invaluable because it will help insulate the plants' roots, protecting them from extreme temperatures.

Earthworms are also attracted to compost, and their presence is vital: they open up the soil, improving oxygen levels and drainage, and pulling organic matter on the surface underground.

DIY compost in 6 months

For your compost bin you have two basic choices, either bought (usually made from plastic, but sometimes wood) or home-made. If you only need small amounts, just one bin is fine, otherwise use three larger bins, each holding 750–1,000 litres (26½–35cu ft). One is used for filling, one will have been already filled and is 'cooking', while the third is used for spreading. Site the bins in a sunny position on forked up ground, giving good drainage and ensuring the presence of earthworms. If making your own bin, use wooden planks, at least 2.5cm (1in) thick.

All are nailed permanently in place to stout posts, except for the front ones, so that you can remove these and turn the compost over with a fork to aerate it. Also add a removable wooden 'lid' to keep the heap dry.

Fill your finished compost bin with shredded woody material (paper, cardboard and dead leaves, etc.) well mixed with about 35–45 per cent of kitchen waste, grass clippings, annual weeds, etc. When dry, sprinkle with water, and do not let any one ingredient dominate. Avoid adding materials such as cooked food which attracts rats, perennial weeds and diseased plants.

ABOVE A compost heap divided by walls into good-sized sections. The sturdy walls can be made from horizontal railway sleepers held in place by stout posts. It is important that there is plenty of room for the gardener to step into each pile and turn it over, getting in plenty of oxygen. A potential problem with such large compartments is keeping the material dry during wet weather.

LEFT A purpose-made compost bin. The door at the base allows you to remove the compost.

TURNING A COMPOST HEAP

1 Start from the front or back of the heap and work toward the other end. You want to make sure that every part is turned.

2 Take a large forkful and lift it up, exposing the area beneath. Turning a heap is more than just rearranging the surface.

3 Toss each clump up and down, getting in plenty of air, preventing the pile from becoming a solid, stagnant heap.

Soil types

Different soils have different characteristics, and it is important to know what you are working with. It is very easy to determine what kind of soil you have simply by holding it in your hand. The two extremes are:

• Clay – the tiny particles stick together enabling you to roll it into a sticky ball that keeps its shape. The good news is that it is potentially fertile, but drainage will be poor, and it takes a long time to warm up in spring. When dry, clay soil is inclined to form cracks on the surface; when it rains it swells and stays sopping wet. Heavy clay soil is also incredibly hard work when it comes to digging and weeding, being more like concrete in summer. It is, however, easily improved by adding composted organic matter, including composted bark and mushroom compost, and horticultural (or 'sharp') grit. Note that mushroom compost is alkaline and should not be used with acid-loving plants.

• Sandy – in complete contrast, it is gritty, light and free-draining with poor nutrient levels, and needs improving by adding lots of well-rotted compost on a regular basis to improve its moisture- and nutrient-holding capacity. This is particularly important if you are growing hungry plants such as roses.

Other soil types include:

• Chalk – it is obvious by the presence of chalky lumps, making the soil very free draining. Again, it can be improved by adding compost.

• Loam – the ideal soil, but all too rarely found, it clings loosely together and consists of clay, sand and silt.

The 'no-dig' philosophy

Organic gardeners dislike digging up beds, taking the 'no-dig' approach. The advantages are that weed seed is not brought to the surface, the soil structure stays intact and nutrient levels remain consistent. The 'no-dig' approach also relies heavily on earthworm activity (which is disrupted by deep digging) and organic mulches, which means that all the action is taking place near the surface. So, there's no danger of the topsoil (with the good water-retention of its organic matter) and the much poorer subsoil getting mixed up when digging. To be really effective, 'no-dig' should be reserved for areas with weed-free, light, free-draining soil. In effect, everyone practises this system in the flower garden. Once beds have been dug up with organic material added, they are not tampered with except when holes are 'trowelled out' for new plants. Some gardeners like to dig larger holes than necessary, using the opportunity to add extra quantities of well-rotted organic compost, but even then this is a relatively small amount of digging compared to the vegetable garden that is traditionally dug up and churned over, sometimes several times, in winter. A good compromise is to 'no-dig' the vegetable patch every other year or so.

Alkalinity, acidity and pH

It is important to know the pH of your soil, because this determines what kind of plants you can grow. If your neighbours grow azaleas, rhododendrons and camellias then the soil is acid, but use a simple pH testing kit to get an accurate reading.

Testing kits come in two kinds: the meter (see the pH test, right) and the colour chart. The latter involves taking a soil sample and mixing it in a test tube with distilled water. Give the tube a firm shake and

RECOGNIZING CLAY, SANDY AND LOAMY SOILS

ABOVE Clay is immediately recognizable, readily forming solid lumps of soil. Press your thumb in and it will leave a clear imprint.

ABOVE Sandy soil is the complete opposite, being open, crumbly and friable. It is easy to work but lacks nutrients.

ABOVE Loam, with a mix of nutritious clay and sand which provides good drainage is what everyone wants but few gardens offer.

LEFT To grow rhododendrons like this, you need a garden with acid soil.

BELOW If you cannot provide acid soil, you must grow the rhododendron in a large container filled with special ericaceous (acid) compost (soil mix).

let the mixture settle. Finally, check the colour of the water against the provided colour chart which gives readings which run from 0 to 14. Note that the pH readings may well vary in different parts of the garden.

Neutral soil has a pH of 7, and most plants will thrive in it; acid readings are below that; and alkaline above it. The higher the reading, the greater the calcium levels. If you have alkaline soil, the best way of growing acid-loving plants is in containers or raised beds filled with ericaceous soil. You can reduce the acidity by adding lime.

pH TESTING

1 The best way to test the pH levels is to take samples from different sites in the garden, digging holes and wetting them.

2 Then trowel the wet soil, getting out any stones, from the first hole and slide it into a container, ready for checking.

ABOVE If the soil has too much lime, plants quickly signal the problem because their leaves turn sickly yellow.

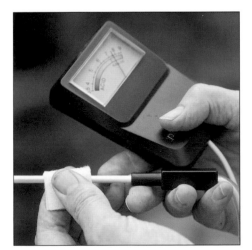

3 Push the switch on the meter to give a pH reading, because many also provide fertility readings.

4 Gently insert the probe into the soil – carefully in case there are still stones in there which might damage it – to find the soil's pH.

Seed Propagation

You cannot propagate plants without trying your hand at sowing seed. It is absolutely essential for growing crops in the vegetable garden – everything from tomatoes and sweet corn to chillies and climbing courgettes – trying out tasty new varieties which you will never get in the supermarkets, and for filling gaps in beds and borders with quick-growing, fun annuals. You can even devote whole beds to annuals, creating interlocking blocks and drifts of bright colours and strong scents, getting a high-voltage, inexpensive display. Growing annuals from seed is perfect for gardeners who get itchy fingers in spring and cannot wait to get going before the temperatures outside have warmed up. Growing annuals also gives you a chance to keep experimenting, trying out different colour combinations and scouring the seed catalogues for the latest introductions.

The following pages tackle every aspect of growing plants from seed, starting with sexual reproduction, the inventive ways in which flowers are pollinated (often tricking insects into lending a hand), how seed spreads to germinate away from the parent, where it has a better chance of surviving without competition for light and nutrients, and the actual act of germination. There is also information about how you can collect seed, and the most effective ways of sowing seed and raising new plants.

LEFT A lively mixture of crops in a potager, all grown from seed, featuring a wide range of shapes and colours.

Sexual reproduction

Plants have evolved extraordinary ways of mating, which basically means transferring pollen from the male to the female parts. This is usually done by insects and/or the wind. But where the wind, and therefore a huge degree of luck, is involved, the plants have to produce even greater amounts of pollen in order to give much better odds of perpetuating themselves.

How do plants reproduce?

Plants can reproduce asexually and vegetatively when they send out runners that root in the ground, or send up suckers around the main plant, for example, producing offspring that is an exact genetic reproduction of the parent. When they reproduce sexually, genetic material from the male and female unites in a seed. The flowers of most plants are bisexual or hermaphrodite. Sometimes a separate, compatible male and female plant are needed (called dioecious), for cross-pollination, and sometimes plants are monoecious, meaning that each individual carries both male and female flowers.

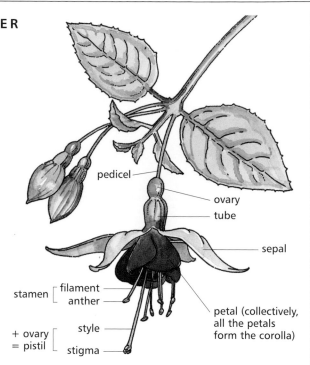

PARTS OF A FLOWER

This close-up of a fuchsia flower clearly shows the male and female reproductive organs. The female reproductive pistil consists of the ovary at the base of the style and the stigma. The male reproductive parts, collectively called the stamen, consist of a pollen-producing anther, usually on a filament.

Some plants are bisexual with the male stamens surrounding the female pistils. When the ovule has been fertilized it develops into seed, which contains enough food to fuel the initial stages of growth.

pedicel
ovary
tube
sepal
stamen [filament
        anther
+ ovary [style
= pistil [stigma
petal (collectively, all the petals form the corolla)

Reproductive structures

The key reproductive parts of angiosperms are kept in the flowers. (Angiosperms are flowering plants whose seed is enclosed in an ovary, unlike the non-flowering gymnosperms, such as conifers, which have naked seeds.) Most flowers, despite their different looks and scents, have the same basic structure, with petals and sepals, whose role is to enclose and protect the inner floral parts. Seed-producing female parts comprise ovaries, and a style that connects the ovary and stigma. The stigma receives the pollen and is usually sticky in order that it safely adheres. The ovary, style and stigma form the pistil. Male parts comprise stamens and pollen-bearing anthers. Hermaphrodite flowers include both male and female parts.

Offspring

The seed has genetic characteristics of both parents, but will not produce offspring that are exact reproductions of the parents. There will be differences, and that is what seed companies continuously investigate in the search for the next big-selling plant. When they can provide seed producing known, uniform plants (particularly important with flowers and

ABOVE We might think it is just a tasty fruit, but an apple is actually a very clever, reliable life-support system. Its prime aim is to help create the next generation of apple trees. The seed will be distributed by animals picking the fruit to eat the flesh.

ABOVE Sweet corn is grown in close groups because it is wind pollinated, with the pollen being blown from the anthers to the stigma.

ABOVE In order to get pollinated by insects, and guarantee the survival of the species, flowers need to provide an eye-catching, colourful and/or scented display. This makes the flower bed a very competitive place, with the different plants vying for attention.

vegetables), it is sold as F1, or the first generation of a cross between known parents. F1 hybrids give good results with vigorous growth, and, in the case of vegetables, large crops, but they are only available for a small percentage of plants, and then mostly annuals. They are tricky to create and are consequently more expensive than ordinary seed.

ABOVE Growing colourful, scented plants is an excellent way of attracting insects, and a house wall covered with a vigorous climbing ivy will erupt in yellowish-green bisexual autumn flowers. They are followed by small, rounded fruits, loved by the wildlife.

ABOVE The tiny pink, purple or white summer flowers of thyme are a major insect magnet, attracting scores of pollinators.

Pollination

This simply means that pollen has been moved from the male anther to the female stigma, and once that happens everything changes. The petals are not needed to attract pollinators, and they fade and fall, revealing the slightly swelling ovary beneath. In the case of an apple tree this becomes the fruit, a juicy, tasty, fleshy, protective case with the seeds within. The seeds themselves are protected from extreme temperature changes and damage by creatures and infection by their own hard outer layer. Most seeds also contain food stores to keep the embryo alive in the soil, and to help it through the seedling stage until it becomes self-sufficient with roots and shoots.

Self- and cross-pollination

Sometimes a single plant actually produces flowers that are either exclusively male or female, sweet corn being the most obvious example. That is why corn is grown in blocks, with the plants in close proximity, about 45cm (18in) apart in the case of taller varieties; the wind blows the pollen from the anthers of the male flowers growing

ABOVE The wide-open flower of a dahlia gives easy access to the sexual organs right in the centre. The petals are called the ray floret and the yellow centre is the disc floret.

at the top of the plant down on to the female stigma growing below, which might be on the same plant or another one. Grow individual plants around the garden, well away from each other, and the chances of getting a crop are severely reduced. Self-pollination, though, is not always in the best interests of some plants, reducing genetic variation, and they have special mechanisms to prevent this happening. The most obvious and most effective involves the male and female parts ripening at different times, a kind of self-imposed segregation. Where self-pollination is important, there is simultaneous ripening.

Animal pollination

The most obvious means of pollen transfer involves the wind (both unpredictable and erratic) and birds, bats and insects (including butterflies, sawflies, wasps, bees,

ABOVE Plants are immobile and cannot go out to find sexual partners, and must attract pollinating insects by colour and scent.

ABOVE The hoverfly feeds on nectar and pollen, and avoids predators by resembling wasps and bees when it is actually just a fly.

ABOVE In midsummer the butterfly bush (*Buddleja davidii*) is covered by long panicles, consisting of scores of tiny scented flowers, attracting pollinating bees and butterflies.

ABOVE The central disc of a sunflower produces copious seed, a food source for birds.

ants, honey and bumble bees), all being attracted by brightly coloured petals, the production of sticky, sugar-rich nectar and nutritious pollen. But while some plants reward their pollinators, others do not. Some orchids trick them. Dancing lady orchids (*Oncidium*) produce

Extra flowers, extra seed

If you want a plant to put out lots of flowers so that you get plentiful seed, grow it in a container, keep it slightly pot bound, put it under stress and it will immediately respond by developing lots of flowers, and seed, trying to propagate. If you want an abundance of attractive flowers from a garden plant, keep taking off the fading ones to thwart the plant's ambition to procreate. It will respond the only way it knows, by developing more flowers (and more seed). If you let the seed develop, the plant will then channel its energy into that. It will not have any need to keep flowering as prolifically.

flowers that resemble an army of bees, and when the real bees see them they charge and attack, so coming into contact with and dispensing the pollen. Other orchids lure pollinators by producing flowers that resemble sexy female moths ready to mate, and even emit a similar scent. More ingeniously, some Mediterranean flowers resemble the rotting flesh of, say, a donkey, with a smell to match, attracting pollinating flies. Some flowers, which only open for the briefest 48-hour spell, put on an incredible show to guarantee they get pollinated quickly, with the Sumatran *Amorphophallus titanum* growing 90cm–1.5m (3–5ft) high with a stink that is just indescribable. But what if there are not any creatures about to carry out the pollination? Fruit trees, for example, produce blossom in spring, but if the weather is too cold for the insects you may have to do it by hand, where possible, on small

trained shapes (for example, espaliers against a wall), using a small paint brush to transfer the pollen to the stigma, to guarantee a good crop. If there is a bad late spring frost, then the blossom will get zapped and you will get a very poor or non-existent crop.

ABOVE Pollinating by hand using a clean brush to transfer the pollen to the stigma, which is often sticky, to make it adhere.

Dispersal mechanisms

The ultimate aim of all plants is to reproduce and expand their territory. The problem is that they are immobile – well, to a point. They might not have legs, but they can certainly travel. Strawberries send out extending shoots called runners that root and produce new plants, while blackberries produce a great colonizing tangle of growth. When it comes to spreading seed to germinate away from the parent, avoiding competition for food and light, plants have found all kinds of ingenious techniques.

Independent spreaders

The Mediterranean sea cucumber (*Ecballium elaterium*) and broom (*Cytisus*) are two of the most inventive seed spreaders. The cucumber has a built-in pressure chamber. It gradually fills with juice as it ripens, until it reaches the critical point when it gets flung from its stalk and whizzes through the air for about 5.4m (18ft). Even better, it trails a mix of slime and seed through a hole, scattering it across the ground. Without help from any external agency, it manages

ABOVE Sea cucumber (*Ecballium elaterium*) likes poor, dry, free-draining ground where it will produce fruits that fling out its seed.

to create expanding colonies of itself. Broom is slightly different and relies on the sun's heat to disperse its seed in different directions. The sides of the pods facing the sun heat up more rapidly than the shady sides, and the internal tension makes the pod burst open and propel its seed away. Legumes also have pods that split on drying with a satisfying snap.

Wind aid

Other plants are dependent on the wind, with poppies producing drying seed heads or capsules with small holes at the top. Prise one head open and you will see that it is packed with masses of seed. As the wind blows the stems, so the heads get tossed and shaken, and the tiny seed goes flying. If you want to scatter the seed in another part of the garden, simply pick the ripe heads and shake them like a salt sprinkler where you want extra colonies. If you want to make sure that at least some will definitely germinate, collect and save it for sowing and raising in pots. Such seed is typically minute

ABOVE The seed heads of a clematis are blown away by the wind, creating distant new plants which will not compete with the parent.

ABOVE Dandelions produce seeds with long, feathery tufts attached to each one. The seed is then dispersed by the wind.

ABOVE The seed head of a broom relies on the sun's heat to create internal tension, which eventually makes it burst open.

ABOVE Most seed heads of a maple spin on the wind and land away from the parent, avoiding the dark shade at the base.

ABOVE When the seed pods of a pond iris break open, those tumbling into the water will float away to germinate on a muddy bank.

ABOVE The sticky goosegrass (*Galium aparine*) is designed to latch on to passing creatures, helping the seed to spread far and wide.

ABOVE Agapanthus seed heads, just about to scatter seed on the wind. In cold climates the seed is best saved and sown indoors.

(so that it is easily whipped away on a breeze) and produced on an amazing scale, increasing the odds that some will land where it can safely germinate.

The spinners

Sycamores (*Acer pseudoplatanus*) and maples (*Acer*) are slightly more inventive and produce one-winged seeds that twist and spin through the air like crazily out of control helicopters. Look inside the sycamore's nut with a hand-held lens and you will see an embryo (which is inside every seed) with two pale green seed leaves (cotyledons) tightly rolled up, waiting to develop. The Asiatic *Anisoptera* has a twin-winged seed, but because the wings are not symmetrical they lurch and spin, and whip the seed away from the parent to a place where it can start to germinate. What we regard as the wonderful silvery seed heads of a clematis are also very efficient kinds of seed dispersal. Plants such as *Clematis tangutica* are partly grown for their spidery seed heads that always get a double approving look

when they catch the sun, but their purpose is not to amaze. The fluffy contraptions get caught by the slightest puff of wind, getting wafted away for incredible distances. The crack willow (*Salix fragilis*) propagates itself by cuttings, sending snapped off twigs flying through the air which root in muddy ground.

Fertile willow

Salix can be so quick to propagate that even tree stakes have been known to take root in wet ground, as can sliced-up horizontal sections of a trunk, that have been arranged on bare soil to make a path.

ABOVE *Clematis tangutica* produces yellow summer flowers followed by silvery seed heads that are easily dispersed by the wind.

ABOVE The crack willow (*Salix fragilis*) is very efficient at reproducing itself, with snapped twigs taking root in damp ground.

Animal digestion

When you plant berrying shrubs for the birds to eat in autumn and winter, you're not only helping them; you're also helping the plants to propagate themselves. Jays carry off acorns and drop them en route to wherever. Birds also eat the ripe fruit and berries, and the seeds pass undamaged straight through the gut and out, being deposited in the droppings well away from the parents where, with luck, they will have more space and light to grow and thrive without competition.

Unripened fruit is too bitter to eat, and is only edible when the seed itself has fully developed. When this happens the fruit signals that it is edible, becomes highly coloured (often turning red as with apples and most tomatoes), the texture softens as starch is converted to sugars, and it often gives off a sweet scent. The moment animals see what is happening, they pounce. They learn to read the signals.

Animal hitchhiking

If you've ever wondered why pets come in at night covered in tiny sticky little balls, the seed heads

ABOVE The brightly coloured, highly visible autumn berries of a hawthorn (*Crataegus*) are a boon to birds; they eat the crop and distribute the seeds far and wide in their faeces.

belong to goosegrass (*Galium aparine*). The heads stick to passing creatures and get carried away to fall off and eventually germinate, a very effective means of distributing the species over great distances and in different directions.

Other means of getting a lift over long distances include seed heads with hooks and spines that latch on to passing traffic. But what happens

when a creature that helps transport the seed of a particular plant is wiped out and becomes extinct? The plant might be wiped out too. It is also worth stressing that being transported by an animal can be a

ABOVE The crop of berries with the seed inside is 'flagged' to hungry birds, with the red contrasted against a pale background.

ABOVE If you want to collect seed to sow your own plants, you will have to be quick off the mark to get it before the birds.

For animals only

The large tropical Malaysian tree *Durio zibethinus* combines prickly, warty thorns and a splendid green capsule (a 'durion') like a large melon on the trunk, and the smell is quite repellent (to us, but not to animals). The flesh is a delicacy and available in Asian markets, but it is banned by airlines. You would not want to be locked up in a metal tube with it!

Nor with the wooden fruit of the *Couroupita guianensis*. Because it grows straight out of the trunk and can be 20cm (8in) wide, it is often called the cannonball tree. The smell of the pulp, for humans, is vile, but wild pigs cannot get enough of it. The seeds have a hairy covering that protects them from the pigs' digestive juices, and they can even germinate in their faeces.

risky strategy, which is partly why a surprisingly large number of plants and fruits are toxic, which ensures that they will not get eaten. They have an amazingly efficient deterrent. Yew leaves and twigs are certainly bad news for horses and cows – but it is the seed which is the most poisonous element, not the red fleshy part around it, in extreme cases leading to respiratory failure. Even chippings and fallen leaves lying in a field are dangerously toxic.

Tree seed

Some seed pods are designed to float, and the buoyant, waterproof coconut (*Cocos nucifera*) is the ultimate little boat complete with a life support system capable of drifting for hundreds of miles. The seed inside has an instant supply of liquid and food. When it reaches land it germinates on the shore. But it is not always that easy for trees to spread quickly by seed.

Some, like elms (*Ulmus*), seldom produce viable seed, and oaks (*Quercus*) often produce huge crops only after a long interval. Some seeds, such as ash (*Fraxinus*) and lime (*Tilia*), only germinate after a two- or three-year period, and others might need light – for example, oak – or shade – for example, beech (*Fagus*). In fact few trees can germinate in the shade of the same species.

But when it comes to colonizing new ground, suckering is just about the most efficient technique. Some trees send up suckers, and they in turn sucker, spawning more suckers, and so on, and gradually a huge area is colonized until what looks like a small wood is actually just one ever-spreading, incredibly prolific,

ABOVE The native British yew makes good topiary but it also has high levels of taxin, a complex mixture of toxic alkaloids.

ancient tree. Just one expanding, multiplying, colonizing aspen (*Populus tremuloides*) in Utah, USA, is thought to cover 106 acres (43 hectares). Other trees create the same effect in response to cutting. A giant ash in Essex, England, over 800 years old in the 1970s, responded to centuries of cutting by producing a great ring of new growth, totalling about 20 stems, around the hollow centre.

ABOVE The burdock produces seed heads with tiny specialized hooks that catch in the fur of passing mammals for easy distribution.

ABOVE Aquilegias have highly distinctive, upright seed heads which eventually ripen and split to scatter the shiny black seed.

ABOVE The North American *Populus tremuloides* spreads and regenerates itself thanks to new suckering growth.

Germination

What converts a seed – apparently completely inert, dehydrated tissue, sometimes so small you can scatter scores of them on a finger nail – into a powerful living plant, capable of drawing up over 500 litres (110 gallons) of water a day, in the case of a mature oak? One process: germination.

The four key factors
Seeds, each containing the embryo of a plant, will not germinate until the surface conditions are right, and they generally need four environmental factors to come to life: water and oxygen, temperature and then light.

Water and oxygen
Penetrating the seed coat, water causes swelling while dissolving nutrients that kick-start the growth process. Because seeds are hygroscopic (expanding when wet, almost doubling in size, and conversely contracting when dry), the availability or absence of water is crucial. It is vital that the soil is kept moist after sowing, but if seed

Timing
Germination times of different plants vary considerably, with the quickest seeds to respond usually coming from the most arid areas of the world where, after a sudden bout of heavy rain, it is in the plant's interests to get its roots quickly into the wet soil and start growing before it completely evaporates.

is continuously locked in sopping wet soil then germination will be tricky because there will be severely reduced oxygen levels. Seed needs to breathe. And good oxygen levels are the second factor, helping the seed to release food and energy for the embryo, which is partly why seeds are sown in a light, open, airy compost (soil mix).

Temperature
The third factor is temperature, but this does not mean that if you zap the seeds of various plants with a high temperature they will all germinate. They won't. Different plants have

ABOVE A propagation case with a sliding cover over a ventilation hole provides a safe environment for growing seedlings.

different, often fairly wide maximum and minimum temperature ranges within which germination takes place, with an ideal band in the middle. The temperature at which germination takes place usually

ABOVE What looks like a scattering of insignificant blobs is a mass of seed, each one capable of producing a vigorous plant.

ABOVE Plants are far more adaptable than we imagine, and self-sown seedlings can emerge in even the tiniest nooks and crannies.

ABOVE A powerhouse of a mature tree growing in the best position, well away from other trees competing for light and water.

equates to the spring temperatures found in a plant's native habitat. Consequently, plants from colder temperate regions need lower temperatures to start germinating than plants from the tropics. If you cannot provide artificial heat for temperate seed to match late spring-time temperatures outdoors, just keep seed trays on a sunny windowsill in mid-spring, where the temperature should be about 15°C (60°F), and you will still get early growth. If you provide temperatures that exceed a seed's ideal range, you will probably get thin, feeble, tall growth or possibly no growth at all.

Light

The fourth factor is light, in combination with rising temperatures. As a good guide, sow seed to the depth of one seed placed on top of it. So, small seed will be near the surface (and some seed is so fine that you can just cover it with perlite or vermiculite), while large seed goes deeper in the ground. Plant fine seed so deeply that light

levels are excluded and it will not germinate. (As ever, there are some exceptions; *Allium* and phlox, for example, germinate only when there is no light.) Provided you are sensible and follow the directions on the packet of seed, light levels will not be a problem. Never leave seed on the surface in the garden because it will promptly get taken by birds and mice.

ABOVE Phlox seeds quickly germinate within a period of 7–10 days, with perennials flowering in their second year.

ABOVE Leave the heads on 'drumstick' alliums when the flowers fade, either for gathering seed or because of their attractive shape.

Built-in repair kit

The first visible signs of seed growth follow imbibition, a process that prompts the swelling of the seed's tissues. This causes the seed coat to split, letting in both water and gases. As the cells hydrate, nutrients are transferred to the embryo, but some of the early activity in a seed is required to repair damage caused by drying.

ABOVE Seeds need light, water, oxygen and warmth to germinate, with room to grow separate, not entangled, root systems.

RIGHT Once the seeds have germinated, they must be separated into individual compartments giving them extra space.

ABOVE Sandpapering seeds with a tough outer covering helps water get in to kick-start the germination process.

ABOVE Alternatively the toughest seed coverings can be nicked with the point of a clean, sharp knife to let in moisture.

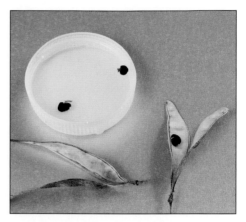

ABOVE Many seeds can be left overnight in a bowl of warm water, prompting the seed to swell and split.

Dormancy

When seeds have been shed, they lie dormant in the soil waiting for the surface conditions to favour successful growth. That is their whole *raison d'être*. But sometimes their needs do not coincide with our needs, or with conditions in the garden. For example, some alpine seed needs a cold period before it will germinate, and other seeds are programmed to develop at staggered times to give better germination rates and perpetuate the species. There are several techniques for helping seeds break dormancy, depending on the nature of the problem.

ABOVE Laburnum species can be grown from seed. It needs to be sown in a container in autumn, which is then placed in a cold frame.

Scarification

The problem with tough, impermeable seed coats, for example the seed of broom (*Cytisus*), *Gleditsia* and *Laburnum*, is that is that they cannot be penetrated immediately by water. The tough coating inhibits quick and even germination. In the wild that is not a problem – there is no immediate need for speedy germination, and the coat gradually decays over a long period – but in the garden it is. Hence the need for scarification, a technical term for cracking through this suit of armour and letting moisture seep in. You can file seeds with the toughest coats, or nick them with a knife, while others can be rubbed between sheets of sandpaper or, as in the case of sweet peas (*Lathyrus odoratus*), you can soak them overnight in warm water or between wet sheets of kitchen paper. When the case swells, softens and splits you will see a flash of white beneath. Immediately sow before the seeds dry out.

Stratification

Other seeds need a period of winter chilling, called stratification (from the practice of putting the seed in strata of sand, to stop them drying out, in the garden), and this particularly applies to alpines, and hardy trees and shrubs. Put the seeds in a plastic bag with some damp sand and refrigerate them in mid-winter, the length of time (ranging from 4–20 weeks, but usually from 6–8) depending on the size of the seed and its natural habitat. When you can see about one-third of the seeds have developed tiny roots they can

Other forms of dormancy

Some seeds (for example, eucalyptus) only germinate after they have been exposed to sudden searing temperatures as fires flash through the cluttered bushy undergrowth in parts of Australia, for example. The fires break open the tough seed cases, while chemicals in the smoke also help some seeds to germinate. The fires destroy most of the competitive growth, giving the new seedlings a good start in the open, with excellent light levels. Other seeds stay in a period of dormancy until they have passed though an animal's gut where the chemical inhibitor, lining the outer coat of the seed case, gets removed. Other seed – for example, hellebore – has an immature embryo and needs a long warm spell before it develops and germination can occur.

Roots

Plants produce a variety of different roots. Their primary aim is to anchor the plant and allow it to feed and drink, the moisture being pumped up and around the top growth. The first root is the radicle, and it sometimes tunnels deeper and deeper as a taproot, while other plants are distinguished by their multi-branching system of fibrous roots. Some plants (the epiphytes) live attached to other plants and have aerial roots that feed off trapped leaf debris in the absence of soil, and absorb both humidity in the air and falling rain, while others (mistletoe) actually root in tree branches and parasitically feed off the host plant. Adventitious roots appear in unexpected places, for example bursting out of a main stem.

ABOVE Eucalyptus are primed to grow very quickly, and take advantage of sudden gaps in the Australian bush caused by fires.

ABOVE Look closely at any ivy growing up a tree or wall and you will see scores of tiny hair-like roots growing out from the stems.

be removed from the bag for sowing. Alternatively, you can just scatter the seed on top of the compost (soil mix) in a pot, and then cover it with sand. Leave it out in an exposed place where it can get frosted, but make sure that the pot will not go flying in a gale. The worse the conditions, the better. That's what it would face in the wild.

Early growth

When growing different kinds of seed, the first thing you notice is that the seedlings emerge in different ways. Courgette seedlings push up, out of the compost (soil mix), with the opened seed case clamped over the leaves. As the leaves open, so they fling it off. Do not be tempted to prise off the case because

you might well damage the tender young leaves. The roots are attached to the base of the seedling. This is called epigeal germination, unlike hypogeal germination where the seed case and the seed leaves (or cotyledons) are left under the soil, with the seedling growing vertically up out of it, and roots growing down out of the bottom.

LEFT Look on the soil around a hellebore and you will find seedlings that can be potted up. Only keep those with the best flowers.

BELOW Courgette seeds shoot up, so do not sow until several weeks before planting out or you will have nowhere to put them.

Collecting and saving seed

If you've got a particularly good species plant in the garden that can be propagated by sowing seed, collect some when it has ripened. Many plants do the job for you, scattering seed, and all you've got to do is carefully lift the seedlings and plant them where required. But to guarantee that happens, try the following techniques.

Gathering seed

The best time to collect seed from healthy, vigorous plants is usually when the seed is ripe. Stick the seed head in a paper bag and give it a good shake until all the seed has fallen out. Collect from species plants where possible, and not hybrids, because the latter will not give predictable results, though you might come up with something interesting. If you've got one good species plant and it is isolated from similar species, you minimize the risk of hybridization and you should end up with a near copy of the parent. The seed heads normally indicate when they are ripe by changing colour from green to beige or brown, though there are some cases where immature seed gives better results than the mature kind. The best days to collect are when it

Fleshy fruits and berries

The seed that is wrapped up in a food parcel, e.g. a pear, that is meant to be eaten by an animal which deposits the seed through its faeces some distance from the parent, needs special treatment. You have to separate the seed from the soft, fleshy covering, and in the case of a rose hip, for example, that is easy enough. In autumn flick the seed out with the point of a sharp knife and put it in a clear plastic bag containing some coir, and keep for about 10 weeks at 21°C (70°F), before refrigerating in late winter for a further four weeks.

ABOVE Ornamental grass stems need to be kept in a cool, dry place for several days before the seeds are stripped off.

ABOVE Even the smallest seed heads can contain scores of tiny seeds. Collect the moment that they ripen.

ABOVE Inspect the seed carefully and, if it is damp, gently dry it on absorbent paper to avoid any risk of rotting.

ABOVE Rose hips, often resembling tiny tomatoes, are packed with fresh seed that needs to be stored in plastic bags with coir.

ABOVE Seed packets usually provide all the growing tips you need on the back; keep in a cool, dry place until ready for use.

ABOVE Keep a close check on the seed heads in the garden, and on their changing colours as they ripen from green to brown.

ABOVE The seeds in the purple, oval autumn fruit on *Callicarpa bodinieri* var. *giraldii* can be sown either fresh or dried.

ABOVE If you're not sure when a seedhead has ripened, keep a close watch and it will open when it is ready for the seed to be sown.

Attractive fruits and seedheads

Many plants provide attractive pods, seedheads or fruits. If you do not want to collect the following, leave the stems uncut with the pods or fruits hanging on.
- *Celastrus orbiculatus* Hermaphrodite Group – orange fruit splits open exposing red seed.
- Chocolate vine (*Akebia quinata*) – fruit turns from plump and green to violet-purple.
- Dead man's fingers (*Decaisnea fargesii*) – deep blue plump fruit.
- Foxglove tree (*Paulownia tomentosa*) – large, acorn-like capsules.
- Indian bean tree (*Catalpa bignonioides*) – slender brown pods up to 30cm (12in) long.
- *Iris foetidissima* – large capsules split to reveal orange-scarlet seed.
- Passion flower (*Passiflora*) – in a long, hot summer it produces egg-like fruit.

Ageing seed

When opening seed packets, there is sometimes far more seed than you could ever need. If you're not giving some away, or growing extra numbers to keep in reserve, simply take what you need and reseal the packet, keeping it in a dry, cool place. But for how long? Fresh seed usually gives the best, most consistent results. In general, you can try keeping vegetable seed for two years in an airtight container at a uniform temperature (but not parsnips – they do need to be grown from fresh seed). Flower seed might keep for slightly longer.

The undeniable fact, though, is that seed deteriorates as it ages, giving increasingly unpredictable results. One way to test this is by scattering some seed on damp kitchen paper and seeing how much of it germinates. If you're still unsure, use new packets of fresh seed to guarantee the best results, especially where you're creating a special feature rather than less obvious, distant gap-fillers.

is dry and fine, without gale force winds. This is not just for obvious, practical reasons but because wet seed can be prone to mould.

Drying seed

If the seed is wet, then dry it gently on kitchen paper but not with a vigorous blast from a hairdryer. Even if it is not wet, let it dry in labelled paper bags (never plastic ones or sealed containers that lead to a build up of humidity which creates mould and rotting) on a sunny windowsill. When storing capsules from the pea family, violas, and impatiens, etc., all of which ping open and can expel the seed right across a room, make sure that the tops of the bags are tied.

Storage

If you need to separate the seed from the chaff and other bits of plant by sieving or winnowing, put everything in an open box and then blow across the surface. The seed

then goes into a sealed envelope, in a cool, dark place, avoiding any humidity, but some kinds need to be refrigerated (mimicking a cold winter spell out in the wild), while others are what's called 'desiccation-intolerant' and need a container with a high moisture and oxygen content.

ABOVE The seed pods of *Lilium regale* are ready the moment the tops crack open; sow immediately or keep until early spring.

Sowing seed indoors

Getting the garden off to an early start usually means sowing seed indoors, where you can control the growing conditions. This is where it all starts. Stick to the rules and you will have more seedlings than you know what to do with.

Timing

There is sometimes a burst of early spring hot weather when it is very tempting to start sowing all your seeds, but be careful when doing this indoors. When the seedlings have shot up they will need to be pricked out and transferred to larger, individual pots, but if you do not have a greenhouse or cold frame you simply will not have enough windowsill space to line them up until it is safe to plant them outside, when both day and night temperatures are reliably warm. Some plants (for example courgettes) shoot up in days and can be left until mid- to late spring while others (chillies) take longer to germinate and need to be started off in early spring to give the first crop time to develop.

ABOVE Nicely spaced out seedlings in a propagating case. Do not completely remove the lid if you have cats because they will curl up on the compost and crush the seedlings.

Containers

Choosing the right container for the right seed is partly a matter of preference. Use seed trays for large numbers of plants that do not mind root disturbance, and sow the seed thinly and evenly to avoid getting concentrated packed clumps of seedlings that are hard to separate and prick out, when they need to be moved into larger containers. The best way to avoid that problem with the tiniest fine seed is to mix it with sand, and scatter it down the fold in a piece of paper. When growing large numbers of plants that dislike being disturbed, choose root trainers, large modules or builder's guttering with lots of holes drilled in the bottom to let the water drain out, sowing the seed at the final spacing. Using all three means you will avoid the task of potting on and the seedlings will be big enough to survive outside. When growing small numbers of plants, just four or five different chillies or tomato plants, for example, grow each variety in a 5cm (2in) wide plastic or biodegradable pot. Put two or three seeds in each pot, and remove the weakest to leave one strong seedling.

Compost (soil mix)

Either sow seed in seed compost, or multi-purpose compost that has been mixed with a handful of

ABOVE Tomatoes are usually sown about eight weeks before planting time in the first few weeks of summer.

ABOVE Chillies and sweet peppers need to be sown at 20°C (68°F) from late winter because they can take 30 days to germinate.

vermiculite or perlite. Fill to near the top of the container, and then level and lightly firm down the surface to eliminate any air pockets using a smooth piece of wood cut to size or the bottom of an empty pot or seed tray. When covering fine seed on the surface, either use sieved compost (soil mix) or vermiculite which lets both light and water penetrate. Water with a fine rose spray, turned upwards, or by standing the containers in pans of water where it will be absorbed by capillary action. To generate a warm, moist, humid atmosphere, put the small containers in a clear plastic

bag in an airing cupboard, or without the bag in a propagator, usually at a consistent 18°C (65°F), and regularly wipe off the condensation. When the seedlings appear, remove the protective cover, and water as necessary, as before. Keep turning the containers in order to prevent the seedlings from growing at an angle toward the light.

Soil depths

The finer the seed, the closer it is planted to the surface, and the shallower the soil covering. The rule of thumb is that a seed should be covered by its own depth.

ABOVE *Rhodochiton atrosanguineus* makes prodigious growth from a spring sowing, and by the end of summer will easily cover a wall.

SOWING SEED IN A SEED TRAY

1 Fill the seed tray to near the top with compost (soil mix) and perlite, and then lightly tap it down to flatten the surface.

2 Sow the seed thinly and evenly across the surface. This gives much better results than packing the seed in tight clusters.

3 Then lightly cover tiny seed with a fine layer of compost, which can be sieved over to remove any grit and lumps.

4 Always add a clearly written label so you know what is in each seed tray, and stand in a pan of water, giving a thorough drink.

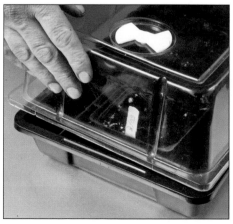

5 Carefully put the clear lid on top, having thoroughly cleaned it on both sides to ensure good light levels.

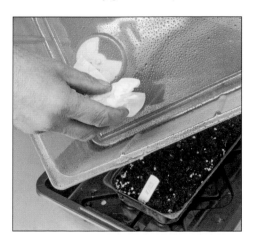

6 The moment you see any condensation on the inside of the lid, promptly remove it, wipe it off and then replace.

Pricking out

When the seedlings have opened their first pair of true leaves, not the small, rounded seed leaves (cotyledons), they can be pricked out. This is a vital step because the growing plant now needs more light, space and compost. Make sure that the compost (soil mix) is on the dry side, and then carefully fork out the seedlings, handling them very carefully by the leaves, avoiding the weak, easily damaged stems. The seedlings go straight into the next size pot, filled with multi-purpose compost, or modules (a 24-module tray is excellent for bedding plants). If putting them back into a seed tray, use fresh compost, and space them out about 36mm (1½ in) apart. Make individual holes with a dibber, carefully lower the seedlings so that they are at the same depth as before, and firm in, before watering again with a fine spray turned upwards. If continuing to grow on a windowsill, keep turning the containers to get vertical growth. Seedlings are incredibly light sensitive and need regular attention.

Composts for permanent containers

If you are growing plants permanently in containers, you have a wide choice of composts (soil mixes). All have several pros and cons.

• Loam, or soil-based compost – the John Innes range is basically a recipe with No. 1 aimed at seeds and cuttings, No. 2 (with double the amount of nutrients) at young plants, and No. 3 (treble the amount) at greedy long-term plants (such as shrubs). However, the nutrients get used up and flushed out after about 12 weeks, at which point you will have to start adding a liquid feed. Some peat is included.

• Peat-free compost – the alternatives include green waste, coir, and composted bark (but not for seeds or seedlings). Green waste is made from recycled household waste, while coir is made from shredded coconut husks (imported mainly from Sri Lanka, stacking up plenty of air miles) and has few nutrients. Coir-based compost is mixed with two parts of loam-based, or multi-purpose, to one of the coir. Use for one-season displays but note that it dries out quickly and needs regular drinks. Ideally choose a bag containing a mixture of different organic materials.

• Peat-based (or loamless or soilless) compost, including the multi-purpose kind – again for one-season displays. It is lightweight but dries out quickly, and has low nutrient levels, although these can be easily supplemented.

• Ericaceous compost – essential for acid-loving plants.

Hardening off

Plants that have been raised in a sheltered, warm environment need to be acclimatized over several weeks to outside conditions before they are permanently grown in the garden. The longer they have been in the warmth, the longer they will need to be toughened up. If they go straight out they will probably suffer a significant check to their growth. The ideal place is a cold frame, but if you haven't got one, initially stand plants outside in a sheltered position with dappled light during the day, for example at the base of a hedge, avoiding any extremes, and bring them in at night, until the night-time temperatures start picking up and they can be left out

ABOVE Some different composts (soil mixes) and additives. Back row: multi-purpose compost, loam-based compost and moss peat. Front row: water retention granules, vermiculite and coarse grit.

ABOVE The ideal place to harden off young plants, and acclimatize them to outside temperatures, is in a cold frame. Regularly open the lid to provide good ventilation, but keep it closed and covered on cold nights.

for the occasional mild night until, finally, these temperatures are not in any danger of suddenly falling. Even if the plants have been hardened off, though, and there is suddenly a bad early summer with fierce, chilly winds, delay planting until the weather returns to normal. If you have got a cold frame, initially keep it closed at night, cover it with old carpet if the temperatures are set to dive, and open it on mild days to give plenty of ventilation.

Aftercare

After all this attention, don't just leave ornamental plants to themselves. Keep a close eye on their development and act promptly if they become lanky. Pinch out their growing tips to encourage more bushy growth from lower down. To create really bushy, prolific flowering plants (for example, fuchsias), you might need to keep pinching out this new emergent growth in early summer.

In addition, if young seedlings are grown with too much warmth and not enough light, you end up with weak, spindly, elongated growth, so keep an eye on these factors too.

PRICKING OUT SEEDLINGS

1 Occasionally, gently brush the tops of the seedlings to mimic the wind. This helps produce sturdier, more resilient plants.

2 When young seedlings develop their first pair of true leaves, not the initial rounded kind, they are ready to be given more space.

3 Carefully prise them out of the compost (soil mix), perhaps using a kitchen fork. Do not damage the roots or crush the leaves.

4 To make the new planting hole, use a pencil or dibber and carefully lower in the roots. They must be at the same depth as before. Water.

ABOVE Young plants can become rather lanky. To generate extra flowering branches, nip back the tops to force out more side growth.

ABOVE A bushy young fuchsia that has been regularly pinched out in the first few weeks of summer, giving a greater mass of flowers.

ABOVE Pelargoniums respond well to regular pinching out in late spring, and they quickly produce extra flowering growth for summer.

Sowing seed outdoors

To get good success rates, it is worth following the accepted way of sowing seed. If you just throw seed about the garden the odds are that little will germinate, and certainly not where you want it, standing only a poor chance of thriving.

Where and when to plant

The first key requirement is deciding whether you are sowing straight into a special nursery seed bed (later transplanting the seedlings, for example hardy biennials, to their final position), or whether you are sowing the plants exactly where they are to flower (for example hardy annuals). But note that *Gypsophila* and parsley, with deep, anchoring taproots, hate being lifted and disturbed. If you do it, you will check their growth.

Next, check whether you are growing hardy plants that can withstand frost and can therefore be sown when the soil temperature is above 9°C (48°F). Half-hardy plants can take the cold but cannot withstand actual frost, and need a

temperature of 15–18°C (60–65°F), while tender plants cannot be sown or planted outside until late spring or early summer (though they can certainly be given an early start by germinating them indoors with the half-hardies). Hardy biennials are sown and planted in the summer, to stay outside all winter and flower the following year. When you are sowing seed where the plants are going to flower, do check their needs, finding out which require full sun, dappled light or shade, which require poor, dry, free-draining soil (at the one extreme) and which require moist, rich ground, with plenty of added organic matter (at the other) and which will give good results in average conditions. Grow the right plant in the right place, and it will thrive. Grow it in the wrong place, and it won't.

The soil

When sowing tiny seed, it needs to be sown in fine, crumbly soil that will let in light and air to help the seed germinate. Dig the ground

ABOVE Before sowing directly outside, mark out the areas for the different plants first, to organize the contrasting blocks of colour.

when the soil is dry because if it is wet and squishy you will badly compact it if you stand on it. One of the reasons for growing vegetables in narrow beds is precisely to avoid this problem. You should be able to keep your anchoring foot on the path and avoid damaging the soil texture. Also make sure every weed and its roots have been removed (far easier to get them out now than later), and then rake over the ground to get out any stones and to break up the soil. If there are any large clods, simply use your rake like a hammer and smash down on them, breaking them into tiny pieces. Poor soil can be given an all-purpose feed, lightly raked into the topsoil. You now need to eliminate any air pockets because if seeds fall into them, they will struggle. Do this by shuffling over the ground to flatten the soil surface, but do not stamp on it. Rake over it again, giving a crumbly soil topping to a depth of 5cm (2in) and you're ready to sow.

ABOVE Everyone wants a garden full of wildlife, but that does not include household pets. Covering these emerging sweet pea plants with netting will help keep off cats and dogs looking for a toilet, and clearly indicates to garden visitors that they must keep clear of the fragile growth.

Lines or drifts

Before sowing, you need to decide whether to scatter the seed in all directions over the area (called broadcast sowing, which is how you sow a lawn), or in neat, precise, well-spaced straight rows. If you are sowing a patch of annuals, then the broadcast method is best so that you get natural and irregular-looking blocks of plants. To mark out an informal area, define it with a stick, leaving lines in the soil, rubbing them out if you make mistakes. If you are creating a more structured, geometric layout then use canes and string to create straight divisions.

When you are happy with the different areas, clearly mark out the boundaries using sand poured out of an old, dry plastic water-bottle.

Sowing

Broadcast the seed on a still day, giving an even covering, always holding some seed back as gap fillers, then lightly rake over so that the seed is not exposed on the surface, label and water (or water before sowing).

RIGHT When planning and sowing a vegetable garden, always think about the range of colours, shapes and heights that will create an attractive, imaginative look.

SOWING SEED IN AN OUTDOOR BED

1 Give the bed a thorough weed, also getting out stones and breaking up any clods by smashing down on them with a fork.

2 Then rake the soil thoroughly lengthwise and crosswise to give a flat, even surface with a loose, crumbly top.

3 Next, mark out the areas for the different plants using a stick. Check that the final look will work from all sides.

4 When you are happy with the final divisions, clearly mark them out using an old bottle filled with dry sand.

5 Scatter the seed over the surface, giving an even spread, though any cluttered seedlings can be thinned out later.

6 Finally cover the entire area with netting in order to keep off hungry pigeons, and household pets and children. Water.

Thinning

Though it might seem an advantage to have huge numbers of plants packed together, you really are better off having slightly fewer, stronger, healthier, more vigorous, better fed, better performing plants than a large number growing so close together that they are fighting over food and water, struggling in periods of drought, and prone to disease. More is definitely less.

THINNING PLANTS

ABOVE Keep a close eye on the emerging seedlings, and when you see a few growing too close together, pull out the weakest.

Weeding

Keep an eye out for weeds, and get rid of them the moment they appear. That is obviously easier when growing plants in straight rows because you can spot a rogue seedling and easily whip it out, or just run the hoe between the rows and leave the upended weed seedlings to shrivel in the sun.

Watering

Also make sure that the seedlings get nicely watered on a regular basis when the ground is dry, though as the roots get longer aim for a good watering every 10 days or so to encourage them to tunnel down deep for moisture. If you pamper the plants and keep the topsoil moist, then the roots will happily stay in the top layer, and the plants will quickly suffer in dry periods because this layer dries out quickest, meaning you have to keep running outside to supply more water. Do not get locked in that cycle. Also note that when giving established plants a good drink it takes a huge amount of water to soak even several inches into the ground. Check by putting a trowel in the soil to see how deep the water has sunk. Also, never water on a hot day because a huge percentage of the water is promptly lost through evaporation. The plants only get a brief drink. Do it last thing at night and the plants have got a good 10 hours to drink. You will immediately notice how much sturdier they look in the morning. To stop lawns from getting brown and patchy, do not keep cropping the grass too severely, but let it grow quite long, resulting in longer roots that go deeper down for a drink.

If there is a water restriction in your area, investigate different ways of using rain run-off channelled into water butts and concentrate on drought-resistant plants, for example growing sweet corn and pumpkins in the vegetable garden.

Keeping out the pests

Put netting over any seedlings where possible, because inquisitive birds can rip them out in seconds. Look out of the window early in the morning and you will see pigeons and crows staggering around the

ABOVE Annual cosmos can be sown directly outside in late spring, and is one of the main ingredients of cottage garden displays.

ABOVE A seed-raised bergenia injecting a colourful touch in spring. Grow it in full sun or light, partial shade.

ABOVE The larger sunflowers produce enormous flowers, nearly 25cm (10in) wide, so avoid growing them in packed clumps.

Stopping slugs

The only foolproof method of stopping slugs from demolishing your seedlings is to stand guard at night – and that's right through the night – and pick them off by hand, unless you want to use large quantities of toxic slug pellets. There are countless other methods of controlling slugs, which can be effective. These include: scattering eggshells or sharp sand over the ground; using saucers or jam jars filled with beer to drown them (sunk into the soil near valuable plants); using upturned grapefruit halves as traps, because slugs love the pith; stretching out lengths of copper slug tape as a barrier; and watering nematodes into the soil – these then seek out and destroy slugs underground (recent research suggests the killing ingredient might actually be a bacterium carried by the nematodes), which also means that older slugs which live on the surface are relatively safe.

Try eliminating slugs' hiding places, for example old pots left lying around the garden, or damp, dark places where slugs congregate. Provided you are not trying to poison them, keep a pond well-stocked with frogs, who slurp slugs down as a delicacy, and encourage thrushes, hedgehogs and ground beetles, which also like haute cuisine.

ABOVE Keep a lookout for slugs in cool, damp conditions, or plants with young soft succulent stems will become a prime target.

Herbaceous plants that are less prone to slug damage

Acanthus mollis
Alchemilla
Bergenia
Dicentra spectabilis
Eryngium
Gaillardia
Hemerocallis
Papaver orientale
Pulmonaria

garden pecking at everything and anything, even if you have scarecrows. Netting should also keep out dogs and cats, and there are ultrasound devices to scare off the latter (that necessitate erecting speakers), although many cats ignore them. Netting, erected over canes firmly fixed in the soil, is also vital if you have young children as a way of telling them and their friends that this is definitely a no-go area.

ABOVE Hostas are prone to slug and snail damage, and are often grown in raised pots topped by gravel to avoid any damage.

ABOVE Annual mallows (*Lavatera*) can be sown outside from mid-spring, and give a long flowery show through the summer.

ABOVE Whenever you have a spare patch of ground to the front of a border, grow richly scented stock (*Matthiola longipetala*) from seed.

ABOVE Love-in-a-mist (*Nigella*) can be sown directly outside either in mid-spring or several months before, in autumn.

Cuttings

If growing plants from seed involves a huge leap of faith (will they/won't they grow?), with cuttings you are halfway there. The job is usually incredibly simple: you just snip off a length of growth and plant it up. There are ideal times to do this, but you can, if desperate, do it at other times, although your chances of success will be lower.

The key point is not rushing the young plants-from-cuttings into the garden, because they can quickly get lost among larger, more vigorous plants, getting shaded and smothered – suddenly, at the end of autumn, you cannot find them. If you have a cold frame or nursery bed, put the young plants in there, giving them time to put on growth. The larger they are when planted out, the better they will be at coping with any extremes, including spells without decent rain and winter nights when the temperatures dive. Cared-for cuttings give the best results, so make sure they are not ignored.

This chapter begins by looking at cuttings basics, tackling everything from the best time to take cuttings, how you take them and the rooting process to raising cuttings in pots. It then moves on to the different kinds of cuttings – greenwood, semi-ripe, and hardwood – and even those that can be taken from leaves and roots. The chapter finishes with four special features on taking rose, conifer, heather and willow cuttings.

LEFT A large reddish-purple *Buddleja davidii* 'Dartmoor' grown from a summer cutting, attracting large numbers of butterflies.

Cuttings basics

You can take cuttings of tips, stems, leaves and roots at various stages throughout the growing season, starting off with the youngest, freshest growth at the plant's tip, usually taken in spring. Once you realize what each cutting needs in order to succeed, it is actually a simple job getting high success rates.

The best growth
Look for a healthy, sturdy, non-flowering shoot (from this year's new, quick growth), which will have better growth potential than a shoot with buds or flowers. If you have a choice of plants from which to take the cutting, select the best, because you're producing a copy. Further, if the parent is now an old, relatively unproductive plant, nip it back one year before. This will generate a fresh batch of better shoots to be used as cuttings.

Timing
Ideally, take cuttings first thing in the morning when the stems are full of water. If doing this later in the day, do not under any circumstances

ABOVE All cotoneasters are easily grown from cuttings, taken from spring to autumn. The showiest kinds make substantial unfussy shrubs or trees with an abundance of berries loved by birds. Others can be used as ground cover or weeping standards.

leave them lying around to wilt in the hot sun. Get them potted up as quickly as possible. They should be about 10cm (4in) long without too much leafy growth. If there is too much foliage there is a danger that the cutting will lose more water than it can take up, making it wilt. It is sometimes advisable to trim off the top halves of the leaves.

Basic principles
The main principles that apply to the different types of cuttings in this chapter – greenwood, semi-ripe and hardwood – are shown here in the step sequences 'Taking tip cuttings from a ficus' (opposite) and 'Taking internodal cuttings from a fuchsia' (overleaf).

When taking the cuttings (e.g. the new young growth from the end of a stem), make the cut just above a leaf node. This means that the parent plant will not be left with an unproductive length of stem that will die back.

If using a side shoot, gently tug it away from the parent so that it retains a 'heel', or sliver of bark at the base. Then remove the lower leaves (give them a quick pull down), so that they do not come in contact with the compost (soil mix) and possibly rot.

The base of each cutting now needs to be trimmed to just below a node. This is crucial because that is exactly where the plant has the greatest potential for new root

ABOVE *Abelia grandiflora* can be easily grown from cuttings, especially if it is rooted in a heated propagator. It should take 1–2 years to flower, and makes a substantial shrub 3 x 4m (10 x 12ft). It is not totally hardy and needs to be planted in a sheltered position.

growth. Plants that do not root easily (and there are not that many) can be given a kick-start by lightly dabbing the end of the cutting in rooting powder. Too much will be counter-productive. The sooner the roots develop, the sooner the cutting will turn into an independent plant.

Internodal cuttings

The preceding cuttings rely on nodes, which means that each length of stem used as a cutting has one node at the base with more at the top. The base node generates all the root growth. But some plants can be grown from lengths of cutting that

do not have a node at the base. The bottom cut is therefore made above a node, and often the entire length of the internodal stem produces roots. The advantage is that the stems produce more cuttings than normal.

Potting up

While the cuttings are developing, they are entirely reliant on you. Use an open-textured seed or cuttings compost (soil mix), which has just the right amount of nutrients. Insert approximately three around the edge of an 8cm (3in) plastic pot, and carefully firm in, making sure that the bare 'leg' of each is in contact

ABOVE Shrubby and perennial St. John's wort (*Hypericum*) can be grown from cuttings, and normally takes 3–6 weeks to root.

TAKING TIP CUTTINGS FROM A FICUS

1 To propagate a new *Ficus*, take a leafy cutting in spring that is about 10cm (4in) long, cutting if off just above a node.

2 Then trim the cutting, making this second cut just below a node, and discard the redundant bottom length.

3 Remove the lower leaves. If too many are left the cutting will lose more moisture through the foliage than it can drink up.

4 Arrange the cuttings in seed or cuttings compost (soil mix), spacing them out equidistantly around the edge of the pot.

5 Water and add a clear plastic covering to keep the cuttings warm and humid, but wipe off any condensation when it appears.

Gardenias

Since gardenias can be expensive, they are worth propagating by cuttings. They root within eight weeks.

with compost (soil mix) and not an air pocket. Then water using a fine rose spray, because if you pour straight from the spout of a watering can you will compress the compost. To ensure that the cuttings go into a warm, humid environment, the pot either needs to go in a heated propagator or be sealed in a clear plastic bag – kept clear of the cuttings by short, vertical canes – and held in place with a rubber band until all have rooted. Periodically wipe off any condensation. With firmer cuttings, for example a pelargonium, the bag is not so necessary.

Aftercare

When young cuttings start putting on new growth, they can be taken out of this 'hot house' and potted up individually. It is vital that they are not put under any stress. Avoid extremes of direct sun and permanent shade, giving them a bright, cool place in a greenhouse or on a windowsill. Keep turning them to avoid the stem angling exclusively in one direction to the light.

ABOVE The rather shrubby busy Lizzie (*Impatiens walleriana*) can be grown from spring cuttings, then treated as an annual.

ABOVE The climbing honeysuckle (*Lonicera*) quickly roots in four weeks. Look for sound, vigorous cuttings that are 5cm (2in) long.

LEFT Every garden needs at least one mock orange (*Philadelphus*) for its rich summer scent. It is easily propagated by cuttings.

TAKING INTERNODAL CUTTINGS FROM A FUCHSIA

1 During the growing season, choose a strong, vigorous, healthy shoot from a fuchsia, with several pairs of leaves.

2 Using a clean, sharp knife, make cuts just above each pair of leaves. Hold the stem very carefully to avoid accidental damage.

3 The bottom piece of stem is left on and not trimmed off as for tip cuttings, because rooting will occur right along its length.

The range of cuttings

Once you understand how tip cuttings are taken and grow, it's time to look at three more kinds. The main distinction between greenwood, semi-ripe and hardwood cuttings is the time when they are taken. Greenwood, as the name implies, means that the new young growth is still green and fresh and has not hardened and become brown and woody. Semi-ripe means that the growth is gradually maturing, and hardwood means that the cuttings can be taken later in the season when the growth has toughened up. All are dealt with on the following pages.

Plants grown from internodal cuttings

Clematis	Hydrangea
Fuchsia	Hypericum
Hedera	Verbena

RIGHT If you have a favourite fuchsia, keep nipping off the growing points when it is young, to create a bushy plant. The following year, use the new shoots as cuttings, creating an even more impressive display.

ABOVE Clematis cuttings are taken from spring to midsummer when the plants are in full growth.

ABOVE Ivy (*Hedera*) is one of the easiest climbers to propagate by cuttings, but keep the cuttings out of damaging direct sun.

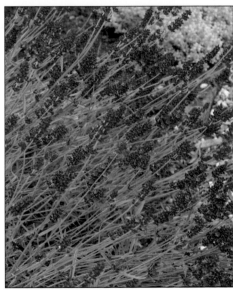

ABOVE Lavender cuttings can be delayed until after flowering; nip off the top growth in spring to encourage more shoots.

Greenwood cuttings

Outdoor plants generate new shoots in early summer, and the tips of this new growth can be used to make greenwood cuttings. They are easier to handle than those taken from spring growth, and less likely to wilt.

Timing
You can basically take cuttings throughout the growing season, the only difference being the degree to which the stems have aged and hardened, and their speed of growth. This will vary from plant to plant, and since the differences between softwood, greenwood and semi-ripe cuttings is not that radical, the most important factor is when you can do the best possible job. Far better to take a mid- or late season cutting when you can tend it well than an early season one that is going to get ignored and perform poorly.

Greenwood cuttings are an in-between, early summer stage, being taken after the tip and softwood kind but before the semi-ripe. Close examination shows a slight difference in texture and colour, and while the rooting takes slightly

ABOVE Elder (*Sambucus*) roots easily from cuttings from spring on, with the pots being stood outside in dappled shade.

longer than the tip cuttings, the stem will be that bit firmer and more mature. Again, it is sensible to take a few extras in case of failure.

Taking cuttings
As with the tip or softwood kind, take the cuttings early in the morning, when the stems are still full of moisture. They should be trimmed to about 10cm (4in) long, just below a node to maximize the chances of successful rooting. Give the leaves on the bottom third of the stem a quick pull down to get rid of them, and if there is plenty of leaf growth, cut it in half, crosswise. If a large, full head of leaves is left on, there is a danger that the plant will wilt as transpiration of moisture exceeds the take-up rate, causing cell damage. The snag left on the parent plant needs to be cut back to just above a node, where new branching will occur. By nipping off this growing end, the parent plant will respond by activating its reserve supply of latent or dormant buds, which is why most trees, for example, react so energetically when they are coppiced, firing out a spray of new growth in all directions.

ABOVE If you need a box hedge or more topiary specimens, then use the early summer trimmings to raise new plants.

ABOVE Gardens cannot have enough richly scented daphnes, and numbers can be increased by taking greenwood cuttings.

ABOVE Grow extra pyracanthas from cuttings to make a robust, spiny hedge packed with brightly coloured berries in autumn.

ABOVE When taking magnolia cuttings, you can help them root by making a light wound at the base of the stem.

Potting up

The cuttings need to be potted up in seed or cuttings compost (soil mix), around three per 8cm (3in) pot. Do not firm the soil down too much because you want a light, open, free-draining texture conducive to good root spread. Water the cuttings in using a fine rose spray, and then place the pot in a warm, humid environment, best provided by a heated propagator or sealed, clear plastic bag. Make sure that it is well supported at the top by short canes so that it does not touch the leaves, and seal it with a rubber band around the base of the pot.

Aftercare

Keep the cuttings in a bright, cool place where there is no danger of wilting or being stuck in the shade. When they start developing, pot them up individually, and keep turning them to avoid angled growth toward the light. However, they cannot go permanently outside at this stage. Gradually harden them off by standing them in a cold frame when the weather has warmed up. For the first few cold nights, bring them indoors. Thereafter cover the lid with old carpet on frosty nights, removing this in the daytime.

Sports

A plant with all-green leaves might suddenly and unpredictably develop a shoot, for example, with attractive variegated foliage. Such a sport, as it is called, is caused by a random genetic mutation, and if you want to propagate this shoot, do so by taking cuttings. When a sport is unstable it can suddenly revert to its all-green state. Quickly remove any branch without the variegated leaves or, in time, the whole plant will be affected.

TAKING GREENWOOD CUTTINGS FROM A KALANCHOE

1 Carefully check the parent plant, looking for likely non-flowering cuttings with firm, vigorous growth and healthy leaves.

2 Take a cutting by slicing straight across the stem with a clean, sharp knife. Do not squeeze and bruise the tissue.

3 Trim the cutting, first getting rid of the largest leaves, and then to leave the shoot about 5cm (2in) long.

4 Hold the cutting by the edge of a leaf, making sure that you do not damage it, and dip it in a rooting/fungicide compound.

5 Now insert it in an 8cm (3in) pot that has been filled with free-draining compost (soil mix) with plenty of added grit. Water.

6 Finally, place a clear, clean plastic dome on top to provide a warm, humid environment. Clean off any condensation.

Semi-ripe cuttings

If you missed the chance to take cuttings earlier in the spring or summer, or suddenly realize that you need more of a particular plant for next year, it is not a tragedy. Semi-ripe cuttings can be taken now, in late summer.

Taking cuttings in late summer

Many deciduous plants are best propagated now, when the new growth has lost its soft, sappy look, and is turning brown and woody though still slightly pliable. Take 15cm (6in) long cuttings, removing them just above a node on the parent plant, and then trim them just below a

node. Or, if using side growth, gently tear it away from the parent so that it is left with a 'heel' of old bark at the base. Semi-ripe cuttings, being more mature than softwood ones, have a higher success rate.

Stripping and rooting

The base leaves now need to be removed, being given a quick pull down, so that the bottom third to half of the cutting is clear. You can also nick the base with a knife to remove a piece of bark and expose the growth cells in the cambium to help generate roots. Tricky plants can have the end dipped in rooting

ABOVE Cuttings of the Californian lilac (*Ceanothus*) are best taken with a 'heel', a sliver of bark at the base, to help rooting.

TAKING SEMI-RIPE CUTTINGS FROM A WEIGELA

1 Weigelas root easily and quickly from cuttings, taking about four weeks. Take the cutting just above a node.

2 Next, trim the cutting just below a node and remove the lower leaves so that none are left in contact with the soil to rot.

3 Insert them in open, free-draining soil with plenty of added grit in a cold frame, and then firm down to eliminate any air pockets.

4 The finished cuttings, each with an array of leaves, look like this. They are well spaced out, giving them plenty of room to grow.

5 Finish off by gently watering in with an upturned rose spray in order to avoid dislodging the cuttings.

Plants propagated as semi-ripe cuttings

Argyranthemum
Berberis thunbergii
Ceanothus
Cistus
Deutzia
Elaeagnus
Forsythia
Pyracantha
Rubus
Salvia officinalis cultivars
Senecio maritima
Weigela

ABOVE One of the most valuable garden shrubs, a berberis can be propagated by taking semi-ripe cuttings in late summer. To get the best autumn leaf colours and an excellent show of fruit, grow it in full sun. Many make very effective dense hedges.

ABOVE Forsythias are versatile plants, making useful shrubs and hedges. Cuttings can be taken from spring to autumn.

Rock roses

Mediterranean rock roses are not reliably hardy, so if you live in a region where you cannot guarantee mild winter temperatures, it is best to take cuttings in case you suddenly lose an impressive plant. Give the new shrub a sheltered hot spot and good drainage.

and they will root well. Remove any fallen leaves, keep the glass free of condensation and cover the frame with old carpet when the temperature dives. Either plant them out at the end of spring or wait until the following autumn. Alternatively, provide warmth and humidity by inserting the pot in a heated propagator or inside a clear plastic

bag. Insert short vertical canes to lift the bag clear of the cuttings, and seal around the base with a rubber band. When the cuttings have clearly rooted, they should be individually potted up and kept in a greenhouse or cold frame over winter.

Aftercare
The following spring, after the last of the frosts, they can be hardened off by placing them in a cold frame before planting out in autumn.

powder, and then be given a light tap to get rid of any excess. Do not apply too much, thinking that it will apply a late-season push because it will have the opposite effect.

Potting up
Arrange the cuttings around the edge of a pot, firming them into cutting or all-purpose compost (soil mix) with added sharp sand to improve the drainage. Water in using a fine rose spray, and nip off the tops if they are very sappy. You can then put the potted cuttings straight in a cold frame, giving them plenty of ventilation on mild days,

ABOVE The spring- and summer-flowering deutzias make excellent border shrubs, with extra plants being raised from cuttings.

ABOVE The rock rose (*Cistus*) tends to be short-lived so periodically take semi-ripe cuttings to guarantee you have replacements.

Hardwood cuttings

You can successfully take cuttings in autumn, when the leaves have fallen, from many deciduous trees and shrubs. They require little effort, though they will not be ready for planting out for possibly one year.

Deciduous trees and shrubs

The best time to propagate such plants is in the second half of autumn, as the leaves are falling, into early winter, though if you miss this period you can still take them through to the start of spring, through the dormant period. This particularly applies to willows (*Salix*) and poplars (*Populus*). Evergreens are best taken in autumn. Of all the cuttings methods discussed, hardwood cuttings are the most trouble-free kind, partly because the stems have sufficient food reserves to generate sturdy root growth, and partly because they require only a pair of secateurs, one spade and a small, spare piece of well-weeded land that you will not need for 12 months.

ABOVE Evaluate the garden at the end of summer and, if you need more topiary, there will still be time to take box cuttings.

ABOVE Elder (*Sambucus*) cuttings, taken with a 'heel', usually give very good results but avoid pithy shoots that tend to rot.

Making the cut

In general, aim for a 15–20cm (6–8in) length of ripe stem that has developed this current year. It will be hard, woody and darker than the softwood kind, will not be pliable, and needs to be pencil thick. Make a straight cut at the base of the cutting, just below a node. Then trim the soft tip, making an angled cut just above a node. Making the one straight and one angled cut immediately indicates which is the top and bottom, should you forget. If you are growing a tree, do not remove the top, but leave the cutting intact to produce a clean, straight trunk. Finally, strip the leaves off the bottom two-thirds of evergreens.

Rooting

Dip the bottom ends in rooting powder. Trickier subjects might need to have the bottom sliver of wood nicked and lifted to expose the growth cells in the cambium. To plant them out, you need to make a simple trench by thrusting the spade into the ground, then pushing it slightly back to create a V shape but with one straight, vertical side. Move it to and fro a few times to make it work. Then pour in sharp sand to line the base to improve aeration and drainage. Insert the stems of shrubs, bottom first and 15cm (6in) apart, into the trench. Leave just the top third exposed, with trees going slightly deeper, just having the top bud showing. Then backfill and firm in, giving the cuttings a good drink.

ABOVE Extra numbers of buddlejas can raised at the end of the season, into the start of autumn. In the garden *Buddleja davidii* can be given a hard spring pruning, back to 30cm (12in) from the base. Less drastic pruning produces taller, less vigorous growth.

The best site

Make sure that the site is in full sun, and that the soil is free draining. To reduce the amount of time spent weeding and watering, try covering the length of the trench with landscaping fabric, and make planting slits in it. The weeds are thwarted by the lack of light, and the plastic acts as a mulch, reducing evaporation from the ground. If the only patch of ground you can spare has heavy clay soil, dig it up in advance, adding plenty of horticultural grit or sharp sand and mushroom compost to improve the structure and drainage. If you cannot use the garden, or you live in a particularly cold, exposed area, then set the cuttings in pots in a cold frame. Avoid using a warm greenhouse or there will be more premature top growth than root growth.

Aftercare

Keep the site weed free, and water in dry spells. Rooting will commence next spring when the temperatures rise, with the plants being transplanted the following autumn. If the cuttings are raised in a greenhouse and given gentle bottom heat, the process is much quicker, with a decent set of roots appearing by early spring.

Plants providing hardwood cuttings

Buddleja
Buxus
Clematis montana
Cornus
Deutzia scabra
Lonicera fragrantissima
Philadelphus
Populus
Ribes
Rubus
Salix
Sambucus
Symphoricarpos
Tamarix
Weigela

TAKING HARDWOOD CUTTINGS FROM A BUDDLEJA

1 Snip off a length of this year's growth from late autumn to winter, when most of the leaves have fallen.

2 Each individual cutting needs to be about 18cm (7in) long. If the tip has not hardened, snip it off. Remove any side shoots.

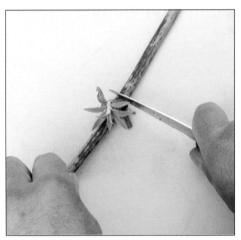

3 Trim the bottom cut just below a node, giving it a horizontal cut so that this end (which will be buried) is clearly marked.

4 Then nip off any growth at the base, because once planted it will simply rot. This will also encourage roots to develop.

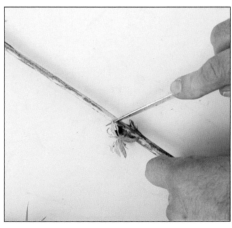

5 Then make a slanting cut just above a node at the top, which will clearly signify where all the top growth will emerge.

6 Finally, insert each cutting in a 15cm (6in) deep hole lined with sharp sand to improve drainage, firm in and water.

Leaf petiole and lateral vein-leaf cuttings

Plants that do not produce stems can be propagated from their leaves. There are two ways of doing this, and both are relatively quick and easy: from the leaf and stalk (or petiole), and from the leaf veins. Rooted plants should be ready for potting up after about two months.

Leaf petiole cuttings

The starting point is one leaf and its stalk (the petiole), typically taken from an African violet (*Saintpaulia*) in late spring or early summer. The new growth – shoots and roots – will appear around the base of the petiole.

Potting and rooting

Take cuttings carefully, slicing off the stalk-cum-leaf with a clean, sharp knife, and note the sharpness is very important. A scalpel is ideal. Then trim the end of the stalk to leave about 4cm (1½in). Dip the end in rooting powder, blow off any excess, and then fill a seed tray with cuttings compost (soil mix). Make a series of small holes, well spaced apart, and then start inserting each stalk, but do so at a slight angle, angling them back at about 60 degrees, to avoid shading.

ABOVE Begonias can be propagated in various ways, by division, seed, stem cuttings and leaf petiole cuttings. When inserting the stalk, make sure that the leaf is resting on the surface. Begonias give a very impressive show indoors or in the conservatory.

TAKING LEAF PETIOLE CUTTINGS FROM A SAINTPAULIA

1 Always start with a healthy parent that has been well cared for, and look for three rich green, nicely rounded leaves.

2 Carefully slice them off using a razor-sharp blade, and then horizontally trim the stalk to a length of 4cm (1½in).

3 Finally, insert the stalks equidistantly, making sure that they are angled at 60 degrees, with the leaf touching the surface.

Plants for leaf propagation

Begonia (petiole)
Gesneria (midrib)
Gloxinia (midrib)
Peperomia (petiole)
Ramonda (petiole)
Saintpaulia (petiole)
Sinningia (midrib)
Streptocarpus (midrib)

Aftercare

Then water in using a fine rose spray, after which the cuttings need high humidity to avoid any drying out. This is best provided in a heated propagator, at just over 19°C (66°F), or place in a clear plastic bag in a warm, bright place, but out of direct sun, or the temperature in the bag could quickly soar to damaging levels. Check that the cuttings are still at the correct angle so that they do not shade or cramp each other. In approximately six or seven weeks you should see the new growth starting to appear above the compost (soil mix). Remove the seed tray from the humid environment to avoid the onset of rot and, when the cuttings are large enough to be handled, transplant into individual pots.

TAKING LATERAL VEIN-LEAF CUTTINGS FROM A STREPTOCARPUS

1 Look for a shapely, well-developed leaf without any blemishes, and cut it cleanly off at the base.

2 Slice it neatly into horizontal sections, but maintain the original shape so that you immediately know which are the tops.

3 Plant them with the bottom end going in the compost (soil mix). They need to go in at a depth that will keep them upright.

4 Firm in and water, and then slide the container inside a clear plastic bag or propagator to maintain good humidity.

Lateral vein-leaf cuttings

This technique is extremely useful for plants with one long central vein and involves dividing it into horizontal sections, and is often carried out on a *Streptocarpus*. The leaves have the ability to produce young plants from their severed veins. Make sure you select a healthy green leaf with no defects, and then start slicing (again with a scalpel to give clean, straight cuts), producing sections never wider than 5cm (2in).

Potting and rooting

Do not forget which is the top edge because the sections are now planted up, with the bottom edges fitting into a narrow slit or trench in the compost. The sections must stand upright, with the bottom 12mm (½in) being buried, the top exposed to the air.

Aftercare

Place the seed tray in a warm, humid, bright environment (a clear plastic bag or a heated propagator), out of direct sun. The new, young growth should appear in about six weeks, when the seed tray can be removed from its humid environment. When the plants are large enough to be handled, they can be moved into their individual containers.

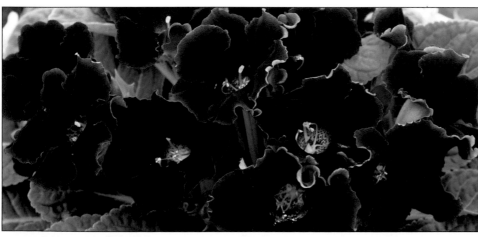

ABOVE A purple-pinkish florist's gloxinia (*Sinningia speciosa*), from Brazil, makes a striking houseplant with flaring, trumpet-shaped flowers in a range of bright colours. The large, velvety leaves have short, dense hairs. Keep it on the dry side over winter.

Leaf sections and midrib cuttings

Short for monocotyledons, monocots are partly distinguished because they often have clearly visible parallel lines on the surface of the leaves. They can be sliced into sections to grow large numbers of new plants. For dicotyledons, take midrib cuttings using the two long halves of a leaf.

Monocot leaf sections

Look for a long, healthy, blemish-free leaf, for example on a mother-in-law's tongue (*Sansevieria*), and cut it off at the base. Leaf sections are certainly quicker to produce new plants of the *Sansevieria* than seed or offsets, though strangely they may

not inherit the parent's variegation. Lie the leaf face down and cut firmly and cleanly across it to produce 2.5cm (1in) wide slices. It is vital that you do not mix them up, as you need to remember which is the top edge.

Planting

Set the leaf sections out in rows in cuttings compost (soil mix), wedging them in bottom edge down so that the top edge is exposed to the air. Water with a fine rose spray. To avoid drying out, place the seed tray in a heated propagator at 21°C (70°F), or in a sealed, clear plastic bag, and give it light but not direct

ABOVE The pineapple flower (*Eucomis*) from South Africa can be propagated by slicing a leaf horizontally into separate sections.

TAKING LEAF SECTIONS FROM A SANSEVIERIA

1 Only take sections from a thriving, vigorous parent packed with leafy growth. Single out one new, well-formed, undamaged leaf.

2 Cut if off cleanly at the base, using a sharp knife, taking care not to squeeze or damage it in the process.

3 Lay it on a clean surface, so that is face down, and then proceed to slice it across the stem into equal sections.

4 You should now be left with a jigsaw arrangement of pieces, clearly showing the tops and bottoms of each piece.

5 Now plant them vertically in mini trenches, making sure that you insert the bottoms in the compost (soil mix) and not the tops.

Plants for propagating by leaf sections

Eucomis (monocot)
Galanthus (monocot)
Gesneria (midrib)
Gloxinia (midrib)
Heloniopsis (monocot)
Hyacinthoides (monocot)
Hyacinthus (monocot)
Lachenalia (monocot)
Leucojum (monocot)
Scilla (monocot)
Sinningia (midrib)
Streptocarpus (midrib)

TAKING MIDRIB CUTTINGS FROM A STREPTOCARPUS

1 Select a fully grown, healthy *Streptocarpus*, and cleanly sever an undamaged leaf at the base of the plant.

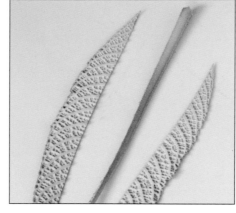

2 Slice along either side of the midrib, so that it can be removed, leaving the two whole side portions.

3 These are now planted lengthways with the edges that were closest to the midrib being inserted in the compost (soil mix).

sun to avoid a sudden escalation of the temperature. After approximately eight weeks new growth should have appeared, and the seed tray can be removed from its enclosed environment. When the young plants are large enough to handle, they can be moved to their individual containers.

Midrib cuttings

Dicotyledons usually have leaves with a midrib. Run a scalpel up one side of the central vein, and then the other, so that it can be removed and discarded.

Potting up

The two halves are then wedged in the compost, with the severed edges going into the mini trenches. Firm in and water. Again, a warm, humid environment is vital.

Aftercare

After approximately eight weeks, you will see new growth appearing along the base of the leaves, at which point the seed tray can be removed from its hot house. Separate the young plants, and move to their own individual containers.

Monocotyledons

Angiosperms – plants with seeds inside an ovary – have two divisions: monocotyledons and dicotyledons. The former have only one seed leaf (called a 'cotyledon'), parallel leaf veins, the absence of cambium and woody tissue, and therefore woody stems, and petals and sepals that are virtually identical. The latter have two seed leaves and cambium, producing thicker (possibly woody) stems. Also, their petals are generally arranged in fours or fives, while those of a monocotyledon appear in threes.

ABOVE Hyacinths can easily be propagated by leaf sections, giving extra scented plants for a spring display.

ABOVE The snowflake (*Leucojum*) is best in groups for a strong spring display, with new plants being raised by leaf sections.

ABOVE Scillas are bulbous perennials giving a gentle spring show, and are available in colours from white to blue and pink.

Leaf squares and leaf slashing

These two techniques are usually reserved for plants with large leaves, and they give good results producing a large batch of new plants from just one leaf, so that the parent plant will not suffer too much.

Leaf squares

Use any plant that has the means to generate new plants from its leaves, and begin by removing one whole, unblemished leaf. The larger the leaf, the greater the number of offspring. Promptly get rid of the leaf stalk, which is not needed, and then lay the leaf face down. Use a new clean scalpel (cleanliness is very important

since this technique can result in rotting), and slice up the leaf into small squares, with the sides approximately 2cm (¾ in) long. Each square must contain a piece of main vein. Leave them on the surface so that you remember which edge is nearest the base of the leaf.

Planting leaf squares

Get the seed tray ready, and fill with cuttings compost (soil mix). The surface needs to be flat but not compressed and squashed down hard. You then have two choices. Either lay the individual squares down on moist cuttings compost in rows, face

ABOVE *Begonia rex*, with its richly coloured large leaves, is a prime candidate for propagation by leaf squares.

up, pinned down by short lengths of bent wire, leaving 12mm (½ in) between each, or, in the case of crinkled, wrinkled leaves that are impossible to lay flat giving good all-over surface contact, plant them vertically. Note that the end nearest the base of the leaf just goes into the compost, with the top end being exposed to the air. Do not bury them too deeply. The aim is simply to get them to stand upright. After watering with a fine rose spray, put the seed tray inside a clear plastic bag to create humidity at a temperature of about 21°C (70°F). Keep it out of direct sun, then wait approximately two months for the new growth to appear. Finally, remove from its humid bag and, when the cuttings are large enough to handle, after a few more weeks, they can be removed and individually potted up.

Leaf slashing

Best reserved for leaves with an all-over network of veins rather than those with one strong, dominant vein running up the length of the leaf, with laterals breaking from it, this simply involves making slashes in the leaf rather than cutting it up into segments.

SLICING LEAF SQUARES FROM A BEGONIA

1 Select a large, unblemished leaf, and remove it by making a quick, clean cut at the base of the stalk.

2 Next, trim off the stalk just below the leaf, taking care to lay it flat so that it is not bruised or damaged.

3 Using a clean sharp scalpel, remove several squares from the leaf, making sure that each one contains a piece of main vein.

4 Finally, lay them flat on the compost (soil mix) surface, weighing them down so that they make full contact.

Planting slashed leaves

Use one large leaf from a rhizomatous begonia (e.g. *Begonia rex*), whose ovate, warty leaves can typically grow 20cm (8in) long, and sever it from the parent at the base of the stalk, which can then be discarded. Only use firm, healthy leaves. Then lay the leaf face down and make a number of 12mm (½in) long cuts, using a clean scalpel, across a dominant vein. Space out the cuts across the leaf so that the new plants are not all packed together.

Potting up

Lay the leaf, face up, on the top of the moist cuttings compost in a seed tray. Pin the leaf firmly down with the slashes in direct contact with the surface. New buds will develop at these points, producing plantlets and roots. Place the seed tray in a clear plastic bag to provide 21°C (70°F) warmth and humidity. After the plants appear in about four weeks, remove the tray and wait until they can be individually potted up.

Aftercare

Grow on the young plants in a shallow container until they are large enough to pot up individually.

RIGHT *Begonia masoniana*, distinguished by a dark brown-blackish mark like the German Iron Cross, can be propagated by leaf squares.

LEAF SLASHING FROM A BEGONIA

1 When slashing a begonia leaf, turn it face down and make sure that the quick, short cuts run across a strong, prominent vein.

2 Then turn the leaf face up and pin it on top of the compost (soil mix), ensuring that each slash is in contact with the surface.

ABOVE 'Etna' is a compact begonia with crimson-brown leaves that are splashed with bright patches of silver and pink.

ABOVE The puckered leaves of 'Helen Rowe' are an even creamy-green with ruffled, dark margins and a striking central mark.

ABOVE The cultivar 'Silver Jewel' needs good humidity at all times or it may shed its leaves, especially during cold periods over winter.

Root cuttings

There is nothing new about propagating from roots. It has been practised for well over 350 years, and though it has never become as popular as taking softwood cuttings, for example, it can be an incredibly successful way of making large numbers of new plants from a relatively small amount of material.

The simplest cut

A good way to show the power of roots to generate new plants is to dig quite fiercely in spring around a *Rubus*, for example, slicing the spade just under the surface. The aim is to sever through the roots. Remove the

ABOVE Phlox make a very impressive border show in cottage and formal gardens, but you will need several plants to create a strong impact. More plants can easily be propagated by taking root cuttings, by seed, softwood cuttings and division.

ABOVE The tender clerodendrums, mainly from near tropical regions, might die over winter so grow replacements as a precaution.

ABOVE The Chilean glory flower (*Eccremocarpus*) is usually grown from seed, but you can also opt for root cuttings.

ABOVE The subshrub *Romnya coulteri* is not reliably hardy; if you live in a chilly area, grow precautionary replacement root cuttings.

ABOVE In late summer *Campsis radicans* has orange-red flowers. Take precautionary replacement cuttings in cold regions.

parent plant, and make sure that the roots left in the ground are well watered in a dry spell. By autumn, they should have generated new growth that will be poking through the ground. Eventually, they can be dug up and replanted.

Timing

Different plants (and there are not that many that can be used for root cuttings) have different times when root cuttings are taken, but as a general rule stick to the end of autumn, and the start of the dormant period. Select a vigorous, well-established plant with a good root system, and carefully fork it out of the ground. If the plant is too large to get out, or the root system is proving immovable, you simply need to be able to get at the roots, in which case dig down until some are exposed.

The cut

With the plant out of the ground, wash or spray the root system to get rid of the mud and expose the growth. Then use a sharp, clean knife to slice off pencil-thick, fleshy lengths of root, taking each one

ABOVE The Indian bean tree (*Catalpa bignonioides*) makes a 10m (30ft) high specimen, and produces striking flowers.

from as close to the plant's crown as possible. Each length should be about 12.5cm (5in) long and at least 6mm (¼in) wide, with the cut closest to the crown and the soil surface being straight and the bottom one, further away in the soil, being angled. This will help you remember which is the top and bottom. The parent plant then goes straight back in the ground, at the same depth as before. Firm in well to ensure there are no air pockets, and water in well.

Potting up

These thick cuttings can then be inserted in pots – with say five to an 8cm (3½in) container – that have been filled with loam-based compost (soil mix) for standing in a cold frame. The pots must be deep enough to sink in the whole length

of root vertically, with the angled cut at the bottom, the straight cut just beneath the top covering of compost finished off with a scattering of grit. If the compost is already moist, do not water, but if it is dry just give a gentle drink. Expect to see results at the top within about 16 weeks, but if you need quicker results in a quarter of the time then take much shorter cuttings, 2.5cm (1in) long, and having potted them up provide mild bottom heat – about 18°C (65°F) – in a greenhouse.

Aftercare

If you have neither a cold frame nor a greenhouse, then cuttings of plants which are quick to produce new

roots – the tree of heaven (*Ailanthus altissima*) and *Rhus typhina*, for example – can be put in the open ground. When this new growth appears, you can start watering.

Horizontal cuttings

Plants with thinner, fibrous roots, such as *Campanula*, can be treated slightly differently. Do not bother making straight and angled cuts, because you do not need a top and bottom. Instead, the 7.5cm (3in) long cuttings are laid 2.5cm (1in) apart just below the compost on a seed tray, and are given a 12mm (½in) covering of grit on top of that. These cuttings might well generate growth at both ends.

TAKING ROOT CUTTINGS FROM A PHLOX

1 Sever the roots using a sharpened knife, making the cut close to the crown, that is topped by the surface growth.

2 To clearly mark a root's crown-end from the base, give the latter an angled cut and the former a straight cut.

3 Plant with the straight (top) cut just below the compost (soil mix) surface and cover with a layer of grit.

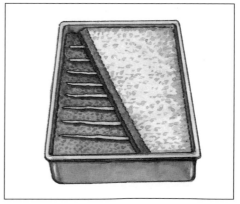

4 When using horizontal cuttings, lay them neatly in rows just below the surface, under a scattering of grit.

Plants that provide root cuttings	
Campsis	Paulownia
Catalpa	Phlox
Clerodendrum	Romneya
Eccremocarpus	

Cuttings checklist

It is worth taking time to run through the dos and don'ts of taking cuttings to make sure you get good results. Most people take cuttings at some time or other, and once you've mastered the basics everything becomes less fraught.

Healthy parents, healthy offspring

Buy one large, new, well-grown plant and you can quickly divide it into several new plants or use it to take cuttings, getting a multitude of new, young plants. This is much cheaper than buying lots of new plants, and is particularly useful when you need formal rows of hedging plants, or want to plant great drifts of one particular plant running into another, in a mock prairie style.

Care of cuttings

Cuttings, which have had part of their tissue cut and exposed, are prone to infection, and the best way of getting a high success rate is by using clean equipment. When you have used a scalpel to take one batch of cuttings, clean it to make sure that there is no possibility of an infection spreading to the next batch. There is nothing more infuriating than seeing a large number of cuttings collapse and die. Good hygiene is essential.

Pots

It is very tempting to grab the first pot in a shed to get on with potting up, but get everything lined up before you start and scrupulously clean everything out.

ABOVE Sit one cutting in the centre of a small pot to give the roots room to spread all around, without being forced to one side.

Taking cuttings

Only use cuttings of non-flowering shoots – if there are none, then quickly snip off the buds – because this gives quicker and far higher success rates. If you cannot put the cutting straight into a pot filled with compost, keep it in a plastic bag which has been sprayed with water so that it is moist and humid inside. But whatever happens, do not let the cutting dry out. When using rooting powder, remember that a little is best. That applies to soft young growth and to hardwood cuttings, which also need to have a sliver of bark left on to help the roots quickly grow and get established. Too great a concentration of these chemicals will damage the cutting. Having applied some, give the powdered end of the cutting a quick shake or a gentle tap.

Compost (soil mix)

Do not think that by using a compost high in nutrients – one suited to nicely established plants – you are giving the cutting a quick boost, energizing plenty of new growth, because that will not happen.

ABOVE When inserting several cuttings per pot, insert them around the outside. Lightly dab the end of each in rooting powder.

ABOVE Insert cuttings into a seed tray, lining them up in neat rows so that you can easily keep a check on each.

ABOVE When using a large leaf to propagate by leaf slashing, you can pin it on compost (soil mix) inside a bright, warm propagator.

ABOVE Propagating cases need to be scrupulously cleaned – both the lid and base – before being used each year.

ABOVE Stand cold frames in a bright but sheltered position. Do not put them in full sun where the young plants will quickly bake.

Stick to a weak formula specially aimed at developing plants or you might badly check, damage or even kill the cutting.

Water

Cuttings only need a drink when the compost is clearly getting dry. Keep it just moist and avoid the twin extremes of over-watering which will rot the cutting, and even 'drown' it, preventing it from getting adequate oxygen, and leaving it so dry that it wilts from dehydration. A humid atmosphere is helpful, because it reduces transpiration (moisture loss through the leaves).

Light and temperature

Cuttings need light, but avoid any extremes that will put them under stress. Avoid permanent shade and direct, fierce sun, sticking to a mild, gentle temperature about 17°C (62°F).

Aftercare

When standing out young plants in a cold frame to acclimatize them to outside conditions, put them on a layer of gravel over weed-suppressant matting. This deters slugs and snails

ABOVE A border packed with neatly ordered lines of bright red lupins, all grown from cuttings. To thrive, they need light, free-draining soil, which can be slightly acidic, and full sun.

from feasting on the tasty new young growth. Keep lifting the pots on a regular basis to check that slugs are not hiding underneath.

Keep an eye out for fungal growths or rotting or dead leaves, and promptly remove them so that they are not left lying around.

ABOVE If you need dozens of the same plant to grow a hedge or wind-break, taking cuttings gives excellent results.

ABOVE Keep checking to make sure that plants do not need potting into larger containers, and that they are well watered.

Propagating roses by cuttings

There are several methods of propagating roses. Some, such as micropropagation and budding, are best left to the professionals. But others can easily be done by the amateur, and are an inexpensive way of building up numbers of a favourite plant.

Why cuttings?

One of the simplest techniques simply involves taking a non-flowering cutting, about 13cm (5in) long, from midsummer. With a cutting, you will not get any suckers of a different plant from the rootstock, which happens with grafted plants. This technique is best for vigorous shrubby types, climbers and miniatures.

Semi-ripe cuttings

Snip off the cutting just below a node that will generate a good supply of roots. Then pull off any leaves up the 'leg' of the cutting, leaving two clusters of leaflets, each on its own stem. If the cutting is top heavy with foliage, cut off some of the leaves to avoid excess transpiration. Dip the base in

ABOVE *Rosa* 'Graham Thomas' was introduced in 1983 and makes a vigorous, bushy, middle-of-the-border English rose. The pure yellow flowers keep opening all through summer. It is named after one of the most distinguished gardeners of the late twentieth century.

ABOVE The Gallica 'Duc de Guiche' has scented wine red flowers and can be propagated by hardwood cuttings.

ABOVE The Damask rose 'Ispahan' has one of the longest flower shows of any Old Rose, with an abundance of pink flowers.

rooting powder and pot up in cuttings compost (soil mix). Finally, either move the pot into a heated propagator or put a clear bag over the top, kept well clear of the foliage, and leave to provide a warm, humid atmosphere. When the cutting starts making root growth after a few weeks it can be removed and hardened off.

Hardwood cuttings

The best time is late autumn when the ground is still warm and the plants are dormant. You need strong, pencil-thick hardwood cuttings from growth produced that year. Old roses

ABOVE 'Stanwell Perpetual' has pretty pink-white blooms and will keep on flowering until the start of the cold winter weather.

ABOVE The single pink flower of *Rosa rugosa*, which makes an excellent bushy hedge about 2.5m (8ft) high.

TAKING ROSE CUTTINGS

1 To grow a batch of hardwood cuttings, make a narrow trench using a spade in crumbly, free-draining, well-weeded ground.

3 Take the cuttings, removing each one just above a node, with each one being about the width of a pencil. Not too thin, not too thick.

5 Trim off the top end, this time with an angled cut so you know which part will poke just out of the ground.

2 Then carefully pour in sharp sand to improve the drainage, but only enough to cover the bottom. You should not fill the trench.

4 Trim below a node with a straight cut, making sure that there are three nodes up the length of the stem.

6 Finally, insert the lengths bottom end first, and firm down the soil around them to remove any air pockets and water.

(e.g. Gallicas) respond best to this treatment. Each should be approximately 25cm (10in) long, being removed from the parent just above a node. Trim below a node, using a straight cut. There should be three more up the stem. You do not need the soft, sappy growth at the end, which can be removed immediately with an angled cut, signalling the difference between the top and bottom. Also remove any leaves. Then nick up a sliver of wood at the base and apply a light dab of rooting powder, and insert the cuttings in a trench in the ground. It needs to be a V shape, but with one side vertical. Simply thrust a spade in the ground and wiggle it backwards and forwards. Pour sharp sand into the bottom, and make sure that the end with the straight cut is in the base of the trench, with the angled cut poking out of the ground. Firm in well and then water. New growth should be evident next spring, but the cuttings will not be ready for transplanting until autumn. Keep watering over summer, and do not let weeds get anywhere near. Alternatively, you could just stick prunings of ramblers in the ground in autumn, and many will root.

Propagating conifers by cuttings

Conifers can be propagated by a variety of methods, including cuttings (also see grafting). Seed takes a long time, and grafting is one for the professionals. This method is relatively quick and easy.

Parentage

Look for a conifer with a particularly attractive shape. If you want to encourage birds into the garden, evergreen conifers are particularly useful. Their close network of branches provides a very effective microclimate for birds in winter, and shelter from raw, cutting winds. They radically improve a bird's chances of survival. But more importantly, note that the cutting that you take will copy the shape of the branch from which it is taken, so a sideways shoot will produce a low spreader while a vertical one will produce an upright. Take your choice. Or for a variety of shapes, take different types of cutting.

ABOVE *Picea glauca* var. *albertiana* 'Alberta' is a 90cm (3ft) high rounded North American conifer. It is ideal when you want a variety of shapes in a Japanese-style garden, or a series of domes that are not immaculately symmetrical to flank a path.

ABOVE The Irish juniper (*Juniperus communis* 'Hibernica') is a good choice for adding thin evergreen vertical shapes.

Timing

Take a semi-ripe cutting (from this year's growth) in late summer or wait until early autumn. It should be approximately 7.5cm (5in) long, and the base needs to have the leaves stripped off, leaving a bare 3cm (1in) 'leg'. You can tear the cutting away from the branch to leave a heel at its base, but some say it isn't strictly essential. Then snip off the top of the cutting if it is soft and sappy before lifting up a sliver of bark at the base and dipping it in rooting powder. Tap away the excess so that it is not thickly covered.

TAKING FULLY RIPE CONIFER CUTTINGS

1 Conifer cuttings can be removed by hand. Give a sharp tug to pull them away, possibly leaving a sliver of bark attached to the base.

2 Use a scalpel to trim the attached piece of wood, then dip the end in rooting powder and insert in a tray of compost (soil mix).

Growing on

Grow the cuttings in free-draining compost (soil mix), standing in a cold frame. Provide good ventilation on mild days, and cover the closed frame with a piece of old carpet on frosty nights. The cuttings should have rooted nicely by the following spring, but need to be nurtured in pots (potting up as required, and never being allowed to dry out) before planting out when they have roughly doubled in height.

The majority of conifers are relatively trouble-free, provided they are well cared for and given the right growing conditions. If growing a hedge of young plants in an exposed site prone to flaying winds and heavy frosts, some form of protection will be necessary in their early years (e.g. a sheltering, protective, temporary barrier). When protecting just one plant with horticultural fleece, wrap it around posts staked firmly around the conifer, and tie in but never be tempted to cover the open top, because it needs excellent ventilation. Once the late spring temperatures start to pick up, promptly remove the fleece, because young plants become more robust when they are ruffled by the wind. Also make sure that the moment it snows, you brush off this weight to minimize damage.

ABOVE The 8m (25ft) high *Cryptomeria japonica* 'Elegans', which is at its best in cold winters when the green foliage being hit by the prevailing wind turns reddish-brown. It is also worth growing for its reddish-brown bark. It can even be coppiced.

TAKING SEMI-RIPE CONIFER CUTTINGS

1 Take cuttings about 7.5cm (5in) long from the current season's growth. For a vertical conifer, select a vertical shoot.

2 Strip off the leaves from the base, then lightly dip the end in rooting powder, tapping off any excess.

3 Plant the cuttings in neat rows in a seed tray, water and, when they have developed roots, start putting each in its own pot.

Propagating heathers by cuttings

The quickest ways to propagate heathers – which need acid soil and invariably look best when planted in large numbers or in their own special bed – are by taking cuttings, layering and dropping. If cultivars are propagated by seed, they might not be exact copies of the parent.

Cuttings

Take cuttings in midsummer to ensure a good stock of new young plants to replace any old ones that are becoming woody and bare at the base. Take your time looking for good material, selecting sturdy, non-flowering shoots just under 5cm (2in) long. Give them a sharp pull, tugging them off the parent, to provide a heel if possible, which then needs trimming with a knife. If the tip of the cutting is soft and sappy, nip it off. Strip the leaves off the base, except in the case of *Calluna*, and then root the cuttings in a seed tray enclosed by a clear, plastic bag. The one potential big problem is rotting, but this can easily be countered by watering the cuttings with a fungicide solution from below. Put the tray in its bag

ABOVE *Calluna vulgaris* 'Alison Yates' makes a strong show of silver-grey leaves, with white flowers from midsummer to the end of autumn.

outside in a cool, shady position, and leave until the cuttings have rooted after about ten weeks. Feed and regularly nip out the growing tips to generate plenty of new, compact, bushy growth.

Layering

If you do not need so many plants, and want a less time-consuming method, opt for layering. In autumn or spring, dig a shallow trench around the perimeter of the plant. The outer side should be vertical, with the inner one sloping up to the parent. Backfill with the excavated soil mixed with sharp sand and garden compost. Water well. Then bend several long side shoots into the trench (wounding is not necessary) and hold them in place with a strong piece of U-shaped wire. New growth should appear, and it can be severed from the parent about 12 months later. But, if you need more plants and another labour-free method, try ...

Dropping

Carefully lift the whole plant out of the ground in early spring, taking care not to injure its roots, and then

ABOVE A multicoloured patchwork showing the range of merging and contrasting colours possible from a massed planting of heathers. Their undulating shapes lead the eye into the distance. Use callunas to flower in summer and autumn, and ericas for winter and spring.

deepen its hole to twice the existing depth and replant (i.e. drop) it back in. About two-thirds of the plant should now be buried. Then backfill, working a mix of excavated soil with horticultural sand and garden compost between the stems, leaving a multitude of shoots poking 3.5cm (1½ in) above the ground. Firm down and water, and keep the site well weeded. These shoots should have rooted by autumn, when they can be separated and potted up.

RIGHT *Erica* x *darleyensis* 'White Perfection' makes a 40 x 75cm (16 x 30in) mound of white flowers from mid-winter to spring.

TAKING HEATHER CUTTINGS

1 Select a vigorous, healthy parent with a good selection of strong, non-flowering shoots that can be used as cuttings.

2 Firmly and gently hold the cutting near the base and quickly tear down, so that a thin sliver of bark is attached at the end.

3 Next, take a clean, sharp scalpel (avoiding any with blunt blades) and carefully trim off the thin sliver of bark, called the 'heel'.

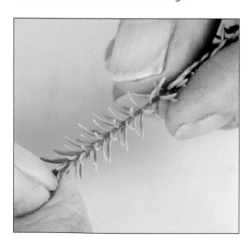

4 If the growing tip is soft, you can pinch it off, holding it between thumb and first finger, to generate more side branches.

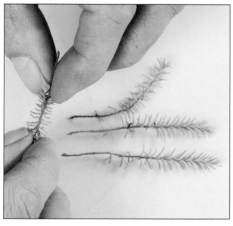

5 Before planting, run your thumb and first finger along the bottom half of the cutting to strip off the leaves and leave a bare leg.

6 Dip the ends in rooting powder and insert in a seed tray filled with 50:50 sharp sand and peat, or an alternative. Water well.

Propagating willows by cuttings

Willows are immensely useful garden plants because some have brilliantly colourful stems, keeping the garden alive in winter, while others can be used to grow all kinds of informal structures.

Why willow?

You can grow long rows of willow cuttings to either side of a path to arch over and create willow tunnels, plant them in circles and create anything from an arbour to an animal hide, or train them around a template to grow giant abstract or animal figures. If it sounds tricky, it isn't. All you need do is buy a large batch of willow cuttings, or rods, online. They are widely available. Or take cuttings from your own plants.

Cuttings

Willow cuttings are just about the easiest kind to take. In the wild, snapped off pieces of crack willow (*Salix fragilis*) fall to the ground and root in the muddy ground, and that is without any pampering from an anxious gardener. To take your own, in autumn or early spring remove cuttings from the most recent growth and divide them into

ABOVE Willow features can range from waist-high fences to large bird hides to huge structures like this tunnel. Use lengths of *Salix viminalis* because it is a quick grower, making 3.6m (12ft) a year. When the willows meet in the centre, tie them together.

ABOVE The goat willow (*Salix caprea*) is a prodigious grower, but can be coppiced to keep it manageable and generate thin rods.

ABOVE *Salix alba* var. *vitellina* 'Britzensis' is best regularly coppiced to generate its mass of brightly coloured new growth.

ABOVE *Salix alba* var. *vitellina* 'Yelverton' is another good candidate for coppicing, producing flame orange-red new shoots.

lengths up to about 40cm (16in) long. Make sure that the end nearest the base has a straight cut, and the top end an angled cut, so you know which is which, though willow is quite capable of rooting at either end. Then prepare a length of weed-free ground, and a trench running up it filled with well-worked soil with plenty of organic material. Pin a covering of weed-suppressant matting over the top, with holes for the rods that go in about two-thirds deep and some 30cm (12in) apart. Rooting powder is not necessary.

Willow fencing

If planting a living fence – and you can reduce the planting distance to 15cm (6in) if required – you will need a system of posts and wires for tying in the new growth. The cuttings soon take, with new growth breaking out in the first year. Keep weaving and tying it in and clipping back when necessary, but if the shape eventually becomes too tangled and blurred, prune back all the stems quite hard the following winter, and new shoots will soon erupt the following spring.

ABOVE The long, thin coppiced rods of a willow can be cut off and used to weave an ornamental fence or windbreak.

TAKING WILLOW CUTTINGS

1 Take hardwood cuttings from late autumn, as the leaves are falling, to late winter if you did not have enough time.

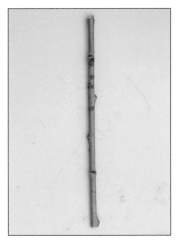

2 The cuttings should be from this year's growth. Trim off the top so that each ends in a strong new bud.

3 The cuttings can be grown in a pot. Note the top end stays at the top, with the bottom end going in the compost (soil mix).

4 Alternatively, set out the cuttings in a cold frame, again ensuring that the bottom end is the one in the cuttings compost.

5 You can also grow the cuttings direct outside, in a trench. The soil must be weed-free and free-draining, in a sheltered site.

6 Line the bottom of the trench with sharp sand, and then insert the cuttings equidistantly, leaving the tops exposed.

7 Backfill the trench, firming in so that the entire length of each cutting is in direct contact with the soil. Avoid air pockets.

8 Finally, water in the cuttings, keep checking them, regularly water the following spring and summer and lift them in autumn.

Division

One of the quickest and easiest ways of propagating is digging up a plant that has become a packed clump of shoots or buds, and slicing it into smaller sections for replanting. Just double check that each division, or new plant, has the means to develop above ground with a few buds, and roots to anchor it in the ground and feed.

Propagating such clump-forming plants does two things. It provides new plants, and is an excellent way of preventing the parent plant (typically a herbaceous perennial) from gradually deteriorating in the centre, becoming a big disappointment, with all the best growth at the fringes. In the wild this does not matter, but who wants a feature border plant that is overcrowded and tangled and unproductive in the centre? Worse, the dying centre can become a breeding ground for pests and diseases. So, after several years of growth, before this happens, and before the plant starts producing fewer, smaller flowers, be brutal. Divide to produce fresh, new vigorous plants and start arranging them around the garden.

To cover all eventualities, the chapter tackles plants with fibrous roots, those with fleshy crowns, plants with suckers, those with rhizomes, plants producing offsets and runners, and ends with a special feature on dividing water lilies.

LEFT A newly divided batch of lilac irises. Give them space to multiply, which will guarantee a bright show and vigorous growth.

Dividing plants with fibrous roots

Herbaceous perennials with a tangled mass of thin, fibrous roots are relatively easy to divide, posing fewer problems than plants with a seemingly impenetrable, dense, thick, tough interconnecting root system. With luck, you can divide the former by hand; the latter inevitably involve a bit of muscle.

New from old

A young plant with fibrous roots has a rather loose crown with an abundance of buds in spring. As the plant gets older, so the crown becomes increasingly woody with fewer shoots. Division discards the old, relatively unproductive centre, and keeps the vigorous outer portions for replanting.

ABOVE Achilleas are mainly herbaceous perennials, and spread to make impressive clumps. But the moment they start to become tired and congested in the centre, dig them up, prise them apart and replant the more productive, younger, outer portions.

Digging up

The first job is to get the old plant out of the ground in early spring, when still dormant, just before it is about to break into new growth. This means that the new, young, replanted sections will quickly recover, while giving them one whole season to get established. Do the digging on a fine, mild day, when you and the plant are not battling with the elements. Carefully dig it up with a fork so that you do not damage the root system. This often sounds much easier than it is in practice, but persevere and it will come out. You might have to resort to a spade, getting it right under the plant before it will come out. Then snip off any dead top growth so that you can clearly distinguish between the old, deteriorating central portion and the newer, more vigorous fringe areas that you want to keep.

Separating

If you end up with a great big solid, muddy root ball (roots), and cannot see what you are doing, spray off some of the soil. If the soil is dry and loose, just shake it off. This helps you see where best to make the

ABOVE *Alchemilla mollis* makes an excellent filler in bare stretches at the front of the border, and tolerates long, dry periods.

ABOVE Essential ingredients in the late summer garden, asters need dividing every other spring to maintain a first-rate display.

Timing

The best time to undertake any activity is generally when you have the time and inclination to do a first-rate job. So if you cannot divide a summer-flowering plant in early spring or autumn, when dormant, or a spring-flowering plant in summer, after it has flowered – the ideal times when you have the best chances of getting a high success rate – then do it at another time, but always make sure that the replanted sections get a good regular drink in dry spells during the growing season.

ABOVE Bell flowers (*Campanula*) give a carefree cottage-garden look with a plethora of blues, as well as pink and white.

ABOVE Chrysanthemums generally need dividing every three years for a middle-of-the-border, colourful late summer show.

ABOVE Established geraniums can easily be divided, creating extra plants to fill gaps as they appear around the garden.

divisions. In the case of a large root system, spear one long fork into the clump, followed by a second, so that they are back to back, and then prise them apart. This might need quite a bit of force, rocking the two back and forth, until the clump splits apart. Each section can then be subdivided, giving several new plants. Check that each one has a few buds and a good root system. If either is missing, do not use it.

ABOVE Heleniums add colour through summer into early autumn, but they can become congested. Divide the clumps every three to four years, keeping the vigorous, outer sections.

ABOVE Hostas are best divided in spring before they have put on too much leafy growth, though late summer is possible.

Topping

If you are dividing a plant when the new sections have plenty of long, leafy top growth, immediately shorten this or the plant will quickly lose more moisture through the leaves than it can take up through the roots. Do not put it under stress at a time when it is still trying to get established.

Irishman's cuttings

Delphiniums and Michaelmas daisies (*Aster novi-belgii*) are good examples of plants that produce new stems, called 'Irishman's cuttings', right at the base, which already have their own root system. All you need do is carefully separate them from the parent, prising them away before planting them up.

ABOVE Fibrous-rooted evening primroses (*Oenothera*) can be divided in spring, adding rich yellow to the summer border.

ABOVE Monardas are very efficient spreaders, adding colourful verticals, and can be divided by severing the new growth.

ABOVE Penstemons are worth propagating because they are not all reliably hardy, and can easily die in heavy soil in a bad winter.

Alternative methods

If the clump is small, then just use a couple of hand forks or trowels. However, if you are really lucky, in the case of *Heuchera* and *Epimedium*, you can just pull the clump apart with your bare hands.

Aftercare

Look after the new plants, and give them the best possible start. If they are being planted in a part of the garden that does not have good, well-worked soil, dig a large hole, fork up the bottom to loosen the soil, plant so that the crown is at the same level as before, and then refill with a mix of the original soil and well-rotted organic material. Make sure that the plants are well firmed in, which will eliminate any air pockets. All this must be done immediately after separating so that the sections go straight back into the ground as soon as possible. Label the plants, water them in, keep the immediate area weed free, and remember to give them a drink

during dry spells. While they are getting established, these new young plants are still largely dependent on you.

Exceptions

If you are replanting in the same piece of ground as before, give the plants a kick-start with a slow-release

fertilizer. In the case of very small divisions, they may be better nurtured in a container in a cold frame (especially over the first winter) until they are larger and more robust, and are capable of surviving a particularly cold spell. Plant them out when they need less cosseting.

ABOVE For an attractive, continuous show of the bluish leaves of *Festuca glauca*, divide the plant every three years or so.

Dividing grasses

Cool-climate grasses (such as *Deschampsia*, *Festuca* and *Stipa*) that flower before midsummer are best divided in the autumn, late winter or early spring. Warm-climate grasses (*Miscanthus* and *Pennisetum*) that flower after midsummer need dividing (less frequently) in late spring. Dig them up, shorten the leaves to make it easier to work, then prise the clump apart by hand. If the roots will not yield, do not tug at them, inflicting extra damage, but slice through the clump with a knife or spade (and if that won't work, try a saw). Such divisions are an excellent way of creating more plants, for a row of grasses to fringe a path, for example.

ABOVE Black-eyed Susan (*Rudbeckia fulgida*) needs rejuvenating every five years or so to maintain its strong show of bright yellow.

ABOVE Speedwell (*Veronica*) can be easily propagated by dividing well-established plants in spring, or later, in autumn.

Fibrous-rooted plants for dividing every few years

Achillea	Lythrum
Alchemilla	Monarda
Alyssum	Nepeta
Armeria	Oenothera
Aster	Ophiopogon
Astilbe	Penstemon
Campanula	Phlox
Chrysanthemum	Polemonium
Delphinium	Pyrethrum
Dicentra	Rudbeckia
Erigeron	Stachys
Geranium	byzantina
Helenium	Tiarella
Hosta	Trollius
Ligularia	Veronica

DIVIDING AN ACHILLEA

1 Carefully fork the plant out of the ground, gradually working around and under it to free the roots on all sides.

2 Use a hand fork to scrape away the thick clumps of soil around the roots so that you can clearly see what needs to be done.

3 Thin the top growth, and remove any dead or dying stems, which can then be promptly discarded.

4 Insert two forks back-to-back, and then prise the clump apart. In tough cases you might need another person to help.

5 Separate the newer, more vigorous outer portions and replant them in well-weeded soil improved with well-rotted organic matter.

6 After firming in, water in well. Keep an eye on them during their first growing season and keep weeds well away.

Dividing plants with fleshy crowns

Plants with a sturdy, thick, compact crown and system of roots with an abundance of growth buds need special handling. When dug up and seen for the first time, you might think the best thing is to stick them straight back in the ground, and that they should not be touched, but these crowns are actually very easily and successfully divided.

Budding plants

The key point when dividing plants with such tough, dense crowns is identifying new sections with a number of growth buds, with the potential to provide vigorous new plants. These sections also need a

ABOVE Astilbes are a colourful mainstay of boggy sites, giving a showy display in colours ranging from white to red, pink and purple.

ABOVE Pretty blue delphiniums can easily be grown from seed, and you can raise all the extra plants you need by division.

decent root system, which both feeds and anchors the plant in the ground. One by itself is not enough.

Being brutal

In early spring, at the end of the dormant season, carefully dig up the plant and then try to get rid of as much soil as possible – hosing might help – so that you can clearly see what you are doing. The fleshy or woody crowns can be so tough that it is impossible to tear them apart by hand, and the only option is to use a sharp, clean knife or spade to slice straight through the crown and root ball (roots) where there is one or more natural divisions. If there are no obvious, natural divisions, then roughly divide the plant into several sections, and slice accordingly, trying

ABOVE The South African agapanthus can be highlighted in an ornamental pot, such as a Versailles planter, but the growth will eventually become so packed that you need to get the plant out or the show will start to deteriorate. Divide and replant in spring.

Plants with fleshy roots

Agapanthus	*Helleborus*
Anthropodium	*Hemerocallis*
Astilbe	*Hosta*
Delphinium	*Lupinus*
Dicentra	*Rheum*

to avoid damaging too many shoots. Do not limit a new section to just one latent shoot in case it does not develop, and you end up with a dud. Then check the roots, and trim any that have been damaged.

Stress management

Always replant the new sections as quickly as possible to avoid any drying out, and to keep stress to an absolute minimum. Larger sections should flower that season, but smaller ones will need another season.

Replanting

The new planting holes should be refilled with well-worked soil and well-rotted organic matter, with the crowns level with the ground and the shoots just above soil level. Do not replant them any deeper than before. Finally, water in well and keep the whole area well weeded. If you need to build up a large quantity of one particular plant, then divide the plant on a fairly regular basis. It is a fallacy that letting one plant build up into a large clump will instantly provide you with all the sections you need, in one go. It will not.

DIVIDING A HEMEROCALLIS

1 When digging up daylilies (*Hemerocallis*), spade the whole clump out of the ground, working around and under the root system.

2 Identify sections with growth buds on top and a batch of roots below, and then sever them away by slicing down with a spade.

3 Select good, solid new sections with their own root system clearly visible and the potential for top growth.

4 They can now be replanted in well-worked ground with some well-rotted organic matter. Weed carefully all around and water in well.

ABOVE The fragrant *Hemerocallis* 'Wind Song' adds a strong show of orange flowers, and contrasts well with rich blues and reds.

ABOVE Rheums are grown for their large leaves and towering flower spikes in bog gardens or areas with moist soil.

Slug patrol

When replanting in damp, shady conditions, do not forget that many plants (hostas being a prime example) are a magnet to slugs and snails. If pests promptly chomp through the new growth of young plants, they will, in time, seriously weaken them, and stop them becoming strong, vigorous specimens. No matter which solution you favour – beer traps, picking off by hand at night etc. – keep on top of the problem. If all else fails, grow the plants in raised containers, wrapping copper tape or strips around the outside to deter the slugs with a minor electric shock.

Dividing plants with suckers

Many shrubs naturally increase by sending out long underground shoots from the roots (as in *Rhus typhina*) or underground stems (*Gaultheria shallon*). They are a terrific source of new plants and are well worth propagating, not least because if left they might well overwhelm the parent.

Wait for the roots

If you spot what looks like one or more new young versions of the parent breaking out of the ground say 30cm (12in) or even further away, then carefully scrape back the soil at the start of spring and trace their origin. You are looking for one underground stem per 'baby' leading straight back to the parent. If left, the new plants will gradually increase in size, eventually forming a thicket, with the new growth competing with the original plant for nutrients and water. If you do not want to propagate them, see the 'Suckers – bad news' box (below right).

Preparing suckers

Having exposed the join, look for a cluster of fibrous roots just below where the suckering stem emerges out of the ground. If they have not developed, firm back the soil and

ABOVE *Amelanchier lamarckii*, with white spring flowers, is best as an eyecatching small tree, without competing suckers.

DIVIDING A SUCKERING SHRUB

1 When the strong framework of a shrub is becoming fuzzy and cluttered with new suckering growth, it is time to act.

2 Scrape away at the soil around a sucker, and check to see that it has developed its own root system just under the soil.

3 Tug the sucker (its root system is obscured in this photo) away from the parent, and sever the length of stem beneath.

4 The new plant, with topgrowth and roots, can now be replanted elsewhere. Water in well and through the growing season.

Suckers – bad news

To get rid of unwanted suckers – and this could apply to trees as well as shrubs, especially if the tree's roots have been damaged in any way, perhaps by close mowing and striking the surface roots, or by close digging – take prompt action. If left unchecked, suckers could eventually turn into trees. Unearth the 'umbilical cord', tracing it back to the parent, then give a sharp tug to pull it away. This is better than a clean cut with secateurs, because the tugging pulls off any dormant buds that might grow at a later date, thus repeating the problem. Also note that suckers on roses (or any grafted plants) from the base will not reproduce the highly attractive top growth, but the rootstock plant, which is very different (the rootstock is like the plant's engine, providing the vigour but none of the glamour). You can immediately spot the sucker on a rose because it has different leaves and stems (in colour, size and shape). Also look out for suckers at the base of cultivars of witch hazel (*Hamamelis*) when it has been grafted on to *H. virginiana*. The leaves on the former will usually hang on for longer than the cultivar's.

ABOVE Lilacs (*Syringa*) give such a good display in late spring and early summer with their scented flowers that it is worth looking out for new suckering growths. When they have developed their own root systems they can be used as new plants.

ABOVE *Cornus sericea* 'Flaviramea' is grown for its yellowish-green winter shoots; it is also a prodigious suckering shrub.

wait for them to develop. The sucker will not survive without its own root system. Given they exist, sever the sucker from the parent with sharp secateurs, and then cut off the long length of sucker below the fibrous root system. This is completely redundant and you can immediately discard it.

Growing suckers

The young sucker can now be planted in the open in well-prepared ground, or nurtured in a container filled with potting compost (soil mix). Water it regularly in dry spells through the growing season. If the parent plant tends to be rather leggy, cut back the young plant to make sure that it becomes thick and bushy, or if the

root system looks too spindly at this stage to support a large amount of top growth. However, it is sometimes worth leaving suckers, for example on the stag's horn sumach (*Rhus typhina*), to create a clump with bonfire-coloured autumn leaves, before they fall.

RIGHT Bay (*Laurus nobilis*) is often grown in pots to avoid the winter wet, but in dry, mild areas it makes a large hedge.

Plants that sucker

Amelanchier	Rhus typhina
Cornus	Robinia
Forsythia	pseudoacacia
Kerria japonica	Salix
Laurus nobilis	Sarcococca
Populus	Syringa

ABOVE *Kerria japonica* makes a substantial shrub, a good 2m (6ft) high and 2.5m (8ft) wide, with a strong show of yellow spring flowers. Keep a constant lookout for its new suckering growth, and rip it away from the parent the moment it pokes through the soil.

Dividing plants with rhizomes

Many plants have thick root systems, often at soil level, resembling horizontal, solid, warped sausages – the branching rhizomes of root ginger being a good example. These rhizomes (often food stores) are actually modified stems, and can be divided to create new plants.

Perennials with rhizomes

The best garden examples are so-called bearded irises (though note that not all irises have rhizomes), and the best time to tackle them is straight after flowering in summer. That is when the new root system starts developing.

ABOVE Rhubarb (*Rheum*) provide plenty of leafy, impressive, subtropical growth in the damp soil around a natural pond or in a bog garden. They are also particularly impressive in summer when they are topped by an erupting mass of tiny, star-like flowers.

DIVIDING A RHIZOMATOUS IRIS

1 Carefully lift the packed clump, making sure that the prongs of the fork do not spear and damage the rhizomes.

2 Lay the sections on the soil, separating the new (with buds and foliage) for replanting; discard the old, unproductive parts.

3 Trim the foliage of the new, vigorous sections so that it will not catch the wind like a sail, and dislodge the rhizome in the soil.

4 Replant into crumbly, free-draining, well-worked, well-weeded soil. Keep watering over summer, while it is developing.

Separation, slicing and laying

Carefully dig up the plant with a fork, inserting the prongs into the ground away from the main clump to avoid spearing the rhizomes. Try to see exactly what you have got, either by shaking off the soil or, on a wet day, when it will not budge, by spraying it off with a hosepipe. Then pull the clump apart, separating the old, exhausted, unproductive rhizomes and those with dead flower stalks (which you will not need) from the new, young growth with buds and leaves (which you do need, for replanting). Handle with care.

Then comes the next stage. The new rhizomes can be sliced up into chunks about 7.5cm (3in) long using a clean, sharp knife (you can dust the cut surfaces with a fungicide to eliminate any possibility of infection and rot), but check that each piece has its own individual set of leaves and roots. The latter need trimming by about one-third if they are long; shorten the foliage to leave just 15cm (6in) of growth. This means that the plants will not lose more water than they can take up through their roots, and will not be blown about in strong winds, loosening the grip of their roots in the soil. Replant in improved soil.

Lay each rhizome horizontally in its own shallow hollow. It needs to be half-buried so that the back of each is visible (like a floating whale, part above and part below the water) with the leaves poking upwards, but the fibrous roots firmly set in the ground. Group them so that they are approximately 15cm (6in) apart.

Aftercare

Being exposed to the hot summer sun means they will dry out very quickly, and need to be regularly watered throughout the season. If you go away for a long, hot period, leaving no one in charge, you will come back to a cluster of dead, baked rhizomes. Do not be tempted to mulch them, covering them in a protective layer of soil, because this is counter-productive.

Crown rhizomes

Other typical rhizomatous plants include peonies and asparagus. Peonies pose a slightly tricky problem because

ABOVE The arum lily (*Zantedeschia*) brightens up areas of moist soil, producing flamboyant late spring and summer flowers.

they do not like being moved. They do best if the new divided clumps are quite big – small ones can take a long time to get established. They need digging up when the end of winter meets spring, when you can easily spot the new buds bulging out of the crown. Each new section must have a few buds (do not rely on just one in case it is not prolific), and again the cut surface can be dusted with fungicide. When replanting, keep the sections about 23cm (9in) apart.

ABOVE Cannas add a subtropical look to summer bedding schemes, with their large leaves and gladioli-like flowers.

Bamboos

These are best divided in mid-spring, but cut back the height of any tall canes or the plant will get rocked out of the ground in a high wind. Bamboos have comparatively shallow, anchoring roots. If you do not want to cut them back, ensure they are planted in a sheltered site to avoid wind problems. Failing that, tie them securely to a stout post, allowing for the fact that strong winds might strike from any direction.

ABOVE Asparagus have fleshy crowns prone to rotting, so avoid wet sites. If there is poor drainage, plant them on raised mounds.

ABOVE Mint (*Mentha*) is such a rampant spreader that it is usually grown in a deep bottomless bucket sunk in the ground.

ABOVE When replanting peony rhizomes, make sure that each has about four buds, and plant them about 2.5cm (1in) below the soil.

Dividing plants with offsets and runners

One of the key ways in which many plants multiply is by offsets and runners. The former is a young plant that is clearly joined to the parent, and which can be simply and quickly detached from it. The latter appears at the end of a long, horizontal stem that creeps across the soil, producing a rooting plantlet at the end.

Offsets

Clump-forming cacti and succulents, and many house plants – including pineapples (*Ananas*) – often produce new young plants at the base of the parent plant. They usually occur where there is a rosette of leaf growth at ground level (called basal leaves). Initially the expanding numbers of offsets can look incredibly impressive on the parent, creating a mounding, multiplying effect, but eventually they can overwhelm it, and you might run out of space.

Separation

To thin out and create extra plants, each of which in time will produce even more offsets, separate the

ABOVE After a mature agave has flowered, the rosette of leaves usually dies, being replaced by its offsets around the base.

ABOVE Many cacti, if given a regular summer feed and watering, produce a cluster of offsets around the base of the plant.

young plant – when it is clearly maturing – from the parent in spring. This can seem quite daunting, a bit like doing a miniature amputation. You should wear thick gloves when working on a spiky cactus. First, scrape back the compost (soil mix) to expose the join where the offset and parent meet. Then use a clean, sharp knife or scalpel, and carefully separate the two. Where the parent has been wounded, the exposed surface can be treated with a fungicidal powder.

Potting up offsets

The offset should be immediately potted up (one per small pot) in a free-draining compost, especially for cuttings. Just firm the base of the offset into the soil, and do not try planting it too deeply. Top the surface with extra grit and, while it is getting established, putting on anchoring root growth, keep it in light shade. This reduces the risk of dehydration, with more moisture being lost than can be taken up.

Runners

The best example of a runner is found on a strawberry plant (*Fragaria*). Neat, orderly rows of strawberries will quickly become a chaotic patchwork of plants if the runners are not kept in check. Strawberry plants usually last for three or four years before they start to decline, and these runners are an invaluable source of replacements.

Horizontal stems

Runners can be kept if you need to fill gaps in a new strawberry bed, or if you are expanding it. Otherwise they can be discarded until you need a new batch of plants to replace the

ABOVE Tender echeverias, often with yellowish-red flowers, can be planted out over summer to line the front of a border.

ABOVE Saxifrage quickly spreads and self-propagates thanks to its offsets, which can be easily removed and replanted elsewhere.

Plants producing offsets

Agave	*Crassula*
Cacti (e.g.	*Echeveria*
Echinocactus	*Phormium*
and	*Primula*
Mammillaria)	*Sempervivum*

ABOVE The blue-flowering *Ajuga reptans* spreads by stems that create new plants as they creep across the soil.

deteriorating, increasingly unproductive first batch of plants. Make sure that the parents are healthy, with flat, all-green leaves. Then, in early summer, select about four runners from each plant.

Potting up runners

Fill a pot with potting compost and set it in the bed, so that the compost is virtually flush with the surrounding ground. Then pin the horizontal stem in place in the pot, securing the plantlet. Make sure that it is watered during dry spells, and after about five weeks it should be ready for severing and planting out.

DIVIDING A SEMPERVIVUM

1 Look around the base of a sempervivum for offsets. Let them mature until they are getting bigger than a thumbnail.

2 With a long, sharp knife, slice one away from the parent making clean, sharp movements. Do not hack it off.

3 Carefully holding it by the edge of a leaf, lower it into cuttings compost (soil mix), firming it into a shallow hole.

4 Apply a scattering of gravel to the surface so that when giving it a drink the top layer of water quickly sluices away.

PEGGING A STRAWBERRY RUNNER

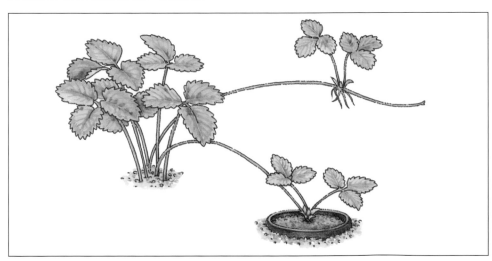

ABOVE Strawberry plants send out long stems (runners) across the soil. When they develop plantlets, insert a pot with cuttings compost (soil mix) in the soil below, and pin the runner in place with a U-shaped piece of wire. In five weeks it will be an independent plant.

Dividing water lilies

It is very tempting to think that you only need divide land plants that are gradually becoming congested, imagining that somehow water plants magically look after themselves. But some will need thinning, especially if they are grown in a small, submerged, aquatic basket. In larger ponds the divisions will make new plants. In both cases, the older, more unproductive sections are discarded.

Overcrowding
When a water lily (*Nymphaea*) becomes too congested every four years or so, its flowering potential significantly

ABOVE When buying a water lily, always check its eventual spread so that it does not choke your pond. Also keep an eye on its growth and performance. After about four years its rhizome might need slicing up, creating several more vigorous plants.

DIVIDING A WATER LILY

1 Hauling the plant out of its basket and out of the pond is the trickiest part. Once you have done that, clean the mud off the rhizome.

2 Either slice up the rhizome into sections, or, as here, remove a bud attached to a middle finger-length of rhizome.

3 Fill the container with aquatic compost and bury the bud, leaving the top exposed, then add a layer of shingle.

4 Then put this container inside a larger one, and fill the latter with water until it just covers the shingle. Keep in a cold frame.

diminishes. What you end up with is an abundance of leaves as the plant tries to absorb even more nutrients, from the water, to make up for the lack of them in the compost (soil mix).

Lifting
Lift the container out of the pond as spring turns to summer (avoid the very cold water before this time and the likelihood of new, young divisions rotting). There should be a new batch of leaves appearing. Carefully lift out the water lily, and then wash the soil off the roots, dipping them in the pond. You will be left with a thick, fleshy crown. The propagating technique is exactly the same as for any rhizomatous or tuberous plant with upward growth from a fleshy storage organ, with fibrous roots at the bottom. Use a knife to cut the organ into pieces; make sure that each one has buds for the top growth and a set of roots (trimming any that are too long).

Potting up
Insert the pieces in fresh aquatic compost, ensuring that there is a thin covering of soil topped by pea

shingle, and then place the container inside a larger one filled with water to cover the shingle. The key point is that the top growth must be able to reach the water surface. If the water ledge is too deep, then stand the containers on a base to raise them up. As the plants mature, and the stems lengthen, so the containers can be submerged in deeper water.

Root buds

Some tuberous water lilies (and other rhizomatous and tuberous water plants) can instead be propagated by means of the small root buds emerging on the root stock. In spring break off a bud and plant it in aquatic compost in a small basket. If using a rhizomatous section, you need the bud still attached to about 8cm (3½in) of rhizome behind it. The bud should be semi-buried, with its growing tip left exposed. Top the surface with pea shingle, and then sit this basket in a slightly larger container. Fill it with enough water to just

ABOVE A water hyacinth (*Eichhornia*) produces the easiest kind of offsets; they can just be pulled off and lobbed back into the water.

cover the shingle, but no more, and keep it in the sheltered environment of a greenhouse. As the bud grows, so the depth of the water cover can be increased.

Plantlets

Some plants, such as water hyacinths (*Eichhornia*) and *Pistia*, produce small offsets that can be quickly pulled

ABOVE The floating aquatic *Pistia stratiotes* from the tropics and subtropics needs to be lifted and kept in the warmth over winter.

away from the parent. They do not need any special treatment, and can be put straight back in the water. Other plants – such as water soldiers (*Stratiotes aloides*) – produce their young like spider plants (*Chlorophytum*), with the parent sending out long stems and new young plants at the end. You can separate them when sufficiently large, with their own root system, placing them in shallow water.

Culling

Since water soldiers can become very large when mature, a good 75cm (2½ft) wide, they can quickly clog up a small pond or water channel with their widespread spiky leaves. In fact by late summer you will find a smallish pond is packed with layers and layers of plants, one on top of the other, making it impossible to see the bottom. A heavy cull is the only solution, keeping the new young specimens. Leave the discarded plants around the pond edge so that any wildlife (including newts) can waddle back into the water. Water soldiers are very good at keeping the water clear and oxygenated.

ABOVE Water lilies come in a wide range of colours from near blackish-red to bright whites. Their leaves help shade the water from the sun, reducing the amount of algae, and provide good hiding places for frogs which congregate beneath them.

Propagating Bulbs, Tubers and Corms

Many bulbs, tubers and corms naturally increase, and some eventually create an incredible spread or clump of colour. But not all are that quick to multiply, and it is often necessary to intervene and propagate, creating extra numbers.

At its simplest, this means detaching the new young miniature bulbs that appear beside the main bulb – and they will be exact copies of the parent, which cannot be guaranteed when taking seed. (Seed also takes far longer to produce a flowering plant.) Scaly bulbs can be tackled slightly differently, actually snapping off the scales that generate new young plants. Non-scaly bulbs can even be scooped and chipped, when they are either sliced up like an orange or have their bottoms scooped out like a hard-boiled egg. Tubers are usually easy to propagate, with shooting sections being separated and planted up. If you've got a handful of striking dahlias and want even more, this is a great way to generate fantastic blocks of colour.

This chapter covers everything you need to know, starting with removing offsets, bulblets and bulbils, before moving on to the best way to scale bulbs. It then explains scoring, scooping and chipping bulbs and, finally, ends with dividing tubers and corms.

LEFT A flamboyant show of *Narcissus* 'Pipe Major', which can be readily propagated, giving an extra show of yellow.

Removing offsets, bulblets and bulbils

Bulbs are highly efficient storage organs. They can survive long periods of dormancy below ground when the surface climate is hostile or unsuitable for growth. They are also capable of producing identical, miniature versions of themselves that provide quicker results than growing young plants from seed.

Terminology

There is occasionally some confusion as to the differences between these three terms. Here, to keep things simple, the young which are either attached to, or grow around the bulb, are called offsets. When they are attached below ground to the stem, they are bulblets, and when they appear above ground in the join between a leaf and the stem, they are bulbils. Crucially, all three can be detached and grown on before the bulb goes dormant, but note that different species have different dormant periods. Most are in active growth in spring and summer.

Why divide?

First, it can avoid an overcrowded, congested clump, with all the bulbs ending up – after many years –

ABOVE The bright orange, downward-pointing heads of *Fritillaria imperialis*. This exotic show is worth highlighting in a large tub.

ABOVE *Cardiocrinum giganteum* is a woodland bulb from the Far East; it likes rich, moist soil, avoiding hot, dry extremes.

packed together while competing for the same nutrients and moisture, resulting in poor performance. Second, you can create new groups of bulbs around the garden.

Offsets

The main characteristic of the offset is that it is usually found growing beneath the papery covering of the bulb (though not all bulbs actually have this), attached to the base, or possibly to the side or even beneath the bulb. Take great care when forking up a clump of, say, crocuses

or crinums, because it is very easy to spear them with the prongs. Then remove the soil to expose the offsets. The larger new ones can be planted out immediately, and should start

Plants producing offsets

Allium	Gladiolus
Cardiocrinum	Leucojum
Crinum	Lilium
Crocosmia	Narcissus
Crocus	Scilla
Fritillaria	Tulipa

REMOVING A TULIP OFFSET

1 Dig up likely bulbs in spring, or after flowering, and look for mature offsets. If they are too small, leave them to grow.

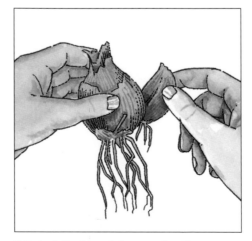

2 Detach the largest, by snapping them off crisply and cleanly. The bigger they are, the quicker they will be to flower.

3 Plant them in a container at about twice their own depth, keeping them well apart so that they have plenty of room to fatten.

flowering the following year, with the smaller ones being nurtured in pots in a cold frame for up to two years. Plant them in groups, at twice their depth, in wide, shallow pots, making sure that each has room to double in size. The compost (soil mix) must be free draining. Water well in dry spells, but keep them much drier while dormant over winter. Otherwise, avoid any extremes that will put them under stress. The parent bulbs go straight back in the ground.

Bulblets

Not many plants produce bulblets, and rarely in big numbers, but do look for young, small bulbs on some lilies on part of the stem beneath the soil. The best time to remove them is at the end of summer. Set them out in a wide, shallow container, about 5cm (2in) apart with a covering of cuttings compost,

ABOVE Brighty coloured tulips need to be grown in decent-sized groups to provide maximum impact in the spring border.

about one and a half times their own depth. After one year they should be ready for planting out, and will flower a few years after that.

Bulbils

Look for these tiny bulbs, which grow above ground on the stem, in the angle with a leaf. They should also be obvious, scattered on the ground where they fall, usually at the end of summer, and can be gathered up, taking care not to damage the tiny roots. Others can be removed direct from the stem. They need to be nurtured in a wide, shallow container, like bulbils.

REMOVING A LILY BULBLET

1 After flowering, at the end of summer, look for small bulbs attached to the base of the stem, underneath the soil surface.

3 Pot them up in a shallow container or small pots, setting them below the surface, at about one and a half times their own depth.

Life and death

Some bulbs (e.g. *Cardiocrinum giganteum*) die after flowering, but automatically supply their own replacement offsets. They can be left where they are to flower.

2 They can be easily plucked off between thumb and forefinger, and then lined up on a clean sheet of paper.

4 Scatter a thin covering of shingle on top, and then stand in a cold frame until they are large enough to be planted out in the garden.

Scaling bulbs

The technique of scaling is an extraordinary way of producing a large batch of new plants (especially lilies) from one scaly bulb, and is a good technique for getting children interested in something that they would normally run a mile from.

ABOVE After propagating bulbs, it is important to remember where you have planted the new sections in the garden. Use large stones that will not get kicked out of the way to mark their position, and then you will not risk digging them up and losing a lily display as good as this.

Clean snaps
Many bulbs (especially lilies) have a quite distinct covering of scales, and well over half, but no more than 75 per cent of those on one particular bulb, can be used to propagate new plants. Do this at the end of summer for plants due to flower next spring/summer, and in spring for the autumn/winter flowering kind. Also make absolutely sure that the parent is a solid, healthy bulb without any defects. Then bend back and snap off the fresh, healthy scales (discarding the discoloured, disfigured outer ones), making sure that each has a piece of the base. Strangely, the parent bulb does not suffer and it will flower as normal, on time, the following year. Its performance is not diminished by the scaling.

Storing
To safeguard the scales, and eliminate any chance of rotting, they need to be placed in a clear polythene or plastic bag and dusted with fungicide. Give a good shake to ensure that all parts are treated. Then pour in an equal parts mix of vermiculite and peat (or a substitute), so that the

bag is just over half full, but no more. If you are propagating a lot of scales from several large bulbs, do not try cramming them all into the one bag; you need to make sure that there is approximately four times the volume of the vermiculite-and-peat mix to the volume of scales. A rough check will suffice. Then blow into the bag until it is fully inflated (but not to bursting point) and tightly seal it. Then keep it in a warm, dry, dark place at 21°C (70°F). If placed in direct sun the internal temperature will soar.

New growth
In approximately eight to twelve weeks, small bulblets (initially tiny white growths that produce roots and leaves) will appear on the scale's base. The bulblets-cum-attached-scales are now planted in free-draining potting compost (soil mix). It does not matter if part of the scale is poking above the compost surface, provided the bulblet is just under the surface, at twice its own

ABOVE Fritillaria michailovskyi, a stocky species from Turkey, reintroduced in 1965, has early summer brownish-purple flowers.

ABOVE Buying large numbers of new lilies can be expensive, which is why it makes good sense to propagate from your own stock.

SCALING A LILY BULB

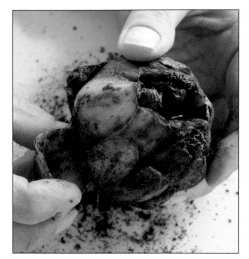

1 When the lilies' leaves have died down in late summer, or soon after, select a firm, healthy bulb and start pulling off the scales.

2 You should now be left with several scales, and provided you do not massacre the parent, it will continue to flower well.

3 When putting the scales in a plastic bag, they need to be treated with fungicide (in liquid or powder form) to prevent rotting.

4 Give the bag a gentle shake so that all sides of the scales are covered with the fungicide. To avoid any damage, don't be too vigorous.

5 Half-fill the bag with a 50:50 mix of perlite or vermiculite and peat (or a substitute). Or just use perlite, as shown here.

6 Finally, blow into the bag to inflate it and tightly seal, and keep in the warmth until small bulblets start to appear.

depth. Finally, top the surface with grit, and stand the pots outside for summer in a cold frame in the shade.

Potting up

The attached piece of scale soon dies, leaving the bulblets, and they can be gently removed for replanting in pots at regular, wider spacings in autumn when the leaves have faded. Then stand the pots in a cold frame over winter. The following spring and summer they can be potted up as necessary, as they grow, being planted out when they reach flowering

size. Or plant out after their third year, but it could take two more years before they flower. Keep an eye out for lily beetles. An infestation of these 8mm ($\frac{1}{3}$ in) long bright red beetles with a black head can ruin the top growth. Pick them off when seen, as with slugs, putting a sheet of newspaper on the ground under the plants to catch any beetles that fall. Immediately crush them.

RIGHT *Nomocharis* is related to the lily, and has scaly bulbs that can be used to create extra clumps of early summer flowers.

Scoring, scooping and chipping bulbs

These techniques might sound like something out of a cookbook, but all three are extremely easy, and are best used on plants that are slow to produce their offsets. They speed things up quite quickly.

Scoring

Simply turn the bulb (for example a fritillary) upside down in late summer, and make two or three slicing cuts, as if you were going to divide the bulb into sections. But the knife should not cut any deeper than 6mm (¼in). The cuts then

ABOVE Snowdrops (*Galanthus*) can be propagated by scoring or scooping, and thrive in sites with plenty of winter and spring rain with hot, dryish summers, though they do not like being baked. Most species flower in late winter or early spring.

SCORING A HYACINTH BULB

ABOVE An upturned hyacinth bulb clearly showing the four shallow cuts on the base plate where the new bulblets will appear.

need to be dabbed with sulphur dust to counter any infection. Finally, spread a thick layer of moist sand in a saucer, just enough to sit the upside-down bulb on, keeping it upright. It then goes into an airing cupboard (or a warm, dry, dark place) for about 12 weeks, when the bulblets will appear. They, and the attached bulb, now need to be planted (still upside down) in a small pot. The compost (soil mix) should just cover the small bulblets. At this point they can go into a greenhouse, being placed in a cold frame in spring. After 12 months the bulblets can be

separated, and given their individual pots. Plant out when they have reached flowering size. This method produces fewer, larger bulblets than scooping, which is the second option.

Scooping

Slightly trickier than scoring. You need an old teaspoon with one sharp edge. Then take a hyacinth bulb, for example, in later summer and scoop out the inner portion of the basal plate, as if you were scooping the top out of a boiled egg. Leave the outer rim of the plate, and the exposed base of the bottom scales.

SCOOPING A HYACINTH BULB

1 Hold a large, healthy bulb upside down and use a teaspoon, ideally with a sharp edge, to scoop out the inside of the base plate.

2 Do not damage the shell or casing of the bulb, but do expose the bottom of the scales. This is then dusted with fungicide.

3 After it has been stood bottom-up in moist sand in the dark, new growth eventually appears, providing firm, young bulbs.

CHIPPING A NARCISSUS BULB

1 Begin by trimming the roots, getting rid of any wispy lengths, but do not damage the base plate. Then slice off the nose.

2 Now cut down into the bulb, slicing it up into equal segments. The key point is that each must have part of the base plate.

3 Each segment must be treated with a fungicide, then insert into a plastic bag with vermiculite. Inflate, seal and keep warm.

That is crucial. The whole of the base is then dusted with fungicide to avoid rot, after which the process is very similar to scoring. The bulb is set bottom-up on a bed of moist sand in a saucer, and kept in the dark and warmth. When a batch of bulblets appears on the cuts, after about 10 weeks, the bulb is put in a pot filled with compost. The bulblets should be just below the surface. Keep the pots in a cold frame until spring. Gradually the parent bulb disintegrates, and the young bulbs can be separated and given small, individual pots. Keep nurturing until they have reached flowering size after three to four years.

Chipping

Sometimes called sectioning, this does actually involve slicing up the non-scaly parent bulb, for example a hippeastrum, which is particularly tricky to propagate. It also has a higher success rate than scaling. Start with a firm, healthy, dormant bulb – and note that good hygiene is very important to avoid the likelihood of infection with this technique. Clean it by stripping off the papery covering (if present), and then trim

off the roots using a sterilized knife, but do not cut into the basal plate. The bulb's nose also needs slicing off. Then divide the bulbs like an orange, slicing it into segments (approximately 12), checking that each has a piece of the basal plate. The segments then need to be treated with sulphur dust in a clear plastic bag or, to be ultra careful, soak them in liquid fungicide and then drain. Finally, moist vermiculite

ABOVE Chipping is an excellent way of propagating an amaryllis (*Hippeastrum*), which cannot be grown from seed.

is added and the bag is blown up, as with scaling, and sealed, being kept in a warm, dark place. Within about three months bulblets will have formed. The segments can then be potted up, so that the bulblets have a covering of 12mm (½in) of compost. As the bulblets grow and develop roots, so the attached segments disintegrate, and each bulblet can eventually be given its own individual pot.

ABOVE Richly scented hyacinths need to be given a sunny sheltered site so that their wonderful scent can linger in the air.

Dividing tubers and corms

Like bulbs, tubers are underground storage organs, albeit structurally different, being swollen roots (just think of a potato) or stems, while the distinguishing feature of a corm (a swollen stem) is that the old corm withers and dies each year and is replaced by a new one. Both tubers and corms can be easily propagated.

Tubers

A dahlia is a typical tuberous plant. Dig it up after just one season and there will be a cluster of tightly packed underground organs, and after a few years of multiplying growth the cluster can become enormous.

If you need to dig dahlias up for overwintering in a cool, dry place before potting up next spring, these large clusters can become a nuisance. It is far better to divide them up, which also generates new individual plants. Each division must have a

ABOVE Tuberous dahlias come in a huge range of colours from the bright and brash to the subtlest pastels, and give a long show through the second half of summer to the end of autumn, when the leaves are blackened by the first frosts.

growth bud or eye, but if they are tricky to spot, lay the clump half-buried in a tray of compost (soil mix) in late winter, provide gentle bottom heat and spray with water. When the shoots develop on a particular tuber, separate it (complete, with roots at the bottom), and plant in a pot, with the new shoot just below soil level. Any cut surfaces need treating with a fungicide, followed by a drying out period when the surface heals.

You can alternatively cut off the young shoot, when 7.5 cm (3 in) long, then trim it just below a node, and treat that as a cutting, again potting it up in its own container. Keep both the potted tubers and cuttings well watered in dry summer spells, only planting them out when they are mature and well established.

Corms

Readily identified because they are shorter, wider and more solid than bulbs, the most crucial fact when it comes to propagation is that the new internal growth emerges from the centre. So, when slicing up a large corm just before it needs planting

ABOVE South African gladioli need a warm site and free-draining soil to thrive; heavy, cold, wet winter soil will rot the corms.

ABOVE Just a handful of freesia corms make a fine indoor pot plant display for spring. Pot up at intervals to give an extended show.

out, divide it into orange-like segments with each one having a bit of the central growing point, otherwise it will be a dud. The cut surfaces need be dusted with sulphur powder, and after drying and healing for 48 hours they can be planted up individually with the tops just protruding above the soil level.

Cormels

Freesias and gladioli readily produce large numbers of cormels (or offsets) between the old and the new corm. The shallower the parent is planted, the more offspring it should eventually produce.

When lifting the corms before their dormant period, remove the cormels and keep dry and frost-free in a plastic bag with air holes, filled with moist vermiculite, until ready for planting out next spring. Do not expect an immediate show of flowers. That might take approximately two years.

ABOVE Choose wisely and you can have crocuses in flower from autumn to spring. Some are gently scented.

DIVIDING A DAHLIA

1 Lift the tubers from the ground. Carefully insert the fork under and around them, taking great care not to spear and damage them.

3 Divide the tubers in late winter. Before making a cut, check that each tuber has an eye that will produce the top growth.

5 Fill trays 10cm (4in) deep with moist, soilless compost and plunge the tubers shallowly into the surface, remembering to label the trays.

2 Once you have dug up the tubers, gently clean the excess soil from them. Ensure that you label them for later identification.

4 In this close-up view, the eye can be seen just to the left of the knife blade. New shoots will eventually be produced from the eyes.

6 Water the compost when it starts drying out, and new shoots should appear quite soon. Ideally, provide bottom heat in a propagator.

Layering

The method of layering is one of the simplest kinds of propagation. Nature occasionally does it for you. When a strawberry plant sends out a runner, you sometimes find that the end, with a batch of fresh, young leaves, has rooted in the soil, producing a new plantlet. All you have to do is sever the 'umbilical cord', carefully prise the roots of the new plant out of the ground and find the best possible site for it. Since this is not that common, layering involves ingenious ways of tricking plants into doing something similar. The good news is that all of the action takes place outdoors.

There are seven basic layering methods described in this chapter. The first two involve simple and serpentine layering, in which stems are bent down to the soil, where they eventually take root and become independent plants. The third involves tip layering, in which just the tip produces a new young plant. The fourth involves stooling, when a plant is cut back to generate new replacement growth, with all the new shoots becoming new plants. The fifth is French layering, in which plants are again cut back but the new growth is stretched out around the parent to produce new plants. The sixth, dropping, involves 'dropping' a plant into a deeper hole to generate new plants. Finally, there is air layering, a rather tricky technique involving stiff, upright stems.

LEFT Grow a wisteria from seed and it may take a good 18 years before it is large enough to flower, but if you layer a new wisteria, not only will it flower within two or three years, but the colour will be exactly the same as the parent plant.

Simple and serpentine layering

A reliable means of propagating which anyone can master, layering takes very little time to set up but does then require a fair bit of patience (about a year) as you let the new plant take root. If you want more camellias, daphnes and jasmine, try it. Simple and serpentine layering both involve using long, bendy lengths of growth that have been wounded, to generate more plants.

Simple layering

This propagation technique could not be easier. If possible, select your parent plant one season before you aim to layer, and prune it back to generate lots of new, vigorous, bendy growth. This flexibility is essential because selected stems have got to be bent right down to the soil without snapping or breaking. Any plant producing long, supple stems can be layered in this way.

The time to act is when the plant is dormant between autumn and the approach of spring. It is probably best to layer one or two extra stems

ABOVE The smoke bush (*Cotinus coggygria*) has richly coloured leaves that turn orange in autumn. It is suitable for simple layering.

just in case the first one does not take successfully, so you do not have to waste time repeating the whole operation.

Selecting the right shoot

Use new, long, straight growth – not too thin and without any side shoots. Bend it gently down to the ground and select a leaf node that is about 30–45cm (12–18in) from

ABOVE *Actinidia kolomikta* is suitable for propagation by layering. It has white and pink new leaves, and white summer flowers, and needs a sunny, sheltered site.

ABOVE The long, bendy growths on a camellia give good results when layered. The new plants need acid soil and a sheltered site to avoid cold winds and damaging frosts.

Plants for simple layering

Acer	Hedera
Actinidia	Magnolia
Camellia	Parthenocissus
Cornus	Pittosporum
Corylus	Rhododendron
Cotinus	Syringa
Daphne	Viburnum
Forsythia	Vinca

the growing tip, and that easily comes into contact with the soil. You do not want to force it.

Weeding

Now you know where the new plant is going to grow, you have got to prepare the ground. Weed a wide circular patch, say 15cm (6in) radius, to make sure there is no competition for water and nutrients, and so that you can clearly see how the new plant is developing.

The patch also needs to be dug over. If the ground had to be improved for the parent plant, make sure the space for the new plant is similarly treated. If it was heavy clay, add some well-rotted compost and grit to break it up and improve the soil structure and drainage. The crumblier it is, the better. If it was too poor and free-draining, again add some compost. You can, alternatively, put a container with potting compost (soil mix) in the ground and root the stem in that. The side of the hole nearest the plant should slope toward it, while the farthest side should be vertical.

Preparing the stem

The part of the stem that is in contact with the soil needs to be damaged or constricted to encourage the growth of roots. The easiest way to do this is by wounding the stem, giving it a little nick or cut on the underside with a sharp knife, just below (i.e. behind) a node. Gently prise back a bit of bark, and then add a dab of hormone rooting powder. Strip off any leaves that might be in contact with the soil.

Then create a 15cm (6in) hole, and gently bend the stem down into it. Pin the wounded piece in place with U-shaped galvanized wire, and fill the hole, covering the wounded section, gently firming the soil down to exclude any air pockets. Give it a drink. The end of the stem, approximately 15cm (6in) long, needs to be tied to a vertical cane.

Clearly mark the area, encircling it with canes and rope to keep people well away so that no one damages the growing tip. If you spot any subsequent weeds emerging through the soil, quickly remove, roots and all.

ABOVE For extra numbers of the Japanese snowball bush (*Viburnum plicatum*), propagate by layering the stems when dormant. Established plants reach 3 x 4m (10 x 12ft).

LAYERING A SHRUB

1 Lay down the stem, identifying where you want the new roots to grow, and the position in the soil for the planting hole.

2 The area for and around the hole needs to be well weeded and, if necessary, add some well-rotted organic matter.

3 Gently nick the stem, where the new roots are to grow, just behind a node. Use a clean sharp knife.

4 Then lift the bark and add a dab of rooting powder beneath it. The easiest way to do this is by using a paintbrush.

5 Make a small hole and pin the wounded section in place and bury it. Ideally, it should be 15cm (6in) deep, but can be shallower.

6 Finally, insert a vertical cane in the ground next to the end of the stem, so that you can tie it in, encouraging upright growth.

ABOVE The long, young, supple, flexible stems of a honeysuckle (*Lonicera*) are suitable for simple and serpentine layering, thus creating extra plants for a row of richly scented climbers. They are ideal for growing into small trees and for training over walls and fences.

ABOVE Clematis can be easily propagated by serpentine layering, which involves multiple woundings in a long stem.

Aftercare

Make sure the patch of ground stays weed-free, and water well in dry spells. It will take 12–24 months for a layered plant to root well. Different plants root at different rates, so be patient. Gently expose the soil beneath to see if it has rooted, and then give it several more months to develop and start growing vigorously. Sever it from the parent, lift and transplant in autumn or spring, being careful not to damage the new roots. It is important that its new growing position is weeded and, to help the plant through prolonged dry periods, add a mulch after the soil has been well watered.

ABOVE The best daphnes have such a ravishing scent that it is worth layering more to feature around the garden.

ABOVE Propagate *Pittosporum* shrubs because they are not reliably hardy, and you might need a replacement after a bad winter.

ABOVE Rhododendrons are an obvious choice for acid soil, and extra numbers can be propagated by simple layering.

ABOVE The climbing grape vines (*Vitis*) are grown for their reddish-yellow autumn leaves and stems, which are easily layered.

Serpentine layering

If you need more than one new plant, or are worried that one alone might not take, serpentine is a basic extension of simple layering. If you can do that, you can do this. It is an excellent technique for plants such as clematis, honeysuckle, rambling roses and wisteria.

Instead of making one wound in the stem, which is then buried in one shallow hole to take root, you use one long length of stem and wound it at regular intervals. Each wounded part creates a new plant in its own

ABOVE The magnificent flowering display of a wisteria can be grown against a wall, over a pergola or even through a sturdy tree, using it as a prop. The Chinese types flower in late spring, and the Japanese several weeks later. Propagate it by serpentine layering.

hole. So, for example, there might be three holes in a row, with the stem snaking in and out of each.

Make sure that the wounds are inflicted between the nodes this time, so that they are clearly visible on the length of stem (which has been stripped of its leaves) between the buried sections.

If these exposed nodes start generating new growth, which will obviously be clearly visible, nip it back so that the plants' energy is channelled into making plenty of root growth instead.

Plants for serpentine layering

Campsis	Lonicera
radicans	Vitis
Clematis	Wisteria

As with simple layering, make sure each buried section has a patch of weed-free ground and is watered in; water again in dry periods. The holes should be 10cm (4in) deep, with both sides being gently slanted. You only need a far vertical side with a cane on the very last hole.

Self-layering

Some plants do the job for you, with ivies often rooting along the ground as they spread. Sever the new plants from each other and the parent, and then transplant or pot up. Keep giving regular drinks, and move into a larger pot when the roots poke out of the bottom.

Tip layering

Blackberries and loganberries naturally propagate themselves when a stem flops on to or trails along the ground, and the tip roots where it comes in direct contact with the soil. This technique simply copies nature, and takes advantage of the fact that such plants have a strong concentration of rooting hormones right at the end of the stem.

Single tip layers

The easiest kind of tip layering simply involves taking one or several long, strong, new arching stems in summer, and bending them down to the ground. Where the tips meet the soil, either dig a hole for each approximately 10cm (4in) deep or fix a container with potting compost (soil mix) in the ground. In both cases make sure the surrounding area is weed-free. If digging a hole, make sure that the side nearest the parent plant is sloping toward it, that the far side is vertical, and that it can be refilled with fine, crumbly, free-draining soil, adding grit if necessary and well-rotted organic matter to improve the structure.

ABOVE Blackberries can be grown in two ways, neatly tying them up or, as here, letting them form massive, coiling mounds which double as an impenetrable hedge at the perimeter of a wild garden where it is a fight between gardener and birds for the crop.

Locking in place

Each tip then needs to be put head-down in the hole, being held in place by a strong piece of U-shaped wire. You can make the stem leading to the hole doubly secure by tying it to a stout cane fixed vertically in the ground by the hole or container.

Water the tip layer, and make sure you give it a regular drink during dry weather. When a new shoot appears above ground approximately three weeks later, check that it has rooted. Now cut the linking stem to the parent, but leave the new, young plant where it is growing until next

TIP LAYERING A BLACKBERRY

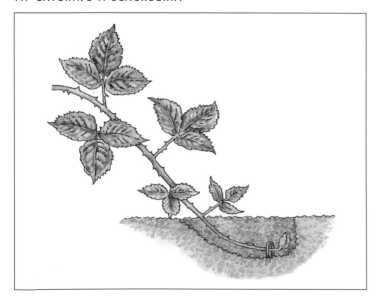

1 Bury the tip of the blackberry in a shallow hole, pinning it in place with a bent piece of wire. Water as required.

2 When the buried tip has developed its own root system and new top growth, it can be severed by the pin, but let it develop *in situ*.

Marking young plants

When the new tip-layered plants have been put in their final position, make sure that their position is clearly marked, because they will initially be quite small, and you can easily step on them and damage the new growth. Either use a cane or place a ring around the new plants using a collection of large stones.

ABOVE *Rubus thibetanus* makes a thicket of white stems, a striking sight that looks best in full sun in winter.

ABOVE The ornamental *Rubus odoratus* grows 3m (10ft) high and wide, and produces pink flowers right through summer.

spring. Then dig it up and plant; make sure that it is well tended throughout its first year.

Multiple tips

If you want a large batch of new plants, it is worth trying the following. Instead of using one long, new stem, select a short stem, about 40cm (16in) long, that has grown this current year. Then nip it back to force out new replacement growth. These new stems can in turn be nipped back, generating yet more new growth. And each one of these tips will now, come midsummer, be used to produce a new plant.

Pinning in place

Though there are several shoots, you need just one hole, or possibly a short trench, in which to bury the tips. Again make sure the tips are pinned in place, and that there is plenty of fine soil for burying the tips, and keep the young plants well watered in dry spells.

Colonization

Blackberries need regular care. They can form impenetrable, spiky mounds with powerful stems that can easily reach 4m (12ft) long. Train them along horizontal wires attached to posts, and cut out the old stems after they have fruited, to make caring (and picking) easier.

ABOVE If you want a cross between a raspberry and a blackberry, try a loganberry.

ABOVE Blackberries can be grown along a system of strong horizontal wires to make the picking process much easier. If left untouched, they will create a large, tangled, self-supporting mound.

Stooling and French layering

Also known as mound layering, stooling is an easy way of generating a large number of new plants from one shrub, and is particularly useful when you need a big batch of young plants to grow a uniform hedge. French layering is equally good at producing multiple new plants from one parent.

Stooling

The technique of stooling is most widely practised by commercial growers to produce virus-free rootstocks for fruit trees, guaranteeing their size and vigour. However, it can certainly be used at home on a few woody plants (for example dogwoods, lilacs and willows) that respond well to an annual cut, and is extremely productive. The most important point is that they are growing on their own roots, and have not been grafted on to another rootstock. If that has happened, you will be reproducing the plant with that particular root (used for vigour, not looks) and not the top, grafted part of the plant.

ABOVE The common lilac (*Syringa vulgaris*) can be stooled for a showy touch in late spring and early summer, before the garden's main display. It is a useful addition in an informal wildlife hedge, where it will attract privet hawk-moths, chaffinches and goldfinches.

The first cut

When using a new plant, let it establish for one season before cutting back the stems the following early spring. This cut needs to be approximately 3.5cm (1½in) above ground. The plant will quickly respond in the only way it knows how, by generating new replacement growth, and once this is 15cm (6in) long you need to act fast and cover 99 per cent of it with a well-prepared mound of soil, blocking out the light. The soil should have been well worked, being fine and crumbly. Avoid using large, solid lumps of

ABOVE Stool *Amelanchier laevis* to make a small tree or large shrub which, in late spring, is thickly covered in white flowers.

ABOVE The shrubby hazel *Corylus avellana* can be stooled to create new plants which have a good winter show of catkins.

ABOVE Rootstocks, grown to produce productive fruit trees at a certain height, are often propagated by stooling.

ABOVE The grow-anywhere Japanese quince (*Chaenomeles*) stands out in spring, with its bright flowers on the stiff, leafless stems.

ABOVE Willows (*Salix*) can be cut back hard for stooling, creating new shoots which gradually become independent new plants.

ABOVE Crab apples (*Malus*), grown for their clusters of brightly coloured ornamental fruit, can be increased by stooling,

clay, which need to be broken up with grit and well-rotted organic matter. Just leave the tips showing, making sure that the soil is firmed down between the emerging growth.

Repeat mounding

As the new growth lengthens, so it will need to be covered probably twice more, with the last mounding happening just after midsummer. Make sure you keep the immediate area weed-free to avoid competition for moisture and nutrients, and always water during dry spells to generate good new growth. Avoid the temptation to keep scraping back the soil to see what is happening beneath because you might well end up damaging the new growth.

Tree coppicing

Stooling and coppicing are often used as interchangeable terms, but that is when they refer to cutting a tree back to near its base. The technique forces the tree to generate new shoots, and this burst of thin growth is then used to make fences or poles. (When a tree is coppiced at head height, that is known as pollarding.)

Winter harvest

When the plant is dormant and the leaves have fallen, gently scrape back all the mounded soil to expose the buried, lower stems that will by now have developed clusters of roots at the base. Using a pair of secateurs, the rooted stems are severed from the parent plant, but make sure that when cutting them away the cut is flush to the stool. Also take care not to damage the roots. Each new rooted section can now be planted in its final position.

STOOLING A HEATHER

1 Make sure that the soil has an added mix of sand and compost or peat, and mound it around and between the stems.

More stools

That is not the end of the story, because the parent can be used to keep producing more plants by the same method. Clean the soil away from the remaining, exposed stub, and make sure that the surrounding soil has been weeded and given an all-purpose feed. If the parent and soil are well cared for, you will get many years of new plants. Plants that can be propagated in this way include *Amelanchier*, dogwoods (*Cornus*), lilacs (*Syringa*) and willows (*Salix*).

2 Leave just the last 3.5cm (1½in) of each tip showing, and keep mounding up as the stems grow. Keep watering in dry spells.

French layering

Similar to stooling, French layering is popular with commercial growers who need a regular supply of a particular rootstock. It is also like serpentine layering, except the latter can be used on plants with supple, bendy growth that can be made to snake up and down into the soil, while French layering is used on plants with stiff, inflexible growth.

The technique is best used by amateurs when they need large numbers of a plant to create an impressive block of colour.

First steps

Using a young, established plant, cut it hard back in spring leaving about 3.5cm (1½in) of growth above ground. This in time will generate a handful of new shoots that will produce the new plants. At the same time, cut back hard any shoots that you do not need. Toward the end of winter stretch out this new growth along the ground, radiating it out from the parent plant. Pin it in position, and wait for new shoots to emerge from along the length of each stem. When the shoots are the length of a little finger, the long, laid-out stems can be carefully released, and the surrounding soil now needs to be well prepared; break it up, hitting any large clumps with the back of a fork, and add plenty of well-rotted organic matter. Make sure all weeds are promptly removed.

Trenching and covering

Dig long, narrow, 5cm (2in) deep trenches where the stem lengths were lying. Each stem can now be laid in

ABOVE The vigorous, deciduous *Hydrangea paniculata* produces a big burst of late summer, early autumn flowers.

its own trench and buried, leaving just the tips of the new shoots showing. As the shoots grow, keep mounding up soil around them, so that light is excluded from the base of each. Alternatively, leave the stems pinned to the ground and mound the soil over them, dispensing with the need for digging a trench. In early winter, when the mounds are about 15cm (6in) high, it is time to gently scrape back the soil to expose the join between the shoot and the laid out length of stem.

ABOVE An essential feature in the winter garden, dogwood (*Cornus*) has a thicket of bare, brightly coloured stems that will be beautifully highlighted in full sun.

Plants for French layering

Not many plants are propagated in this way, but they include:
Cornus
Cotinus coggygria
Hydrangea paniculata
Prunus tenella
Pyrus
Salix
Viburnum

And rootstocks of:
Malus
Prunus (cherry and peach)

Separating new plants

With all the underground growth now completely visible, the join between the underground stem and the parent is severed with secateurs. Then each new plant (the vertical growth and the roots at the base) can be severed from its neighbours for replanting. If you are going to need even more plants, the new, vigorous growth from the centre of the parent will become the next batch of stems for laying out. Once you have set out the new young plants in their final positions, keep watering thoroughly in dry spells so that the roots are not tempted to stay near the surface.

ABOVE The smoke bush (*Cotinus*) has the twin benefits of bright autumn leaf colours and a mass of tiny flowers, giving a blurring effect.

ABOVE *Prunus tenella* is one of the smallest cherries, just 1.5m (5ft) high and wide. The pink flowers are followed by velvety fruit.

FRENCH LAYERING A CORNUS

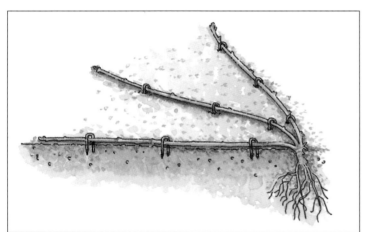

1 Cut back the top growth hard, just above soil level, to generate a batch of vigorous new shoots which are pinned to the ground.

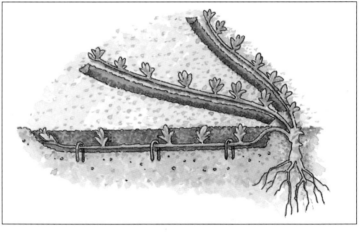

2 When new shoots have started emerging, dig a trench for the stems and keep mounding soil up above the new growing tips.

3 Keep repeating the mounding process. You can instead make individual soil mounds around the new growth and dispense with the trench.

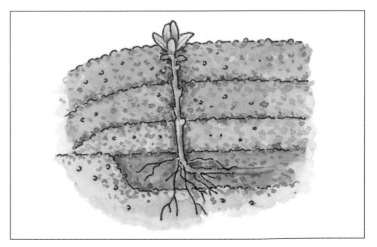

4 Eventually, you will have a series of new plants, each with its own set of roots. Sever these plants from the parent for replanting.

Dropping

Rarely practised by amateurs, dropping is well worth knowing about. It is ideal for a range of short, woody plants that do not produce long flexible stems for bending down to the ground for propagating by layering. Instead, you bury a plant, remove the new, young rooted growth, and then completely discard the parent.

Why drop?

When a short, shrubby plant is clearly past its best, with a rather desolate, open, unproductive centre, and straggly growth to the sides, do not abandon it. Instead, use it to generate a batch of vigorous young

ABOVE *Erica carnea* at its late winter best, with a great spread of purple flowers. It will tolerate mildly alkaline soil.

ABOVE *Erica vagans* 'Valerie Proudley' has a bright mix of yellow leaves and white flowers from midsummer through autumn.

replacements. Start by giving the plant a hard, all-over prune in winter, while dormant, to force out plenty of replacement growth the following spring that will root far more readily than the old, unpruned growth. Alternatively, you could buy one young, productive, bushy plant specifically for the purpose of dropping, and use that to produce up to 12 new ones.

ABOVE Heathers (*Calluna*) are ideal for brightening up the garden through the second half of summer to the end of autumn. There's a choice of over 500 cultivars, and all need acid soil in a sunny site. The more extensive the spread, the more room you will need to stand back and enjoy it.

ABOVE The smaller rhododendrons can be replanted in an enlarged hole to create a batch of new young plants.

Plants for dropping

Berberis x stenophylla 'Irwinii'
Calluna
Cassiope
Daboecia cantabrica
Erica
Gaultheria
Kalmia angustifolia
Rhododendron, dwarf varieties
Vaccinium

The burying stage

This next stage involves digging up the old plant, with its roots intact, in early spring. Do not wait for the plant to start firing out new growth. Dig it up before that happens. Then roughly measure the distance from the bottom of the root ball to the top of the stems, but exclude the top 3.5 cm (1½ in) of growth. This top part will not be covered. Finally, fork up the bottom of the hole which will also facilitate good drainage and carefully drop the parent plant into the larger hole. Gently refill with crumbly, broken-up fine soil, firm down and water.

ABOVE The whortleberry (*Vaccinium corymbosum*) makes a large shrub, 1.5 m (5ft) high and wide, with late spring white flowers.

DROPPING A HEATHER

1 Carefully fork a heather out of the ground when it is dormant, making sure that the roots are not damaged.

3 Enlarge the hole so that when the plant is dropped back in only the top 3.5 cm (1½ in) remains visible above the soil.

2 Go over the top growth with a pair of secateurs, nipping back any stems that are particularly congested or straggly.

4 Backfill with sand and garden compost or peat mixed in with the soil, and leave the stems to develop their own root systems.

Arranging the stems

If possible, arrange the stems poking up through the soil into a rough circle. This immediately makes clear what is valuable growth, and what are weeds, should any start bursting up through the soil around the plant. It is vital that all the weeds are promptly removed to avoid any competition from the vigorous, quick-growing plants.

The rooting stage

Over the next few months the buried stems will start rooting just below the soil surface. To ensure this happens, water the plant in dry spells over summer, keeping it well looked after. If there is a danger that you might accidentally start forking around the area, or that children might run over the buried plant, arrange a number of vertical canes around the plant and tie coloured string around them.

In autumn the plant will be ready for digging up. Carefully lift it out of the hole, and start cutting away the young growth, each with a batch of roots at the base. These plants can now go into a container or be planted out in the garden, where they need to be clearly labelled. The parent plant can be discarded.

Air layering

Propagating by air layering sounds tricky, but it isn't. Instead of bending growth down to the ground, often covering it with soil, all the action takes place on a stiff, upright stem. It was probably first practised in China 4,000 years ago, and is an excellent way of getting children interested in the art of propagation.

House plants

Air (or 'Chinese' or 'marcottage') layering is traditionally used to propagate a new plant from the top section of a house plant, especially when it has outgrown the available space, becoming much too tall.

Selecting a shoot

The key to success is selecting a young, not too woody stem, and then pinpointing a section about 25–30cm (10–12in) from the tip. There are then two possible ways of 'girdling' the stem. You can either use a clean, sharp knife to carefully remove a ring of bark 12mm (½in) wide, or use it to make an upward slicing cut into the bark. It needs to be about 2.5cm (1in) deep, going just less than halfway through the stem. Since this can quite tricky if you have not done it before, it might be worth trying this out on another not particularly productive stem.

ABOVE Camellias need acid soil, but if you cannot provide that, grow one in a tub specially filled with ericaceous compost (soil mix).

Plant support and rooting

If the stem is thin and weak, the length above the cut might bend right back and snap off. If that looks likely, tie a thin stick to the affected part to prevent any accidents.

The next stage involves applying a dab of rooting powder with a soft, clean paint brush around the cut surface. Then wedge a matchstick in the cut to keep it open.

Wetting the moss

You need a ball of sphagnum moss, available in all garden centres, which needs to be soaked in warm water for several hours to get it thoroughly moist. Then take it out and pack it

AIR LAYERING A MAGNOLIA

1 Use a very sharp thin-bladed knife to make an upward slice through the bark. Do this about 30cm (12in) from the tip.

2 Having dabbed rooting powder on the cut, keep the flap wedged open using a matchstick, but do not snap it off the stem.

3 Next, pack a ball of sphagnum moss which has been soaked and squeezed and opened into two halves, around the cut.

4 Wrap black polythene around the moss to keep it in position, and then tie or tape it up to make sure that it is completely airtight.

Plants for air layering

Likely contenders include:
Camellia
Cordyline fruticosa
Ficus elastica
Gardenia
Hamamelis
Hibiscus
Ilex
Magnolia
Schefflera

together, giving it a good squeeze, and use your two thumbs to open it out in two halves. They are then packed around the cut. While holding it, you will need another pair of hands to wrap a piece of black polythene around the moss, holding it in place.

Then tape up the overlap so that, in effect, the polythene forms an airtight bag. It is then held in place at the top and bottom using twist ties, but make sure you do not tie them so tightly that you are in danger of damaging the stem.

ABOVE A prolific berrying holly (*Ilex*), which adds bursts of bright colour to the winter garden and attracts large numbers of birds.

ABOVE Some of the more robust hibiscuses can be grown outside, but in cold climate areas they will need protection over winter.

ABOVE *Magnolia* x *soulangeana* is a multi-stemmed shrub that flowers in the second half of spring when the new young foliage is just emerging. Even young plants that are three years old produce a very good show. It is one of the easiest magnolias to grow.

Aftercare

Do not imagine that the plant now needs to be hot-housed to promote a good batch of roots. If anything, excess heat is damaging, so if the plant is in direct sun try wrapping a piece of aluminium foil around the polythene to give protection. Normal room temperature is fine. Occasionally, carefully unseal the polythene to make sure that the moss is still moist, and spray it if necessary. After several weeks (air layering indoors is obviously much quicker than outdoors, when it could take six months), when the roots have formed around the slice in the stem and started poking out through the moss, it is time to remove this section.

Removing the new plant

Make the cut just below the roots. You will then need to cut off the remaining length of stem on the parent plant, snipping it off just above a bud to help force out new growth. Remove the packaging – the polythene and aluminium, if used – and finally set the plant in a container filled with potting compost (soil mix). Do not try to remove the moss, because you might accidentally damage the roots.

Grafting

The use of grafting – taking two different plants and getting them to fuse together and function as one – is an excellent solution for those plants that cannot be easily propagated by other means, i.e. by seed or vegetative cuttings. The best way to see what a grafted plant looks like is by examining the base of a rose (and most garden roses are 'customized'), at the thick swelling at the bottom of the stem. This is the join (called the graft union), linking two different plants. The top growth (the scion) provides the big attractions, the colour and scent, and the bottom (the rootstock), the power and vigour, and often disease-resistance.

To graft two different plants, you need to master one basic surgical trick. Both sections must have their cambium (just beneath the bark, where the cells keep dividing, producing the essential new ones that cement the two sections together) exposed, and firmly bound together. Grafting is usually carried out when plants are dormant, through winter to early spring, or sometimes in midsummer. Ideally the scion will be dormant (not in leafy growth) with the rootstock just coming into growth. Get this right and the rest, in theory, is easy.

This chapter takes you through a wide range of techniques, starting off with the splice graft and then the whip and tongue, apical wedge grafting and side-veneer grafting, chip-budding and shield- or T-budding, and finally top grafting and approach grafting.

LEFT Almost every garden apple tree will have had its scion grafted on to a rootstock, which acts like an engine, providing all the power. It also determines the eventual size of the tree.

Splice, and whip and tongue grafting

There are several different kinds of grafting, and while they can be quite fiddly and tricky, some could not be easier. The best way to get started is by trying the splice graft.

Splice (or whip) grafting

An extremely simple graft, in which the two ends to be joined have the same diameter and a slanting cut, about 2.5cm (1in) long, so the one fits impeccably on top of the other. Use a sharp, sterilized knife so that each cut surface is smooth and flat, and then bind the two together immediately before they can dehydrate. Use grafting tape or alternatively a rubber band (though many gardeners still favour raffia or wax), and promptly remove it when the graft has callused over and healed. Always use a stable surface for cutting on, with good lighting, for this and the other techniques.

ABOVE Depending on which rootstock you choose, you can have the same variety of apple tree growing at a wide range of heights.

Benefits of grafting

Grafting is expensive, but most fruit trees are propagated this way for the following reasons:
• Grown on their own root systems, many would be excessively vigorous.
• Cultivars will not usually breed true from seed.
• A fruiting plant can be produced in a shorter period of time.
• Some weak-growing cultivars can be invigorated.

Whip and tongue grafting

For those good at carpentry, this is a very popular and effective way of propagating fruit trees and ornamentals, and is also a good alternative if a bud graft has not worked. Because the graft is made outdoors it is called field grafting. Instead of the two smooth, flat, joining surfaces of a splice graft, here each section has three exposed surfaces, and when joined they make a very effective bond.

Diameters

Again, note that the diameters of the scion and rootstock where the two join must be the same, up to 2.5cm (1in). Start by preparing the rootstock one year before, planting it where you want the tree to grow. Keep removing any side growth. When it is time to graft, in late winter or early spring, again remove any side growth and then cut off the top about 23cm (9in) above the soil. This must be a slanting, 3.5cm (1½in) long cut.

SPLICE GRAFTING

1 The stems of the rootstock and the scion must both be 12mm (½in) or less. Look for two matching plants to give an exact fit.

2 Make two slanting, matching cuts at the bottom of the scion and the top of the rootstock. The graft union must be an exact fit.

3 Finally, bind the two lengths together using grafting tape or raffia. You want a solid join without any wobble.

Trees for splice grafting

Acer palmatum	Pyrus
Hamamelis	Sorbus
Malus	Thuja
Picea	Wisteria

WHIP AND TONGUE GRAFTING

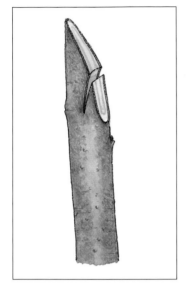

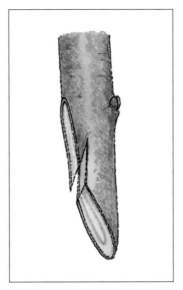

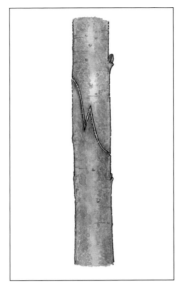

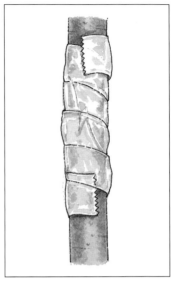

1 In late winter cut off the rootstock's top, 23cm (9in) above the soil. Make an upward-slanting cut 3.5cm (1½in) long. Then make a shallow incision one-third of the way up.

2 The bottom of the scion, which has three or four buds, needs a matching angled cut. Then make the shallow incision, so that the protruding tongue slips into the slot below.

3 Pair the two together. There needs to be complete contact of the exposed cambium wood, so carefully slice away any bumps to give an exact fit. This can be tricky, so take your time.

4 When the two lock together, they need to be firmly bound while the cambium surfaces gradually merge together. Use grafting tape. It can be removed after about eight weeks.

Scion

The scion needs to be a stout, strong, unblemished one-year-old shoot, about 23cm (9in) long, with three to four buds, the top one eventually becoming the leader. If collecting the scion before you are going to graft, keep it safe by planting it in the soil, leaving 6cm (2½in) exposed above ground. Make the top cut just above a bud, and the bottom, slanting cut 3.5cm (1½in) below a bud, and the same length and angle as the cut on the rootstock. But instead of firming the two together, as with the splice graft, do things differently. One-third of the way up the sloping cut on the rootstock make two short downward cuts, removing a narrow V-shaped wedge. Make a similar cut at the base of the scion, so that the two can firmly and perfectly lock together, and then bind them together with grafting tape. It will take about eight weeks before the tape can permanently be removed.

ABOVE Whip and tongue grafting is commonly applied to fruit trees, such as this plum, using hardwood shoots before new growth appears. The technique is also sometimes called field grafting for the simple reason that it is done outdoors. The best time is late winter or the start of spring.

ABOVE When growing cherry trees, only prune in the growing season; if done when dormant, silver leaf disease might strike.

Apical wedge grafting

A technical name for what is essentially very simple, apical wedge grafting is used by commercial growers for woody ornamentals, including rhododendrons, witch hazel (*Hamamelis*) and crab apples (*Malus*), and climbers, giving good results.

The cut

Choose a strong, healthy scion that is pencil thick and one year old. Make the top cut just above a plump, fat bud (that will become the trunk) and the bottom cut below a bud. The final length should be about 15cm (6in). The bottom must now be cut into a pointed V shape that is 3.5cm (1½in) long. Next, the rootstock needs to be carefully lifted without damaging the roots. Then slice across the top of its stem – which needs the same diameter as the bottom of the scion – about 3.5cm (1½in) above the roots. Finally, make an inverted V in the centre of the stem so that the end of the scion can wedge perfectly into it. All four exposed cambium surfaces should have maximum contact.

ABOVE Most hibiscuses are tender shrubs, but if you live in a cold climate, use the sturdy, erect and hardy *H. syriacus* 'Diana', with its large white flowers and dark green leaves. It can be trained into a standard, and propagated by apical wedge grafting.

Bonding

Lock the scion and rootstock in place with grafting tape, and then pot up the plant in a container filled with potting compost (soil mix). The warmer the conditions in which it is now kept, the quicker the graft will take. Stand the container in a sheltered cold frame, greenhouse or gently heated propagator kept at 13°C (55°F), but do not go above 16°C (60°F). The tape can be removed when the graft has callused over in about six

ABOVE Beech makes excellent deciduous hedges, which can be clipped into various shapes. They like chalk or free-draining soil.

ABOVE The rowan tree (*Sorbus aucuparia*) makes a large 15m (50ft) tree with white spring flowers and reddish berries. Rowans are a marvellous source of striking clusters of aerial fruits, which are quickly taken by hungry birds with the onset of autumn.

weeks. Carefully peel off so that none is left. Thereafter keep nurturing it, watering as necessary, before planting out the following year. As with all forms of grafting, it is essential that you use a sharp, sterilized knife, and wash your hands before starting. Avoid touching and possibly infecting the exposed wood.

Saddle graft

A specialized variation on the apical wedge, it is worth understanding how evergreen rhododendrons (species and hybrids) might be tackled. Start by checking that the rootstock and scion have the same diameter, and are approximately pencil thick, but this time the cut is more of a rounded U than a sharp V-shape, with a matching concave U-shape at the bottom of the scion. Any large leaves should be cut in two horizontally to reduce moisture loss. When the graft union has finally taken, you can carefully remove the grafting tape.

ABOVE Propagate azaleas by apical wedge grafting, with the scion being wedged into the sliced-open top of the rootstock.

ABOVE Always buy a grafted wisteria, because those grown from seed can take up to 18 years, or even longer, to flower.

Trees, shrubs and climbers for apical wedge grafting

Actinidia	Cotoneaster	Malus (crab apple)	Rhododendron
Aesculus	Fagus	Parthenocissus	Rowan
hippocastanum	Hibiscus	Prunus, flowering	Wisteria

APICAL WEDGE GRAFTING

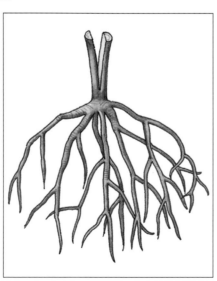

1 Use a healthy scion, nipping off the top above a bud, while slicing the base into a sharply angled V shape.

2 The V shape in step 1 now needs to be inserted into an upward-pointing V shape in the rootstock, with the same diameter as the scion. It is vital that there is an exact fit if the graft is to be successful.

3 Now lock the two together, ensuring that the exposed cambium surfaces make full, excellent contact.

4 The join needs to be held firmly together using grafting tape, and the whole plant is potted up to promote new growth. Stand it in a bright, warm place, water as required and plant out the following year.

Side-veneer grafting

Used to propagate a wide range of fairly small plants, the specialized technique of side-veneer grafting is mainly applied to evergreen and deciduous trees and shrubs, including conifers that cannot be grown from seed and which are difficult to raise from cuttings. It differs from previous techniques in that the graft is made right at the side of the rootstock.

Rootstock

Carefully dig up the rootstock with a pencil-thick stem in late winter, when it is still dormant, and bring into a greenhouse for potting up. Unlike previous techniques it is not beheaded. Only give a gentle drink, but do provide some heat – no more than 16°C (60°F) – to generate extra root growth.

Scion

The strong, vigorous, one-year-old scion with a shoot at the top should have a base with a diameter matching, or possibly slightly less than, the

ABOVE Acers give a range of striking effects, from those with shedding, scrolling, papery bark to bold autumn colours before the leaves fall. Propagating acers can be tricky, with layering and side-veneer grafting two of the more popular methods.

rootstock. The base of the rootstock then has a sloping, downward, 2.5cm (1in) long cut made into it at an angle of 10 degrees, about 6cm (2½in) above ground. This upward-pointing flap needs to be removed at the base by making a horizontal cut no more than halfway in, forming

a shelf. The scion now needs to have its base stripped of any side growth, with a thin, 2.5cm (1in) long tongue cut to fit exactly against the slice taken out of the rootstock. The two are then firmly bound together with grafting tape or a rubber band, and are given a warm, humid environment at 13°C (55°F) in which to fuse together.

Matching growth rates

When selecting the scion, make sure that it comes from a plant that has a similar growth rate. If it suffers in comparison, or is much more vigorous than the rootstock, then there will be an imbalance, and in time the part with the poorer growth will be overtaken and overwhelmed.

Practice cuts

Making the thin slice in the rootstock at a downward sloping angle can be tricky, and it is worth having several practice attempts on other shoots before tackling it for real. Make sure that the cambium layer is clearly exposed.

ABOVE The optimum time for grafting conifers is late winter, when the roots are putting on growth but before new shoots appear.

ABOVE A white-stemmed birch (*Betula*), showing why they are so highly regarded, especially as the autumn leaves change colour.

ABOVE The one-species ginkgo (*G. biloba*) has existed for over 200 million years, and has been cultivated since 1754.

ABOVE *Picea pungens* 'Hoopsii' makes a small to medium-sized tree with a conical shape and striking bluish leaves.

ABOVE A sorbus, at its best in autumn mornings when the mists slowly lift and the red berries burst through the gloom.

Aftercare

Regular watering will not be necessary. Once the join has callused over after about eight weeks, remove the tape and nip back the top of the plant (i.e. the rootstock, not the grafted-on scion) in stages until it is level with the top of the graft. This will give a nicely shaped plant. Do not do this radically all in one go, because you will be removing the plant's photosynthetic, leafy, feeding factory. It can also come out of its warm, humid environment, gradually being given a cooler site with regular drinks.

SIDE-VENEER GRAFTING

1 The rootstock needs to have an angled, sloping cut sliced into it, just above soil level, with a horizontal shelf or base.

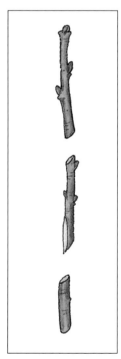

2 For the scion, remove a central section, leaving a sloping top cut and a shaved base.

3 Slip the base of the scion into the angled cut in the rootstock, and firmly bind the two together with tape.

Trees and shrubs for side-veneer grafting

Abies	*Hamamelis*
Acer	*Larix*
Betula	*Magnolia*
Cedrus	*Malus*
Daphne	*Picea*
Fagus	*Pinus*
Ginkgo	*Robinia*
Gleditsia	*Sorbus*

Side-wedge grafting

Similar to side-veneer grafting, side-wedge grafting differs in one key respect. Instead of making a very narrow shelf that the tongue at the end of the scion fits snugly against, the side-wedge has an upward-pointing flap in the rootstock into which the scion's tongue slips.

Chip-budding

A good example of a grafting technique practised by professionals when tackling fruit trees and various ornamentals, it has now become much more popular and widespread than T-budding because you can carry it out over a longer period, through the second half of summer – it has a high success rate.

Healthy growth

Start by selecting the most appropriate commercially available rootstock (which should be at least two years old), when dealing with fruit trees, and the scion from the current season's growth. Both should show strong, healthy growth, and the pencil-thick diameter of the rootstock stem should match that of the scion. In midsummer, remove all the growth from the bottom portion of the rootstock, flush to the stem, leaving a bare 30cm (12in) long leg.

The wedge

What you are looking for now is a fattening bud on the scion. Get rid of the soft end growth, and then the

Extension growth

If the new bud produces a flowering shoot, promptly get rid of the flower bud. You want the new section to put all its energy into developing valuable extension growth, creating a sound framework, not an attractive show. That comes later.

leaves, leaving stubs, and make the first cut 2cm (¾in) below a bud. It should angle up at 30 degrees, and only slice in to a depth of 5mm (¼in). The second cut starts 5cm (1½in) above the first one, and comes down at the same angle. In effect you are cutting out a triangular wedge with a bud and short, sliced-off leaf stalk. Take care not to damage it because this is going to be the new growth point that is inserted inside the rootstock.

Insertion

Locate the exact position where you want the bud to be inserted on the rootstock. Slice a wedge in the bark, just above a bud, and then carefully

ABOVE The advantage of a white-flowering hawthorn (*Crataegus*) is that it grows virtually anywhere, from cities to coasts.

slice up from beneath it so that the gap is exactly the same size and shape of the insertion.

The scion is then slotted in snugly so that the exposed lengths of cambium are in direct contact with each other. The insertion must be bound firmly in place with grafting tape, but make sure that

ABOVE The best laburnums are worth propagating for their shock of dangling yellow flowers as spring turns to summer.

ABOVE Both the scented and non-scented magnolias, grown for their lavish flowers, can be chip-budded to create extra numbers.

ABOVE The crab apple (*Malus*) makes an ornamental show with brightly coloured fruit, and will even fit into small gardens.

ABOVE Give pears a warm, sheltered spot, ideally against a sunny wall, and the fruit will juicily ripen through the autumn.

ABOVE An ornamental cherry tree, above a mass of daffodils, giving both spring blossom and later autumn leaf colours. Two of the best cherries include *Prunus serrula*, because of its shiny brown bark, and *P.* 'Shirotae', with its cloud-burst of flowers and fresh, apple-green foliage.

you do not tape over the bud or petiole. This stays on until the bud scion and rootstock have firmly joined, when the leaf stalk drops off. The bud also begins to swell, and this normally takes about eight weeks. The warmer the weather, the quicker the join.

The final cut

At the end of winter the rootstock is then cut back just above the new bud, provided it has taken successfully. Use an angled cut that will direct drops of rain and moisture away from this bud, to the opposite side, and not directly on to it. Keep an eye on the tree and get rid of any new growth emerging from below the bud when it starts exceeding 10cm (4in) long. If the bud did not take, the most likely reason is that the two exposed lengths of cambium were not in full contact. Get this right, and you should have a high success rate.

CHIP-BUDDING

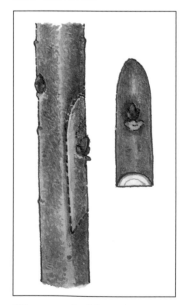

1 Remove a bud from the scion. Make a downward-angled cut below it, then cut down behind the bud from above.

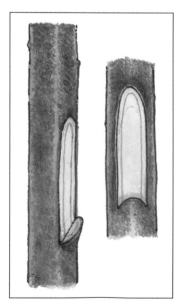

2 Make a matching cut to one side of the rootstock, cutting deep enough to expose the cambium layer beneath the bark.

3 Slip the bud into the cut on the rootstock, making sure to line up the cambium layers. It should be a snug fit.

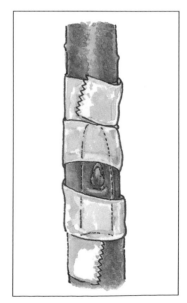

4 Wrap grafting tape around the rootstock to hold the bud in position, but take care to leave the growing point exposed.

Shield- or T-budding

An excellent technique for grafting roses and fruit trees. Though it can only be carried out when the bark of the rootstock is easily prized up, there is still a good time slot in late midsummer. Do not miss it.

Rootstock

Make sure that the rootstock (which should be two years old or more) is growing in the right place at least one year before making the graft. Its stem should be approximately pencil thick. Over a few weeks before starting work in early summer, to midsummer at the very latest, make sure that it is well watered whenever there is a dry spell. This is crucial to avoid hardening of the wood.

Scion bud

The bud that needs to be removed comes from this year's growth. Cut off a stem and then remove the foliage but leave 12mm (½in) of stalk, which you can use as a handle. You now need to carefully remove a mature bud (possibly halfway up the stem).

ABOVE Medlars need an open, sunny site, avoiding frost pockets that might ruin the spring blossom and potential crop. Do not pick the latter until it has been autumn-frosted.

About 12–18mm (½–¾in) below the bud, slice into the bark at an angle, so that you are going behind the bud (but not damaging it), then up, round and back so that the knife comes out well above the bud. In practice you will find that once the knife has gone in, it is easier to lift up a strip of wood with the bud, and then cut it off, leaving a short tail. It should be a clean, simple extraction. Then turn over the bud and have a close look. If there is any woody tissue, scrape it away, especially when dealing with roses. (The worst case scenario is when the bud comes away with it, which means it is not mature and viable, so quickly look for a replacement.) Keep the bud fresh and safe in a moist plastic bag while making the next cut.

The T-cut

Next, strip off all the side growth up the bottom 30cm (12in) of the rootstock, and three-quarters of the way up this clean leg make a T-shaped cut in the bark. First make the 12mm (½in) wide horizontal cut, and then the vertical, 2.5cm (1in) cut. You need an old table knife or spatula to lift up the flaps and expose the cambium, whereupon the bud can be inserted just below the cross of the horizontal and vertical

ABOVE An unpruned apple tree on a spare patch of ground might not be as productive as an espalier, but it adds a carefree touch.

ABOVE Roses are easily propagated using shield-budding, but pull away any suckers from the parent the moment they appear.

cuts. If the bud will not fit exactly because there is a snag or tail of wood attached to it, slice it off flush with the horizontal cut. An exact fit is vital. Then secure it in place using grafting tape, but do not cover the bud itself. After about five weeks the scion and rootstock will have joined, and the tape is removed.

The final cut

Finally, cut back the rootstock in late winter, just above the new bud. Ensure that you make an angled cut to direct any moisture away from the shoot, down the opposite side of the rootstock. Also remove any growth emerging from below the new bud when it is more than 10cm (4in) long, and any flower buds on the new shoot. The aim is to produce good new extension growth.

Correct timing

Some gardening techniques are best done when you are in the right frame of mind but some, such as shield-budding, must be done at set times. Wait too long and you won't be able to lift the bark flaps for the new bud.

SHIELD-BUDDING

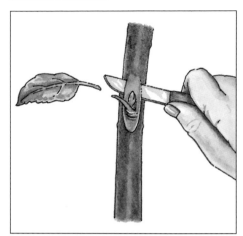

1 When removing the bud in early summer, leave a leaf stalk to act as a handle. Slice out the bud from below, going right behind it.

2 Then mark the insertion point in the rootstock, starting with the horizontal cut, and then make the vertical slice.

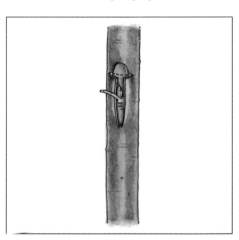

3 Lift the flaps to slide and wedge the bud in place. If there is a long wooden tail attached to it, slice it off to make a good fit.

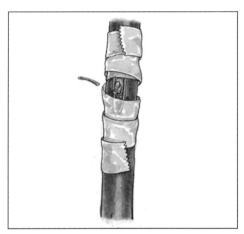

4 Finally, tape the bud in place leaving the growing point free to emerge and develop. In late winter, cut back just above the bud.

ABOVE Once you've got a successful graft, plant damsons in soil with plenty of organic matter to help retain some extra moisture. The fresh fruit is very tart, so use it cooked to make jams and sauces.

ABOVE Peach trees are often best grown in a greenhouse, but it needs to be cool so that they can lie dormant over winter. For outside, use a midsummer-fruiting kind trained against a sunny, sheltered wall.

Top grafting

Sometimes it is necessary to change the cultivar of a mature apple tree, and possibly introduce a more effective pollinator, and the advantage of this technique is that the graft becomes productive quite quickly because it benefits from a well-established root system.

Cutting branches back

The first job seems quite brutal. All the branches are cut back (called 'dehorning') almost to the trunk, losing almost all of the top growth, in early spring before the big rush of sap. But do leave two of the less developed branches that will help pull up the sap, enabling the joins to take quickly. Use a sharp saw.

ABOVE Apple trees are ideal for top grafting, and those on a dwarfing rootstock can even be grown in a small garden.

ABOVE Having propagated a plum tree, add a thick spring mulch around the trunk to lock moisture in the ground and suppress weeds.

Taking the scions

You will need three or four dormant scions, with a final length of 10cm (4in), but tackle one at a time. When taking the first, make sure it has three nodes, and then slice a sliver off the bottom quarter, cutting down from just underneath a bud, leaving the bud below (on the opposite side) intact. The top of the scion has an angled cut, not pointing down on to the bud beneath but to the opposite side.

First insertion

Make a 2.5cm (1in) long slicing cut down from the edge of the sawn-off trunk, and then loosen the bark, carefully lifting it up. Prise it away with the side of a blunt old table knife but do not do this too vigorously and tear or splinter the bark. Provided you do this in early spring there should not be a problem. The aim is to expose the cambium. Then insert the first length of scion, checking that the exposed surface of the bottom of the sliced-off piece is in direct

ABOVE When propagating apple trees, make sure that the vigour of the rootstock is compatible with the size of your garden. M26 is one of the most popular rootstocks, giving an ultimate height of 2.4–3m (8–10ft). M27 and M9 give shorter growth, but both can be rather feeble.

ABOVE To give new, propagated quinces the best conditions, add an organic mulch to keep the roots cool and moist.

Final cuts

When the scions start growing – and they should make good progress powered by the established root system – look for the most vigorous. The next winter saw off the weakest scions, flush to the first cut when the trunk was sawn off, leaving just the most vigorous to grow away. Because these grafts are not the firmest, take care not to knock them. You might even find that they need a support, such as a cane tied firmly in place, as a temporary measure.

You can use top grafting on ornamental trees, but it does tend to change their shape, so think twice before trying this technique. With fruit trees it does not matter.

ABOVE Give crab apples a prominent position in full sun, because the brightly coloured fruits make a strong visual feature.

contact with the rootstock's cambium. Continue working around the sawn-off trunk, adding the other scions at regular intervals. When the final one is in position, wrap grafting tape firmly around the end of the sawn-off trunk, locking all the scions in place. Also carefully seal the exposed, raw end of the trunk with grafting wax or grafting paint to keep it waterproof and prevent it drying out. The tape should be ready to come off after five to eight weeks.

TOP GRAFTING

1 You need to make three clean, slicing vertical cuts in the bark, about 2.5cm (1in) long, an equal distance apart.

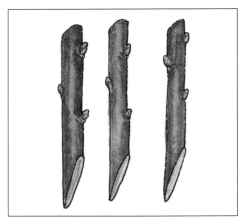

2 Line up the 10cm (4in) long scions, each with three buds and angled cuts on the bottom and top.

3 Insert each scion. Wedge the bottom end into the cut, with the angled cut making full contact with the cambium. Slide right down.

4 Tape the scions in place and then seal the end of the branch with grafting wax or paint. Eventually remove the weakest two scions.

The cleft variation

You can alternatively make a cleft or cut across the top of the sawn-off stem, about 2.5cm (1in) deep, and then insert two scions in that, one at either end. Make the cut using a wedge and mallet. The cut will be sufficiently springy to close up tightly, holding the scions in place. You will then need to paint over the top of the sawn-off stem with grafting wax or paint in order to exclude moisture and eliminate drying, and eventually remove the weaker of the two scions.

Approach grafting and grafting tips

If you get hold of an old propagators' handbook, you will find all kinds of highly specialized grafting methods, many that are no longer used or taught. But some are good fun and worth knowing about, and are definitely worth a try.

Appproach grafting

This technique can be used to propagate a particularly important dying tree, and anything else that is proving tricky by other methods, including pot plants. In the case of the latter, start by standing the two plants next to each other, and look for two stems that easily touch. Both should be this year's growth. It is very important that you do not try and force them together in case they snap or get damaged. Then carefully slice off a 3.5cm (1½ in) long strip of the outer bark on one to expose the cambium, and then do exactly the same to the other, checking that they are going to be in full contact. Next, bind the two exposed areas together with grafting tape.

ABOVE Hollies can be propagated in various ways, one of the simplest being an approach graft, in which two plants, one with an established root system, are conjoined.

Continued growth

While the two cambiums join, both plants carry on growing and there is no danger that either will dry out. When the join has taken, after 10 weeks or so, remove the tape and make two cuts. First, remove the top of the rootstock, just above where the two plants now join. Then sever the scion just below where the two join, retaining the leg and roots of one plant, and the top growth of the other. Keep the soil around the rootstock well watered during dry spells in the growing season so that the new plant is not stressed. Add a thick mulch after a night of heavy rain to lock moisture in the ground.

APPROACH GRAFTING

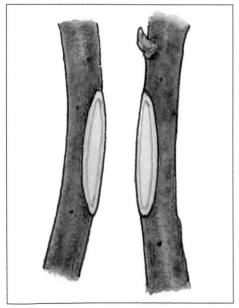

1 When standing two pot plants side by side, select two facing stems. Slice off 3.5cm (1½ in) strips to expose the cambium.

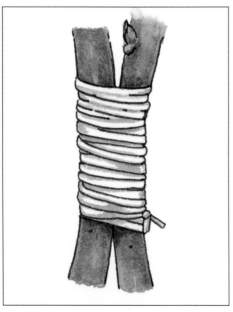

2 Gently bring them together, so that the exposed lengths are in full contact, and then bind together with grafting tape.

3 After about 10 weeks, remove the head of the rootstock plant above the tape, and the bottom of the scion plant below it.

Grafting tips

Infection

Make sure that you always use sharp, sterilized equipment. Anything that touches the exposed cambium can theoretically pass on an infection. Given how much skill, care, effort and time can go into making a successful graft, it is ridiculous to ruin everything when just a few minutes at the start, and throughout the operation, can eliminate a potential hazard.

Scions and rootstock

It is important that scions are healthy and vigorous. Do not perpetuate any problems. That equally applies to the rootstock, which must be virus-free. Both sections must also be compatible.

Vigilance

Do not let new growth appear on the rootstock below the scion. You want to channel the plant's energy into making the new bud take and then grow away strongly, without it being diverted to other shoots.

Full contact

The key to success is making sure that the exposed cambium on the scion and on the rootstock are locked together firmly, before being taped in place. If there is a gap between the two, they cannot join together. And when you have made the two cuts, act quickly or the wood will dry out.

Forced wait

If you are taking large quantities of scions before it is time to make the implants, you can keep them in good shape by tying them together in bundles, with the bottoms together. Label the batch, noting the cultivar and the date taken. Plant the bundle in the soil, leaving 6cm (2½in) exposed above ground.

RIGHT When propagating, it is sometimes easy to forget that you might be creating magnificent giants such as these conifers.

Directory of Plants for Propagating

It is impossible to give an exhaustive list of all the available plants for propagation, but there should be enough variety in the following pages to keep most gardeners happy and give first-rate results. This directory includes everything from self-seeding, quick-spreading cottage garden plants to the incredibly chic, with colours ranging from the quietest pastels to the bright and brash. Whatever look you want, you can create it from the following lists.

To make sure that the garden stays in excellent condition, there are scores of growing and propagating tips throughout, explaining how old plants can quickly be replaced by the new and vigorous, enabling you to keep creating extra, smartly planted beds. There are also special feature boxes – including information on what to plant where, different garden styles, choosing containers, hanging baskets, creating borders and border plants, annuals and biennials, bulbs, deadheading and pruning, underplanting with climbers, supports and garden styles – to help you use the newly propagated plants in the most practical and inventive ways. They cover all areas of the garden, from those dedicated to special containers to beds with exciting winter colours.

LEFT A rich pink display from a newly propagated rhododendron. Rhododendrons can look spectacular, and while many are large, there are also superb smaller varieties that are suitable for tubs.

Flowers and foliage plants

ACANTHUS
Bear's breeches
Large, vigorous perennials, with the hardy *A. spinosus* one of the best. It sends up dramatic stems with brown bracts going right to the top, like hoods with white flowers peeping out, in the first part of summer. They get about 1.5m (5ft) high, adding plenty of clout to any border, being backed up by the long, deeply cut shiny green leaves that can reach 60cm (2ft) long. Do not confuse it with the Spinosissimus Group, which only usually flowers well given a long, hot summer. A good variation is 'Lady Moore' with its near-white new leaves that gradually turn dark green over summer. Grow in rich, well-drained soil in full sun. One of the distinguishing features of acanthus is the set of deep roots, and when moving plants some always get left behind. In time they produce new plants. To propagate, cut off 5cm (2in) long sections of root and set them vertically in pots filled with compost. Water regularly, and keep in a cold frame. Alternatively, divide plants. Species can be sown from seed at 18°C (64°F).

ACHILLEA
Yarrow
Easily grown perennials producing many daisy-like summer flowers in flat heads in a range of colours including white, yellow, pink, orange and red. Though the taller kind have stiff stems they might need support to stop them flopping on shorter plants in front. *A. filipendulina* is a tall, hardy upright with even better cultivars, including 'Cloth of Gold' and 'Gold Plate', both of which get 1.5m (5ft) high and are good for cutting. The 60cm (2ft) high hardy *A. millefolium* has dozens of shorter, excellent cultivars that invariably change colour as they fade. 'Epoque' (red fading to yellow), 'Heidi' (pink fading to white), 'Kelway' (red), 'Mondpagode' (creamy yellow), and 'Summerwine' (reddish-purple fading to pinkish-purple) are among the highlights. All like average, free-draining soil in full sun. The best way to propagate is by dividing plants on a regular basis every four years or so. While self-seeding can be prodigious, the seedlings will not amount to much, and it is best to cut off the flower heads the moment that the colour fades, to avoid what is tantamount to an invasion of weeds.

ACONITUM
Monkshood
Perennials grown for their typically bluish summer sepals (the flowers are much smaller), some lasting to early autumn, making a strong, unmistakable border show. For a rich blue at the start of autumn, the hardy *A. carmichaelii* 'Arendsii' – which grows 1.2m (4ft) high – is unbeatable, as is the slightly taller 'Kelmscott'. The 90cm (3ft) high 'Bressingham Spire' starts flowering slightly earlier, and has spikes of violet-blue flowers. For a midsummer monkshood, try 'Newry Blue', with its 1.5m (5ft) high growth and deep blue flowers on 60cm (2ft) long spikes. Use it to contrast with rounded and horizontal shapes. All make 30cm (12in) wide plants, like rich, moist soil in full sun, and can be propagated by autumn divisions, with the species being grown from seed. Note that monkshood is highly toxic, and gloves must always be worn when handling them, even when dealing with the roots.

AEONIUM
Aeonium
A winter conservatory plant that can be stood outside over summer, the most popular form is the tender succulent 'Zwartkop'. In ideal conditions it can grow 1.8m (6ft) high and wide, though much shorter when its roots are restricted in a pot, with long, branching stems being topped by an array of deep, dark purple leaves that look black from a distance. Established plants will

GARDEN STYLES

Before deciding what you're going to grow and where, the number of beds and artificial structures etc., be clear about the style. Get that right and everything should blend. The basic choice kicks off with formal, geometric gardens with clear-cut lines of view and paths, strongly structured shapes (including smartly 'shaved' or topiarized evergreen hedges) and clearly marked borders, where everything knows and sticks to its place. As a variant, the planting within the design could be relatively free-and-easy, softening the effect. At the other extreme is the wild garden, with rough grass and trees and shrubs and wild flowers, often with an adjacent cottage garden.

Though it might look spectacularly chaotic in midsummer, the cottage garden has to be cunningly manipulated to prevent it from going haywire. Plants need deadheading and cutting back, and if they are not controlled, a sumptuous mix of colours could end up as a jungle, with exquisite little plants being swamped by high-voltage neighbours. Alternatively, opt for minimalism, where less should mean more, subtropical gardens featuring large-leaved exotica (many of which will be tender plants, needing some form of shelter over winter), or modernism, with strong colours and contemporary materials with angular shapes.

Acanthus mollis

Achillea millefolium

Aconitum napellus

Aeonium arboreum 'Atropurpureum'

Agapanthus 'Loch Hope'

Ajuga reptans

produce yellow flowers. If standing it outside, take care not to let it get blown over and damaged, with stems snapping off. Heavy clay pots are essential. Water regularly over summer but keep dry in winter while it is dormant. While it can be propagated by seed, it is far quicker to snip off a rosette of leaves at the end of spring with a bit of stem attached, and plant up in compost for cactus cuttings that will be very free draining. Keep at 19°C (65°F) until roots form.

AGAPANTHUS
African blue lily

South African perennials creating bold, exotic, eye-catching clumps of strap-like leaves topped by upright flower spikes – often 90cm (3ft) high and 45cm (18in) wide – in shades of purple, blue, silver-grey or white. There are over 300 named species and cultivars, but the differences between them can be slight in the extreme. They are often used as feature plants in large Versailles tubs or ornamental containers, or to flower amongst architectural plants. The best include the hardy 'Headbourne Hybrids' and 'African Moon' with pale violet-blue flowers. New plants keep appearing like the pale blue 'Blue Ice', first seen in 2003, and the violet-blue 'Black Pantha' (2004). The deciduous kind tend to be the hardiest (*A. campanulatus* and *A. caulescens*): they die back in autumn to a compact clump of buds on underground rhizomes, and remain dormant until next

spring when they shoot up, but they need to be given a protective winter mulch. The evergreens are more tender, with next year's buds being enclosed in the base of the leaves, and they remain above soil level. In both cases, late summer is the prime flowering season for the agapanthus. All need free-draining soil, with plenty of well-rotted organic matter and an open, sunny position, ideally to the front of a border where they will not be shaded. If they are potted up for winter, do not set them out again in the garden until the soil has warmed up in late spring. Those being kept in pots need a minimum 15–20 litre container because they are strong, vigorous plants needing plenty of root space. Eventually, when they fill even large pots they need to

be taken out and divided, and the whole process of potting on starts all over again. In spring sow seed at just under 16°C (61°F) and protect the young plants in a cold frame in their first winter, before they are planted out. Seed-raised plants flower in three, or possibly two years. Collected seed in the garden will not always replicate the parent, but it is worth trying to see what you get. Also take divisions in spring.

AJUGA
Bugle

The perennial, evergreen *A. reptans* at 15cm (6in) high and 75cm (2½ft) wide and its many cultivars are ideal for groundcover, providing late spring and early summer flowers (often with a later flush), and brightly coloured

foliage. *A. r.* 'Atropurpurea' is virtually dark purple, 'Burgundy Glow' greenish-red, 'Catlin's Giant' bronze-purple, 'Ermine' white, and best of all, 'Multicolor' a mix of green, bronze, cream and pink. Grow them around ponds, partly because they hate dry soil and spread producing a multitude of leaves that help provide hiding places for amphibians. Also grow in wild gardens and on new banks to bind the soil. The kinds with coloured leaves need full sun; those with purple tints end up turning green in shade. Plants rarely need propagating because they are such effective spreaders, but if more are needed then either divide or look for newly rooted sections and sever from the parent, and transplant in spring or autumn to well-weeded sites.

DIVIDING AGAPANTHUS

1 When an established agapanthus does not flower as profusely as it should, dig up the old clump with a fork, without damaging the roots.

2 Use a spade, two forks inserted back to back, or a knife and slice down creating sections with roots and buds for the top growth.

3 The outer more vigorous sections with the best flowering ability can now be replanted around the garden. Firm in, water and keep well weeded.

Alcea rosea

Alchemilla mollis

Alstroemeria aurea

ALCEA
Hollyhock

Ideal ingredients for cottage gardens, hardy biennial hollyhocks send up tall spires, often getting well over head high, with mallow-like flowers in a range of colours running from white, to yellow and pink to near black. They

sometimes develop rust on the leaves, and can be treated with a fungicidal spray, but that is not usually necessary. Plant them anywhere in the border, even toward the front, because you can easily see between the thin spires as long as they are not packed too closely together. They can even be

grown in gaps in paving providing there is space to walk around them. Average soil is fine, but full sun is a must. Sow seed in midsummer where you want the plants to flower, or in pots and move to their final position in autumn. Thereafter the plants will self-seed; either let the seedlings grow in the soil or collect the seed and sow in pots and keep in a cold frame over winter for planting up the following spring.

ALCHEMILLA
Lady's mantle

A highly rated front-of-border hardy perennial where its large lime-green leaves make attractive mounds, 60cm (2ft) high and slightly wider, especially when filled with early morning dew. They are liberally topped by sprays of sweet-scented greenish-yellow flowers all summer, and it is best to shear off the growth after the first flush of flowers for two reasons. This gives a second burst of fresh foliage, which is a prime attraction, and it stops the flowers from scattering seed across the garden. It thrives in rich, moist ground, and if being grown in drier soil, needs to be regularly watered in long, dry spells. If you need more plants, either leave a few plants to self-seed, and then carefully dig up the seedlings and move to their new site, or divide established clumps, or grow from seed in autumn, standing pots in a cold frame. Always sow more than you need because success rates are variable.

ALSTROEMERIA
Peruvian lily

A South American hardy perennial getting 90cm (3ft) high, it is an exquisite plant ideal for cottage gardens and provides excellent cut flowers. The modern *A. ligtu* hybrids – 50cm (20in) high and 75cm (2½ft) wide, with increasing numbers that keep appearing – flower for much longer than the species, with the Little Princess Series being ideal for the front of the border and pots. The 70 or so species (not that often grown) come in a wide range of sizes and colours, with the inner petals being a different

shape, with a different colour, to the outer ones. *A. psittacina* and *A. brasiliensis* are among the more popular ones, and both have tall stems – 90cm (3ft) and 75cm (2½ft) high – with red and green, or red with black streaked flowers. To attract pollinating hummingbirds they have a long uppermost petal, with the lowest being the shortest, with the nectar in the petal bases. When being grown in containers in cold-climate gardens, stand them in a sheltered site over winter. Excellent in a warm, sunny border, while in cold areas they need the shelter of a sunny wall. In open sites give them a protective winter mulch. Leave plants undisturbed after planting; they may take some years to establish. Divide clumps of the hybrids in spring or autumn, making sure they are replanted in ground that will not stay cold and soggy in winter, which will be fatal. *Alstroemeria* species can be grown from seed. Sow it fresh (avoid dry seed because it can be slow to germinate) in autumn, having soaked it for 12 hours in tepid water, at 5–10°C (41–50°F). Once the seedlings appear, they still need to be kept in these cool conditions, as in the wilds of Chile. If dividing the species, do so in spring.

ALYSSUM
Alyssum

Good range of half-hardy annuals and evergreen perennials for the front of a cottage garden scheme, producing ankle-high growth packed with colourful, scented flowers in spring and early summer. Wide range available, including 'Carpet of Snow' and

---

ORIENTAL STYLES

If you do not want a Western garden, try the Oriental look. There is no single Eastern look; they range from the massively extensive ancient Imperial gardens, covering thousands of acres, created by countless slaves and highly skilled gardeners building hills, lakes and palaces, even villages, to a small town, or scholar gardens created by the elite. Both were gardens where people could play, party and argue, with real water (unlike Japanese gardens with their heavy emphasis on symbols). The prime aim was to evoke nature and go on a spiritual self-improvement course, and the main ingredients were rocks, water, ancient twisted trees, and highly stylized scenes often glimpsed through an opening in a wall. Japanese gardens were often more for looking at than living in, and since 75 per cent of the country is uninhabitable

mountain and valley, the trick was to scale down and replicate a famous view. But gardens also had a rich, spiritual life. They were a kind of horticultural version of yoga, calming and transporting, wafting the essence of a quiet, still universe out of an open, artful area filled with dry gravel (signifying the sea) and stones (mountains). They were created to perpetuate and elide layers of meaning. The key ingredients were the tea house, metamorphic rock, stones, paths, gravel and granitic sand with bamboos and trained, clipped shrubs, trees thinned and pared down to their essential shape and, above all, cherry blossom. Japanese gardens were constructed by phenomenal patience, restraint, natural observation, sensibility (or a highly tuned, alert kind of choreography) and rules. Nothing was accidental.

SOWING ALYSSUM SEED

1 In spring or autumn fill a container, making sure that the seed compost (soil mix) has added grit for good drainage, and level.

2 Scatter on the seed, giving a wide distribution to avoid packed clumps of seedlings and the likelihood of damping off and fatalities.

3 Cover the seed with a thin layer of compost. If you can sieve it on to remove any lumps even better. Water with an upturned rose spray.

'Sweet White', and packets of mixed seed with pastels and sharper colours. Needs a sunny hotspot and good drainage; very effective in cracks between paving. In autumn or spring sow seed in containers and stand in a cold frame. Germinates in about three weeks. Plants which are densely packed together when grown *in situ*, without being thinned, are prone to mildew. Also take early summer cuttings of perennials.

AMARANTHUS
Love lies bleeding

A. caudatus is a fun, flamboyant annual ideal for a conservatory (being highlighted in a pot) or a sheltered, exotic garden where it gets the maximum amount of summer sun. Well-grown plants easily reach anything from 75cm–1.1m (2½–4ft) high and 45–75cm (18–30in) wide, and

stand erect with large leaves and long dangling panicles to 60cm (2ft) long of deep purple-crimson flowers. Keeps going right through summer, into autumn. Site at the front of a border where it can be fully seen, and because people love to finger the flowering lengths of blood. Very effective with brugmansias and cannas. Sow seed in early spring at 18°C (64°F) or *in situ* in mid-spring; germinates in 14 days for flowering that summer. You can also put a large tray beneath the tassels and rub the flowers to collect the seed.

ANEMONE
Windflower

Grow a wide range of anemones and you will have colour in early spring, summer and autumn. The hardy wood anemones (the rhizomatous *A. nemorosa* and its

cultivars) give a beautiful show of spring flowers low down, about 15cm (6in) above ground, 30cm (12in) wide, just above the grass, and are always grown in woodland gardens around trees and shrubs, giving a gentle start to the year. There are countless forms in white, pale blue, lilac, soft blue and mauve, with 'Royal Blue' in rich blue making a good contrast with any of the whites. They like a damp, cool site. Plant the rhizomes the moment they are bought because they must not dry out, and water in well. They quickly form clumps, and you can create even more plants by lifting and dividing in autumn. The hardy, suckering *A. hupehensis* and its cultivars – all about 90cm (3ft) high and 40cm (16in) wide – flower in late summer, and the slightly taller *A. × hybrida* opens from late autumn

to mid-autumn. 'Honorine Jobert' (pure white) is one of the best, mixing well with *A. hupehensis* 'Hadspen Abundance' (purple-pink). The spring-flowering, tuberous *A. blanda* is a dwarf anemone about 5–10cm (2–4in) high and wide, with divided leaves and flat flowers in shades of blue, pink and magenta or white. They like dappled shade in humus-rich soil, avoiding cold, wet clay. The best way to propagate anemones is by lifting and teasing them apart in spring, replanting immediately 2.5cm (1in) deep. Seed from the plants produces variable results.

ANTHEMIS
Anthemis

Excellent range for the cottage garden, with a prolific show of daisy-like flowers. Given full sun and average, quick-draining ground, they will keep flowering through early summer. The hardy perennial *A. punctata* subsp. *cupaniana* flowers from mid-spring to midsummer, giving a massed, cheery display of white flowers with a yellow eye and growing 30cm (1ft) high and 90cm (3ft) wide. The 90cm (3ft) high Golden marguerite (*A. tinctoria*) has several fine cultivars in white, lemon-yellow and bright yellow, with 'E. C. Buxton' widely grown. It has two shades of yellow, the darkest hue in the centre. Because it tends to be short-lived it needs to be propagated, and that is easily done by dividing clumps in spring, using two back-to-back forks. Or try sowing seed at the same time, at 18°C (64°F), with flowers for midsummer.

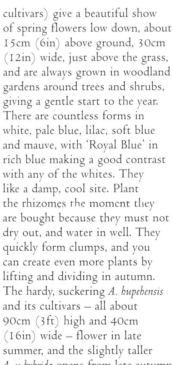

Alyssum spinosum 'Roseum'

Amaranthus caudatus

Anemone blanda

Anthemis tinctoria 'E.C. Buxton'

ANTIRRHINUM
Snapdragon

Most seed catalogues contain a wide range of these extremely good value, compact, summer-flowering hardy annuals and perennials. They keep flowering from spring to autumn, provided they are regularly deadheaded, at heights from 20–90cm (8in–3ft) with widths ranging from 30–45cm (12–18in). The Sonnet Series has pure whites, and mixes well with the blood-red leaves and red flowers of 'Black Prince' or the even darker red leaves of 'Bull's Blood'. In autumn or spring sow seed in pots in a cold frame, or in late spring in open ground when the nights are warmer, and the temperature stays above 10°C (50°F); it germinates in about three weeks. Alternatively, sow indoors in spring at 18°C

Antirrhinum majus

(64°F) for quicker results. Take cuttings of shrubby antirrhinums in summer. Beware rust.

AQUILEGIA
Columbine

Traditional cottage garden perennials for the front of a border, giving an excellent choice. Colours range from the quiet pastels to brazen oranges and yellows, with wonderful mixes of blue and white, and burgundy and white in between. Look for the newish Songbird and State Series besides old favourites like 'Nora Barlow'. Many have long, striking spurs. The Songbird Series get about 40cm (16in) high and 45cm (18in) wide, and include the pure white 'Dove', rose-pink and white 'Chaffinch', lavender and white 'Skylark' and mid-blue and white 'Bluebird'. The State Series are slightly taller, at about 55cm (22in), and include the red and pale gold 'Kansas' and deep purple and white 'Colorado'. The Cameo and Fantasy Series are a good 25cm (10in) shorter, ideal for containers. Aquilegias in the garden freely hybridize, and it is always worth seeing what the seedlings turn into. In summer sow fresh seed in containers in a cold frame – germination takes about three weeks – and plant out in early spring. (The seedlings of the Songbird Series need low night temperatures to flower that summer.) You can dig up named cultivars and try splitting them, but do not expect the plants to bounce back with a good display, because they hate being disturbed.

Aquilegia vulgaris

ARUNDO
Arundo

The hardy perennial giant reed (*A. donax*) looks more like a bamboo. It fires up high-powered stems that easily clear 3.6m (12ft) in one season, even when starting from scratch in spring, though it stays evergreen in mild climates. There is a variegated form if you need something even more distinctive. It is remarkably unfussy, thriving in most soils, but full sun and moisture get the best out of it. It is most impressive when a gentle breeze can send it rustling, but avoid the complete opposite of open, exposed, windy sites. Either grow from seed, sowing it in spring, or dig up a young clump in spring, before the growth begins, and divide. Given clumps can get nearly 1.8m (6ft) wide, it is best to divide before they become too big.

ASTER
Aster

Essential perennials for the late summer and autumn garden, they generally form woody clumps with new growth bursting up from the base of the previous year's flowering stems. The heights vary from just above the ankle to over head high, with most in the 1.2m (4ft) high by 90cm (3ft) wide range. The two most popular groups are the hardy New England asters (*A. novae-angliae*) and hardy Michaelmas daisies (*A. novi-belgii*), so called because they flower in north-west Europe around Michaelmas Day, September 29.

Arundo donax

A. novi-belgii is often found growing as a weed, brightening up railway cuttings and areas of rough land with its violet-blue flowers. The colours of the garden forms range from white, through all shades of pink, to pale and dark lavender-blue and purple. One of the best of the taller varieties is the pale lavender-blue 'Climax', while 'Jenny' is a good dwarf with purplish-red flowers. Other top choices include forms of the 75cm (2½ft) high, 30cm (1ft) wide hardy perennial *A. ericoides*, from North America, especially 'Blue Star' with pale blue flowers, 'Golden Spray' in white, and the mauve-pink 'Pink Cloud'. The hardy, slightly shorter *A. × frikartii* includes some vigorous hybrids, the outstanding 'Mönch' having large, lavender-blue flowers carried freely on branching stems. It is an excellent companion to shrubby lavateras. The similar blue 'Wunder von Stäfa' usually

Aster x frikartii

DIVIDING ASTRANTIA

1 Astrantias eventually make very decent clumps that can be divided in spring, before the new growth appears. Fork out of the ground.

2 Split them into several sections by hand, prising them apart so that each has a good batch of roots with buds for the leaves and flowers.

3 Prepare the new planting holes. Make them slightly larger than the root balls and when refilling add some well-rotted compost.

needs staking, and the hardy *A. laterifolius* – also at 90cm (3ft) high and 30cm (1ft) wide – has an unusual habit. The erect stems produce flowering sideshoots, almost at right angles, giving a tiered effect. The flowers are white to pale lilac. 'Horizontalis', which is rather more spreading, has pale lilac flowers. An extra bonus is the coppery tinges acquired by the leaves as the weather turns colder. Perennial asters need full sun in soil that will not dry out completely, and in the wild they constantly regenerate by expanding into new, fresh soil via seedlings or creeping roots. Gardeners can help them do this by dividing clumps every other spring, discarding the older woody central parts and replanting the younger, more vigorous outer sections. You can

also propagate by taking late spring or early summer cuttings, keeping them in a cold frame until the following spring. Note that the New England kind need regular spring and summer fungicide sprayings to counter mildew, right through the growing season, especially prevalent in hot, dry weather. Also nip back the growth of *A. novae-angliae* and *A. novi-belgii* to generate bushier growth and hide any stems that are suffering from mildew.

ASTRANTIA
Masterwort

The most commonly grown kinds are the summer-flowering hardy perennials *A. maxima* and *A. major* and their cultivars. They have airy sprays of pincushion flowers on tall, upright stems – 30cm (12in) and 45cm (18in) high – varying from white to pinkish-white and, in the case of 'Hadspen Red', deep, dark reddish-purple. They are invaluable in moist, rich soil in dappled shade, for example beneath apple trees, where they make good clumps – 35cm (14in) wide – and freely self-seed and hybridize. Where possible let the seedlings flower to see what you've got, and discard inferior plants. The first batch of flowers can be snipped back to the next buds lower down, after which plants can be cut right back for another show. Water well in dry periods. Propagate by spring or autumn division. Note that the

new growth is slow to appear each year, so leave a marker where plants grow to avoid weeding and spearing what is about to emerge. Propagate by dividing plants in spring or autumn, or sow species in autumn and stand pots in a cold frame to germinate after some six months.

Astrantia major

BERGENIA
Elephant's ears

Hardy, usually evergreen perennials, with many (for example the deep pink 'Eric Smith') at their best in winter when the large leathery foliage reddens up. Alternatively try *B. cordifolia* 'Purpurea' with its sprays of magenta flowers in spring and red leaves. One big advantage is that these front-of-border plants, ideal growing around a pond, thrive in almost any conditions, in sun or partial shade. They grow about 45cm (18in) high and wide, and spread slowly, making thick clumps with a long shelf-life, which is why they are highly regarded as groundcover plants, especially in gravel gardens, where the large leaves contrast well with the scatterings of stone and any verticals. In early spring, sow fresh seed, though dividing four-year-old clumps in spring or autumn will be much quicker because seed-grown plants can take three years to produce a fully productive specimen.

Bergenia 'Bressingham White'

BETA
Swiss chard

Though this is a vegetable, the hardy annual *B. vulgaris* subsp. *cicla* is increasingly grown at the front of a border thanks to the remarkably flashy bright red stalks set against the rich green leaves. Failing that, it is a must in a potager which mixes flowers, fruit and vegetables in colourful arrangements. Other forms are available with yellow, pink, white and orange stems, Bright Lights being an excellent seed mix. They grow from 23–45cm (9–18in) high, with a similar spread, and can be cooked as a vegetable, but when using the leaves for salads they must be harvested before they are over 5cm (2in) long. More leaves will resprout provided you do not cut too close to the ground. Grow in sunny, moist (watering in dry spells), fertile ground. If they show signs of bolting, just cut back and they will quickly regrow.

Beta vulgaris

Brassica oleracea

TAKING BRUGMANSIA CUTTINGS

1 Take cuttings of a brugmansia in summer, or even as late as autumn – they take very quickly – making the cut just above a node.

2 Trim the cutting, making a second cut just below a node. Aim for a length about 10cm (4in) long. Large leaves are cut horizontally in half.

3 Pot up and water in. The cuttings do not need special treatment, and normally root quite quickly on a bright windowsill out of direct sun.

Sow in late spring (having run the seed under a cold tap to wash off a chemical inhibitor) where the plants are to grow, or before that at 16°C (61°F) in trays to get an earlier crop, and the seeds quickly produce shoots.

Bidens ferulifolia

Briza minor

BIDENS
Bidens

A summery perennial, *B. ferulifolia* makes a generous burst of thin, wiry stems about 30cm (12in) long, with small, bright yellow, daisy-like flowers above the slender leaves. Excellent in window boxes and hanging baskets where it pokes out scatterings of colour with an open, airy look, combining well with just about anything, whether chunkier, more substantial plants to make a lively contrast or other wiry subjects. Move plants under cover over winter to keep them out of the worst weather, but in any event sow seed in spring at 19°C (66°F). Established clumps can be divided in spring, but you can also take cuttings.

BRASSICA
Ornamental cabbage

The hardy annual *B. oleracea* – about 45cm (18in) high and wide – provides some of the flashiest autumn colours. It is not grown for the kitchen because the leaves are bitter and the striking colours quickly get washed out when cooked, but for the way the leaf colours (white, red and pink) radically intensify when the cold weather strikes in autumn. Because they are quite short, grow them in rows to the front of a border. The Osaka Series have bluish-green outer leaves. They are easily grown from seed in spring at 19°C (66°F), and quickly germinate.

BRIZA
Quaking grass

B. maxima is a delightful hardy annual grass – 60cm (2ft) high and 25cm (10in) wide – with an attractive scattering of tiny seedheads that start off pale green but gradually acquire a purple tint. It adds a gentle touch when growing around the base of fruit trees, or when planted in wild gardens or informal borders. It can also be used in dried flower arrangements. In spring or autumn sow the seed *in situ*, making sure that the soil is free-draining. Once clumps are well-established, they will do the propagating for you, scattering seed and new plants around. Perennial brizas can be carefully divided in mid-spring.

BRUGMANSIA
Angel's trumpets

Easily grown from autumn cuttings (quicker than seed in spring) a few inches long, they quickly root and will give a prolific display over the following summer. They really stand out when the season goes out on a high. The 4m (12ft) or so high, thin, woody stemmed *Brugmansia × candida* (and cultivars) offers height, large flappy leaves and a great whoosh of long, flared, trumpet-shaped flowers in white, pink, tomato red and soft yellow, and in the early evening there is a strong, sweet scent. Plants get about 1.8m (6ft) wide. Mature, pot-bound, well-fed plants (they

Calamagrostis x acutiflora 'Karl Foerster'

Campanula latiloba

BORDER PLANTS

Unless you are creating a border exclusively featuring a specific kind of plant, for example summer annuals, most need a mixture of ingredients to keep them interesting through the year. They need different heights, generally working up from the smallest plants at the front, with the tallest dead centre only in the most formal arrangements. Use a mixture of shrubs to give all-year-round structure, perennials to fire up new spring growth, and annuals to fill the gaps with different colours each year. Make sure each plant is given enough room to spread so that it does not overwhelm and badly shade the neighbours.

respond well to seaweed fertilizer) give the best results. Water well over summer, especially on hot days when they can quickly wilt. Because the plants are too tender for cold, wet winters, bring into a cool conservatory where they go dormant. Cut back as hard as necessary, keep barely moist, start watering again next spring and they reshoot strongly.

CALAMAGROSTIS
Reed grass

The top pick is C. × *acutiflora* 'Karl Foerster' – 1.8m (6ft) high and 60cm (2ft) wide – a hardy, upright grass with deep green foliage and plumes of flowers that will sway in the slightest breeze. As with most grasses the flowers turn beige in autumn, and these are best left over winter to add structure before being cut down to allow the new growth to spurt up next spring.

Staking is not necessary because it stands resolutely vertical. Use in long lines to create garden divisions, or to the back of borders. 'Overdam' is very similar but the leaves have a vertical white edge, though the flowers are said to be less robust. Propagate by dividing an established plant into several clumps in spring or autumn, with each having a number of shoots for the top growth and a good set of roots.

CAMPANULA
Bellflower

A huge range of annuals, biennials and mainly perennials for spring and summer flowering, with most of the annuals flowering in white or blue in early summer and midsummer. Excellent in all kinds of borders, from formal to cottage, helping to offset bolder, stronger plants, and in mixed schemes. The

giant is the frost-tender chimney bellflower (*C. pyramidalis*), a biennial that can get 3m (10ft) high and 60cm (2ft) wide, and self-seeds the following year, saving you the trouble. The best of the perennials include the hardy, compact 'Burghaltii' – at 60cm (2ft) high and half as wide – in greyish-blue, and forms of the slightly taller, hardy *C. latiloba*, especially the bluish-purple 'Hidcote Amethyst'. In spring sow seed in containers in a cold frame, while the alpine kind need sowing in autumn. Divide established plants in spring or autumn, while perennials can be increased by means of basal cuttings in spring.

CANNA
Indian shot plant

Cannas make flamboyant, exotic, tender perennials with large paddle-like leaves and small

brightly coloured gladioli-like flowers on top of the tall, vertical stems. In their native tropics they are evergreen, but in cold-climate gardens they die down in autumn. The top growth needs to be cut back after the frost has blackened the foliage. In milder regions they can be left in the soil, given a thick mulch for winter protection, but if the soil is cold and wet the rhizomes need to be dug up. Keep them in trays covered with sand in a dry, frost free place (such as a garage), giving them the occasional spray so that they do not completely dry out. The following spring bring them out and pot up in a warm greenhouse and they will quickly reshoot. To propagate, slice up the rhizomes making sure that each section has both buds for the top growth, and roots.

PLANTING CANNA RHIZOMES

1 Cannas grow from underground storage organs (rhizomes) that can be propagated in spring before the new growth appears. Dig them up.

2 Look along the length of the rhizome for a section with roots below and a couple of buds or eyes above where the shoots will appear.

3 When they have been sliced up with a sharp knife, apply fungicide to the wound, plant and give bottom heat to generate new growth.

Canna 'Black Knight'

CARDIOCRINUM
Giant lily

The one to get is the hardy *C. giganteum*, a giant of a Himalayan lily that, in ideal conditions, can get over 3m (10ft) high and 45cm (18in) wide. Found in Himalayan, Chinese and Japanese forests, it sends up stout, sturdy, vertical stems with large, richly scented white flowers (striped inside), up to 20cm (8in) long. It needs a cool, sheltered position, out of direct sun, with rich, moist soil. If you cannot provide these conditions in a border, try it in a large pot, making sure it is kept out of baking sun. Plant the bulbs in autumn, just beneath the soil, and water well in dry periods. You can sow fresh seed in deep trays in a cold frame (they may take 7 years to flower), or detach offsets after flowering, when the parent dies, and pot up (for flowers after 4–5 years). Add a protective winter mulch.

Cardiocrinum giganteum

Centaurea cyanus

CELOSIA
Cockscomb

Cultivars of the tender perennial cockscomb (*Celosia argentea* var. *cristata*) produce outrageous, flamboyant clustered flowers that from a distance look like a genetically engineered party piece. Though technically perennials, they are usually grown as annuals, being planted in sunny summer bedding schemes or exotic borders. The smallest are ankle high, with taller ones (the Kurume Series) 1.2m (4ft) high. Sow in late spring where they are to flower, or earlier under glass at 17°C (63°F), and provide rich, fertile soil.

CENTAUREA
Knapweed

This mix of annuals and perennials, and even shrubby plants, are ideal for poor ground, especially dull soil that is quick draining. Mostly from the Mediterranean, the thistle-like

Celosia argentea var. cristata

Cerinthe major

ANNUALS AND BIENNIALS

What is the difference? Annuals give quick results, but they only live for one season. They germinate, shoot up, flower and set seed all within a few months, usually being sown in spring and ending up on the compost heap in autumn. Biennials live a bit longer, taking two seasons to complete their life cycle, being sown one year to flower and die the next.

To get a quick crop of annuals (which includes vegetables), sow them in the warmth in early spring in a greenhouse or warm up the garden soil. Use sheets of clear plastic or cloches, but you do need soil that is capable of warming up quickly, and which ideally is in a sunny, sheltered site. Cold, wet clay will not really benefit from this approach, nor will soil that has been improved with plenty of added organic matter (which helps retain moisture), though that is certainly no reason not to improve the ground. Cover each individual bed with a sheet of plastic four weeks or more before sowing, weighing it firmly down with rocks, and tuck the edges into the soil or they will be whipped up in a gale. You can even cut planting holes in the plastic for sowing, or put in young seedlings. The extra heat means that weeds will quickly appear, but they can be promptly removed, roots and all. Avoid using black plastic because, first, it needs to be in complete contact with the soil to generate any extra heat and,

second, slugs often quickly congregate beneath it. If you want to wait until nature has warmed the soil for you, wait for the first batch of weed seedlings to appear. They are like a gardening barometer. If they germinate, so will your seeds.

Covering seedlings with fleece does little to trap warmth, but it does provide some cold and wind protection while giving good light and, crucially, lets in the rain. The problem of sowing direct in the garden is not just possible poor germination rates due to unseasonably bad weather but pests (especially mice and pigeons) gobbling down the seed, or slugs and snails lurching toward the tender young shoots.

Whichever means of protection works for you, do not let up.

flowers come in a range of colours including blue, violet and yellow, and make a medium-high informal clump, approximately 30cm–1.5m (1–5ft) high, in a wild or cottage garden. The hardy annual *C. americana* 'Aloha' has an open shaving-brush effect. All are particularly useful when you want to attract butterflies and bees, and are best sown in spring where they are to flower; allow up to two weeks for germination.

CERINTHE
Honeywort

C. major 'Purpurascens' is a shortish annual, growing 60cm (2ft) high and wide, that is ideal for any colour scheme requiring blue-green (the colour of the leaves) or purple (the flowers). It flops and spreads, and keeps flowering right through summer, and needs to go right at the front

of the border where it can be seen. Once grown from seed, either being sown where it is to flower, or in trays at 17°C (63°F) to get an earlier show, you do not have to worry about propagating more because it is a prolific self-seeder. The following spring you will find scores and scores of seedlings, and it is a case of getting on hands and knees and whipping out those you do not need.

CHRYSANTHEMUM
Chrysanthemum

There are scores of showy, perennial chrysanthemums for the garden, many making excellent cut flowers, providing a wide range of marvellous colours, getting about 60cm–1.2m (2–4ft) high and 30–60cm (1–2ft) wide. They excel in the second half of summer and early autumn. You can grow chrysanthemums for

Chrysanthemum 'George Griffiths'

architectural displays and even modern gardens with all kinds of geometric shapes benefit from their late-season show. There are scores of hardy hybrids, and they include the anemone-centred, orange 'Curtain Call', the reddish-pink 'Glamour', the early-flowering pink 'Mei-kyo', 'Pennine Oriel' and 'Primrose Allouise'. The early-flowering, half-hardy 'George Griffiths' has large, deep red flowers. All like free-draining soil and full sun, the taller ones needing support. Propagate by dividing established plants in spring, about every three years, sow seed or take basal cuttings.

CITRUS
Lemon

These trees – actually shrubby plants that can kept in a pot or grown in a conservatory border where they can easily get 1.8m (6ft) high and wide – give a good crop. When you buy a young plant – for example the small, bushy, slow-growing, extremely tasty *C. × meyeri* 'Meyer' (a cross between a lemon and possibly a mandarin) or 'Four Seasons' – nip off all the flower buds, making it fire its energy into body building, producing more flowering, fruiting growth. Later, let the flowers open (and they will keep opening in bursts all year) and you will get white, waxy flowers smelling of jasmine. The lemons take 9–12 months

Citrus

to ripen. You do not need a hothouse or conservatory and can stand them outside over summer, but keep checking the pot to make sure that ants are not marching inside. Once they start nesting in the compost it is a job getting them out. If a potential problem, stand the pot on a wire basket. Give the shrub excellent winter light indoors, some humidity by standing it on a pebble-filled plastic tray filled with water, and only give it a drink when the leaves start to wilt. Keep at 10–12°C (50–55°F). Over-watering is the big killer. Specialist nurseries sell a range of different lemons as well as sweet oranges, grapefruits, kumquats and tangors (like spicy mandarins). The easiest way to get a copy of the parent is to take semi-ripe summer cuttings, though they will not be as vigorous as the parent because it will probably be growing on a rootstock. Plants grown from seed take 7 years to flower. Feed all year, especially with a nitrogen-high feed in summer to boost bushy growth. Without a regular feed they will crop badly and be unable to support the fruit. Where most people go wrong is in trying to grow them in the hot, dry atmosphere of a lounge with poor natural daylight. Given how expensive well-established plants can be, it is ridiculous to then ignore their growing needs.

exhibition with enormous blooms, but that requires specialist techniques. For most gardeners, chrysanthemums are far better out in the borders than on greenhouse benches, providing fulsome sprays of mauve, red, white, yellow and orange, in flower forms ranging from large balls to open stars like large daisies, to spidery shapes with thin, dangly petals. Patio gardens, cottage gardens,

SOWING CHRYSANTHEMUM SEED

1 Fill seed trays in spring with seed compost (soil mix). Tap it down and level off, using the bottom of another tray as the leveller.

2 Carefully scatter the seeds into your hand before picking them out, one by one, and placing equidistantly apart on the surface.

3 After the seed has been sown, cover with a thin layer of sieved compost, water and keep at 13–16°C (55–61°F).

Cleome hassleriana

Colchicum autumnale

Convallaria majalis

CLEOME
Spider flower

Highly impressive border plants, the tender annuals *C. hassleriana* get 1.2m (4ft) high and 45cm (18in) wide, being ideal for the middle of the border. The flowers have four upright petals, and they catch the eye both because they look so unlike anything else, and because they come in a lively mix of colours. Give them a place in full sun, and pinch out the growing tips when young to make them bushier and more flowery. Do beware the surprisingly vicious spines at the junction of leaf and stem. A large batch of plants can be sown in spring at 19°C (66°F), though success rates do vary. A delayed planting gives shorter plants (if required).

COLCHICUM
Naked ladies

Mainly autumn-flowering corms, they produce large, goblet-like flowers at just 15cm (6in) high before the leaves appear, hence the common name. When the summer leaves do appear, they can easily spread 45cm (18in), so to give them room to spread do not jam them close up against other plants. The best include *C. × agrippinum* – 10cm (4in) high and 8cm (3in) wide – an early autumn purple-pink that will make a very effective clump. The meadow saffron (*C. autumnale*) also flowers in early autumn, growing fractionally taller, but because its flowers easily get toppled by rain, it is best grown in grass to provide some support. A better bet is the pinkish-purple *C. speciosum*, which has bigger, more robust, more rain resistant flowers, and at 18cm (7in) high and 10cm (4in) wide, it makes the biggest impact, especially when planted in large groups. 'Album' is the white form. All like full sun in fertile, well-drained soil. They propagate by producing new offset bulbs, but you can propagate them by sowing fresh seed in containers in an open frame, growing them in a special bed until they reach flowering size, or lift and divide an established clump in summer, planting them 10cm (4in) deep.

COLOCASIA
Taro

Tender perennials, they are now being increasingly grown as highly dramatic foliage plants – potentially getting 1.5m (5ft) high and 60cm (2ft) wide – for subtropical gardens. The best form by a long way is *C. esculenta* 'Black Magic', which has 60cm (2ft) long black leaves, and needs to be planted among whites or yellows to highlight the impact. Alternatively, grow it in a large pot, but do not stand in full sun, so that it gets roasted over summer. Give it a place in dappled shade. It certainly is not grown for the flowers that rarely appear in gardens and, in any event, they cannot compete with the foliage. Water well and give regular summer feeds. The tubers should be lifted in autumn, like a dahlia, and kept in a dry, frost-free place over winter for planting up the following late spring/early summer. Propagate by dividing the tuber in spring, but carefully check that each portion has both buds for the top growth and a good set of roots. Always give it a prominent, eye-catching position.

CONVALLARIA
Lily-of-the-valley

C. majalis is the top choice for a shade-loving plant, thriving under trees in rich, moist soil. The dark green leaves appear first, followed in spring by the richly scented white flowers. Give it a prominent position and some dappled light that will make it even more vigorous. It grows to 23cm (9in) high by 30cm (12in) wide, and will keep spreading if it is happy, but you can easily dig out unwanted sections. It makes good cut flowers. To sow fresh seed, separate it from the flesh, though it is far easier to separate the rhizomes in autumn and replant where required. Failing that, grow them in pots until ready for planting out.

DIVIDING CROCOSMIA CORMS

1 Crocosmias can be divided in spring or when the foliage is yellowing in autumn. Dig up congested clumps with a fork.

2 Carefully lift them out of the ground, taking care not to damage the roots, and haul out any weeds rooting among them.

3 Separate the packed clumps, making sure that each separated corm can feed via its own set of roots and that it has a bud for top growth.

4 Replant the corms in well-worked soil with plenty of added organic matter to help retain some moisture and firm in.

Cortaderia selloana

CORTADERIA
Pampas grass

A giant grass and a hardy perennial that needs plenty of space to make an unmissable clump. It is best used as a centrepiece in a bed fringed by richly coloured late summer flowers, like dahlias, where its arching swish of green leaves can shoot above them, with the white or pinkish plumes erupting above the foliage. Younger plants tend to be more vertical, older ones increasingly arch up and over. Good forms include *C. richardii*, a 1.2m (4ft) high and 3m (10ft) wide New Zealander with cream plumes all summer, and *C. selloana* 'Sunningdale Silver', a 3m (10ft) high, 2.5m (8ft) wide whopper with silvery plumes in mid-autumn. Grow them in moist ground, in an open position without any shade. If you need to propagate, divide plants before they get too big. Digging up and dividing an established clump is very difficult, and you can easily cut yourself on the viciously sharp edges of the leaves.

Cosmos bipinnatus

COSMOS
Cosmos

For a scented, dark red almost reddish-brown cosmos, grow the 75cm (2½ft) high, 45cm (18in) wide tender perennial *C. atrosanguineus* from Mexico. Give it a place in full sun (with free-draining soil) and the long thin wiry stems angle out all summer with the open flowers on top, smelling of vanilla and chocolate in the heat. Excellent in window boxes and tubs. You will need to bring the tuber under cover over winter, storing it in sand in a garage, giving it the occasional drink. In mild gardens with open soil it can be left outside, but add a thick mulch on top to provide some extra warmth. Take basal cuttings in spring to propagate more. For the annual *C. bipinnatus*, which is not scented but has slightly taller cultivars in a range of colours, including white, pink and red, sow seed in spring at 19°C (66°F) to generate quick results or outdoors, in well-weeded sites, where the plants are to grow.

CROCOSMIA
Montbretia

Excellent hardyish perennials for adding strong border colour, usually in red or orange, in mid- and late summer at heights ranging from 60cm–1.2m (2–4ft), with a spread of 8cm (3in). The most popular are the flashy hothouse colours of the cultivars of *C. × crocosmiiflora*, like 'Carmin Brilliant', 'Lucifer' and 'Queen of Spain' (though there are softer pastels if needed), in subtropical gardens with large-leaved cannas and banana trees bursting above them. All like a bright, sunny site and moist soil to flower best. They quickly

Crocosmia 'Lucifer'

Crocus tommasinianus

multiply, and the easiest way to propagate is to divide the clumps. This is particularly important when the flower power starts to diminish and the corms need more space to expand.

CROCUS
Crocus

Select well and you will have the ankle high, hardy perennials in flower from autumn to spring. They give exquisite, detailed elegance, sturdy, robust shapes and intricate purple feathering on whites, yellows with mahogany veins, lilacs, and blues, etc., but no red. There are over 200 different kinds available, and new ones keep appearing, like the terrific pale blue *C. baytopiorum* that flowers for three weeks from late winter. The current top choices are the forms of *C. chrysanthus*. Try 'Cream Beauty' with gorgeous, soft yellow-creamy flowers, 'Prins Claus', white with a beautiful blue mark outside, and the exquisite 'Zwanenburg Bronze', orange inside, and outside purple-mahogany. The main season is late winter to early spring. Given the right conditions – a fertile, free-draining light soil in good sun – they will multiply; 20 corms this year gives 40 in three to four years, and they do not become a nuisance. For a bit more presence try the large Dutch Hybrids and the 'tommies', *C. tommasinianus* though this can be a prodigious spreader. Buy the autumn crocuses in late summer. They tend to be smaller and need very good light

PERENNIALS AND TREES

If a plant lives for more than two seasons, it is called a perennial. Perennials are different from shrubs and trees because both the latter have a permanent above-ground structure, whereas perennials, with their soft, non-woody stems, have to start from scratch each year. They die down and re-emerge, and when they do, every cell is alive, unlike a tree, because four fifths of its cells are dead. Just a part of it is alive. It retains the dead parts, though eventually it might shed unnecessary limbs and the inner heartwood. The other crucial difference between a perennial and a tree is that trees need substantial quantities of the chemical lignin. Without it, those huge, long branches and trunks would collapse. Lignin is the crucial toughening agent that helps keep trees up, enabling them to lift up the crown to get maximum light.

and drainage. (Note: colchicums are sometimes called autumn crocuses, but they are larger, usually pinker, and more like goblets than true crocuses.) Plant crocuses 10cm (4in) deep in groups. Vigorous spreaders need to go in the grass. Cut out three sides of an area of turf, peel it back, fork over and loosen the soil, sink in the corms, and replace the turf. Many self-seed, and clumps gradually get bigger. Dig up excess corms and replant where required.

Dahlia 'Fascination'

DAHLIA
Dahlia

The tender dahlias – about 1.2m (4ft) high and 60cm (2ft) wide – from Mexico and Central America add an incredible range of colours (from white to bright crimson, with many bicolours) to formal and cottage gardens. In cold-climate gardens they are dug up at the end of autumn when frost has blackened the foliage, with the tops being cut off. Turn the roots and stems upside down to dry before storing in a cool, frost-free place over winter in trays of sand. Treat with a fungicide to stop rotting, and do not completely ignore but give an occasional spray with water. The following spring bring into the warmth and shoots will appear. Pot up, start gentle watering and they will produce some growth when they can be hardened off. Nip off the tops to make plants bushier and generate more flowers, and add a tomato feed when the first buds appear. Beware slugs that can savage the new stems. In mild gardens with free-draining soil dahlias can be left in the ground all year, but do provide a thick winter mulch as protection. Either propagate by taking cuttings of the new spring growth, or divide the clusters of tubers ensuring that each has both growth buds and roots to create new plants.

DELPHINIUM
Delphinium

Tall, hardy perennial, back-of-the-border plants – 90cm–1.7m (3–5½ft) tall with spreads 45–75cm (18in–2½ft) – with soaring spires for cottage gardens, usually in a shade of blue, they make a great sight in sunny gardens with free drainage. There are many excellent hybrids, with the clump-forming Elatum Group having almost flat flowers in dense, upright spikes in the first part of summer – 'Blue Nile' is a classic pale blue, 'Clifford Sky' has Wedgwood blue flowers, 'Finsteraarhorn' is cobalt-blue with a hint of purple, and 'Mighty Atom' has solidly packed spikes of semi-double, lavender-blue flowers with brown eyes. Cut them back after flowering and you might get a second show in autumn. The Belladonna Group have branched stems and loose sprays of flowers in early and late summer – 'Casablanca' is a pure white with yellow centres. Delphiniums need supporting to prevent the tall, thin stems from snapping (this must be done before they get over 30cm [12in] high) and good border access for keeping a lookout for slugs that can destroy a large cluster overnight, chomping through the new growth.

1 To create extra clumps of this flowering grass, dig up an established plant in spring or autumn, getting beneath the roots.

2 Provided the clump is not too large and solid, insert a hand fork into the centre and lever it to and fro, creating several sections.

3 When you have identified two or three sections you can finish the job by hand, pulling them apart without destroying the roots.

4 When you have several decent sections, each with a good set of leafy growth and established roots, plant out and water.

In general, avoid enriching the soil too much or plants will put on lush growth and will not survive over winter. Propagate the tall kind by taking cuttings or divisions in spring, separating clumps into about three pieces. Delphiniums are easily raised from seed, but the seedlings usually differ from the parents, though this might well mean that you come up with a striking plant.

DESCHAMPSIA
Hair grass

A good choice for any collection of grasses because it flowers early, producing an airy show of flowers at up to 1.5m (5ft) high. The most popular species – both hardy perennials – are the tufted hair grass (*D. cespitosa*) and *D. flexuosa*. The first includes the excellent 'Goldschleier' – 1.3m (4½ft) high and wide – with its long, strappy, green leaves and summer purple flowers with a silver tinge that turn silver and then buff, standing out well against a dark background. The second flowers through the first part of summer, to the middle of the season, with silver-tinted panicles, and gets half as high. Both like full sun in soil that can be dry or moist. Cut back in late winter before the new growth begins. When propagating, divide a clump into fairly large pieces for the best chance of success.

DIANTHUS
Carnation/pink

Mostly long-flowering hardy perennials, growing about 45cm (18in) high, the best (usually old-fashioned) garden pinks have a deep scent of cloves. They can be highlighted in beds or borders, or in special containers such as old kitchen sinks or Victorian chimney pots. There are dozens of good choices, including 'Bovey Belle' with double purple flowers, the scented 'Brympton Red' that is crimson with darker markings and the scented white 'Dad's Favourite' laced with maroon. Also try the pink 'Dawlish Joy', the bicoloured 'Doris' with pale pink flowers and a maroon centre, large-petalled 'Excelsior' with

Delphinium 'Clifford Sky'

Deschampsia cespitosa

pink flowers, salmon-pink 'Freckles' delicately blotched with red and clove-scented 'Gran's Favourite' that is white laced with maroon. 'Joy' has salmon-pink flowers, 'Louise's Choice' has crimson-laced pink flowers and the miniature 'Mendlesham Maid' has white flowers with frilly edged petals. The bicolour 'Monica Wyatt' has phlox pink flowers with a magenta centre, while 'Ricardo' is a border carnation with red and white flowers. 'White Ladies' has clove-scented, double white flowers that are even purer white than 'Mrs Sinkins'. All make a marvellous flowery show in sunny cottage gardens, and the more you keep deadheading them, the more they keep on flowering. Because they demand free-draining (ideally chalky) soil, they might need to

BULBS

Bulbs – including rhizomes, tubers and corms – are underground or soil-level storage organs. They need to store food to survive the long periods of dormancy when the above-ground weather is unsuitable for growth. Though gardeners might think that nothing is happening, the bulbs are more often than not developing their next year's flowers inside the 'casing'. In Namaqualand, south-west of the Kalahari Desert, it is savagely hot, but if you get a spade and dig, there are underground layers with bulbs and corms, freesias and amaryllis, layer on layer, waiting for it to rain. The moment it does, they erupt into growth and flower, then become a lumpen thing again, dormant until next year, living on stored-up energy. Bulbs range from tiny blobs to flattened, frazzled cowpats, with no indication of what might happen. Some actually grow 20 times their height when dormant, and in a matter of weeks.

TAKING CUTTINGS OF DIANTHUS

1 Extra numbers can be easily propagated by taking softwood cuttings in spring. Gently pull away a soft new young shoot.

2 It should be about 7.5cm (3in) long, with several leaves emanating from one growing point. Trim off the bottom with a sharp knife.

3 Arrange several cuttings around the edge of a small container filled with cuttings compost (soil mix) and added grit to improve drainage.

be grown in large tubs filled with open, gritty compost or in rock gardens. Heavy soil that stays cold and wet over winter is fatal. The best way to propagate is by taking spring cuttings. Also try Sweet William (*D. barbatus*), growing 60cm (2ft) high and 30cm (1ft) wide, which is either grown as a biennial (being sown one year to flower and die the next) or as a short-lived perennial in free-draining soil. The flowers are long lasting, followed by self-seeding, but if that is a problem simply nip off the fading heads. Since the season is limited to midsummer, plants such as adjacent dahlias are required to help plug the gap when they have finished flowering. Sowing seed is the easiest method of propagation. The seedlings will be more vigorous than cuttings and, provided there has been no cross-pollination, will be good copies of the parents. Sow toward the end

of spring in a cold frame, and shoots appear three weeks later. Plant out in autumn for an early display the following year, and use it as a good, colourful foil for major spring bulbs, such as tulips.

DIGITALIS
Foxglove

Common foxgloves (*D. purpurea*) – 1–2m (3–6ft) tall, with a spread of 60cm (2ft) – provide early summer thickets of spires of purple, pink or white flowers with beautiful dark speckling inside, being particularly useful because they flower in early summer in partial shade or a woodland garden. They are happy in most soils, avoiding dry and wet extremes, and should prolifically self-seed. This is good news because they are short-lived hardy perennials or biennials. Keep a lookout for the young seedlings and move (if necessary) to where they are required. Alternatively,

remove the seed capsules before they split and open them and scatter where you want more foxgloves, or sow in pots in a cold frame in spring.

DIPSACUS
Teasel

Self-seeding biennial teasels (*D. fullonum*) provide a fun show in wild gardens, and rocket up 2m (6ft) high, thin spires, about 75cm (2½ft) wide, with long, narrow leaves and hollows in the join where they meet. After any shower rainwater collects there, often filled with drowning insects. The fuzzy, oval, blue, thistle-like flowers are a honey pot to bees. Leave the attractive seedheads over winter for birds. Sow seed in autumn where you want the plants to grow. Once established, just go round the garden in spring looking for the seedlings, and either eradicate or move them to where they are required.

Dianthus 'Mrs Sinkins'

Digitalis purpurea

Dipsacus fullonum

ECHINACEA
Coneflower

Highly effective hardy perennials producing clumps of upright or drooping growth, with tall stems topped by brightly coloured flowers attracting butterflies. They have an array of open petals around a prominent, central cone (*echinos* is Greek for spiny and is the word used for hedgehog). Make sure you plant them in the right place because they dislike root disturbance when being moved. The most popular kind are the cultivars of *E. purpurea*, at 55cm (22in) high and 30cm (12in) wide, with 'Kim's Mop Head' in white, 'Leuchtstern' in purple-red and 'Magnus' in reddish-pink. Grow in full sun in a border packed with plenty of well-rotted organic matter, with good drainage, and keep deadheading. Propagate by taking root cuttings at the end of autumn or sow seed at 19°C (66°F) in spring. Division is not always successful.

Echinacea purpurea

Echium vulgare

UNDERPLANTING CLIMBERS

Flowering high up, not down at ground level, climbers can become quite leggy at the base when grown against a wall. To cover that, and give shape and colour low down, plant perennials by the stems with a long flowering period, like penstemons. Penstemons also benefit from the protection of a wall, the heat that bounces back off it, and the good drainage. Also try bending the lower branches of a climber out in a horizontal arc to encourage shoots to break out, and give extra cover and more flowers. This is particularly important when you are growing richly scented climbers and want to get close to smell them, or take cut flowers.

ECHIUM
Echium

The echiums are a mixed group of annuals and biennials, with perennials and shrubs, and the star is the tender, biennial tree echium (*E. pininana*) from the Canary Islands, where it grows at high altitudes on mountains. It produces a generous batch of long, lush, silver-green leaves in rosettes that are a terrific eye catcher, and in the second year fires up a massive summer flower spike that can get 4m (13ft) high. It is packed with tiny funnel-shaped flowers, initially pinkish then blue, and is so completely disproportionate to the cluttered leaves that it often looks as if another plant is bursting out amongst it. Once *E. pininana* has flowered it dies, but it does produce a prodigious amount of seed. If the plant is growing in a sunny, well-protected part of the garden with average but fast-draining soil (because it hates cold, damp winters) then there is a good chance the seed will germinate; if not, collect it for sowing in late spring at 18–20°C (65–70°F). It should germinate in two weeks. When large enough to handle, transplant to pots. Overwinter in a cool greenhouse, and plant out the following spring at 90cm (3ft) apart.

ELYMUS
Wild rye

A varied group of plants consisting of over 150 perennial species, with *E. magellanicus* one of the best. It makes a clump of semi-evergreen or, in cold regions, deciduous bluish foliage poking out of the ground like a porcupine's quills, getting nearly 60cm (2ft) long. It demands sun and excellent drainage, and does well in gravel gardens, where it grows well and looks good, and needs to be spaced out to give good air circulation. Do not cram the plants in cheek by jowl because they will not grow that well, and avoid rich soil. It thrives in coastal gardens and dislikes high humidity in cities in summer. The quickest way to propagate plants is by lifting a well-established specimen out of the ground, using two forks held back-to-back to prise it apart. With tough clumps, you might need someone to help you. Seedlings often sprout out of the ground around the parent, and they can be carefully lifted for planting up.

EPILOBIUM
Willow herb

E. glabellum is a good choice for cottage gardens or wild areas where you need a hardy, semi-evergreen perennial that links star performers. It produces a gentle scattering of white or pink flowers on reddish stems getting about 20cm (8in) high, with plants needing a space again about 20cm (8in) wide. *E. angustifolium* is a larger, more showy version, excellent for slightly wild areas, and easily grows 1.5m (5ft) high and 90cm (3ft) wide. It too has white flowers, but you will need to allow more room for its spreading rhizomes. If it threatens to expand too far, the excess growth can be cut through with a spade. To propagate, separate the offshoots from the parent in spring (not the autumn, because they may rot). If you need a lot of new plants, take root cuttings.

Elymus magellanicus

Epilobium angustifolium

EPIMEDIUM
Barrenwort

These spring-flowering hardy perennials for the woodland garden include four 'musts'. First, *E. grandiflorum* – from deciduous woodlands in East Asia and relatively low growing at 35cm (14in) – which makes a 30cm (12in) wide clump of leaves with spiny edges and pointed tips, with 16 flowers per stem. They hang down, and come in purple, pink, pale yellow or white, but there are dozens of cultivars in specific colours. 'Rose Queen' has bronze-tinted young leaves and rose-purple flowers, 'White Queen' has large white flowers, 'Nanum' is a slightly shorter small white, and *E. g.* f. *violaceum* has large lilac-purple flowers. *E. × perralchicum* is 40cm (16in) tall by 60cm (2ft) wide, and makes a dense clump of tough, leathery leaves with bright yellow flowers held well clear of the foliage. It is fine in dry gravel and Mediterranean-type gardens where it quickly spreads. *E. pinnatum* subsp. *colchicum* is fractionally smaller, and a slow spreader, generating bright yellow flowers and, again, is happy in dry soil. *E. × rubrum* – at 40cm (16in) by 30cm (12in) – has bright red young leaves and striking red and yellow flowers. In autumn the leaves turn reddish-brown. Unless otherwise specified, they like semi-shade and rich, moist soil; in dry ground they will not flower as profusely. Do not put young plants in soil that is too wet because they may rot. Propagate by dividing plants that make tight

DIVIDING EREMURUS

1 Either as the leaves fade or the new growth appears, dig up a clump and look for gaps where you can create the new plants.

2 Use a clean, sharp knife to start slicing down, through the fleshy roots, making sure that the new sections have roots and top growth.

3 When you have finished slicing through the original clump, start planting the new sections, giving them plenty of room to expand.

clumps every four years in autumn. This gives vigorous young sections, and helps maintain a good display. The spreaders can have their rhizomes cut into sections, each with buds for the top growth and roots. Raise in pots in a shady part of the cold frame, and keep moist to help them through winter.

ERANTHIS
Winter aconite

In mild weather, *E. hyemalis* will produce solitary, upright yellow flowers in late winter, though in a cooler year the flowers may wait until early spring. The flowers are held just above a ruff of leaves, on a 10cm (4in) high stalk. Very effective when it appears, growing in rich soil that stays damp over summer in light shade. Plant the tubers 5cm (2in) deep, and when propagating in spring, when the flowering is over, simply lift them up and divide, making sure each section has both top growth and roots.

EREMURUS
Desert candle

Grown for their long, thinnish spikes, packed with hundreds and hundreds of tiny flowers, they make an incredible sight in late spring and early summer when they erupt above their leaves. Some get 3m (10ft) tall, with the buds opening from the bottom of the spike up. *E. robustus* is the biggie, getting over 2.5m (8ft) high, and has 1m (3½ft) long leaves and a candle of light pink flowers. If that is a tad too big, *E. stenophylla* gets about 1.3m (4½ft) high and has bright yellow flowers that make a spurting flash of colour in early evening, while *E. × isabellinus* has hybrids at 1.8m (6ft) high. All like rich soil with well-rotted organic matter and plenty of sun, in a sheltered site, where the tubers can bake in summer. When planting, make a wide, shallow hole to accommodate the spread-out roots and rest the tubers on an 8cm (3in) mound of grit, keeping the crown at soil level. To propagate, lift clumps in spring or autumn and make divisions with a knife, separating the individual crowns, but handle the roots with care because they are easily damaged. Replant the larger ones immediately, but nurture the smaller ones in deep trays (not pots).

Epimedium grandiflorum

Eranthis hyemalis

Eremurus stenophylla

Eryngium bourgattii

Erysimum bicolor 'Bowles' Mauve'

ERYNGIUM
Sea holly

Indispensable annuals, biennials and perennials for gardens with good drainage, they make a strong show with their tiny blue flowers. The latter are packed together in a rounded flowerhead, surrounded by an array of spiny bracts, being invaluable in cut flower displays. Since the spines are quite sharp they're best kept away from paths when young children are charging around. There are excellent forms of *E. bourgattii*, especially the 40cm (16in) high, 30cm (12in) wide 'Oxford Blue'. Grow in gravel and Mediterranean-type gardens where there is high-voltage sun and poor soil, or in seaside gardens. Drought is not a problem. Propagate by dividing the woody crowns in early spring making sure that each has a good set of roots or, in the case of species, by ripe seed. Alternatively, take 8cm (3in) long root cuttings in late autumn, laying them horizontally and equidistantly on a tray of compost (soil mix). Keep under cover over winter and they should produce decent shoots next spring.

ERYSIMUM
Wallflower

E. cheiri, the excellent, short-lived hardy wallflower, and its wide range of cultivars, make terrific blocks of spring colour and a background show for tulips, growing 25–80cm (10–32in) high and 35cm (14in) wide. Get up close on a warm day and you will detect the scent. It thrives in poor, free-draining ground in full sun. Though technically a short-lived perennial it is usually grown as a biennial, producing mounds of growth. If it threatens to become rather leggy, trim it back after flowering. Sow it outside at the end of spring, into early summer, in a special seedbed and move to its final flowering position in mid-autumn, making sure it has free-draining soil.

ERYTHRONIUM
Dog's tooth violet

These American bulbs (said to resemble a dog's tooth) are beautiful spring-flowering plants, most not exceeding 30cm (12in) high and usually 10cm (4in) wide, for woodland conditions.

E. dens-canis – at 15cm (6in) high – appears slightly earlier than most, and bears one single flower in white, carmine, lilac or rose, with coloured zones in the centre. 'Snowflake' is a pure white. Give them a prominent position where they will not get overlooked. *E. revolutum* can get twice or three times as high, and is much better at spreading and multiplying across the soil, and stands out with its brown mottled foliage and deep pink flowers with a dash of yellow. Make sure that they are grown in ground with plenty of added leaf mould, which stays cool and moist in dappled shade through summer. When plants have multiplied to form decent clumps, carefully lift them and separate the new young bulbs. They can be raised in a special bed until they reach flowering size, for planting out at a depth of 10cm (4in).

EUPHORBIA
Spurge

There is an enormous range of euphorbias, noted for their unusual flowers and usually strong shape. The hardy perennials are good value, especially *E. characias* and its many very different cultivars, with the lime-green, 1.2m (4ft) high and wide, sun-loving, evergreen *E. c.* subsp. *wulfenii* giving a long summer display, even when the flowers are over. Also look out for the 75cm (2½ft) high and slightly wider *E. griffithii* 'Fireglow' and slightly taller *E. schillingii*. The first has

orange-tinted bracts and reddish leaves, at its best in autumn, while the latter makes a mound of lime green flowers. There are also dwarf forms like *E. myrsinites* that gets just 10cm (4in) high and 30cm (12in) wide, and is good for growing or flopping over

Euphorbia characias subsp. *wulfenii*

DIVIDING ERYNGIUM

1 Divide the plants in spring (not autumn to avoid all the spiky top growth). Dig up just as the new growth is appearing.

2 Very carefully finger through the clump, separating the pieces of root that should have some of the new top growth clearly visible.

3 Arrange the new plants and, given their size, either replant in well-weeded soil, keeping a close eye on them, or in pots until bigger.

a wall. For heavy shade try *E. amygdaloides* var. *robbiae* at 60cm (2ft) high and wide, which is perfectly happy in poor, dry ground where it generates a mass of lime green leaves and spreads and spreads, making good ground cover. Propagate by taking spring cuttings or divisions, while species can be grown from seed; leave to germinate in pots in a cold frame in autumn. Note that euphorbias bleed a white sap when cut that often produces a nasty skin rash, so wear rubber gloves when handling. If it does get on your skin, quickly wash off.

FESTUCA
Fescue
Ideal choice of hardy perennial grasses for a dry, sunny site with free-draining soil. The most colourful is *F. glauca* 'Blaufuchs' with its evergreen bristle of silver-blue leaves poking out of the ground, making a fairly neat clump 25cm (10in) high and wide. Grow it in a prominent position, to the front of a border, alternating with the near-black *Ophiopogon planiscapus* 'Nigrescens', or dotted about a gravel garden. *F. g.* 'Elijah Blue' is a striking silver-blue and can front taller, more dramatic shapes. Plants need to be regenerated every three years or so to keep them fresh and vigorous, and that is the time to propagate by dividing the clumps

Festuca glauca

DIVIDING FESTUCA

1 To keep festucas looking fresh, dig them up every three years, in spring or autumn, getting right under the root system.

2 You can be surprisingly brutal, slicing off the outer sections using a spade. If the clump is very tough, stand on the spade to force it down.

3 You should end up with several outer new sections, all of which are replanted giving them room to expand. Discard the old inner part.

into smaller sections. Discard the inner, exhausted portions and retain the newer, more vigorous ones to make new plants.

FRANCOA
Bridal wreath
Giving a gentle display of cottage garden flowers, frost-hardy francoas are found in the wild on cliffs where they make a rosette of hairy leaves at the base. In gardens grow them in borders or containers, with the two main choices being 'Confetti' and *F. sonchifolia*. The former gets 75cm (2½ft) high and 45cm (18in) wide, and sends up long spikes packed with tiny white flowers right through the second half of summer. The latter is slightly taller with pink flowers, though 'Alba' gives white flowers and Rogerson's form purple. All like a mild, sheltered site with free-draining soil with added well-rotted organic matter to improve the moisture content. Sopping wet winter soil is fatal, so don't even think about growing it on untreated, unimproved clay soil. To propagate, either take seed from the species for sowing or divide the plants in spring.

FRITILLARIA
Fritillary
Striking bulbous (usually hardy) perennials, these have nodding plum to orange to white bell-shaped flowers, some being

bicoloured (*F. michailovskyi*) and others chequered (*F. latifolia* and the snake's head fritillary, *F. meleagris*). The best for a border include the hardy perennials *F. imperialis* and *F. persica*. The former grows to 1.5m (5ft) high and 30cm (1ft) wide, and produces a batch of orange petals above a tuft of dark green leaves on a stout stem, and looks good in large (Versailles) tubs. (Stand the hollow bulbs upright or lie on their sides when planting at four times their own depth or they might well rot.) The latter is a good 60cm (2ft) shorter, with flowers verging on black. The equally hardy 30cm

(12in) high, 8cm (3in) wide *F. meleagris* is the one for naturalizing in a field, and produces downward dangling lanterns. The above three like fertile, well-drained soil. Propagate by dividing clumps, removing the rice-like offsets and growing them in individual pots until large enough for planting out. You can also score the bulbs, turning them upside down before slicing into the surface, making 6mm (¼in) slashes as if they were going to be quartered. Stand on a tray of moist sand, place in an airing cupboard and healthy young bulblets should appear in about 10–12 weeks.

Fritillaria meleagris

Galanthus nivalis

DIVIDING GALANTHUS

1 When a group of snowdrops multiplies and ends up too congested, with more leafy growth than flowers, start dividing.

2 Do this as the leaves start to yellow, fade and die down. Fork up the clump, getting the whole of the root system out of the ground.

3 Using your fingers, carefully separate the original clump into smaller, more manageable sections for replanting in the lawn or border.

GALANTHUS
Snowdrop

There are over 400 kinds of named snowdrops, with 18 species found in the wild from the Pyrenees to Iran, and while the differences can be incredibly subtle and slight, the beauty is in the detail. The three most popular kinds are the hardy perennial common snowdrop (*G. nivalis*), *G. plicatus* and *G. elwesii*. The first flowers in winter, gets 10cm (4in) high and wide, and has an inverted green mark at the tip of each inner petal, with *G. n.* f. *pleniflorus* 'Flore Pleno' being a robust spreader that soon makes large clusters. The second grows twice as high and wide, flowering at the end of winter into spring, and has a single green mark on the petal. The third is characterized by large flowers in late winter and broad grey leaves, and is slightly larger. Of the other named kinds, 'Atkinsii', about the

same size, is another good bet, and is typically robust and prolific, creating large clusters. New bulbs are usually sold 'in-the-green', meaning they still have their leaves, before going dormant and shedding them. They're not particularly demanding, and the ideal planting site is in light or partial shade to avoid hot, dry ground. The bulbs invariably do the propagation for you, freely multiplying underground, but the clusters can become congested, in which case they need to be dug up and separated after flowering while they still have leaves attached. You can also chip. This involves stripping off the papery covering, and then trimming off the roots using a sterilized knife, without cutting into the basal plate. Then slice off the nose, and divide the bulbs like an orange, slicing it into about eight segments; each piece needs to retain a sliver of the basal plate.

Apply a fungicide in a clear plastic bag, and add moist vermiculite. Blow up the bag and tie, and keep in a warm, dark place. When the new bulblets have formed, pot them up under 12mm (½in) of compost (soil mix).

GERANIUM
Cranesbill

It is impossible to tackle this huge range of annuals, biennials and perennials in a short space, but they basically divide into those with leafy spring growth at ground level with flowers on top of the vertical stems, and those without this batch of basal foliage with stems that lie across the soil. The most popular garden kinds tend to be hardy perennials, but distinguishing some takes an expert eye. Look out for the sprawling 'Ann Folkard' – 60cm (2ft) high and 90cm (3ft) wide – setting magenta flowers with a black eye against the yellowish-

green foliage, the taller – 1m (3½ft) high – magenta *G. psilostemon*, and the many excellent cultivars of *G. × oxonianum*, *G. pratense*, and *G. sanguineum* among others. When buying, it is worth visiting a specialist collection to pick out the best of the pastels (many in pale blues and pinks, often with darker rays on the petals) and stronger coloured kinds. 'Johnson's Blue' is a sprawling 45cm (18in) high and 75cm (2½ft) wide lavender blue (flowering through the first half of summer) that stands out best in part shade where the colour is that much richer and stronger. 'Orion' has a slightly longer flowering period, its lavender-blue flowers having a white centre and purple veins. The most architectural geranium is *G. maderense*, a half-hardy biennial with a 60cm (2ft) high woody stem, 60cm (2ft) long leaves and mauve flowers. Do not hide it

Geranium 'Johnson's Blue'

DIVIDING GERANIUM

1 Geraniums are among the easiest plants to divide. Look for the point where new growth and shoots emerge out of the ground in spring.

2 Use a spade to slice cleanly down, working around a group of the growing points, and separate them from the rest of the cluster.

3 Lift this clump out of the ground, checking that it has a decent set of roots. It can be further subdivided giving even extra plants.

Geum 'Mrs J. Bradshaw'

away in the border but use it as a feature plant in a container where it is given a prominent position by the front door. Keep an eye on its roots and pot up when they look like they're being restrained, to get the most out of the plant. Do not hold it back. Geraniums with particularly attractive foliage can be sheared back in midsummer for a second flush of fresh leaves. Many make excellent groundcover, with rhizomes that slowly creep through or across the soil, sending out new growth. To stop geraniums flopping over, falling on to neighbouring plants and leaving a bare middle, stake them using twiggy branches in spring and, by midsummer, the leafy growth will have grown over the support, completely obscuring it. The range of growing conditions varies, but average soil with good drainage in full sun should be fine. Propagating by division when plants are dormant is usually the easiest and most successful method. Raising hardy perennials from seed can produce variable results.

GEUM
Geum

A good choice for lovers of hardy perennials in hothouse colours to get the early summer garden off to a sparky start. The heights are generally in the 15cm (6in) to 75cm (2½ft) range. They like moist, rich soil in a bright, open site, but sopping wet soil is definitely not what is required. The names are generally a good indication of what you will get with 'Fire Opal' in orange-red, and 'Flames of Passion' and 'Red Wings' in red, but also look for 'Mrs J. Bradshaw', a bright scarlet.

If you keep deadheading without let-up the flowering should keep going all summer. Propagate by dividing plants in autumn or spring; seed can be problematic, except in the case of 'Mrs. J. Bradshaw' and several others. Sow in pots in a cold frame in autumn.

GLADIOLUS
Gladiolus

The hardiest gladiolus is *G. communis* subsp. *byzantina*. A hardy Mediterranean perennial, it makes a bold flash of magenta in the middle of a border, getting about 90cm (3ft) high and 8cm (3in) wide, quickly making decent clumps. It flowers in the first half of summer, and mixes well with yellow daylilies, white rocket and Oriental poppies, coming into flower just as the larger alliums start losing their petals. It needs to be planted in autumn, about 13cm (5in) deep, in quick-draining ground, so that it can get a good baking over summer, making gravel and Mediterranean gardens a natural setting. Propagate by digging up clusters of plants when dormant, and look for new, young corms. Carefully separate from the parent for growing in a nursery bed until large enough to flower.

GYPSOPHILA
Gypsophila

A huge group of annuals and perennials, with the most popular including the hardy perennial *G. paniculata*. Its cultivars make a marvellous airy show, 90cm (3ft) high and wide in the case of

'Bristol Fairy', with a starburst scattering of thin, wiry stems and panicles of small white flowers. They open in midsummer, and are worth growing beside plants that have just finished flowering so that they can quickly fill the gaps. Have a number of reserve plants in their own bed specially for taking cut flowers. Make sure you site the plants in the right place, because the deep roots hate being moved. There is no time for bad decisions. Poor, free-draining soil is vital ruling out chunky, heavy, poor-draining lumps of clay. To propagate, try taking early summer cuttings with a heel, but do not count on a high success rate. The professionals have to rely on tissue culture, beyond the realms of the amateur.

HAKONECHLOA
Hakonechloa

Found on Japanese mountains, especially around Mount Hakone, this highly rated ornamental grass with bamboo-like leaves makes a mound of graceful, cascading stems, growing about 90cm (3ft) high. *H. macra* has several forms, the most popular being 'Alboaurea' with its yellow, white and green striped foliage. It grows 35cm (14in) high and slightly wider, and can be used as a pot plant. 'Aureola' (the same dimensions) has yellow-variegated leaves with a few green stripes, and 'All Gold' has all yellow leaves. Easy to grow, they just need moist soil in full sun. Propagate plants by dividing in spring, slicing into clumps before the new growth emerges.

Gladiolus

Gypsophila paniculata

Hakonechloa macra 'Alboaurea'

HEDYCHIUM
Ginger lily

An exotic scented perennial from Asia, the various species have large leaves, up to 60cm (2ft) long, making them ideal in subtropical gardens with architectural plants like cannas and bananas, and the flowers are a big bonus. They are highly scented, orange, yellow, reddish or white, being packed together in a long spike that can easily get up to head height. *H. gardnerianum* has late summer flowers, and gets about 2m (6½ft) high and 90cm (3ft) wide. Hardiness is an issue, but in a mild, sunny site with rich, compost-enhanced, free-draining soil, they should survive the winters. Too much winter wet weather and they will quickly rot and die. Always mark where they are growing to avoid the risk of spearing them when weeding. Provide a thick mulch for winter protection, but if there is any risk, dig up the chunky rhizomes in autumn and keep in a frost-free garage. When planting, set the rhizomes about 10cm (4in) deep in

Hedychium gardnerianum

Helenium 'Indianersommer'

cool climates, shallower elsewhere. To propagate, divide the rhizomes in spring, making sure that each section has both buds for the top growth and a good set of roots.

HELENIUM
Sneezeweed

A mix of annuals, biennials and perennials for the cottage garden, being immensely popular for their brownish-orange, rust-red colours. The petals radiate from a central cone, with some flowering in midsummer, others in autumn, the 1.2m (4ft) high and 45cm (18in) wide *H. autumnale* and its cultivars being particularly good at fleshing out the end-of-season garden. Toward the end of spring, plants need to be nipped back to create short, bushy growth and hide bare or mildewed stems. Also deadhead to generate even more flowers. Always give them compost-enriched soil in a sunny site. To maintain the plants' flowering display and propagate them, divide the clumps on a three-year basis using two forks back-to-back. Prise them apart. Replant the outer, more vigorous sections and discard the inner, exhausted parts. If you need more plants in other years, take spring cuttings.

HELIANTHUS
Sunflower

There are two kinds of hardy sunflower, the annual 'flagpoles' (*H. annuus*) and the perennials. The annuals come in a range of colours and sizes, from reddish-bronze to flaring yellow, from bushy low-growing kinds to those fighting to get in *The Guinness Book of Records*. Sow seed in spring where they are to flower, and you should see growth in about two weeks, or to get an earlier batch sow under cover at 12°C (55°F). Always sow far more than you need because slugs chomp through the young stems. Grow them in rich, moist soil in full sun and they quickly shoot up. They are very effective bursting out of

clumps of dahlias and cannas. The perennial kind have similar flowers in late summer and autumn, but the plants make bushy clumps. The vigorous 'Miss Melish' grows 1.8m (6ft) by 1.2m (4ft), while 'Monarch' gets a good 90cm (3ft) bigger, but for a smaller clump of yellow try 'Morgensonne'. They can be grown in drier ground, again with full sun, and can be propagated and kept in good condition by being divided every three years using the back-to-back fork technique. This also stops any excess spread. Replant the outer, vigorous sections and discard the inner exhausted parts. For extra plants, take spring cuttings.

HELICHRYSUM
Helichrysum

A wide mixture of hardy to frost-tender annuals, biennials, perennials, shrubs and even short trees, they need to be grown in

Helianthus annuus

DIVIDING HEDYCHIUM RHIZOMES

1 Ginger lilies grow from underground storage organs, which need to be carefully dug up so that they are not damaged.

2 Look for clusters of shoots on top, and then take a clean, sharp knife and slice down between them, cutting through the rhizome.

3 It should be possible to get two or even three sliced-off sections from one mature plant. Cut down carefully avoiding the buds on top.

4 The two key ingredients for each new plant are a healthy set of roots, which act like the engine, and buds to produce the amazing flowers.

PLANTING TIPS

When positioning a new plant, first hold it up and decide which side is going to be the front, and face out, giving the best display. Plants are very rarely uniformly attractive, and because no one spends hours in a nursery regularly turning them around to ensure uniform growth, bought plants usually have one fuller, stronger side. When using a young plant that you have propagated, grow it in a special nursery bed where it can slowly develop without tough competition from its neighbours. If you put a young cutting straight into an empty patch in a border in spring, you will be amazed how quickly you forget it is there, not least because the neighbours quickly grow and swamp it. Wait until it is a good size and then plant it so that it can compete with the other plants for water, light and space. When you do plant, always firm in the soil around the roots to make sure that they are in direct contact with earth and to avoid any air pockets.

Helichrysum 'Schweffellicht'

Heliotropium arborescens

Helleborus orientalis

and wide, with thick, tightly bunched flowers (in a range of colours) giving off the most amazing whiff of vanilla. They can be grown to the front of a border in full sun in rich, moist soil, but being half-hardy need to be lifted in autumn for keeping under cover. They can also be grown as a pot plant, or as a standard with a bare leg and a ball of growth on top. Either grow as a short-lived shrub or as an annual. In either case, take cuttings that quickly root in summer to generate more plants, or sow seed in early spring at 17°C (63°F).

HELLEBORUS
Hellebore

The Christmas rose (*H. niger*) flowers in late winter, making clumps about 30cm (12in) high

by 45cm (18in) wide. The low, nodding flowers mean you have to get down low to lift them up to get a look. *H.* × *hybridus* flowers at much the same time. The highly collectible forms grow about 45cm (18in) high, and the colours are much more excitingly varied, running from white to pink, mauve, grey, red, purple and even blue-black. The Lenten rose (*H. orientalis*), with a similar height, has more mid-winter to early spring greenish-white flowers for a shady area, while *H. argutifolius* has an impressive cluster of 1.2m (4ft) high evergreen growth and light green flowers that keep the show going from mid-winter to mid-spring. Every four years or so it needs replacing because it will gradually deteriorate. To propagate, you can

raise hellebores from seed but note that cultivars hybridize in the garden and you never know exactly what you've got until the plants start to flower. It is unlikely they will be copies of the parent. Keep the good kinds, and discard those with feeble or washed-out colours. You can easily let the plant do the propagating for you, and just dig up the young seedlings and position them where required. If collecting seed, sow it fresh and then stand the pots outside to give a chilling. Germination might take six months. *H. niger*, *H.* × *hybridus* and *H. orientalis* and the named cultivars can also be divided at the end of summer, and they will give exact copies of the parent. *H. argutifolius* needs to be propagated by seed.

hot sun and poor, free-draining soil. The pick of the woolly-stemmed perennials is the hardy 'Schweffellicht' with its silvery leaves smelling like a ready-mix of curry powder, and bright yellow flowers that turn increasingly orange. Either grow to the front of a border – it gets 40cm (16in) high, spreading by 30cm (12in) – or let it pop out of a gravel garden. Easily propagated, it can be divided into several sections in spring or you can take cuttings at the end of summer.

HELIOTROPIUM
Cherry pie

H. arborescens and its excellent cultivars make shortish, shrubby plants, about 45cm (18in) high

SOWING HELIANTHUS SEED

1 You can sow sunflower seeds outside but few seedlings survive pigeons or slugs, so sow them in containers in spring.

2 The pointed end faces upwards, but if you are not sure lay them on their side and the new shoots will quickly head for the light.

3 Give the seedlings good sun and you should end up with a large colourful flower, packed with seeds that you can save for sowing.

Hemerocallis 'Jake Russell'

Hesperis matronalis

Heuchera 'Pewter Moon'

Hyacinthoides non-scripta

HEMEROCALLIS
Daylily

The hardy perennial daylilies do what they promise. They flower for just a day (strictly speaking there are the day-opening kind, and those that open at the end of the day until the following morning) but keep producing more buds, and flower for a long summer period. The species plants tend to flower in bronze-red to orange and yellow, but the thousands of cultivars provide a far greater range of colours. On average, they get 60–90cm (2–3ft) high and 45–75cm (18in– 2½ft) wide. If possible visit a specialist grower in summer when you can see exactly what you are buying. Good choices include 'Jake Russell' with golden-yellow flowers with a velvety sheen in mid- to late summer, 'Lusty Leland' produces an abundance of scarlet and yellow flowers over a long summer period, 'Prairie Blue Eyes' is semi-evergreen with lavender-purple flowers in

midsummer, 'Scarlet Orbit' has bright red flowers with yellow-green throats in midsummer, and 'Stafford', one of the best in its colour range, has rich scarlet flowers with yellow throats in midsummer. All like loose, open, well-composted, neutral soil (possibly slightly acidic) in an open, sunny position. Keep watering in dry spells. The quickest way to propagate is

by dividing established clumps at the end of summer. If growing species from seed, sow in spring in a cold frame. Protect young plants from slugs and snails.

HESPERIS
Sweet rocket

Do not confuse it with the rocket grown in the vegetable garden; *H. matronalis* is a cottage garden favourite that adds a gentle, relaxed touch with clumps of dark green leaves and clusters of gently scented white or lilac flowers. Plants generally grow about 90cm (3ft) high and half as wide. While the original plant will not last that long, it will self-seed around the garden doing the propagation for you. If the seedlings are growing in the wrong place, simply dig them up and replace where required in sun or shade on average soil. Alternatively, grow from seed in early spring at 19°C (66°F) to get plants in the ground as soon as possible, or wait and sow the seed directly in the ground when the soil has warmed up at the end of spring.

HEUCHERA
Coral flower

These North American evergreen perennials, about 75cm (2½ft) high and 45cm (18in) wide, have given rise to dozens of hybrids that are grown for their clumps of coloured leaves (especially in winter) and airy sprays of small flowers. Many have silvery leaves, the patterning being caused by trapped air bubbles, with 'Pewter Moon'

and 'Silver Light' being good choices. Others, such as 'Chocolate Ruffles', have rich brown leaves (purple beneath) with ruffled edges, while 'Amber Waves' have a yellow top surface that is bronze below. 'Burgundy Frost' is one of the most striking with a mix of purple-bronze set against patches of silver. All need free-draining soil, and if you have heavy, lumpen clay that stays cold and sticky over winter, you will need to grow heucheras in containers or they will promptly die. The easiest way to propagate is to divide plants (essential in the case of cultivars) in autumn. Species can be grown from seed in spring at 20°C (68°F).

HYACINTHOIDES
Bluebell

There are two hardy perennial bluebells, the Spanish (*H. hispanica*) and the English (*H. non-scripta*) kind. The Spanish is basically the more robust, taller and straighter kind, growing to 40cm (16in) high and 10cm (4in) wide. To distinguish the two, check to see if the plant flowers right around the stem and can't stop multiplying. That is the Spanish kind, and it should be avoided as it hybridizes with the English bluebell, which in many areas has become a threat to the native population of wild flowers. The slightly shorter, nodding English bluebell knows its place and is traditionally grown in clumps around shrubs and trees, especially silver birches (or anything with white bark). Both like light,

DIVIDING HEUCHERA

1 Heucheras are easily divided in autumn with nothing more than a spade. Lift the clump cleanly out of the ground, roots and all.

2 Use the spade like a giant knife to separate the different sections. Move back the top growth to see clearly what you are doing.

3 You should end up with several new sections, each with plenty of leafy growth, and roots for anchoring in the ground and feeding.

Hyacinthus cultivars

1 Before a spring sowing, break up the seed compost (soil mix), and incorporate plenty of horticultural grit, sand or vermiculite.

2 Do not pour the seed straight from the packet on to the compost lest it comes out in great lumps. Separate it in your hand.

3 Having scattered the seed widely on the soil, water and add a propagating lid. Keep at 17°C (63°F).

flickering shade, and should not be confused with hyacinths. The old bulbs are automatically replaced by new flowering ones each year. You can also lift and divide when the foliage has turned yellow and died down. Do not try doing this in spring, because you will damage the tender new growth. Look for offsets, and set them out in the ground, where they will flower in about two years' time, planting them about 8cm (3in) deep in rich, fertile soil with decent drainage. Sow seed of the English bluebell in containers from late spring to early summer. It is illegal to collect plants from the wild.

SUPPORTS

Always think about adding plant supports in late spring or early summer for taller, floppier plants before they put on too much growth. Doing it while you can see what you are doing means you do not risk spearing through any plants, and you can easily get to those that need help.

The value of supporting plants is that it stops the long growth from flopping on to other plants, preventing them from being clearly seen, and it simultaneously means that the floppers do not end up with a bare, bald middle exposed by the outward-arching foliage.

All kinds of metal supports are on sale, although you can also use twiggy branches cut from forsythia, for example, to give a more natural look. After midsummer, the supports will be hidden by the foliage. They will be clearly visible while the plants are dormant, however, so make sure they are attractive.

HYACINTHUS
Hyacinth

There is one great reason for growing hardy, perennial hyacinths, and that is their amazing, rich scent in spring when little else is about. There are hundreds of cultivars about 20–30cm (8–12in) high and 8cm (3in) wide in reds, pinks, blues, white and apricot, their spikes packed with scores of tiny flowers, and while they can be grown as pot plants they also make a terrific garden show. Just make sure they have an enclosed, sunny site where the scent will hang in the air, and are close to the house. The very worst position you can give them is an open, exposed, chilly, windy site where the first whiff of scent promptly gets blown away. Plant the bulbs in autumn 10cm (4in) deep, and make sure that they have free-draining soil in full sun. You can also buy specially prepared bulbs that will flower in containers or baskets indoors in winter. You can propagate by lifting and removing offsets after the foliage has petered out, or alternatively try chipping. This involves stripping off the papery covering, and then trimming off the roots using a sterilized knife, without cutting into the basal plate. Then slice off the nose, and divide the bulbs like an orange, slicing large ones into about 12–14 segments; each piece needs to retain a sliver of the basal plate. Apply a fungicide in a clear plastic bag, and add moist vermiculite. Blow up the bag and tie, and keep in a warm, dark place. When the new bulblets have formed, pot them up under 12mm (½in) of compost (soil mix).

IBERIS
Candytuft

For a scented garden filler, go for the hardy annual *I. umbellata*, about 23cm (9in) high and wide. It can be planted in gaps in the rock garden or paving creating mounds of small, scented flowers in a variety of colours. The Fairy, and the Flash Series, also have a good range of colours with white, pinks and reds. Sow it at 17°C (63°F) in spring in trays to germinate in about two weeks. Grow in poor to average soil in a sunny, open site.

INULA
Inula

Hardy perennials for a cottage garden, they produce flat, open rays of yellow petals around a yellow eye; the smallest are ideal for rock gardens, the taller kinds for wild gardens, and those like the medium-high *I. hookeri* – 75cm (2½ft) high and 60cm (2ft) wide – can be grown in beds and borders. Given deep, rich soil with added compost in a bright position it can become invasive, but it can easily be kept in check with a spade, slicing down through the excess growth. For an even showier display at the back of a border try the clump-forming *I. magnifica* that gets 1.8m (6ft) high and half as wide, or *I. racemosa* 'Sonnenspeer' that will outstrip it by another 1.2m (4ft). If clumps start bulging out of their allotted space, or you need extra plants, divide them in spring or autumn, and replant immediately.

Inula magnifica

Iris pallida

IRIS
Iris

The bearded varieties (with a furry, fuzzy growth on the falls, or petals), getting to 50cm (20in) high, are the most popular kind for the border. They produce a good eight weeks of flowers from mid-spring, and there is a huge choice with many new forms regularly appearing. 'Impetuous' is just one good example from scores, with violet-blue and white flowers with purple veins and a dash of yellow. The hybrids usually flower for about eight weeks toward the end of spring into early summer. All the bearded irises are grown from a thick, tough rhizome that creeps and spreads through the free-draining soil (that is essential), just below the surface. They need direct sun, so do not shade them with other plants. If extra plants are required, propagate every three years (after flowering), when the rhizomes can be dug up and sliced into 10cm (4in) lengths, but make sure that each section has both buds and roots. Horizontally snip off the top half of the fan of leaves when replanting. This is essential to avoid wind rock, with the top growth catching the wind like a sail. Dividing is important to prevent clumps becoming overcrowded.

KNAUTIA
Knautia

K. macedonica is an eyecatching hardy perennial that is ideal for cottage gardens, where it has small, rich red pincushion flowers all summer on top of branching stems, never getting more than 75cm (2½ft) high and 45cm (18in) wide. Use it as part of a border scheme with contrasting colours both to highlight its presence, with adjacent neighbours also providing support for its stems. Grow it in the right conditions – light, sandy, free-draining ground in an open, sunny position – and it will thrive with self-sown seedlings popping up all around the parent plants. If growing it in clay soil, you will have to dig it up in autumn and keep in a pot over winter, until next spring. Gently hand-fork them out of the ground and replant where necessary. Alternatively, propagate by sowing seed in autumn, leaving the pots in a cold frame to get a winter chilling, but this is notoriously unreliable, and basal spring cuttings give better results.

KNIPHOFIA
Red-hot poker

These are striking summer perennials that send up spikes topped by dozens of often short-lived flowers. Most are vivid fiery colours – hence the name – but there are also pale yellow and lime-green shades. Plants quickly produce impressive clumps, with architectural strappy foliage rising up before taking a snappy U-turn and pointing down at the ground. They are too weak to stay vertical. Good choices include *K. uvaria* 'Nobilis', which is capable of getting over 2.4m (8ft) tall with its towering flowers like red and yellow traffic lights on top of stout stems. One mature plant will easily get 1.5m (5ft) wide with dozens of packed leaves (always check deep inside because they make terrific hiding places for armies of slugs and snails), and plenty of flower spikes. Grow among other strong colours and architectural shapes, particularly plants with large horizontal leaves. Also grow against dark backgrounds. The deciduous species generally have narrow, grassy foliage and the evergreens folded leaves. The 1.2m (4ft) high and 60cm (2ft) wide *K. caulescens* has unusual blue-green foliage and orange buds producing cream flowers in dense spikes, but its most important distinguishing feature is the ability to form a trunk, like a yucca, that gradually loses its

Knautia macedonica   *Kniphofia*

Lathyrus odoratus

leaves. If cut right back it will reshoot. Other good choices include 'Atlanta', a typical poker with yellow flowers and orange buds, also 1.2m (4ft) high and 60cm (2ft) wide. 'Prince Igor' is 60cm (2ft) taller, a fun cherry red, ideal for autumn, while the one that generates the strongest reaction is the orange 'Erecta', 90cm (3ft) high and nearly as wide, because the flowers do not hang down but point up, creating a remarkable upsurging shape. The yellows are equally striking, and they range from the cool to the bright flashy yellow. 'Yellow Hammer' (the same size as 'Erecta') is particularly startling because the bright yellow flowers emerge from greenish buds in summer. If you do want a pastel to offset the eye-grabbing stronger colours, try the creamy, 1.2m (4ft) high 'Maid of Orleans' and the slightly shorter 'Strawberries and Cream', with coral pink buds and cream flowers. Provide full sun and deep, rich soil that will hold on to moisture over summer, but which will not stay sopping wet in winter because that can be fatal. Propagate by making divisions of plants in spring before they get too established, because digging out a giant root system will take plenty of muscle, and trying to separate it might take more than two back-to-back forks. Seed sown in spring usually has a high germination rate, and while the plants will not be exact

copies of the parents, because they hybridize, they might well be very attractive when they start flowering in their second summer.

LATHYRUS
Sweet pea

A short, hardy annual sprinter that only gets about 1.8m (6ft) high, the sweet pea (*L. odoratus*) is essential in any garden because of its lashings of extraordinary scent. Choose carefully because some kinds (mostly the modern varieties) are not scented, and some only mildly so, but those said to have a strong scent on the seed packet will have just that. Go for the old varieties, especially the maroon and mauve 'Matucana', red and white 'America', and pink and white 'Painted Lady'. Between autumn and spring, sow three per 7.5cm (3in) pot and keep at 15°C (59°F). To speed up the germination process, first soak the seed overnight, or carefully rub the casing with sandpaper or nick it with a knife opposite the 'eye'. Alternatively, 'chit' the seeds by laying them between moist sheets of kitchen towel, wait until the casing splits, and then sow. The autumn sowing is then kept in a cold frame over winter, and gives a head start over the spring batch. After the second pair of leaves has appeared on the spring-sown seedlings, pinch out the tops to generate bushier growth and flowering side shoots. Plant out in late spring, after the frosts, and train up twiggy sticks on to a 1.8m (6ft) high wigwam of canes or similar support, and tie in. Keep deadheading for more, richly scented flowers. Grow in fertile soil and water well in dry weather.

LEUCANTHEMUM
Leucanthemum

An excellent choice for a mass of white daisy-like flowers in beds or pots right through summer. Available as annuals and the popular cultivars of the hardy perennial *L. × superbum* in a variety of shapes including singles, doubles, and anemone-centred. They range from just over 30cm (1ft) to nearly 1.5m (5ft) high

with a spread up to 1.2m (4ft). All have a very effective combination of dark green leaves and the yellow-eyed white flowers on top of long, thin stalks. Keep an eye out for 'Phyllis Smith' with its quirky, long, thin, twisty petals and 'Wirral Supreme' which nearly gets shoulder high. They must have rich, free-draining soil under

an open sky, and will quickly die out in heavy clay. The best way to propagate the perennials is by taking basal cuttings or making divisions in spring. Annuals can be sown in spring, giving shoots within 10 days, when kept at 15°C (59°F), though they can also germinate out in open beds where they are to flower.

Leucanthemum x superbum

Leucojum aestivum

Liatris spicata

LEUCOJUM
Summer snowflake

The hardy perennial *L. aestivum* is a spring-flowering bulb (forget summer) growing up to 60cm (2ft) high and 8cm (3in) wide, but if you want an even taller one, go for 'Gravetye Giant' because it will get 30cm (12in) higher. The first sign of flowering is when a leafless stem shoots up with possibly eight white, dangling bells. To thrive it needs bright sun and rich soil that stays damp. The spring snowflake (*L. vernum*) does just what it says and flowers in spring, getting up to 30cm (12in) high. Small and robust, it has green-tipped white flowers and shiny, dark green leaves. Like *L. aestivum*, it also needs rich, damp soil. The autumn snowflake (*L. autumnale*) is very different, and gets just 10–15cm (4–6in) high and 5cm (2in) wide. The short, thin, grass-like leaves emerge with the two to four white flowers, and they open from the end of summer into the start of autumn. It needs radically different conditions, thriving in a gravel, rock or Mediterranean-type garden with poor, stony or sandy, free-draining ground and hot sun. To propagate, wait until the green foliage has turned yellow and faded, dig up a clump and divide.

LIATRIS
Blazing star

A good choice for cottage gardens, with flower spikes packed with fluffy blooms that open from the top down at the end of summer, attracting bees and butterflies. The hardy perennial *L. spicata* is the best bet with 1.5m (5ft) high growth by 45cm (18in), but if you do not want pinkish-purple opt for one of the shorter cultivars, especially the white 'Alba' or 'Floristan Weiss', or the violet 'Floristan Violett'. All make good cut flowers, especially the Floristan Series. Grow in mixed or autumn borders with large-leaved exotica. All need average, stony ground with excellent drainage. Do not attempt to grow in heavy soil that stays cold and wet in winter. Propagate by sowing seed in spring and standing pots in a cold frame, or for quicker results keep them at 17°C (63°F) until they germinate. Alternatively divide plants in spring.

LILIUM
Lily

Hardy lilies include the best-scented summer bulbs. Amateurs tend to be put off thinking they're too exotic, but most could not be easier. You simply make a small hole in the soil, pop in a bulb, and backfill. *L. regale* is a top choice, producing strong, vertical stems about 1.4m (4½ft) high with arching, rich green, strappy leaves and large, trumpet-like white flowers flushed purplish-brown on the outside, with an amazing scent. If you haven't got room in the border, grow as many as you can in pots. Also try the short-lived *L. auratum*, at the same height, with white, yellow-streaked flowers. The meadow lily (*L. canadense*), from 1–1.6m (3–5½ft) high, is ideal for moist ground and dappled shade where its yellow flowers stand out, and on close inspection you will see they've got dark speckling. The Madonna lily (*L. candidum*), which can get slightly taller, is a beautiful pure white with a lavish, sweet scent that has been grown since the time of the ancient Greeks. The flowers are particularly pronounced because they sit at the tops of the tall stems, well clear of the leaves. When planting this lily, the top of the bulb goes just beneath the soil surface, approximately 12mm (½in) deep. *L. duchartrei*, from mountainous western China, at 90cm (3ft), is a scented white with purple spots, and the white exterior gradually acquires a purple-reddish hue. This is a particularly good choice when you want to let the initial planting multiply because the underground sections produce new bulbs about 30cm (12in) away, and it therefore needs room to invade new ground, in semi-shade. The 1.2m (4ft) high Japanese *L. hansonii* has a thrilling show of deep orange-yellow, waxy, scented flowers that demand light shade. If grown under a glaring sun the colour loses its impact. *L. henryi*, under ideal conditions, can get 3m (10ft) high, though it can be as short as 1m (3ft) above ground, and has striking black-spotted orange flowers that add plenty of impact to the late summer garden, especially among cannas and dahlias. The 75cm (2½ft) high richly scented Easter lily (*L. longiflorum*) is one of the most beautiful of all lilies with long funnels highlighted by the yellow stamens, but it needs to be kept in a conservatory in cool-climate gardens in winter, being stood outside in summer when the temperatures pick up.

For a lily with a completely different colour, try the rose-pink *L. mackliniae*, which is more purple-pink outside, at no more than 60cm (2ft) high. The flowers appear in very attractive clusters of up to six, and it steals the

---

POTTING UP LILIUM SCALES

1 Dig up a lily bulb and clean it at the end of summer, being very careful not to damage the scales packed around the exterior.

2 Then lever back the scales, one by one, until they snap off. Each one must have a part of the base. Discard any with defects.

3 Put either in a plastic bag filled with compost (soil mix) at just under 21°C (70°F) or in modules, and top off with horticultural sand.

Lilium candidum

show in any semi-shady position. The 90cm–2m (3–6ft) high Turkscap lily (*L. martagon*) is a gentle beauty producing huge clusters, usually totalling about 25 flowers, though possibly many more, in pink or shades to darker purple-red, with highly distinctive swept-back petals. *L. nepalense*, from between northern India and the Himalayas, is a ravishing plant that varies between yellow to greenish-yellow or even greenish-white, but it needs to be grown in a conservatory border in cool climates for two reasons. It is not fully hardy, and it produces creeping underground stems that snake through the soil and then launch vertical flowering stems. Give it plenty of room to spread.

The last of the species is *L. speciosum* – look out for the white var. *album* and red var. *rubrum*. Both produce stunning, scented, swept-back flowers at the end of summer, into early autumn, but they do need acid soil. There are scores of beautiful

hybrids and they include 'African Queen', a 1.6m (5½ft) high yellow, and 'Citronella', which is also excellent in large tubs. It sends up tall, thin stems with a multitude of extraordinary, downward-facing, bright yellow flowers that look from a distance like huge, hovering, exotic butterflies. 'Casa Blanca', a pure white, and the crimson-pink

'Journey's End', both get 1.2m (4ft) high. American breeders and the cut-flower trade are continually producing new plants. One prodigious newcomer is the 1.5m (5ft) high 'Black Beauty', which can produce up to 40 flowers per stem, and is dark crimson, verging on black. Keep checking bulb catalogues for new introductions.

Most lilies like rich soil with plenty of well-rotted organic matter and good drainage. A few need or prefer acid conditions. Lilies being grown in pots need gritty compost to help the water sluice out. When making the planting holes, they need to be at twice the depth of the bulb if planting on heavy soil but go slightly deeper, at three times their depth, on light, free-draining ground. Because they like to have their heads, or flowers, in the sun and their roots in the shade, it is worth planting them among groups of perennials that they can quickly shoot through.

The two big potential problems are the lily beetle and slugs. The bright red beetles with black legs and wings nibble through the foliage from the tips to the stem, and should be picked off the moment they are seen, while slugs and snails chomp through the stems, one excellent reason why lilies are often grown in pots on tables to provide extra protection.

Propagate by removing healthy scales (discarding the discoloured, disfigured outer ones) from the parent by snapping them off at

the end of summer. Keep them in a plastic bag with multi-purpose compost (soil mix), and store in a warm, dry, dark place at just under 21°C (70°F). When tiny bulbs have grown they can be planted in free-draining potting compost (soil mix). Some lilies produce tiny bulbs in the leaf axils, and they can be collected in late summer and grown for one year on the surface of potting compost, being covered by a layer of fine grit. Other lilies produce new bulblets on the portion of stem underground, and they can be detached in early spring and grown on. Carefully lift the plant, remove the next generation of bulbs, and replant the parent. Grow the bulblets in a frost-free cold frame, in free-draining soil, until ready for planting out during the autumn, with smaller ones taking longer to mature.

L. longiflorum can be increased by taking leaf cuttings, and treating them like shoots. Plant them vertically, with the end that was nearest the plant being inserted by one-third in a pot of vermiculite, and the end that was furthest away sticking up. Water, put in a plastic bag and keep at 16°C (61°F) until the leaves have produced roots. Carefully take them out and you should spot the baby bulbs right at the base of each leaf. These can be planted in potting compost, and kept in a bright, cool place for one year.

When trying to grow lilies from seed, note it can take up to five years to get a flowering bulb.

Lilium canadense

Lilium martagon

Lilium longiflorum

Limnanthes douglasii

LIMNANTHES
Poached egg plant
The hardy annual *L. douglasii* provides a shock of yellow. It gets just above grass level, at 15cm (6in), and has a white outer fringe around the petals with bright yellow in the centre. It can be sown around the edge of a flashy border, in patio paving gaps, rock gardens or even in the lawn, and in all cases freely self-seeds, taking over new territory if unrestrained. It loves open, sunny ground and average soil avoiding extremes of moisture and dryness. Scatter the seed where it is to grow and flower in spring.

LIMONIUM
Sea lavender
A good choice for a sunny Mediterranean or gravel garden, it includes annuals, biennials, perennials and subshrubs. *L. platyphyllum* is the most popular, a shortish, hardy perennial that

will not get above 60cm (2ft) high and 45cm (18in) wide. It generates a terrific mass of lavender-blue flowers at the end of summer – a good antidote to borders with end-of-season flash reds and yellows – on its wiry stems, and is quite happy in seaside gardens on free-draining soil. It can suffer from powdery mildew, producing a white fungal growth on the foliage. Good in cut flower arrangements. The best way to propagate is by sowing seed straight into the ground where the plants are to grow, and you should get a good crop of seedlings within three weeks. Alternatively, raise new plants by division or root cuttings 12.5cm (5in) long. When taking the cutting, make a straight cut for the end nearest the crown of the plant, and an angled one for the furthest part. This will help you plant the root cutting, with the angled end going head first into the compost (soil mix) and the top (the end with the straight cut) being just beneath the surface of the compost, which needs to be covered with a layer of grit. It should take about four months before you start to see any new growth appear, but you can get slightly quicker results if you provide gentle bottom heat in a propagator.

LINARIA
Toadflax
Available as annuals and biennials, with the hardy perennial *L. purpurea* providing summer-long light purple flowers. It gets 90cm

(3ft) high and 30cm (1ft) wide, but must be grown with caution being a furious self-seeder, scattering new plants around, though the problem is easily solved by nipping of the fading flowers before they have time to multiply. (Other forms of toadflax, especially *L. dalmatica*, can be particularly troublesome.) *L. p.* 'Canon J. Went' is pale pink with silvery leaves and 'Springside White' has white flowers set against more silvery foliage. The 60cm (2ft) high and 15cm (6in) wide hardy annual *L. maroccana* 'Northern Lights' comes in a mixture of colours, including pink, orange, red, white and pale blue, and is very effective inside

formal box hedging or in a cottage garden. All like sunny sites with free-draining soil. Collect seed of the species and sow when ripe in a cold frame. Perennials can be easily divided to produce extra plants in spring or autumn.

LIRIOPE
Lily turf
A marvellous woodland plant, *L. muscari* is a hardy perennial from East Asia, where it thrives in the moist, acid soil and shade beneath the trees. It flowers in autumn, and often carries on into winter, when it sends up shortish flower spikes no higher than 60cm (2ft) tall and 45cm (18in) wide, packed from the top to the

DIVIDING LIMONIUM

1 When buying a new limonium, it is often more cost effective to pay the extra for a large, well-established plant.

2 You can immediately pull it apart by hand, separating it into two plants, each with a nice set of roots and leafy top growth.

3 They can either be planted out or, if one is slightly small, repot it and grow in a cold frame until it is large enough for the border.

Linaria purpurea

bottom with tiny violet-blue flowers. The colour is nicely set off by the rich green, strap-like leaves. A few plants will quickly spread, making propagation unnecessary, but if they start barging into neighbouring plants the excess growth can quickly be sliced off with a spade. The division – each must have both roots and top growth – can then be replanted where required, ideally in part-shade, though the ground must not be too wet. Good drainage is important. Alternatively, plants can be grown from seed in spring.

LUNARIA
Honesty

Two similar kinds are grown in gardens, the annual or biennial *L. annua* and perennial *L. rediviva*. The first is an essential cottage garden ingredient, making its presence felt with 90cm (3ft) of growth, and a width of 30cm (1ft), giving a casual, open look with sweet-scented white to pale purple flowers at the end of spring, and in summer. Good forms include the white var. *albiflora*, the variegated 'Variegata' with its green-and-white leaves, and the deep reddish-purple 'Munstead Purple'. The perennial form has pale purplish-white flowers. What distinguishes both kinds is the seedhead or pod, a flat papery disc which is almost transparent, and is widely used in flower arranging. When plants self-seed themselves around the garden in great numbers, these pods make a terrific show. Honesty is easily grown in any decent soil in sun or

even light shade. It is unlikely you will have to propagate since the plants do it for you, but just in case the perennials can be divided in spring, or both kinds can be grown from seed. Sow it when fresh where it is to grow in the open ground, and the seeds will promptly germinate the following spring, but if you cannot quite decide where you will want to place them, grow instead in pots in an open cold frame.

LUPINUS
Lupin

Guaranteed to make a lively summer show, hardy lupins are available as annuals and perennials and even subshrubs. The most popular kinds are the perennials, producing spikes or spires packed

with scores of small flowers creating an iconic sight in cottage garden borders. There is a huge range of colours, from white to pink, purple and red, with many bicolours, and when planted in clusters they send the eye skipping around the garden from group to group. The amazing range of garden hybrids date back to the work of George Russell (1857–1951), who spent some 25 years developing strong plants with strong colours. Also look out for the midsummer-flowering Band of Noble Series, to 1.2m (4ft) high and 75cm (2½ft) wide, with single and bicolours, especially the blue and white 'The Governor', the pink and white 'The Chateleine', and the red 'The Page'. The French

'Gallery Series' are much shorter, at just 25cm (10in) high, and include the eponymous 'Gallery Blue', some with a white bicolour, 'Gallery Red', 'Gallery Yellow' and 'Gallery White'. Large aphids that live on lupins can devastate whole plants, so keep an eye out and take immediate action or you will not have any plants left. When propagating, carefully divide the crown at the start of spring, or take basal cuttings using the new shoots but make sure that you remove each with a thin slice of the rootstock. To avoid any possibility of rotting, do not plant in compost but use containers filled with perlite. If sowing seed, the seed coat needs to be nicked with a knife or soaked for 24 hours to aid germination.

SOWING LUPINUS SEED

1 The best way to get the spring seed to germinate is by nicking it with the point of a knife. Hold it firmly to avoid slashing your finger.

2 Alternatively, soak the seed for 24 hours in tepid water so that they swell, facilitating germination. It takes longer but is much less fiddly.

3 Sow in seed compost (soil mix), making sure that the seed is lightly covered in sieved compost, at a depth equivalent to its own height.

Lunaria annua

Lupinus

Lychnis coronaria

LYCHNIS
Campion

The best-known forms are the 75cm (2½ft) high rose campion (*L. coronaria*), the 1m (3½ft) high Maltese cross (*L. chalcedonica*) and 75cm (2½ft) *L. flos-jovis*, all hardy perennials getting about 60cm (2ft) wide. The first is either grown as a biennial or short-lived perennial, and it is a big favourite in cottage gardens, where it provides a mix of silvery stems and leaves that highlight the small, flat, open, bright red flowers in midsummer. A good companion is the white 'Alba', or a white with a pink eye ('Angel's Blush' and 'Blushing Bride'). If you're not too fussy about the amount of pink, try the Oculata Group. Plants rarely get above 90cm (3ft) by 45cm (18in) wide, and when grown in drifts or groups in a border they provide strong focal points, helping the eye move from area to area. The one problem is that they're at their best in the second year, and after that are not worth persevering with. The good news is that the scattered seed generates scores of seedlings and fresh, new vigorous replacements. The Maltese cross is slightly taller (needing some support) with stiffer, upright growth and green stems and leaves with clustered bright red flowers in the first half of summer (the four petals are shaped like a cross). Pink forms ('Carnea', 'Dusky Salmon' and 'Salmonea') are available for pastel schemes. Again, it is a prolific self-seeder. *L. flos-jovis* is the shortest of the three, and has whitish stems with reddish-pink flowers. All like full sun with free-draining soil, except for the Maltese cross that prefers moister ground. Propagate by divisions after flowering or by taking basal cuttings. Since the plants are prolific self-seeders, it is rarely necessary to sow your own, but they can be raised at 10°C (50°F) if you prefer to do it yourself. If they have poor colours, promptly remove.

Macleaya x kewensis

CONTAINER CARE

Always check that containers have enough drainage holes. Attractive pots that were never designed to take plants need to have holes hammered or drilled into the bottom, while old pots that were stacked in the garage need to be scrupulously cleaned before re-use to stop the potential spread of pests and diseases. Also check that clay pots have been glazed inside, not just outside, or they could easily get damaged in icy weather. Any moisture seeping into the surface will turn to ice and crack the pot. If in doubt, line the inside with plastic to act as a barrier and a protection but, again, make sure that drainage holes have been punctured in it. When filling the pot with compost (soil mix), put a deep layer of old crocks in the bottom to help the water sluice quickly out through unblocked holes. Also add slow-release

fertilizer because the nutrients will get washed out of the compost after six to eight weeks, depending on the compost, and water-retaining gels that will radically cut down the need for giving regular drinks in summer.

MACLEAYA
Plume poppy

Nothing like a traditional poppy, the big, bold *M. cordata* is a 1.8m (6ft) high hardy perennial that gets about 90cm (3ft) wide. It sends up an airy show of cream-white flowers in midsummer on its grey-green stems, and needs to be grown to the back of a border where its two-tone leaves are not completely obscured because they are greyish-green above and pinkish-grey beneath. Provide rich, moist soil and light shade since it comes from woody areas in East Asia. It can be propagated in various ways, by seed sown in spring, standing the pots in a cold frame, or give gentle bottom heat to speed up the germination process, or divide plants in spring. Water while getting established.

MALOPE
Annual mallow

Essential in cottage gardens, the hardy annual *M. trifida* looks like a short hollyhock, getting 90cm (3ft) high with a 15cm (6in) spread. The dark purple-red flowers, with darker veins, open from summer to autumn, being set against the rich green leaves. Completely unfussy, plants happily grow in average soil avoiding extremes of dryness and moisture. They also do particularly well in seaside gardens, being immune to the winds and salt spray. If you can provide some protection with shrubs, or by planting in a sunken area, even better. Use to fill gaps in the middle of the border, and propagate by sowing seed either where the plants are to grow, or earlier under glass to get a quicker batch of seedlings.

SOWING MATTHIOLA SEED

1 Sowing stock directly outside in spring can be a problem where mice and early morning birds grab anything tasty. Instead sow in pots.

2 Scatter the seed thinly over the surface, and then gently cover with a thin layer of compost (soil mix) so that the seed is near the light.

3 Water and stand the pots in a propagator at about 15°C (60°F) to provide some gentle heat, until the new growth starts to appear.

MATTHIOLA
Stock

The annual night-scented stock (*M. longipetala* subsp. *bicornis*) is one of the most valuable plants in the scented garden. A short, hardy annual at just 30cm (12in) high and wide, it comes in pink, mauve or purple, though the shape and colours do not amount to much. But in early evening it releases a rich, powerful scent, making it absolutely essential beneath windows, and beside paths and ponds, in fact anywhere that people congregate. *M. incana* also has a fantastic scent of cloves, and the different Series at a range of heights up to 75cm (2½ft) offer a range of colours with plenty of whites, purples, lilacs, pinks and reds. Grow in decent soil,

avoiding extremes of damp and wetness. Propagate by sowing in spring where the plants are to grow, or earlier in the season in gentle warmth to get an earlier crop.

MECONOPSIS
Meconopsis

The hardy Welsh poppy (*M. cambrica*) thrives in moist, shady areas where it produces an abundance of yellow flowers on 45cm (18in) high stems, with a 25cm (10in) spread. An easily grown, highly attractive perennial, it reliably self-seeds around the garden. The hardy Himalayan blue poppy (*M. betonicifolia*) is one the great sights in any garden but is notoriously tricky to grow. It has clear blue midsummer flowers on top of 1.2m (4ft) high stems, with a spread of 45cm (18in), and stands out wherever it is grown, ideally against a contrasting background that will highlight its colour. It is a special plant that needs siting with care. Though classed as a perennial, it behaves like a biennial when grown in poor conditions and quickly dies out. Sow in late winter, scatter the seed on peat-based compost (soil mix) with added grit, and cover with perlite because it needs to be near the light. Keep the soil moist and at a minimum of 7°C (45°F). It also needs a cool summer, regular moisture and leafy soil slightly on the acidic side. Whatever happens, do not try it in open, free-draining ground where the soil dries out. When using fresh seed, sow immediately and keep in pots over winter in a cold frame.

Meconopsis cambrica

MELIANTHUS
Melianthus

The perennial honey bush (*M. major*) is one of the best architectural plants, easily capable of getting 2.4m (8ft) high and wide. It has multi-fingered, arching leaves like no other, up to 50cm (20in) long, with a soft greenish-bluish-grey tone. The not-that-exciting reddish-brown flowers will not reliably appear, needing an excellent summer, but when they do the spikes shoot up to 75cm (2½ft) long. Because it is not reliably hardy, especially when young, plants need to be given a sunny, sheltered site, ideally against a wall among some protective shrubs, and a thick winter mulch to protect the crown and roots. The top growth

dies back in winter in cold climates, but if it does not, cut it back in spring to generate fresh, new growth. It is technically a shrub but behaves like a perennial unless being grown in warm climates. Grow in rich, moist, well-drained soil and propagate by dividing plants at the start of spring. Alternatively sow seed in spring at 17°C (63°F), though the divisions obviously give quicker results.

MIRABILIS
Four o'clock plant/marvel of Peru

This perennial from South America is not reliably hardy, but it is easily grown for its scented, colourful growth that gets about 60cm (2ft) high and wide. The flowers can be red, pink, yellow or white but do not open until late in the afternoon, hence one of its common names. It can either be grown at the front of a border or as a pot plant, and needs good drainage and an open, sunny position. In mid-autumn cut back the top growth and keep the tuber over winter in a frost-free place, planting it up again the following spring, giving it warmth, light and gentle drinks. When propagating extra plants for borders or containers, divide the tubers in spring, making sure that each portion can generate both roots and plenty of flowering top growth.

Melianthus major

MISCANTHUS
Miscanthus

An absolutely essential group of hardy perennial grasses ranging in heights from the small to 4m (12ft) high, the bigger ones adding plenty of shape and muscle to the border, often colourful autumn hues and plumes of late summer flowers. They can be used in all kinds of garden styles, from cottage gardens to the sensory deprivation of a minimalist design to the latest sculptural look. They can also be used in drifts across large gardens, but when they are grown too close to each other they promptly lose their individual shape, one of the main reasons for growing them. The best include forms of *M. sinensis* – and there are approximately 90, though new forms are constantly being introduced in Europe and America – that are capable of growing to 3m (10ft) high and 1.2m (4ft) wide. They have an elegant, arching shape, rich autumn colours and airy flowering plumes. Look out for the following, but visiting a specialist nursery is essential if you need a specific size and shape to complete a garden design jigsaw. *M. s.* var. *condensatus* 'Cosmopolitan' (found in Japan in the 1940s) stands out because of the bold, cream-white edge to the leaves that are capable of growing in excess of 2.4m (8ft) long, while 'Ferner Osten' is grown for its green leaves that turn deep orange in autumn, making a flamboyant show, and for its pinkish-silver late summer flowers. 'Flamingo' is another

Miscanthus sinensis 'Kleine Fontaine'

with variegated leaves, this time a white stripe up the centre of the 1.8m (6ft) long, vertical foliage, but 'Gewitterwolke' (the same height) is a much chunkier grass making an unmistakable clump of orange in autumn, and is well worth its own island bed in a large lawn. 'Ghana' gets 60cm (2ft) higher, and sends up vertical leaves that arch at the top, turning beige in autumn. If you need a medium-size grass, then 'Gold und Silber' is a 1.2m (4ft) high neater shape for smaller borders where it stands out in autumn when the foliage turns orange. A good alternative is 'Kleine Silberspinne' (the same height) with its narrow leaves and reddish-orange autumn show. When buying the widely grown 2m (6½ft) high 'Gracillimus', try buying one that is a decent size so that you can see what you are getting because the shapes can vary from the arching to those with a greater width than height, though all have a white vein running up the length of the long, thin leaves. The 2.4m (8ft) tall 'Grosse Fontäne' has spectacular, tall, arching leaves with an airy show of flowers that are well clear of the foliage, and a lively autumn show with tints mingling purple, orange and red. 'Morning Light' (the same height) is widely grown because of its elegant shape and

white striped margins. It was grown for over a century in Japan before it was introduced to the West in 1976, and is the variegated form of 'Gracillimus'. 'Silberfeder' is a top choice where a reliable show of airy flowers is needed, and the silver plumes open in late summer, well clear of the foliage. One of the most striking shapes is the 1.8m (6ft) high 'Strictus', which is called porcupine grass because of its firmly upright leaves, and they are stamped with yellow horizontal bands, while 'Zebrinus' offers the same with arched leaves. Correctly positioned, it is incredibly striking. 'Undine' is another with orange-yellow tones in autumn, and 2m (6½ft) of tall, elegant, arching growth. All can be left standing over winter, adding extra shapes, but do not forget to cut them back in late winter to let the new growth shoot up. Let them grow in full sun, especially those with strong autumn colours, in average soil. To perpetuate a vigorous show and propagate new plants, divide the clumps in spring every three years. If you let the clumps grow for much longer, the ease with which they can be dug up and split lessens, and in extreme cases you will not be able to divide them with back-to-back forks but will have to use a spade with plenty of

Molinia caerulea

power to force them apart. Alternatively, collect the ripe seed in autumn and immediately sow in pots in a cold frame.

MOLINIA
Moor grass
Hardy perennial grasses, and the most commonly grown kinds are purple moor grass (*M. caerulea*) and its cultivars. (What was once called *M. c.* subsp. *arundinacea* is no longer considered a separate plant, but is the same – it only looked different because it was grown in richer, more fertile soil producing stronger growth.) They grow from 45cm (18in) high to over 1.8m (6ft) high with a spread of about 45cm (18in). They add elegance, body and structure to the garden over summer, making architectural clumps of bright green with late summer, purple-green flowers after which the foliage turns yellow-orange-red in autumn. Good cultivars include the 2.2m (7ft) high 'Karl Foerster' with its arching foliage, the slightly taller 'Skyracer' with its stiff upthrust of vertical foliage with leaves turning rich gold in autumn (which is why it needs to be planted where it is picked up by the sun to highlight the effect), the 2m (6½ft) high 'Transparent' with a particularly airy show of flowers, and 'Windspiel' (the same height) with supple flower stems that sway and bend in the wind. All take a good two to three years to reach full size, and stand out

against a contrasting dark background (for example a copper beech hedge with dark leaves, or dark green conifers). They thrive in cool-climate gardens with full sun, and like plenty of moisture during long, hot, dry summer periods. Propagate by dividing youngish plants in early spring before the new growth begins, but if you wait until they are established garden features they will be hard to dig out and slice through because of their dense root systems. Keep the new sections well watered to avoid putting them under stress. Alternatively collect the ripe seed and immediately sow in pots in a cold frame.

MONARDA
Bergamot
Highly distinctive hardy annuals and perennials with clusters of spidery petals around a central disc, they give a strong display of colour – getting 90cm–1.2m (3–4ft) high and about 45cm (18in) wide – from midsummer to the start of autumn in white, pink, red and violet. Each flower has an upper hooded petal and a lower one with three lobes. All inject plenty of fun into cottage gardens, attracting bees and butterflies. The best include the bright red 'Cambridge Scarlet', with more reds from 'Ruby Glow' and 'Squaw', while the 'Beauty of Cobham' is pale pink, 'Marshall's Delight' bright pink, 'Croftway Pink' rose-pink, 'Schneewittchen'

Monarda 'Cambridge Scarlet'

white and 'Violet Queen' bright violet. Many monardas have leaves with a pronounced citrus scent, and can be used in a pot-pourri. They need reasonably damp (not sopping wet), rich ground in cool, dappled shade where they will not bake in midsummer. Mildew is a perennial problem, though some plants in some locations might be lucky. Monardas self-propagate,

increasing by underground stems that inch through the soil, creating decent clumps, so always give them room to expand when planting. If they exceed their allotted space, you can spade down through the excess growth and use that for new plants. Alternatively, take spring cuttings, said to be more resilient to mildew, and discard the parents.

DIVIDING MONARDAS

1 In spring look for vigorous new shoots and carefully scrape back the soil to see if there is a tiny cluster of roots at the base.

2 If so, prise it gently out of the ground. You should have a whole plant in miniature with its top growth and a set of feeding roots.

3 Plant it up in a container and water, standing in a sheltered position in dappled shade until it is large enough to be planted out.

Musa

MUSA
Banana

Few think that a banana tree is actually a perennial, but that is what it is. Forget the crop unless you have a huge heated greenhouse or live in the tropics, and grow them instead for their spectacular leaves with the potential for getting 3m (10ft) long and 30cm (1ft) wide. Use in architectural schemes with other large-leaved species, and plants such as cannas and a coppiced tree of heaven (*Ailanthus altissima*) with its 60cm (2ft) long leaves, *Paulownia tomentosa* and *Tetrapanax papyrifer*. The top banana choice is *Musa basjoo*, a suckering hardyish plant that can reach 5m (15ft) high with a possible width of 4m (12ft). It needs full sun in a sheltered, enclosed space because if exposed to strong, flaying winds the leaves get battered and ruined. In areas prone to frost, cut off the foliage in autumn and wrap chicken wire around the stem, then pack it firmly with straw as insulation. Remove it the following spring after the last of the frosts, and it will soon put out a new batch of fresh green leaves. Alternatively, you can lift the whole plant and keep in a conservatory pot over winter. Propagation is remarkably easy because the plants send out suckers that can be detached from the parent in spring. Before severing, scrape back the soil to make sure that it has a decent set of roots or it will not survive. If unsure, wait a bit longer and then double check.

GREENHOUSES

While being terrific for raising plants, greenhouses are also ideal for pests and diseases. They need to be thoroughly cleaned out twice a year, in spring and late autumn, and that means taking everything out and scrubbing all surfaces. If pests and diseases take hold in the protected, warm environment, they can be hard to eradicate, so make sure they never get a chance. Use biological controls in summer for whitefly, red spider mite, mealybugs and aphids (never in combination with pesticides because the toxins might kill the parasites), but note that they are living creatures and need to be used promptly, so only order them when you spot a problem. Most controls need to be used at about 20°C (68°F). Do not worry that they will fly out of the first open window, because all, except for *Cryptolaemus*, can be relied on to stay put. Also use sticky traps among the plants and high up to catch flying insects. French marigolds (*Tagetes patula*) will deter whitefly, if not already present.

Myosotis

MYOSOTIS
Forget-me-not

Available as annuals, biennials and perennials, the one for dry land is *M. alpestris*. A short-lived hardy perennial getting 20cm (8in) high and 15cm (6in) wide, it has clusters of tiny dark blue flowers attracting bees and butterflies, and thrives in full sun, though it also does well in light shade. The soil should be free-draining though never bone dry, possibly on the acid side. To make sure you always have a good show, keep propagating, raising new plants by seed sown in autumn. Stand the pots in a cold frame for germination when temperatures pick up next spring. Alternatively, take stem cuttings in spring. Both methods have high success rates.

NARCISSUS
Daffodil

There are thousands of daffodils on the market. Most are hardy perennials for growing outdoors, and the colour range is wide: apricot, lemon, orange, pink, white and yellow. Flower shapes vary; there are 11 botanical groups, and a twelfth for the miscellaneous. *N. triandrus* looks like a fuchsia, with tightly pulled back petals, and 'Broadway Star' like a marvellous, comical lollipop. Heights range from the tiny, 10cm (4in) high delicate little North African white *N. watieri*, to the knee-high *N.* 'Stratosphere', at 65cm (26in). And they can be grown in different ways.

The dwarfs are best in pots in a cold greenhouse where you can see them clearly. The fast spreaders, such as *N. bulbocodium*, can be grown in a spare patch of ground, and the rich, powerfully scented, such as *N. × odorus*, in corners and courtyards; avoid windy areas that quickly disperse the scent. The best daffodils include the late spring, nicely scented *N. poeticus* var. *recurvus*; it grows 35cm (14in) high, and has crisp white petals with a sharp yellow cup and red rim. The double kind flowers slightly later. The prolific 'Tête-à-Tête' is a yellow trumpet shape, at half the height, and a good alternative. The garden show starts with the white-lemon 'February Silver' and rich yellow 'February Gold', both 30cm (12in) high.

Narcissus cyclamineus

REMOVING NARCISSUS OFFSETS

1 If you need more daffodil bulbs then go straight to a cluster in the garden, and dig them up in early summer as the foliage dies.

2 Break off the new young bulbs attached to the parent bulb. Replant the parent bulb, if plump and firm. Otherwise, discard it.

3 Dust the broken edges with fungicide to prevent rotting, then grow in a special nursery until they reach flowering size.

N. cyclamineus is a small, bright yellow, 20cm (8in) high, sprouting a long, thin, distinctive trumpet, that flowers in early spring and likes slightly acidic soil. 'Peeping Tom' is twice as tall. Mix them with the late 'Tricollet', 38cm (15in) high, which looks absolutely outrageous. It has six creamy petals and a bizarre, orange T-shape on top. When naturalizing bulbs, remember that you have got to endure long grass. Mowing round the daffodils is necessary for at least six weeks after flowering. You have got to let the bulbs store up energy for next year's display. The pick of the scented daffodils are the tazettas (though not all are reliably hardy) and hardy jonquils, both with several small flowers per stem. Bulb merchants stock big selections such as

Narcissus papyraceus

'Geranium' (tazetta), 'Baby Moon' and 'Bobbysoxer' (jonquil), and the paper white (*N. papyraceus*). Without a sun-facing border in a mild region, backed by a sheltering wall (where the tazettas can bake over summer), and where the scent hangs in the air, grow these bulbs in pots, under glass, giving frost protection though winter. When planting any daffodil in grass, roll back the turf in autumn and plant the bulbs one and a half times to twice their own depth, in a sunny position, from 20–30cm (8–12in) apart, or closer, giving them room to multiply. They need at least 15cm (6in) of soil above because in mid- and late spring, in periods without any rain, the topsoil quickly dries. Below that level the bulbs can fatten and drink all they want. Well-drained ground is essential, and fine grass is better than choking, vigorous growth. On poor soils, sprinkle an all-purpose feed after flowering, before the foliage dies. The best way of maintaining a clump of daffodils, and of stopping them from becoming congested (and thereby propagating more), is to carefully dig them up just as the foliage is dying, when you can clearly see where they are. Separate the clump and look for small, new, young bulbs that need to be removed from the side of the parent, but leave the roots intact. Then place in a special bed with free-draining soil where they can be grown until they reach flowering size for planting out in autumn.

NECTAROSCORDUM
Nectaroscordum

The hardy perennial bulb *N. siculum* subsp. *bulgaricum* makes an excellent background or combination plant that is not quite good enough to be the centre of attention, but which is nonetheless an essential in cottage gardens. The stems get up to 1.2m (4ft) high and 10cm (4in) wide, and the clustered flowers are initially wrapped up in a sheath that fattens and swells until it falls off, leaving the flower stalks to bend up to the horizontal and vertical. The bells are more interesting than the colours, which are cream with purple and green, and need to be to the front of a border because people love to touch them. The flowers then fade to brown. Buy a handful of bulbs for planting in well-drained soil in full sun and they soon self-seed and create decent clusters. Excess plants can easily be dug up and moved to other sites, but if you need even more, sow ripe seed in autumn, cover the compost (soil mix) with grit and stand the pots in a cold frame for germination next spring. Water as they come into growth.

Nectaroscordum siculum

NEPETA
Catmint

Guaranteed to produce a comical, exaggerated display of crazy cat behaviour, which can temporarily ruin a plant, catmints are very good border plants. The three most popular kinds are *N. × faassenii*, *N. racemosa* and 'Six Hills Giant'. The first makes an upright or spreading clump – about 45cm (18in) high and wide – with a lovely mix of violet-blue flowers right through summer, set against the grey-green foliage. The second is about half as high, with similar coloured flowers, and there is an even shorter lavender-blue form – the 15cm (6in) high 'Little Titch' – and the white, 30cm (12in) high 'Snowflake'. The one that makes the showiest display is 'Six Hills Giant', a big burst of upright growth topped by lavender-blue flowers, again set against grey-green foliage. It grows about 90cm (3ft) high and half as wide.

SOWING NICOTIANA SEED

1 Nicotiana seed is very fine and best mixed with horticultural sand before being scattered on compost (soil mix) to give even distribution.

2 Because it needs good light to germinate, cover the seed in spring with a thin layer of vermiculite before watering and giving gentle heat.

3 Some nicotianas make substantial plants, so only propagate those which you have room for in the garden. Do not get carried away.

Once established, it is reliably drought-tolerant, also making it a good ingredient in gravel and Mediterranean-type gardens. It is often used in narrow borders to flank paths. All like wall-to-wall sun and free-draining soil, but if you've got cats, put the plants where a good battering will not detract from the rest of the border. New plants are easily raised by taking cuttings of new growth at the start of summer, though clumps can also be divided. If sowing seed, do so in spring at 17°C (63°F) for germination within three weeks.

NERINE
Nerine

N. bowdenii are hardy South African bulbs giving a gentle autumn show with pink flowers. (Others are less hardy.) The stems get about 45cm (18in) high, with a spread of 8cm (3in), and after the excess of summer they might seem slightly odd for having just a flowering stem, but the foliage follows soon after when winter kicks in. It likes to bake in a sheltered, sunny position (for example at the foot of a wall) with excellent drainage. Courtyard gardens are ideal, as is the base of an evergreen hedge. When planting, leave the neck of the bulb visible above the soil, but in regions with frosts it will need protecting. Plant it slightly deeper so that it is not so exposed. When the flowering show has finished, clumps can be dug up and divided, and while fresh seed can be sown, dividing gives much quicker results.

NICOTIANA
Tobacco plant

The short-lived, tender perennial *N. sylvestris* is high on the list for sweetly scented plants, and it has a strong presence with up to 1.5m (5ft) of growth, a spread of 60cm (2ft), and long-tubed white flowers. Plant it to the front of a cottage garden border where you can get your nose close for a good whiff, and also because its angled, upright stems add a quirky, see-through touch. Make sure it has plenty of sun in rich, free-draining soil. It is not hardy enough to last outside in cool climate gardens over winter, but new plants (raised as annuals) are easily propagated by collecting seed in autumn. Either sow them in late spring where they are to grow in the garden, or to keep a

Nepeta racemosa

Nicotiana sylvestris

Nigella damascena

Oenothera biennis

close eye on the seedlings and to get an earlier crop, sow in early spring at 20°C (68°F). Sow the seed on the compost surface and cover with perlite to give good light. If only a few germinate after 10 days or so, prick them out and wait because more may follow later. They can be erratic.

NIGELLA
Love-in-a-mist
A cottage garden favourite, love-in-a-mist is a shortish – at 50cm (20in) high and 23cm (9in) wide – hardy annual with gentle sky blue flowers. There is a shorter version, 'Blue Midget', at half the height, and 'Mulberry Rose' in cream-pink, while a packet of Persian Jewel Series provides pastels in white, pink, rose and lavender-blue. It is extremely good at filling gaps at the front of a border, and for a massed planting in a small island bed with a flamboyant centrepiece, like a large standard brugmansia. Note that the flowers are followed by very attractive, rounded seed pods or capsules, much used in dried flower arrangements. Also use for cut flower arrangements. Grow in average soil, and keep deadheading to promote more flowers right through summer. Sow the seed in late summer where you want it to flower, because it dislikes being moved, but do not cover the seed because it needs a winter chilling. It germinates the following spring.

NOMOCHARIS
Nomocharis
About 10 different species are usually available, mainly from specialist nurseries, but you are likely to find just one in gardens, *N. aperta*. A bulbous perennial from western China introduced in the 20th century, it produces exquisite pale pink flattish, nodding flowers with some delicate spotting in the centre. It gets about 30cm (12in) high and 10cm (4in) wide. Plant the bulbs 15cm (6in) deep in humus-rich, acid soil in partial shade so that the soil stays moist in summer without being wet. If you are lucky enough to have such a site, and can grow rhododendrons, try a scattering of nomocharis around them. Sow seed at 10°C (50°F) in spring or autumn, but you will have to allow a good three to four years before you see any flowers.

OENOTHERA
Evening primrose
Another highly scented cottage garden plant, *O. biennis* is a hardy annual or biennial with a delicious perfume at the end of the day when the flowers open for the evening. It needs space because it grows 1.5m (5ft) high with a spread of 60cm (2ft), but it has an open, see-through shape, and self-seeds prolifically around the garden. Other good hardy perennial choices include

O. fruticosa 'Fyverken' and *O. f.* subsp. *glauca*, both of whose flowers open during the day, and *O. macrocarpa* whose flowers stay open until mid-afternoon. The first grows 45cm (18in) high by 30cm (12in) wide, and is so named because it is covered in red buds that ping open giving yellow flowers, while the new leaves are tinged red. The second grows fractionally taller and has young reddish leaves and small clusters of yellow flowers, while the third is a low-growing trailer that will not get above 23cm (9in) high, while spreading up to 45cm (18in). It is packed with bright lemon-yellow flowers. All flower right through summer (the flowers only last a day but new ones keep appearing) and thrive in full sun (though light shade is not a problem) with average to rich soil. Because all kinds are prolific self-seeders, you do not need to worry about propagating more. Just look out for seedlings and move those required to the right place,

carefully forking them out of the ground so that their root systems are kept intact. Get rid of the excess soil. You can also divide plants and, when sowing the first batch for the garden, germinate them at 13°C (55°F) for shoots within 14 days.

PLANTS FOR SCENT

Grow scented plants in a still, enclosed space so that the scent hangs in the air and does not get blown away. The best places are near seats, by the back door, and as close as you can get to windows. For heady, powerful scents try *Daphne odora* 'Aureomarginata' with a big gorgeous perfume in mid-spring. It has mauvish-purple flowers, and forms a mound about 1.2m (4ft) high and wide. All the daphnes are good (some exquisite), and this is one of the best. If your soil is acid, and all your neighbours are growing rhododendrons and azaleas, then go for *Rhododendron*

luteum. It is tall at 1.8m (6ft), and a woodland kind of plant, one for the back of the border. It has bright yellow spring flowers with a scent that wafts in the warmth and the leaves turn red in autumn. Also include a wisteria, lilacs, jasmine threading through the protection of an evergreen hedge, Mexican orange blossom (*Choisya ternata*) and mock orange (*Philadelphus*) for whiffs of marzipan and vanilla, with sweet peas (*Lathyrus odoratus*), lilies and *Viburnum* x *bodnantense* with its pink winter flowers on the bare winter stems and a lung-filling, ravishing scent.

Onopordum acanthium

1 Nip off the tops of several young osteospermum shoots in late spring or, failing that, in late summer, taking the cutting just above a node.

2 Trim off just below the bottom node, discarding the unused lengths of stem. The larger leaves can be reduced, cutting off the top halves.

3 Then dip the ends of the stem in rooting powder, blow off the excess and plant up in separate containers. Eventually move to a cold frame.

ONOPORDUM
Scotch thistle

For those with large gardens and large borders, this thistle provides a very tall, see-through, angular spread of branches. The two choices are *O. acanthium* and *O. nervosum*, both hardy biennials, with the latter having silver-grey leaves, the former grey-green ones. Both have thistle-like flowers, and the main stem shoots up well over head high to about 2.5m (9ft), with a spread of 90cm (3ft). They certainly will not suit every border, but fun, quirky ones and cottage gardens that thrive on the unexpected make very good settings. They like fertile soil with good drainage, and plenty of sun. Since they scatter their seed around the garden, look out for seedlings in spring and carefully fork them up and move to where required. If you are sowing, then do so at the end of summer, either where you want them to

grow or in pots, and keep in a cold frame, and they will germinate next spring. If self-seeding is a problem, promptly remove the flowers (or the majority) the moment they start to fade.

OPHIOPOGON
Lilyturf

What looks like a black grass is, in the case of *O. planiscapus* 'Nigrescens', actually a hardy evergreen perennial. It makes a short, 20cm (8in) high spreading cluster of outward-pointing near-black leaves, getting about 30cm (12in) wide, and has an extremely good range of design possibilities. It can be used in gravel gardens or be arranged at the front of a border with silver-leaved plants or white flowers behind, but wherever it is positioned, make sure that the black stands out and is not lost against a dark background. Alternatively use the arching, green and cream striped

O. jaburan 'Vittatus', which is three times the size, though it is not fully hardy. Completely unfussy, it thrives in average soil with light or dappled shade, and can be easily propagated by dividing plants in spring.

ORNITHOGALUM
Star-of-Bethlehem

The hardy bulbous perennial *O. nutans* is ideal for cottage or gravel gardens, especially plantings of silvery whites. Spring-flowering, it can reach 90cm (3ft) high in ideal conditions, and is also used as a follow-on from daffodils and for growing among shrubs, where the pale flowers contrast with the emerging green foliage. It demands free-draining ground, though soil fertility is not that crucial, with plenty of sun or even light, occasional shade. With the right conditions the initial batch of bulbs will quickly multiply, but if plants do start exceeding their

allotted space they can be quickly hauled out. To propagate, lift an established clump and look for new, young offsets, planting them out 10cm (4in) deep where they are to flower. Alternatively, raise in pots or a nursery bed until they reach flowering size.

OSTEOSPERMUM
Osteospermum

South African osteospermums inject a showy, cheery dash of large, daisy-like flowers usually in white, pink or yellow. A mix of annuals, perennial and subshrubs, they are not completely hardy but are easily kept from year to year. In mild, sheltered areas where there is average, free-draining soil, especially in stony ground, they produce a mass of stems topped by open flowers. 'Whirligig' has white spoon-shaped outer petals, a white centre and a blue central disc, and 60cm (2ft) height and width. If you like the colour

Ophiopogon planiscapus

Ornithogalum nutans

Osteospermum hyoseroides 'Gaiety'

Paeonia lactiflora 'Whitley Major'

scheme but not the spoons, try the potentially larger *O. ecklonis*. 'Buttermilk' is pale yellow and 60cm (2ft) high and wide, 'Nairobi Purple' dark purple and 15cm (6in) high and 90cm (3ft) wide, and 'Cannington Roy' white tipped purple, turning purple-pink (the same height but 60cm/2ft) wide. If you cannot grow them outside all year – and they need a mild, sheltered, free-draining, sunny site – either keep them in pots for moving under cover over winter, or dig them up and pot up for a winter out of the cold and wet. New plants are easily raised by taking cuttings in spring or at the end of summer, though you can also sow seed in spring at 18°C (64°F).

PAEONIA
Peony
Well-loved hardy perennials, spring- and early summer-flowering peonies are among the most sumptuous garden plants, many with a fantastic scent. The bowl-shaped flowers come in a wide range of colours, from white and pink to yellow and deep scarlet, with a highly distinctive flash of stamens. The foliage is another plus, especially when it first emerges, and in autumn when it is tinged with red. At 90cm (3ft) high and wide at most, they need to be grown beside plants that will take over when they finish flowering to avoid gaps in the midsummer border. There are hundreds and hundreds of different kinds available, and the best way to make a selection is by using a specialist catalogue or visiting a specialist nursery. Many are sold by just one or two nurseries, and if you want one of the rarer peonies put your order in quick before they sell out. Grow them in deep, rich soil but never set the crown more than 36mm (1½in) under the soil. If they produce lots of leaves but no flowers you've probably planted them too deeply, or piled mulch over the top, in which case scrape back the soil. Moving plants is not a good idea because they have big, fleshy roots but, if you are going to do it, do so in autumn, and dig right around and under the plant so that all the roots stay unmolested, packed in a ball of soil. They may well sulk the first time they're meant to flower after being moved, but in future seasons normal service will be resumed. Other causes include excess shade or high nitrogen levels. The best way to propagate is by dividing plants in autumn after the faded foliage has been stripped off. Lay the plant on the ground, spray the soil off the roots, and cut the crown into sections, each one having 3–5 buds that will produce the top growth next year. The cuts need to be treated with fungicide to exclude any chance of rotting. Then replant so that the buds are about 36mm (1½in) below the surface. You can also grow plants from seed, but it takes five years for flowering.

PANICUM
Panicum
The hardy perennial switch grass (*P. virgatum*) comes from the American prairies, and has many cultivars – 90cm–2.4m (3–8ft) high and up to 1.2m (4ft) wide – grown for their tall, slender, upright leaves and airy haze of purple-beige flowers. 'Cloud Nine' has blue-grey foliage turning golden-yellow in autumn and keeps a good shape over winter, while 'Prairie Sky' has even bluer foliage though it tends to be slightly floppier. 'Rehbraun' stands out because its green leaves acquire a reddish tinge come autumn, while the foliage of 'Shenandoah' becomes intense red. If being grown on moist ground, the autumn seed readily germinates, eliminating the need for propagation, but there is no guaranteeing that they will be copies of the parents. To get exact reproductions, divide the plants in autumn or spring, digging them up and using two forks back-to-back to prise them apart.

DUSTING PAEONIA TUBERS

1 Divide tubers in autumn. Dig them up, and hose down so you can clearly see what you're doing. Look for clusters of three buds or more.

2 Then, using a clean, sharp knife, cut the tuberous root-stock into sections, each with enough buds to generate plenty of top growth.

3 Finally, dust the cuts with a fungicide to prevent rotting. The lengths are now replanted, with the buds going just below the surface.

Panicum virgatum

TAKING PELARGONIUM CUTTINGS

1 Look for a healthy length of new growth after spring, and snip it off just above a node. Then trim the cutting just below a node.

2 You now need to remove the leaves growing from the base of the cutting, otherwise when covered in compost (soil mix) they will rot.

3 Dip the end of the cutting in rooting powder, tap off the excess and plant up. Keep watering and stand on a bright windowsill.

PAPAVER
Poppy

The best of the hardy perennial Oriental poppies – up to 1.2m (4ft) high and wide in the case of the big, brash Goliath Group – give a large cluster of hairy leaves and multiple stems with sensational flowers in reds, pinks and purple as spring moves into summer. Real showstoppers. The colours are often highlighted by contrasting dark blotches at the base of the petals. There are scores of cultivars, many having been given the Award of Garden Merit by the Royal Horticultural Society. In the wild the species grows in full sun on rocky or thin soil, but rich garden soil produces the best results with plenty of well-rotted organic matter. Avoid growing the Oriental kind in heavily fertilized soil because that just produces an excess of floppy leaves. (Also avoid growing them in pots because they have long tap roots.) Even when perfectly grown, there is the problem of what happens when the flamboyant large clump with big, bold, dashing flowers collapses. You need adjacent plants that will start flowering in the lead-up to midsummer, to fill the gaps in the border. The best way to propagate and get a copy of the parent is to take 5cm (2in) long root cuttings in autumn. When taking the cutting, make a straight cut for the end nearest the crown of the plant, and an angled one for the farthest part. This will help you plant the root cutting, with the angled end going head first into the compost (soil mix) and the top (the end with the straight cut) being just beneath the surface of the compost, which needs to be covered with a layer of grit. Annual alternatives include the Icelandic poppy (*P. nudicaule*), with slender stems 30cm (12in) high, getting 15cm (6in) wide, holding up saucer-like flowers predominantly in yellow or white, with some in orange and pale red. There are various strains, including the pastel Constance Finnis Group from Australia, the large-flowering Oregon Rainbow Group, and the Meadow Pastels Group. They make good

Papaver somniferum

cut flowers, and should be cut as the buds begin to open, with the stem bases being dipped in boiling water and then stood in cold water. *P. rhoeas* Shirley Series – 90cm (3ft) high and 30cm (12in) wide – came from one wild flower found in Surrey, in the UK, in 1880. Many selections later and the Shirleys emerged, all easily distinguished by their lack of a black blotch at the base of the flower. Many have a second shade around the edge of the petal. The opium poppy (*P. somniferum*) is the source of opium, though you can safely use the seed when making home-made bread. It gets to 1.2m (4ft) high and to 30cm (12in) wide. Perennial poppies like rich soil with well-rotted organic matter, but never try to make it too heavy and rich, while the annuals (especially the Icelandic poppy) tend to need well-drained soil, with both kinds in full sun. All can be grown from fresh seed in late summer, scattering it where the plants are to grow in poor to average soil, or wait until spring.

PELARGONIUM
Geranium

There is a huge range of tender perennial geraniums that are either grown as houseplants, or in pots and window boxes for standing outside over summer and bringing indoors in winter. They include the bushy Angels, the trailing Ivy-leaved kind, the Regals (also very bushy), those with scented leaves, the shrubby Uniques and the Zonals (with dark bronze-green or maroon markings on the leaves). The Ivy 'Summer Showers' come in a range of pinks (light and dark), reds and white, and can be used to trail out of hanging baskets or pots attached to walls, or be grown up a cane wigwam in a large pot. The Horizon Series provide good Zonals for containers and borders, and have a distinctive dark outer ring on the foliage and flowers, making a lively show in red, pink and white. Many annuals take a battering in wet weather, but this Series stands up well to the wet. All love bright sun and grow well, when established, in containers filled with John Innes No. 2. The range of colours means you can create stunning combinations from pastels to riproaring reds, and there are several interesting species with smaller, less flamboyant flowers. Water well in full growth and give a weekly feed, but give just the occasional drink over winter when dormant. If being planted to the front of flowerbeds, the soil needs to be fertile and free draining. Pot them up and bring indoors over winter to avoid cold, wet conditions that are fatal. Propagate by taking spring and early summer cuttings. They quickly root, and in the act of taking the cuttings and nipping back the parent, you will make a bushier plant with more flowers.

Pelargonium 'Moon Maiden'

PENNISETUM
Fountain grass

Aptly named, because these not-quite-fully-hardy annual and perennial grasses (mainly from tropical areas) produce fountains of flowers from a mound of leaves. The heights range from the short at 45cm (18in) for the front of a border to those at 1.5m (5ft) high for much further back. *P. alopecuroides*, at 90cm (3ft) high and 60cm (2ft) wide, has dark green leaves that flare reddish-orange in autumn, before ending

up beige-brown over winter. The late summer, early autumn flowers come in yellow-green to purple-brown. There are shorter cultivars, for example the variegated, 30cm (12in) high 'Little Honey', and the prolific self-seeder 'Moudry'. It has dark purple flowers and will be surrounded by an abundance of seedlings when it is grown on moist soil. The Oriental fountain grass (*P. orientale*) from East Asia is generally shorter and more compact, but it flowers in white over a longer period, starting in

summer and ending with the frosts. In autumn it 'burns' deep yellow before ending up beige. Its cultivars include the taller 'Karley Rose', at 1.2m (4ft), with its pink flowers, and 'Tall Tails' (the same height) with its flowers that start off pinkish-brown and end up white. All like free-draining soil in full sun. Cut them right back in late winter to get rid of the old growth and clear the way for the fresh, new foliage. You can either look for seedlings growing around the parents, or divide the plants.

Pennisetum orientale

AUTUMN COLOUR

Buy new plants for the garden every few months when they're in flower, and that way you will have a garden with a long flowering period. Specifically look for plants that keep flowering in autumn. They include …
Anemone x *hybrida* (Japanese anemone)
Aster
Dahlia
Fuchsia
Gaura lindheimeri
Penstemon
Sedum
Salvia uliginosa
Tricyrtis
Viburnum farreri

Also try *Dracunculus vulgaris*. The flower might have an atrocious smell when you get close but, in late summer, it produces lovely green berries that suddenly ripen to scarlet. *Iris foetidissima* (stinking gladwyn) has pods that ping open revealing tiny bright scarlet seeds. Crab apples (*Malus*), hawthorn (*Crataegus*), cotoneasters, pyracanthas and sorbuses also have brightly coloured berries.

For autumn leaf colour there is …
Acer, especially 'Senkaki' with its thin, burgundy red new branches
Amelanchier
Berberis
Cornus
Cotinus
Euonymus (deciduous)
Fothergilla
Liquidambar
Prunus (ornamental cherry)
Rhus (sumach)
Tilia (lime)
Vitis (vine)

Never cut the entire herbaceous border back to the ground. Leave a silhouette of assorted shapes, of spines and fat seedheads, of grasses and branches so they can icily stand up in the frost.

Aster

Cornus

Cotinus

Dahlia

Euonymus

Fuchsia

Liquidambar

Sedum

Vitis

TAKING PENSTEMON CUTTINGS

1 If any of your penstemons are in danger of not making it through a cold, wet winter, take tip cuttings in autumn just below a node.

2 Then trim the cutting, slicing off any leaves at the base, and pinch out the growing tip between finger and thumb to generate bushy growth.

3 The finished, cleaned-up cutting is now ready for planting. Keep in a frost-free greenhouse over winter; new growth appears next spring.

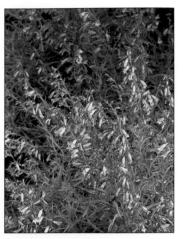

Penstemon 'Evelyn'

PENSTEMON
Penstemon

Rarely reliably hardy perennials, penstemons are the mainstay of the summer border making terrific clumps, up to 1.2m (4ft) high and wide, with most between 60–90cm (2–3ft). They flower prolifically right through the season, and can be used as stand-alones or in drifts. Most flowers are bicolours with a white throat, sometimes making a garish contrast with the rest of the flower, sometimes gently leading into a pastel. They are ideal in small gardens, and mix well with shrubs and other perennials. The one problem is that unless you have a sunny, sheltered position with excellent drainage they will not survive the winters when cold, wet soil is completely fatal. Severe frosts are rarely that big a problem, especially if you add a thick, protective mulch above the roots. If you cannot guarantee a dryish winter then plants can be dug up and kept in pots in a cold greenhouse. It is thought that cultivars with narrow leaves (such as 'Evelyn' and 'Schoenholzeri') are hardier than kinds with broader leaves ('Alice Hindley' and 'Osprey'). The toughest include 'Pensham Eleanor Young' (crimson with a white throat), 'Pensham Freshwater Pearl' (pink with the white throat) and 'Pensham Edith Biggs' (deep dark red). New selections keep being introduced from the USA, though there is still no large-flowered yellow. Expert growers either tend to cut back plants six weeks into spring, or cut them back by one-third late in the year with a more drastic cut in spring, to promote more bushy growth. If you have heavy clay soil, guard against the risk of plants dying over winter by taking 10cm (4in) long autumn cuttings with 3–4 pairs of leaves. Strip off the lower leaves and nip off the top just above a leaf and keep safe through winter. When planting out, surround the young perennial with annuals, when there is space before it really fills out.

PETUNIA
Petunia

A mix of half-hardy annuals and perennials, with most being grown for temporary summer displays in pots and window boxes, and in bedding schemes at the front of a border. There is a wide choice of different Series, for example the early flowering Flash and trailing Surfinia – both about 30cm (1ft) high and to 90cm (3ft) wide – and they're all easily raised from seed. All need fertile, free-draining soil in full sun. Sow the seed at the start of spring and keep at 20°C (68°F). Shoots should appear within 10 days, and plants can be gradually hardened off in a cold frame at the end of spring for planting out in summer. Give a tomato feed in summer to generate more flowers.

Petunia x *hybrida* 'Storm Lavender'

SOWING PETUNIA SEED AND PRICKING OUT SEEDLINGS

1 The seed is sown at the start of spring, being scattered thinly over the compost (soil mix) surface. Prevent the seed falling in clumps.

2 When you have gently watered the seed with an upturned rose spray, clearly label the pot and grow at 21°C (70°F) until growth appears.

3 When you have grown a batch of seedlings, they can be pricked out, taking care not to damage the roots, for planting in the next size pot.

Phlomis russeliana

PHLOMIS
Phlomis

Definitely a front of border plant because the arrangement of flowers is so unusual. They appear clustered in a circle or whorl (with a pair of leaves) around the stem at fixed intervals, and each has a hooded upper petal and open lower one. The hardy perennials feature four species, starting with the 90cm (3ft) high and 60cm (2ft) wide *P. cashmeriana* and its woolly, slightly sticky, long, thin yellow-grey leaves and pale pink midsummer flowers. The pale yellow *P. russeliana* is much the same size, and the thick leaves are even more impressive, getting up to 25cm (10in) long, being longest and most slender at the top. It has a long flowering period, but growth is slow to emerge in spring, so mark its position to avoid accidentally spearing it with a fork. *P. samia* (same size) is decidedly sticky with dark green, 15cm (6in) long leaves and summer-long burgundy flowers with a hint of pink in the usual whorls. *P. tuberosa* is the tallest of the bunch, growing 1.3m (4½ft) high. The arrow-like leaves have deep veins and the purple or pink flowers open in summer. All demand excellent drainage in full sun, being a good choice for a sunny slope that has been terraced. All are also easily propagated by seed sown in early spring, being covered with perlite to germinate at 18°C (65°F). Harden off in a cold frame before planting out. Plants can also be divided in spring.

PHLOX
Phlox

Hardy perennial phlox are quintessential cottage garden plants for flowering in spring or late summer. Heights vary to 1.5m (5ft), with the most popular kind being cultivars of *P. paniculata* that generally get above 1.2m (4ft) high, and about 82cm (32in) wide, with the taller ones needing staking to prevent them from flopping over. Good choices include the large white flowers of 'Alba Grandiflora', 'Alex Owzat' in mauve, the pinkish red 'Brigadier', the reddish-purple 'Dodo Hanbury-Forbes', lavender 'Eventide', bright pink 'Flamingo' and pale purple 'Hesperis'. 'Lizzy de Pauley' is a white suffused with pink around the edge, 'Prince of Orange' is an orange-red and 'White Admiral' is a late white. Grow them in average soil that is on the moist side in either sun or light shade. The one problem with all phloxes, especially these cultivars, is powdery mildew that strikes in dry weather on free-draining soil. Two ways of lessening the chances of an attack are by choosing mildew-resistant plants (though they do not give 100 per cent protection) and by thinning out congested clumps to give good air circulation. Where the stems are packed close together, you can remove 30 per cent. This only applies to well-established plants, and young ones that have not yet bulked up can be left alone. When propagating the cultivars, take autumn root cuttings. They need to be set out horizontally on sand that is been sprayed with water to moisten it, and while this might seem unnecessary it is the only

Phlox paniculata

Phormium tenax

way to prevent the spread of eelworm. The hardy annual phlox (*P. drummondii*) – 10–45cm (4–18in) high and to 25cm (10in) wide – and its cultivars produce small flowers, but they are packed in colourful clusters giving a continuous supply all summer. To increase the effect, nip off the growing tips of young plants to generate extra flowering sideshoots. They can be grown from seed at the start of spring, at about 19°C (66°F), for flowering about 3 months later.

PHORMIUM
New Zealand flax

The not-reliably-hardy phormiums make strong architectural perennial plants with their stabbing growth of sword-like leaves breaking out of the ground, many even more eye-catching because of their multi-coloured leaves. 'Sundowner' has green leaves with red and pink stripes running up the edges, and 'Maori Sunrise' is a pink turning to yellow with a hint of bronze at the edge. Do not confuse these cultivars, which range from 45cm to 1.8m (18in–6ft) high, with *P. tenax*, a potential 4m (13ft) high giant with long leaves well over 1.8m (6ft), and dull red flowers towering above them. It is an unmistakable feature plant. Various cultivars have purple in the leaf, but to be really flashy try the 2.5m (8ft) high 'Variegatum' that is striped cream-yellow and white. All need soil that is on the moist side and good sun. Shelter is important to help it survive a

winter in cold-climate gardens, as is a thick winter mulch to insulate the roots. Propagate in spring by division, keeping an outer section with leaves and roots, preferably before the plants become so big that you need a Sumo wrestler to separate them into chunks.

PHYSALIS
Ground cherry

Though there are about 80 species, the one that is grown in gardens is the Chinese lantern (*P. alkekengi*), a vigorous, hardy perennial that gets 75cm (2½ft) high and 90cm (3ft) wide with upright stems and bell-shaped flowers. The real surprise comes when the berries appear in large, orange, papery Chinese lanterns (botanically called calyces) about 5cm (2in) wide, used for cut-flower displays. While the berries are edible, other parts will adversely affect your stomach. Provide average, moist soil – they tolerate a wide range of growing conditions – but do not be tempted to overfeed or the growth becomes lax and floppy and you will need to start staking. There are other forms that are even more striking: *P. a.* var. *franchetii* is slightly taller with more pointed lanterns; the cultivar 'Gigantea' has the biggest lanterns; and 'Variegata' has variegated leaves. When planting, make sure they have room to spread, which they reliably do via underground stems snaking through the soil, sending up vertical shoots creating large clumps. If the spread threatens neighbouring plants, slice down through the excess growth with a spade, and these sections (with roots and top growth) can be used as new plants for replanting elsewhere.

Physalis alkekengi

PLATYCODON
Balloon flower

P. grandiflorus is a 60cm (2ft) high by 30cm (1ft) wide hardy perennial for cottage gardens. Its position needs to be marked because it is slow to appear, with no immediate sign of growth in spring, and if you get carried away with forking up and weeding, there is a danger the plant could be speared. And why the common name? The gradually swelling flower buds that get rounder and fatter, ever inflating. When the blue flowers appear they are 5cm (2in) wide with dark blue veining, and it helps if the stems are supported by twiggy sticks to keep them upright. To make sure the buds are easily seen, group them to the front of a border, and make sure they have free-draining soil. There are various good cultivars including two blues – 'Apoyama' and 'Mariesii' – the white 'Fairy Snow' and the Astra,

Fuji and Hakone Series offering blues, pinks and white. Once planted, all should be left undisturbed in light, sandy soil in full sun to build up decent clumps. To propagate, take a basal cutting but make sure that a piece of the crown is attached. To grow from seed, in spring sow in pots topped with a scattering of vermiculite and then stand in a cold frame. Avoid heavy watering until shoots have appeared.

POLEMONIUM
Jacob's ladder

Invaluable cottage garden plants in blues, lilac and white growing 30–90cm (1–3ft) high in spring and early summer. (Look closely and you will see that the rich green leaves are so arranged that they look like the rickety steps up a ladder.) They quickly form strong clumps, and there is a wide range of hardy annuals and perennials with many new

introductions. The blues include *P. caeruleum*, which has sprays of soft blue flowers, as does 'Northern Lights', while *P. foliosissimum* is more violet-blue with a longer flowering period. The lilacs include 'Glebe Cottage Lilac', 'Hopley's' and 'Lambrook Mauve', and for a white try *P. caeruleum* subsp. *caeruleum* f. *album*. The perennial problem with plants that finish flowering in early summer is what to do about the gaps that will persist through the rest of summer, into autumn. An adjacent star performer is a must. All are perfectly happy in average, free-draining soil, out in the open, where they get full sun, or in light, dappled shade. Propagate the species by sowing fresh seed in autumn, or later in spring, and giving it a covering of vermiculite, standing the pots in a cold frame. The cultivars can be easily raised by dividing established clumps in spring or autumn.

Polemonium caeruleum

POLYGONATUM
Solomon's seal

One of the best spring plants for a damp, shady site or woodland garden, the most popular kind

---

WINTER COLOUR

Most of the flowering plants are dormant, but there is still plenty of interest from plants such as …

Acer griseum – peeling bark
Anemome blanda – flowers
Arbutus x *arachnoides* (strawberry tree) – white flowers, brownish-red peeling bark
Betula utilis – white bark
Camellia sasanqua – flowers
Choisya ternata (Mexican orange blossom) – glossy evergreen foliage
Conifers – evergreen foliage in light and dark green, bluish-greys and striking yellow-greens
Corylus avellana 'Contorta' – corkscrewing branches and catkins
Eucalyptus niphophila – white bark
Garrya elliptica – evergreen with long catkins
Helleborus niger – Christmas rose
Ilex – evergreen, berrying hollies
Iris danfordiae – flowers
Jasminum nudiflorum – yellow flowers
Mahonia – scented flowers
Narcissus (daffodil) – the earliest have late winter flowers
Rubus cockburnianus – white-coated stems
Sarcococca hookeriana var. *digyna* (winter box) – scented flowers
Skimmia japonica 'Rubella' – red buds
Viburnum x *bodnantense* – scented flowers which are clearly visible on the bare, leafless stems

Acer

Anemone

Betula

Corylus

Ilex

Mahonia

Skimmia

Viburnum x *bodnantense*

Polygonatum x hybridum

is the vigorous, spreading *P. × hybridum* that can hit 1.5m (5ft) high by 30cm (1ft) wide. It hides itself away in dark corners where its long, arching stems dangle a row of white flowers with green lips, followed by blue-black berries. For a more striking show, try 'Striatum' with its variegated leaves. Plants can also be grown in pots so that they can be more clearly seen. Given moist, rich soil with plenty of well-rotted organic matter, the plants spread very effectively by underground rhizomes to make attractive clumps. You can sow seed in containers in a cold frame in autumn – plants can take up to five years to flower – or divide them at the start of spring. Each bit of rhizome needs both roots and buds for the new top growth.

POTENTILLA
Cinquefoil

The hardy perennial potentillas give a good range of colours, many strong and flashy, for the summer border at heights up to 90cm (3ft). The most striking is the crimson 'Gibsons Scarlet', a clump of brash flowers at 45cm (18in) high that inject plenty of life through summer. 'William Rollison' is a dusky orange, 'Jean Jabber' yellow-orange, with yellows from the 23cm (9in) high by 15cm (6in) wide *P. megalantha*, and *P. recta* 'Warrenii', which gets three times bigger. The perennial

potentillas are basically the same as the shrubby kind, but they die back at the end of each year while the latter retain their woody framework. All like average to good soil with free drainage in full sun, while the shortest kinds at ankle height need poor, stony, free-draining ground, being better suited to gravel gardens. While the species can be propagated by seed sown in autumn, with the pots being stood in a cold frame, right through winter, or from a spring sowing at 19°C (66°F) to give germination within 10 days, the cultivars should be propagated by division in spring or autumn.

PULMONARIA
Lungwort

Making extremely effective groundcover in damp, shady ground – not too shady or the numbers of flowers will be reduced – with plenty of well-rotted organic matter, it gradually spreads by underground rhizomes covering the earth with its (often) spotted leaves and pastel flowers in late winter or spring. They include shades of blue, lilac, violet, purple, pink and red, with the occasional white, the flowers appearing just above the leaves on short stalks. Just a few of the many excellent forms, all hardy perennials about 30cm (1ft) high and 45–60cm (1½–2ft) wide, are the rich blue 'Blue Enisign', violet-blue 'Lewis Palmer', coral-red *P. rubra*, and pure white 'Sissinghurst White'. Very effective in tricky-to-plant areas of bare soil or edges of woodland; if it is grown in hot, dry conditions powdery mildew is a big problem. While various treatments are available, the best remedy is to grow the plant in the cool and shade. The quickest and easiest way to propagate is by division, and this simply involves spading and separating the outer growth away from the original clump. Make sure that each section has good roots and top growth, and replant where required, giving it room to spread slowly. Water in well, and make sure the ground stays moist while it is getting established.

PULSATILLA
Pasque flower

The hardy perennial *P. vulgaris* has yellow-eyed purple flowers (or sometimes white) on short stems in spring. It also has silky foliage and wonderful silvery-spidery seedheads. It will not rise more than 20cm (8in) high with a similar spread, and needs to be grown in full sun, right at the front of a border where taller plants behind will not flop on top of it, or in a rock or gravel garden that will also provide the essential, excellent drainage. Good cultivars include the white 'Alba', deep red 'Röde Klokke' and clear pink 'Barton's Pink'. The first plants need to be given some room because they will form clumps, so do not jam them in a tight space. They also dislike being moved, so once you've decided where you're going to plant them, double check and then stick to your decision. Propagating by fresh seed (snipping off the plumes) gives quicker and better results than cuttings. Stand the pots in a cold frame and you should get seedlings within a fortnight. Plants with multiple crowns can be sliced into separate sections in spring, each one needing roots and buds for the top growth. Excellent drainage is important, so make sure they are raised in gritty compost (soil mix). Or add approximately one handful of perlite or vermiculite to each handful of compost.

Potentilla fruticosa

Pulsatilla vulgaris

Rehmannia elata

RANUNCULUS
Buttercup

Besides the pond and moisture-loving buttercups, others can be grown in rock gardens and borders, with *R. aconitifolius* 'Flore Pleno' and the lesser celandine (*R. ficaria*) a good choice for shady, woodland areas with rich, moist soil. The former is a hardy perennial with sprays of double white, button-like flowers in summer, above a mound of dark green leaves, getting 60cm (2ft) high and 45cm (18in) wide. The latter is even more striking, with the tuberous 'Brazen Hussy' producing bright yellow spring flowers above the shiny brown leaves down at ground level where it gets just 5cm (2in) high, though it spreads to 30cm (12in) and more. To avoid a mass of inferior seedlings popping around the plant, diminishing the effect, shear over when the flowers are past their best. Other good buttercups include the half-hardy tuberous Persian buttercup (*R. asiaticus*) that grows about 30cm (12in) high and 20cm (8in) wide. It is hard to find and needs to be tracked down from specialist nurseries, and has five white petals (though it is also available in red, pink and yellow) with a dark eye. It should be grown in pots of John Innes No. 2 with added grit, being stood outside over summer, but kept in a conservatory over winter. To propagate, divide the plants when the flowering is over, and check that each section can survive with its own root system and buds to produce top growth.

REHMANNIA
Rehmannia

The (just about) hardy perennial Chinese foxglove (*R. elata*), that can get 1.5m (5ft) high by 50cm (20in) wide, really does look like a foxglove, with very similar pinkish-purple (spotted within) flowers in late spring and early summer. There are two ways of growing it, depending on your conditions. Sheltered sites with free-draining, rich soil in full sun should mean you can leave it in the ground all year, though if there is the possibility of frosts, then a thick winter mulch is essential. If the ground is likely to be cold and wet, then dig up the plants and pot them up over winter, standing them in a cool greenhouse. Give the occasional drink, but nothing more since it will be dormant, and gradually increase the watering next spring as temperatures rise. Plant out when the frosts have finished. To propagate, take basal cuttings in early spring before the flowers appear. You can also raise from seed, making sowings in late winter at 15°C (59°F), but note that the plants will not flower until the following year.

RUDBECKIA
Coneflower

A big attraction in late summer and autumn, the hardy perennial coneflowers have a spread of drooping yellow petals arranged around a prominent brown, black or green cone. Non-invasive spreaders, they make very good clumps, growing anything from 60cm (2ft) to 2.5m (8ft) high. The head high *R. laciniata* 'Herbstonne' makes a good back-of-the-border bright yellow, and hits 1.8m (6ft) high and more, and 90cm (3ft) wide, so stake it in exposed, windy sites and give it plenty of space, but if that is too tall you can always nip out the growing tips making plants shorter but bushier. Other good choices include the slow-spreading *R. fulgida*, with a prominent cone, one for the middle of the border at 90cm (3ft) high, with *R. f.* var. *sullivantii* 'Goldsturm' (the same height) a deep yellow that starts flowering in midsummer, carrying on until mid-autumn. The black-eyed Susan (*R. hirta*) is a short-lived perennial, again at 90cm (3ft) high, flowering all summer, that is often grown as an annual. If you want to keep growing it, you will have to propagate on a fairly regular basis, every few years. All like plenty of sun, and decent soil with well-rotted organic matter to help retain moisture. This is very important because the moment the soil starts to badly dry out the plants promptly flag and wilt, and in the case of the taller kinds this looks quite dramatic. All can be propagated by various means, including spring-sown seed at 10°C (50°F) or basal cuttings, again taken in spring. Established clumps should be divided every five years or so, using the back-to-back fork technique, immediately replanting the new, outer sections. This helps keep each plant fresh, vigorous and productive.

Ranunculus ficaria 'Brazen Hussy'

Rudbeckia fulgida

GARDEN PESTS

There are two main options when dealing with garden pests, and that is either to adopt a quick-fire spray-with-toxins approach, or to encourage a wide range of creatures in the garden, so that every pest is a meal for a different creature. Roses, for example, often get covered with tiny sap-sucking insects, and while you can spray them immediately, you will also possibly infect and kill any birds and beneficial insects in the food chain that take them. Far better to create a range of different habitats in the garden, including patches of long grass and weeds, etc., with areas for old, rotting logs for all kinds of different insects, and a few well-grown conifers because they provide excellent winter cover for birds. That mesh of twiggy branches is a life saver, and even bare branches can keep roosting birds quite warm, with rooks saving between one quarter and half their fat compared to a night out in the open. Do not be too fussy about the ultimate well-manicured garden and be prepared to wait, and the aphids will get eaten by natural predators, keeping the food chain intact. Only introduce toxins as a final, desperate resort.

SALVIA
Salvia

Gardens needing an extra boost of gorgeous colours need a high dosage of salvias. It is hard to generalize because the range of plants is so wide (with over 900 species, including annuals, perennials and shrubs), the most common being *S. officinalis*. The flower colours veer mainly to blue, with the more tender kinds providing reds and purples. The stems are often square being topped by spikes of flowers, with the showier kind having a top and bottom lip. *S. coccinea*, usually grown as a summer-flowering annual, about 60cm (2ft) high and 30cm (1ft) wide, has red flowers, though there are cultivars ('Snow Nymph') in white. It makes a strong blast of colour when grown in blocks, but for a blue go for the deep, richly coloured *S. patens* or its pale blue form, 'Cambridge Blue'. Also reaching some 60cm (2ft) high, they can, like all the shorter salvias, be grown in containers. For a really jazzy-flashy burst of shortish salvias, *S. splendens* — at 40cm (16in) high — is a fun, bushy bright scarlet, with other cultivars in a range of colours including pink, purple, pale blue and white. *S. × sylvestris* (twice as tall) has pinkish-violet flowers through the first half of summer, while the best salvias for the back of the border are the 1.5m (5ft) high *S. guaranitica* and slightly taller *S. uliginosa*. The former has deep blue flowers through the end of summer, into autumn, and the latter clear blue flowers. Two very different salvias are *S. discoloris* and pineapple sage (*S. elegans* 'Scarlet Pineapple'). The latter flowers bright red from winter to spring, on stems 90cm (3ft) high, and has the most amazing scent of freshly cut pineapples from its leaves. It needs a minimum of 5°C (41°F), and is usually grown in a greenhouse or conservatory, where it makes a bushy clump in a large container or border. The former is half the height and slightly hardier, cannot take temperatures below 0°C (32°F), but has extraordinary, late summer, inky black flowers and a strong whiff of blackcurrants. All salvias need as much sun as they can get, with excellent drainage being far more important than soil type, though it should never be too rich or you will get more leaves than flowers. Any that are not reliably hardy, and that is all those mentioned here, need to be moved into a frost-free greenhouse or conservatory over winter because cold, wet soil is fatal. In areas with mild winters they can be left outside, but they

Salvia elegans

need a sunny, well-protected site, for example at the foot of a wall, and a protective mulch. Salvias are remarkably easy to propagate by taking spring and summer cuttings, though you can also divide established clumps using two forks, locked into the plant so that they are back-to-back, easing them apart to split the crown into several sections. You can also propagate from seed, sowing it at 15°C (59°F) for germination within 2–3 weeks, but given the ease with which they take from cuttings, it is hardly worth the effort and wait.

Salvia officinalis

Scabiosa atropurpurea

Schizostylis coccinea 'Sunrise'

SANGUISORBIA
Sanguisorbia

Not on most hit lists of essential garden plants, but *S. obtusa* is a very beautiful hardy perennial for the front part of the border, where it gets 60cm (2ft) high and wide. There is a gentle mix of fluffy, pink plumes or bottlebrush flowers in the second half of summer and 50cm (20in) long, divided grey-green leaves. Being on the short side it makes a nice alternative to the larger callistemons, and needs to be given a prominent position where it can be clearly seen, for example by a pond where its reflection can be caught, or bordering a path. *S. menziesii* gets slightly taller, and has dark red flowers that stand out as they open in late spring, a good antidote to all those yellow daffodils. Both like average soil but it needs to be damp, and must not dry out, which is why the plants are often grown in light, dappled shade. Adding well-rotted organic matter helps the soil stay damp. The best way to propagate is by division is spring or autumn (where different varieties grow together in the garden there is no telling what their hybrid offspring will be like if propagating by seed).

SCABIOSA
Pincushion flower/scabious

Two particular pincushions, *S. atropurpurea* and *S. caucasia*, both hardy perennials, make first-rate front-of-border flowers with their thin wiry stems topped by rounded flowers attracting bees

and butterflies. Eye-catching cultivars of the first include the near-black 'Ace of Spades' and deep, dark purple 'Chile Black' and, provided they are regularly deadheaded, they will keep on flowering right through summer. *S. caucasia* has given some lovely pastels, particularly the lavender-blue 'Clive Greaves' and pure white 'Miss Willmott'. All get about 60cm (2ft) high and wide, with *S. atropurpurea* at 90cm (3ft), and they need to bask in full sun in very free-draining soil. There is no point trying to grow them in heavy soil because they will not survive the first winter. In fact *S. atropurpurea* will not survive too many winters even when it is being grown in ideal conditions because it is naturally short-lived, and it needs to be regularly propagated so that you do not run out of plants. All can be propagated by cuttings, the best method for the cultivars, though they can also be increased by division in spring or autumn. The species can be grown from seed in early spring at 20°C (68°F) to germinate fairly quickly, within two weeks or so.

SCHIZOSTYLIS
Kaffir lily

The hardy perennial *S. coccinea* is sheer delight in the late summer garden after all the showbiz furore of early summer. It sends up spikes of scarlet flowers, but there are many cultivars in pink (including 'Viscountess Byng'), pale pink ('Pink Princess') and white ('Snow Maiden'), with

others in red and reddish-pink. All gradually make decent clumps, getting 60cm (2ft) high and possibly half as wide. If it is still flowering with the frosts on the way, use as cut flowers. Alternatively grow in cool conservatory borders and the flowers will keep on appearing through the start of winter. Avoid fast-draining dry soil, which produces very poor results, and add some well-rotted organic matter to help retain moisture. Propagate by dividing clumps, making sure the new divisions go into a bright, open space where they get full sun.

SCILLA
Scilla

Essentially short, spring-flowering blue bulbs, though there are exceptions with some non-blues and some that flower in autumn. The not-completely-hardy *S. peruviana* has early summer clusters of small, purplish-blue or white, star-like flowers with a yellow eye on top of 30cm (12in) high stems, well above the lush, green, strap-like leaves that start appearing in autumn. Plants get 10cm (4in) wide. Make sure they are well protected from the worst

that a cold-climate garden can throw at them, with a sunny, sheltered position and free-draining soil. It comes from the northern Mediterranean – Portugal, Spain and Italy – and North Africa, which means it hates lengthy cold, wet periods. The hardy *S. siberica* – 15cm (6in) tall – has bright blue flowers for spring, though there is a deep blue and a white form. Try it in rock gardens or in gaps in patio paving. All need to be planted 10cm (4in) deep in free-draining ground in a sunny position, and like a dry dormant period. Dig up established clumps and discard the inner sections, saving the new, young, more vigorous offsets that can be grown in a nursery bed until they reach flowering size, or plant them straight out where they are to flower.

SEDUM
Stonecrop

There is a huge range of sedums, most being succulents, with the hardy kind being grown in rock gardens and borders. If you're only going to grow one, stick to the hardy perennial ice plant (*S. spectabile*) because it is a magnet to bees and butterflies

WATERING

Most plants need to develop roots that go deep down in the soil where moisture stays longest, and the best way to encourage the roots to bury deep is to give them long drinks. If you keep giving them a small drink, the roots will stay near the surface where the water quickly evaporates, necessitating even more drinks. It becomes a self-perpetuating problem. And what might seem like a decent watering is often the opposite. To test how much water you are actually giving plants, use a trowel to dig down and see just how much of the soil is wet. In most cases it will be shallower than you expect, and certainly not deep down where the roots are. Provided you are giving plants what they require, it should not be necessary to water that often, especially when you apply a thick mulch to reduce the rate at which the moisture evaporates from the soil surface. Concentrate on newly planted trees and shrubs, and bedding plants – mature plants with deep roots

should not need watering, and lawns, though they may turn brown in dry periods, will suffer no harm, especially if you cut them fairly long. The best time for watering is early evening, giving the plants a good 12 or more hours to drink before the sun gets to work. If unsure when to water, get a water meter. Don't wait for plants to wilt.

Scilla siberica

Sedum 'Herbstfreude'

with its flat-topped bunches of sweetly scented pink flowers right through the second half of summer. At 45cm (18in) high and wide it is just the right size for the front of any display, and mixes well with the various cultivars, including the bright pink 'Brilliant' and purple-pink 'Septemberglut'. 'Stardust' is white. Good alternatives include 'Herbstfreude' injecting more flat tops of pink flowers, turning brown as they fade, in late summer and early autumn. Free-draining soil and poor fertility are required by 99 per cent of all sedums, or you will get an excess of floppy foliage and poor flowers. Full sun gives the best results though they can be grown in light shade. The larger kind are easily propagated in spring with a spade, slicing into a clump and removing portions with a good set of roots and top growth, though you can also take stem cuttings at the same time.

SEMPERVIVUM
Houseleek

The essential plant for growing in dry stone walls, rock gardens or gravel beds because they make low, spreading growth and demand fast, effective drainage. The leaves are packed into tactile, geometric, swirling rosettes, and short, thin stalks shoot up with small, delicate flowers. If you haven't got any of the above, then use a trough or an old kitchen sink, making sure the drainage hole is not blocked, and fill the base with stones or crocks so that the water quickly sluices out. There are hundreds and hundreds of cultivars, each one often available from only one nursery; less than 1 per cent have won the Award of Garden Merit from the Royal Horticultural Society, though that does not mean there are not some stunning little plants. Try the hardy perennial common houseleek (*S. tectorum*), which spreads across the soil with its multiplying rosettes, never more than 10cm (4in) wide, with blue-green leaves often tinged reddish-purple and reddish-purple flowers. 'Commander Hay' is equally impressive with its deep reddish-purple leaves and greenish-red flowers. All like full sun and poor, gritty, stony soil. Note that the rosettes die after flowering but are automatically replaced by the offsets. Since the plant does the propagation for you, all you might possibly need to do is carefully slice away the offsets with a sharp knife, ensuring they have some roots, to replant in a new site where you need extra houseleeks.

Sempervivum tectorum

TAKING SEMPERVIVUM CUTTINGS

1 Sempervivums generate a multitude of offsets. Separate one, using a scalpel, cutting it away from the parent in spring.

2 The offsets come with a long, slender stolon; shorten to just below the roots and leave the cut surface to dry in the sun.

3 If there are no roots, sever where it joins the parent. Pot up in gritty compost (soil mix); keep well watered for about five weeks.

HEALTHY LAWNS

Flowers need to be set off, and no matter how well they've been grown from divisions, cuttings or seed, they will never appear as good as they could if they're surrounded by a poor lawn that makes everything look rather tatty. Opt for a regime of regular mowing, aiming for a blade height of at least 2.5cm (1in). Never shave the lawn too fiercely because that encourages short roots, and if the grass cannot get enough to drink it quickly turns brown in hot, dry weather. Putting it under stress also makes it easier for weeds to invade. Carry on mowing, even in winter, because the grass still grows, though it will just need the tops taken off. Set the blade height to about 30mm (1¼in). Do not mow when the lawn is wet, however, because you will compact the surface, badly affecting drainage and aeration.

SENECIO
Senecio

A wide group of annuals, biennials, succulents, perennials, shrubs and climbers, occupying a diverse range of habitats. Two invaluable annuals are *S. cineraria* (actually a shrubby plant, but it is grown as an annual) and *S. elegans*. The former is frost-hardy and is grown for its silver-grey leaves, making a 60cm (2ft) high and wide mound that is often used to the front of a border or as a border divider, or even to weave through borders making separate compartments filled with stronger colours. 'Silver Dust' is even more striking because the leaves are deeply divided and silvery. Both produce mustard-yellow blooms, but many gardeners prefer to cut the flower stems off before the buds open, and just use them as foliage plants. *S. elegans* (again not completely hardy) is very different; it has green foliage and reddish-purple petals around a yellow eye or disc. At 60cm (2ft) high and 30cm (1ft) wide it makes a good gap filler in cottage gardens. All the plants described here like full sun and free-draining soil, and the annuals can be grown from seed sown in spring in a greenhouse at 20°C (68°F) to flower that summer. The perennial senecios — especially the South American *S. pulcher* — include some fun, medium-high plants. The latter gets 60cm (2ft) high and wide, and has magenta-mauve petals around an unmistakable yellow eye. It is not completely hardy and needs protecting in cold-climate gardens. Give it excellent drainage and a sunny, sheltered

Senecio cineraria

position so that it does not get locked in cold, wet ground. If in doubt, dig up in autumn and pot up over winter, keeping it in a frost-free greenhouse and giving the occasional drink while dormant. Replant outside toward the end of next spring. Propagate in one of two ways, by dividing the plants in spring or by taking summer cuttings, which is worth doing in any event in case the parent does not survive the winter.

SIDALCEA
False mallow

Looking like miniature hollyhocks, the annual or perennial sidalceas make medium-size bushy plants with two different kinds of leaves, the lower ones being rounded and those on the flower stems being divided. The first burst of flowers open on tall, thin spikes in midsummer, with more to follow several weeks later. The pick of the species is *S. candida* (pure white flowers opening in early and midsummer), with the hardy perennial cultivars providing 'Elsie Heugh' (rich pink), 'Loveliness' (shell pink), 'Mrs Borrodaile' (rose-magenta), 'Sussex Beauty' (pink) and 'William Smith' (light pink), all adding a summery touch to cottage gardens. All are in the 60cm–1m (2–3½ft) height range, with spreads being no more than 45cm (18in). They like an open, sunny position, out of the shade, with soil that is moist and well-drained but never solid, lumpy

Sidalcea 'Elsie Heugh'

and heavy. If the ground is on the dry side add some well-rotted organic matter to help it retain moisture over summer, though it does not want to be too wet in winter. The moment the first flush of flowers is over, cut them back to generate a second batch. Propagate the cultivars by lifting and dividing plants in spring or autumn, inserting a couple of forks back-to-back to prise them apart. The species can be grown from fresh seed, sowing it in pots and standing in a cold frame in autumn, or wait until the following spring.

SILENE
Campion

You cannot stock a border entirely with star plants, you need some extras, and campions make very good extras. There is a range of annuals, biennials and perennials for all kinds of situations, with the top choices including the following hardy four. *S. dioica* makes a 75cm (2½ft) high clump that is 45cm (18in) wide, with red flowers from late spring to midsummer, and since it likes moist ground and dappled shade it is ideal at the edge of a woodland or a similar position. *S. fimbriata* fills a similar space, flowering at the same time in white, but it prefers dry ground in light shade. *S. schafta* is much shorter, getting just 25cm (10in) high, but it is liberally covered with an incredibly striking blast of rich magenta flowers through late summer, into early autumn, giving the best results in full sun with its roots in free-draining ground, and the colour contrast with gravel is a big plus. If you need something even shorter, the 20cm (8in) high and wide white sea campion (*S. uniflora*) is just right for containers, seaside gardens and even gravel gardens because it demands smart drainage. Cultivars offer alternatives with double flowers and variegated leaves. Propagate the species by sowing seed in autumn, making sure that the compost (soil mix) has 50 per cent added sand, and that the seed is topped by a light covering of sand. Leave outside to germinate

Silene dioica

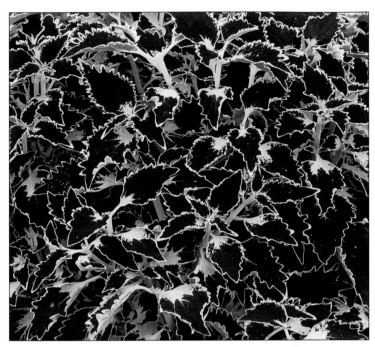

Solenostemon scutellarioides 'Glory of Luxembourg'

the following spring. Cultivars can be raised by lifting plants after flowering and dividing them into sections, or alternatively take cuttings in spring.

SISYRINCHIUM
Sisyrinchium

Cheery, bright plants for the border, they are immediately distinguished because of their clumps of grassy or iris-like foliage and small, star-like flowers. They mainly come from the Americas, with the most commonly grown kind being 'Biscutella', 'Californian Skies', 'E. K. Balls' and *S. striatum*. 'Biscutella' is one of the tallest of this group at 75cm (2½ft) high,

and 15cm (6in) wide, and has a prolific show of cream and brown flowers held above the narrow leaves making a solid burst of summer colour, ideal for filling border gaps. 'Californian Skies' will not get above ankle high, at 15cm (6in), and stands out with its yellow-eyed blue flowers. 'E. K. Balls' is slightly taller, and just as distinctive with purple petals around a yellow eye. *S. striatum*, from Chile and Argentina, equals 'Biscutella' in height and almost colour, being cream or pale yellow, with a brown stripe down the petals. All like open sun and soil that is well-drained; standing in cold, wet soil over winter is fatal. Self-seeding

can be a problem, in which case nip off the fading flowers before they get a chance to propagate. If you need more plants, let a few self-seed and then carefully dig up the seedlings, either potting them up while you decide where to move them or planting straight into their new site. Alternatively, wait until spring, dig up the cultivars and divide them into sections for immediate replanting.

SOLENOSTEMON
Coleus

Tender plants from the tropics, they are grown as garden annuals to provide fun, brightly coloured leaves, often in jazzy patterns, either at the front of a border

or in pots, or as perennials for indoors. The heights are generally in the 30cm (1ft) to 75cm (2½ft) range, with the foliage colours including red with yellow fringes, and yellow-green around purple-brown blotches. 'Display' has some of the largest (dark orange) leaves at 7cm (3in) long. Grow from seed in spring, at 19°C (66°F), leaving it uncovered on top of damp compost (soil mix). You can also take summer cuttings. To get the best display of the flashy leaves, pinch out the tops to make the plants even bushier, and snip off the flower stems. Give a nitrogen-high feed to generate even more leafy growth.

Sisyrinchium 'Californian Skies'

DIVIDING SISYRINCHIUM

1 In spring dig up a cluster of plants, just as the new growth is emerging through the soil, taking care not to damage the roots.

2 Then, using a clean, sharp knife, slice down into the clump creating sections so that each has a healthy burst of leaves and a set of roots.

3 Finish the job with your fingers, teasing the sections apart, taking care to leave the roots intact. If it proves tricky, dunk in water.

STACHYS
Betony

One of the best garden plants, especially for a gravel or Mediterranean-type garden, the 45cm (18in) high and 60cm (2ft) wide lamb's ears (*S. byzantina*) needs to go right to the front where it can be stroked again and again. The felt-like, tactile leaves are as soft as a lamb's or rabbit's ears, being just about the same length but silvery greyish. The pinkish-purple, felty flowers are modest but pretty; however, some gardeners prefer to cut these off as soon as they appear, so that all the plant's energy is channelled into the foliage. It absolutely demands poor, gritty, free-draining soil, where it quickly spreads, creating very effective ground cover. 'Big Ears' has leaves that get twice as big, almost 25cm (10in) long. The slightly taller *S. macrantha* is a complete contrast with its dense spikes of purple-pink flowers from late spring, right through summer, above dark green leaves, and while it too loves a belting hot sun, it needs fertile soil. Propagate by lifting clumps in spring and dividing them into separate sections, replanting immediately, and keep an eye out for slugs and snails that can ruin the new, emerging foliage.

DIVIDING STIPA

1 The ornamental grass *Stipa* can be easily divided. Wait until the parent plant is well established before digging it up.

2 Either pull the plant apart by hand or, if that proves tricky, use two forks back to back, and force both outward to split the plant into two sections.

3 The new divisions can either be planted directly out in the garden or in pots for growing on until they are well established. Water well.

STERNBERGIA
Sternbergia

There is just a faint resemblance to the related daffodil, though sternbergias are actually more like large, yellow crocuses. The bulbs produce strap-like foliage with the flowers in autumn, after the dormant summer period, though in some species the foliage does not appear until the flowering has finished. The two species most commonly seen are the not-quite-hardy *S. lutea* and *S. sicula*. The former never gets above 15cm (6in) high and half as wide, and produces the wine glass-like rich yellow flowers after the end of summer. To make it stand out, plant the bulbs against a dark green background, such as a yew hedge. The latter is similar but slightly shorter. Both are found around the Mediterranean and therefore need a warm, sunny position with good shelter and good drainage. Propagate by lifting clumps and looking for offsets. They can be planted 15cm (6in) deep until they reach flowering size.

STIPA
Feather grass

An extremely useful group of grasses, with 50 clump-forming species for open, dry, sunny sites, their airy heads easily getting caught in the wind, bending and swaying, and self-seeding around the garden. Do not miss the hardy perennial golden oats (*S. gigantea*) – the largest and most spectacular *Stipa* species – a 2m (6½ft) high and 1.2m (4ft) wide evergreen sending up airy, loose, see-through spikelets and plumes of oat-like flowers from the end of spring to midsummer. They emerge gold but gradually turn straw-beige. It is highly effective almost anywhere in the garden from a front-of-border position to one at the back, but it does need full sun and a dark background (like a yew hedge) to bring out the best of the colour. With a smaller space to fill, use the hardy perennial *S. tenuissima*, a 60cm (2ft) high and 30cm (1ft) wide gentle patch of wiry, upright, evergreen leaves with beautiful soft plumes

Stachys byzantina

Sternbergia lutea

of pale greenish-white flowers all summer. (Avoid rich soil or it becomes far too floppy.) Also use as a massed planting in a bed, interspersed with taller, richly coloured feature plants, creating a soft, low, billowing background. If you want something fractionally shorter, try the 45cm (18in) high silver feather grass (*S. barbata*) from Spain. It makes a small mound of thin leaves and excels in midsummer when it is in flower. It is best grown in drifts in full sun. Can be cut back after flowering because it can look rather untidy. For an intermediate 1.2m (4ft) high species, try *S. calamagrostis* with its summer-long, arching flower stems and greenish-white flowers above the 90cm (3ft) wide clump of green leaves. All like well-drained soil

under an open sky, with all being best propagated by fresh seed in late summer, or at 15°C (59°F) the following spring, though in cool climates not all set viable seed. *S. tenuissima* is short-lived but generally self-seeds prolifically, so it is just a case of looking for seedlings and moving them to the right position. Unusually for grasses, all dislike being divided because they have shallow roots. If attempting it, make sure the divisions are on the large side.

SYMPHYTUM
Comfrey

A doubly useful hardy perennial, both making incredibly useful groundcover and all-purpose fertilizer with more punch than farmyard manure. If you have a

patch of open space in dappled shade and need it to be filled quickly, then *S. caucasicum* with its typically coarse, hairy leaves and upright, then sprawling stems, about 60cm (2ft) high and wide, and clustered spring and summer tubular blue flowers will give very quick results. The one problem is that if you then decide to revert to other plants and dig it up, any of the deep roots left behind will regrow. 'Hidcote Pink' flowers in pink and white in spring. Do not confuse either with common comfrey (*S. officinale*) or the Russian kind (*S. × uplandicum*) because the former gets 1.2m (4ft) high or more, spreading by 1.8m (6ft) and more, while the latter gets to 1.8m (6ft) high with a 1.2m (4ft) spread. If you've got space behind a shed though, grow common comfrey to make a high-powered liquid feed. They can be used with nettles, using 1kg (2½lb) of top growth to 10 litres (2¼ gallons) of tap water. Put all the leafy growth into a container and cover it with water, give the occasional stir and cover with a lid. The moment the growth has rotted down, pour the mix through a large sieve and

Symphytum officinale

save the liquid. It can now be used as a fertilizer, but because it is so concentrated and intense, mix one part of the comfrey liquid to 10 parts water. Do not be tempted to use it undiluted, and beware: it has a powerful, foul smell. The simplest method of propagation is to slice down through the growth with a spade, lifting a clump of top growth with roots, and replant.

NATURALIZING BULBS

Bulbs can be grown in pots, borders or in grass, where they can be left to form natural-looking drifts. They gradually increase in numbers as they develop offsets (that can also be dug up, usually in the autumn, and used for new plantings, or when the bulbs become packed so tight together that they need to be spaced out).

The best way to create that natural-looking drift is to take a handful of bulbs and gently scatter them on the lawn, planting them where they land. You can either use a special bulb planter, which takes out a plug of lawn and soil, letting you insert the bulb before replacing the plug, or peel back the grassy surface to expose the soil beneath.

The latter is the best method when you have lots of small bulbs, and simply involves using a sharp spade. Cut an 'H' shape where required, and then peel back the two sections of lawn to the middle cut, scuff up the soil surface with the prongs of a fork, plant the bulbs and then replace the turf. Water the area well, helping the lawn's roots sink back into the soil.

When growing bulbs in a lawn, and they can spread to cover large areas in the case of prodigious spreaders like *Crocus tommasinianus*, you must be prepared to let the grass grow long among them for several weeks while the leaves are emerging and dying. It is absolutely essential that you leave the foliage on the plants even after flowering has ceased, because it is being used to build up energy for next year.

If you promptly cut off the still-green foliage, then next year's flower show will be adversely affected. Do not remove the foliage until it has turned yellow and is clearly dying.

Also note that when planting bulbs under a tree the soil will be particularly dry, and when the bulbs cannot get a good drink they are also being denied nutrients. Water well during dry spells, and apply a foliar or scattered granular feed if necessary while in full growth, and while the leaves are green.

Stipa gigantea

Tagetes patula

Tanacetum parthenium

TAGETES
Marigolds

Bright, brash, half-hardy summer annuals for the front of a border or container, they mainly come in shades of orange, mahogany and yellow. There are four main groups, the African marigolds that flower right through summer, getting some 45cm (18in) high, and the 30cm (12in) high French type. It includes two good Series, the Favourites (in five colours) and Mischief (in six), and the striped Victorian kinds. The taller ones can get 90cm (3ft) high, and are excellent for cutting. Third come the hybrids between the African and French kinds, growing to 30cm (12in), and, finally, the slightly taller Signet Group. All like average, well-drained soil in full sun, and with constant deadheading will keep on flowering over a long

season. Cultivars hybridize in the garden, so you will not get exact copies when you collect and sow the seed, but it is worth trying to see what you get. Germinate it at 20°C (68°F) in spring and you should get a good batch of seedlings within 10 days to flower about 10 weeks later. Alternatively, scatter seed where the plants are to flower at the end of spring when the temperatures consistently pick up.

TANACETUM
Feverfew

Mainly hardy perennials with a few annuals, they grow in a wide variety of settings from cliffs to streamsides and produce daisy-like flowers. Some, especially the perennial, 60cm (high) and 30cm (12in) wide *T. parthenium* 'Aureum', are also grown for their excellent yellow-green foliage.

When designing gardens, there are several tricks that can be used to make a smallish space seem larger. To make the distance from one end to the other seem longer, use taller plants in the foreground, gradually reducing the heights, with the shortest in the far distance. You can also use stronger, bolder hothouse colours in the foreground, with increasing numbers of pastels in the distance. It helps if the whole of the garden is not immediately visible the moment you enter it. A small space can be made to appear infinitely larger and more varied if paths double-back, curve and snake through it, entering and exiting

special hidden areas, so that first-time visitors never quite know exactly where they are, with a number of contrasting places that could include the pond surrounded by tall grasses, the kitchen garden, gravel garden, seated and play areas, and flower beds. The more you keep forcing the eye to look up and down, around and through specially engineered gaps, the more intricate and exciting a smallish space becomes. It needs to contain a rich mixture of surprises, and that will not happen if the whole design is laid bare and is immediately visible the moment you enter it. Keep your visitors guessing.

The white flowers with a yellow eye appear from midsummer until mid-autumn. 'Rowallane' is the double version. The 75cm (2½ft) high pyrethrum (*T. coccineum*) and its many cultivars flower in midsummer, and the pick of the bunch includes the pink 'Eileen May Robinson' and the scarlet 'James Kelway'.

All like full sun, poor soil and good drainage. If they start looking tired in midsummer, just strim them back for a second burst of fresh new leaves. To propagate, sow seed of species in spring at 10°C (50°F), but named forms are best propagated either by taking spring basal cuttings or by dividing plants.

TELLIMA
Fringe cups

There is just one hardy, semi-evergreen perennial species, *T. grandiflora*, which comes from North America. It grows about 75cm (2½ft) high and 30cm (1ft) wide, and thrives in lightly shaded woodland conditions with rich, moist soil (you can also grow it in dry shade, but it will not be quite so effective), where it makes creeping groundcover, spreading by self-sown seedlings. The oval leaves are up to 10cm (4in) long, being topped by tall, thin spires

1 In spring sow just a few seeds to each container, keeping them well apart. Give each room to grow separately from its neighbour.

2 Give a thin covering of vermiculite to give the seed plenty of light to help it germinate. Finally, water with an upturned rose spray.

3 Put the container inside a clear plastic bag to provide humidity and keep at 20°C (68°F). Remove when the seedlings emerge.

carrying greenish-white flowers giving an open, airy display. The various cultivars have attractively tinged leaves, notably 'Forest Frost', with silvery leaves that acquire a red tint in winter, the Odorata Group with red-tinged leaves, and 'Purpurteppich', with darker red leaves. There is no need to propagate because the plants do it for you. Remove any that threaten to give excess numbers, and carefully dig up and transfer any that are required elsewhere in the garden. To get exact copies of the cultivars, propagate by divisions taken in spring, while the species can be sown from ripe seed; scatter it on compost (soil mix) in pots, and let it germinate in a cold frame.

THALICTRUM
Meadow rue
An exceptional tall, thin, airy plant for the late summer cottage garden, *T. delavayi* easily grows 1.5m (5ft) high, and half as wide, and sends up thin, erect stems carrying a haze of tiny lavender flowers. There is a white version ('Album'), and a double, also in lavender ('Hewitt's Double'). For an even more spectacular display, get *T. rochebruneanum* that can grow anything from 1.8m (6ft) to well over 3m (10ft). It has similar flowers to *T. delavayi* and can be used almost anywhere in the garden, to the front or middle of schemes to filter the view through

Thalictrum lucidum

DIVIDING TRICYRTIS

1 The plants can be divided when they are dormant, but if you forget wait until there is some top growth and fork it out of the ground.

2 Hold it firmly in two hands, press your thumbs into the centre and ease it apart into sections, making sure each has a good set of roots.

3 Replant them in pots, so you can take good care of them, turning them regularly and watering while they are getting established.

and beyond, or toward the back. Stake the tallest kind, especially when they are being grown in rich soil that might produce lax growth, and leave the stems over winter to remind you where the plants are because the new growth emerges surprisingly late at the end of next spring. (If they are cut right back, you might forget where they are and damage them when tidying up in spring.) Propagate using the autumn seed, though the results can be unpredictable. Dividing the taller species (not the shorter ones) can be tricky because the rootstock becomes rather woody.

TIARELLA
Foam flower
These two woodland plants, *T. cordifolia* and *T. wherryi*, are top choices for shady, rich, moist ground where spring and early summer flowers are needed. The former is a 30cm (12in) high and wide hardy perennial with 10cm (4in) long leaves and spikes of tiny white flowers. The latter is slightly shorter and more compact, with white to pink flowers, and 'Bronze Beauty' is even better because it combines reddish-bronze leaves with the white flowers. Propagate plants by making spring divisions, replanting them immediately, but it is not usually necessary to increase *T. cordifolia* because it naturally spreads by runners.

If you do need more, then just remove the young plantlets where they have rooted, and plant them where required.

TRICYRTIS
Toad lily
Ridiculously undervalued, the late summer and autumn-flowering perennial toad lilies stand out because they are so completely different. They have patterned, often spotted, orchid-like flowers in a range of colours, including purple, lavender, pink, yellow and white with new Japanese forms constantly coming on the market. Look closely and you will see there are always six petals creating a funnel, out of which burst the stamens and styles. The best place to start is the hardy *T. formosana*, 80cm (32in) high and 45cm (18in) wide. It loves moist, rich soil in dappled shade, and produces flowers with six petals, all thickly covered in purple spots against the white background. It looks too exotic to grow in cool climate gardens, but a cool site is just what it needs. To help lock moisture in the soil, add a thick mulch after a night of heavy rain in spring. Make sure you put them in the right position, because they hate being moved and disturbed. It is worth finding a specialist grower to check the range of different colours. 'Gilt Edge' has gold-edged leaves spotted purple, while the Stolonifera Group

are purple-pink with plum spots. The latter start flowering in midsummer, finishing in early autumn, and do not get checked by a sharp, early frost. Give all toad lilies, especially the latter, space to spread, because a large clump makes a terrific feature, and the Stolonifera Group are among the most aggressive spreaders. The best way to propagate is by dividing established clumps when dormant, or by taking early summer cuttings. You can also grow the species from seed, but it could take several years before you get a flowering plant. Vegetative propagation is by far the quickest method.

Tricyrtis formosana

Trillium grandiflorum

Tropaeolum majus

TRILLIUM
Wake robin

A spring-flowering perennial for the woodland garden, all have three petals and three sepals, with colours ranging from white to deep, dark maroon red. The flowers are followed by fleshy, berry-like, toxic fruits. While there are a large number available, only a few are really popular, with *T. grandiflorum* – to 40cm (16in) high and 30cm (12in) wide – notching up the highest sales. It stands out in the shade with its bright white flowers and yellow eye that sit on top of the 30cm (12in) long, dark green leaves. It thrives in moist soil that had

well-rotted leaf mould forked into it, as in a woodland setting, though summer dryness is not a problem. To propagate, stick to divisions because seed-raised plants take too long to flower. Dig up plants after flowering, and nip off the end bud (which stops the buds behind it from developing) with a piece of rhizome. Then treat the two cut surfaces with fungicide to eliminate rot, and replant the end bud. Immediately replant the length of rhizome, and its buds will start developing, which you should do anyway to create extra flowering stems. But they can also be used to create new plants.

TROPAEOLUM
Tropaeolum

These high-value, high-impact annuals or perennials can be used to trail, climb or spread in any direction, or plug border gaps with their bright colours all summer. The half-hardy annual *T.* 'Empress of India' (derived from *T. majus*, the nasturtium) is a rich red getting 30cm (12in) high and 45cm (18in) wide, and can be used in subtropical schemes to add extra brazen colours at ground level. The tender, annual Whirlybird Series is also very effective, at much the same height, adding reds, yellows, creams and orange, their large,

open faces held up so you cannot miss them. Both like endless summer sun in average soil. The best of the perennials include the half-hardy, scarlet Scottish flame creeper (*T. speciosum*) and frost-tender *T. tuberosum*. The former is best planted at the side of a wide path or with its rhizome beneath a hedge so that its prodigious growth, capable of spreading 3m (10ft) a season, can ramble across or up through the branches so that from a distance the hedge glows red. Since it likes having its roots in the shade and its head in the sun, a hedge makes the ideal setting. The latter is half as vigorous, but if you grow *T. t.* var. *lineamaculatum* 'Ken Aslet', expect more like 8m (25ft) of growth with red and orange flowers. The tuber needs to be dug up in autumn and kept in a frost-free greenhouse for planting out again late next spring. Raise the annuals from seed in early spring, sowing them at 15°C (59°F), or wait until the end of spring and sow them where they are to flower. The tuberous kinds can be propagated by dividing them up in autumn, the rhizomes by slicing them up in spring checking that each section has both roots and top growth.

TULIPA
Tulip

The best way to buy tulips is by mail-order through a specialist bulb supplier. A well-organized catalogue will distinguish between the 15 different groups, or Divisions, as they are called, starting with the Single Earlies. They flower in early and mid-

DIVIDING TROPAEOLUM

1 The tuberous tropaeolums can be divided in spring by digging up a plant, when the top growth appears, but do not damage the roots.

2 Carefully separate the below ground growth, disentangling the roots. If that is tricky, dip it in a bowl of water to wash off the soil.

3 You should end up with a batch of new young plants. Pot up while they get established to prevent them getting swamped in the garden.

PATHS

Plants are considerably enhanced by well-made paths that help set off borders (that back on to something) and beds (that are surrounded by gravel or grass). There is a wide range of choices for possible materials. You can use clearly edged bare soil for the rustic, easy-going, cottage garden path (though it will be slippery and muddy when wet), paving for a more formal look (leaving gaps for newly propagated plants and annuals, specially those that release their scent when stepped on), frost-proof bricks in various patterns (again leaving gaps for scented and low-growing spreaders), or cobblestones. You can break up a long path by using a combination of different materials. When using decking or circular slices of tree trunk, it is inadvisable to lay it in the shade, because when it gets rained on it can take a long time to dry out, staying very slippery. Fallen wet leaves are an additional hazard.

One of the easiest surfaces is gravel, certainly on paths that have awkward shapes and corners, but you cannot just spread it on the ground and leave it. You need to excavate a flat surface to build up a 5cm (2in) layer of gravel that is flush with the nearby surface. But, to stop the gravel being pressed right into the soil and disappearing, you first need to insert a well-firmed, compacted layer of hardcore, or hoggin – a mixture

of sand, gravel and clay – with a sheet of weedproof membrane going on top. This lets rain through the tiny holes but stops most weeds becoming a problem for a couple of years. They will then start seeding in the gravel surface, but can be easily yanked out, especially after a shower of rain. Dandelions, and perennial weeds with long roots that are difficult to remove entirely will die eventually if you pull off the top growth regularly every week – this can take time, but meanwhile the path looks tidy, with just tiny weeds re-emerging – or you can spray with a systemic weedkiller for quicker results.

Tulipa 'Queen of Night'

Tulipa Darwin Hybrid Group

spring, getting 20–40cm (8–16in) tall, most being species. The Double Earlies tend to be closer to 40cm (16in) and flower a few weeks later, and being double they have greater staying power, not getting ruined by heavy rain. The Triumph Group come later still, toward late spring, getting slightly taller at 50cm (20in), with the orange 'Fire Queen' and rich orange 'Fidelio' giving a strong show. The vigorous Darwin Hybrid Group, introduced from 1943, flower at the end of spring and get to 70cm (28in) tall, with 'Apeldoorn' a very reliable red. The Single Late Group, for late spring, has a wide colour range, including the near black 'Queen of Night', with fractionally taller flowers, and the Lily-flowered Group (again, for late spring), 45–60cm (18–24in), stands out with its pointed petals. The pale yellow 'West Point' is traditionally

grown with the shorter blue *Myosotis*, making an unbeatable combination, with 'Ballade' (reddish-magenta), 'China Pink' (very beautiful pink) and 'Red Shine' (strong red) all good choices. The Fringed and the Viridiflora Groups were only

launched in 1981, with flowers about 40cm (16in) high right at the end of spring. The Parrot Group – 35–65cm (14–26in) in late spring – is just what you need if you want something flamboyantly different, with 'Estella Rijnveld' and 'Flaming Parrot' a whirling mix of red and white, and red and yellow. The other groups include the late spring Double Lates, at 35–60cm (14–24in) high, particularly good in containers, and finally the smaller species, the Kaufmanniana, Fosteriana and Greigii. The final three, and the Darwin Hybrid Group, can all be left in the ground, but the rest may need to be dug up after flowering for their dormant period. Make sure that the foliage has time to die down naturally, so that the bulbs can build up energy

for next year, whereupon the stems, foliage and petals are promptly removed to avoid any possible attacks of tulip fire. (Tulip fire rots the new growth of tulips before they flower. Immediately destroy any affected bulbs. As a protection, grow tulips on a new site every third year.) Store the bulbs in a mouse-proof box in a cool, airy greenhouse before replanting in late autumn or early winter. If planted earlier, they might well shoot up in the early autumn warmth and get zapped by frost. The bulbs go 10–15cm (4–6in) deep and 10cm (4in) apart. Propagate by looking for new offsets when the bulbs are dug up, and grow them in a nursery bed (lifting them when dormant in summer) until they are large enough to flower.

POTTING UP TULIP BULBLETS

1 When digging up tulip bulbs after the foliage has turned yellow and died down, for storing over summer, look for any bulblets.

2 Separate those that are near flowering size (the same size as the parents), and the immature ones that need to be grown separately.

3 The latter can be grown in their own pots until they reach maturity, away from competing growth, letting you keep a close eye on them.

VALERIANA
Valerian

Though there are about 200 species of these annuals, perennials and shrubs, the only kind you're likely to see is the common valerian (*V. officinalis*). It is a hardy perennial making some 1.5–1.8m (5–6ft) of growth, with a spread of 75cm (2½ft), with an airy show of summer-long pink or white flowers. Unlike many herbs – especially the Mediterranean ones – it likes dappled shade and moist soil. Propagate by taking basal cuttings in spring, or alternatively by dividing the plants, and then replant the different sections immediately.

VERBASCUM
Mullein

The most impressive mullein, and one of the best sights in summer, is the 1.8m (6ft) high hardy *V. olympicum*, with a spread of 60cm (2ft), powering up its greyish-white stems and filling out with its huge, greyish-white leaves, with a sprinkling of tiny yellow flowers. It needs a prominent position where you cannot miss it, and it is worth growing or buying a new one each year, for a few years, because it will not flower until its second or third summer. It is a biennial or short-lived perennial, usually dying after it has flowered in cool climates, which is why you need to have the next one getting ready to perform. Excellent in gravel gardens where it rockets out

of the stony ground, well away from any competing eyecatchers. Other hardy perennial verbascums tend to be in the 45cm–1.5m (18in–5ft) high range, and are excellent ingredients in cottage gardens, where they send up spires covered with colourful flowers. New introductions keep appearing. Look out for 'Gainsborough' with its tallow flowers and grey-green leaves at 1.5m (5ft) high, the 90cm (3ft) high pink 'Helen Johnson' again with grey-green leaves, and the vigorous Cotswold Group. They date back to the 1920s and come in a wide range of colours, but mainly white and yellow. All verbascums need poor, free-draining soil in full sun. Avoid heavy soil that stays cold and wet over winter because that spells instant death. The one problem is that they have a short shelf-life, and propagating is vital if you aren't to keep buying new plants each year. The species can be grown from seed, while cultivars can be increased by division, though that can be tricky. It is generally easier to take root cuttings in late autumn. Slice off pencil-thick, fleshy lengths of root, about 5cm (2in) long, from close to the plant's crown. Make the cut closest to the crown and the soil surface straight and the bottom one, further away in the soil, angled to help you remember which is which. Insert in pots filled with compost (soil mix) for standing in a cold frame. Expect to see results next spring.

Verbena bonariensis

VERBENA
Verbena

Coming in a wide range of sizes and colours, some verbenas are annuals, some perennials, with the most fashionable being the South American, short-lived *V. bonariensis*. It is a 1.5m (5ft) high plus not-totally-reliably hardy perennial, with vertical, pencil thin, four-sided stems making an open, see-through plant carrying clusters of lilac-blue flowers attracting scores of butterflies. It can be grown just about anywhere in the garden, to the front of borders giving a filtered view, or in drifts in gravel gardens. It can be left outside all year in mild, sheltered areas. Shorter perennials, such as 'Sissinghurst', can be used in containers and hanging baskets where they dangle over the sides, down to 75cm (2½ft), though they can also be grown up a cane wigwam fixed in a large pot, quickly covering it with pink flowers by midsummer. The half-hardy annuals come in different Series, usually to 25cm (10in) high, in various colours, and again make an excellent show in hanging baskets and window boxes etc. All like an open sunny position with good drainage. *V. bonariensis* is an

excellent self-seeder, and on light soil there should be packed clusters of seedlings each spring. To be on the safe side, pot up the parent in autumn, cut back, and stand in a cool greenhouse, as with the other perennials (that are propagated by spring cuttings or divisions). Water occasionally while dormant. The annuals are grown from seed in early spring at 19°C (66°F), and once sown need to have the light excluded by covering the pot with black plastic. Keep checking for seedlings, whereupon the plastic is immediately removed.

VERONICA
Speedwell

Most are grown for their tall, thin spikes of flowers held well clear of the foliage, with the hardy perennial *V. spicata* making shortish clumps 45cm (18in) high and wide. The clear blue flowers appear in summer, and it mixes well with the various cultivars in white ('Alba'), deep pink ('Heidekind') and red ('Rotfuchs'). 'Shirley Blue' is slightly shorter but intense blue, and the cultivars of *V. austriaca* tend to be 30cm (12in) high, with 'Royal Blue' deep blue. There are also short,

Valeriana officinalis

Verbascum olympicum

GARDEN BOUNDARIES

A good boundary is as crucial to a garden as a frame is to a painting. Choose the wrong boundary and the whole effect can be instantly ruined. It sets the tone of the garden, and either needs to wrap around and enclose it, reaffirming the look or, in the case of rural or seaside gardens, for example, open out so that the garden is not enclosed but merges and filters into the surrounding landscape, making what is out there an extension of the view. Formal gardens are traditionally enclosed by formal hedging, often using topiarized shapes that have been battlemented,

or have crisp flat tops. Alternatively, they can gradually ease out into areas of more informal planting, with the garden edges being filled by shrubs and trees, suggesting semi-wildness. Cottage gardens use the same semi-wild look, with more oriental designs using bamboo. Walled gardens are a *fait accompli*, unless you knock them down, and provide a fantastic opportunity to grow all kinds of climbers. Modern gardens need contemporary materials, including galvanized steel and sheer stretches of coloured plaster to emphasize the look of the upmarket, upbeat 'outdoor room'.

Viola odorata

spreading kinds with the hardy perennial *V. prostrata* 15cm (6in) high with a spread of 40cm (16in), and various cultivars in blues, white and pinks. A good alternative is the *V. gentianoides*, a taller spreader getting 45cm (18in) high, with cultivars in white and shades of blue. All are remarkably unfussy, though rich, moist soil is best under an open sky. If the soil is on the dry side,

Veronica spicata

the plants quickly wilt. Propagate species by seed, sowing it in spring at 15°C (59°F), and cultivars by taking spring cuttings, or divide in spring or autumn.

VIOLA
Viola/violet/pansy

First, the distinctions. Pansies are basically annuals or perennials with a short lifespan, and the flowers often have a central blotch. Violas are perennials, and they quickly form small clumps; the flowers do not have the central dark blotch but they do have dark lines or rays and sometimes a gentle scent. Violets have smaller flowers than violas and no rays. Annual pansy cultivars of *V. × wittrockiana* come in various Series, generally no more than 23cm (9in) high, and they are excellent for pots, hanging baskets and front-of-border schemes. Some flower all summer, some in autumn and winter, and some in winter and early spring. They range from in-your-face primary colours to the fun Joker kinds to pastels,

often in bicolours. Now for the hardy perennials. The 10cm (4in) high 'Bowles Black' is a sumptuous, velvet black pansy with a yellow eye, and though short-lived can be easily propagated by taking spring cuttings. (Other good blacks include the bushier 'Blackjack', 'Molly Sanderson' and 'Roecastle Black'.) *V. cornuta*, a 15cm (6in) high, bluish violet with a long end of spring to mid-autumn flowering season, makes excellent groundcover; there are some cultivars in white (Alba Group) and pale mauve ('Minor'). 'Huntercombe Purple' is an extremely attractive violet-purple viola, again at 15cm (6in) high, with the vigorous, short-lived 'Jackanapes' (same height, viola) a fun mix of red

and yellow. The quick-spreading, self-seeding *V. odorata* (violet) is a 20cm (8in) high violet or white (with cultivars in other colours). It does not mind summer shade, while the rest like summer sun, all enjoying well-drained soil with well-rotted organic matter. Keep cutting back the dead flowers of violas (not violets) to promote a longer burst. Propagate according to type. Violet species can be grown from seed sown in autumn, with the pots being placed in a cold frame. Sow seed of violas in midsummer. Sow seed of early spring and summer pansies in late winter, and for winter flowers in summer. Initially exclude the light until seedlings appear in both cases. Propagate cultivars by spring cuttings or division.

SOWING VIOLA SEED

1 When sowing viola seed, drop no more than two or three seeds in each compartment, pulling out the feeblest when the growth appears.

2 Cover the tops of the sections with a sheet of black plastic to exclude the light, and only remove when the new growth appears.

Trees, shrubs and climbers

ABELIA
Abelia

Though they are not reliably hardy, needing wind-sheltered, sunny gardens and good drainage, abelias do flower over a long period. *A. schumannii* makes a large, 1.8m (6ft) high by 3m (10ft) wide deciduous shrub, covered in lilac-pink flowers, while *A. × grandiflora* is a vigorous semi-evergreen with dark green leaves set off by pinkish-white flowers from midsummer into autumn. The best of its cultivars include 'Francis Mason', 'Hopleys', and the striking 'Gold Spot' with all-yellow leaves. Propagate by taking spring or summer cuttings that will root quickly, keeping them in a cold frame, but make sure they do not get frosted over winter.

ABIES
Silver fir

The hardy, evergreen giant fir (*A. grandis*) really is a giant, hitting 60m (200ft) high and 8m (25ft) wide in ideal conditions. It makes a tall, slim shape, being covered by dark green needles that smell of orange when crushed. It shoots up extremely quickly, and needs a huge space. The Korean fir (*A. koreana*) is completely different, being shorter at 10m (30ft) high and 6m (20ft) wide, and slow growing. Both like protection from cold and fierce winds, and need a sunny site. The best way to propagate is by ripe seed that will need chilling for 21 days before being sown in a cold frame.

TAKING ABUTILON CUTTINGS

1 The quickest way to propagate is by spring cuttings. Nip off a length of new young growth, about 10cm (4in) long. Trim just below a node.

2 Remove the lower leaves, just leaving a batch at the top, and then lightly dab the base in rooting powder, tapping off any excess.

3 Insert in cuttings compost (soil mix), giving each its own container. Water and keep turning, avoiding one-sided growth.

ABUTILON
Flowering maple

This is an excellent range of shrubs, both evergreen and deciduous, many of which are frost-hardy. The latter can be grown outside all year (often being planted in large, colourful groups), provided they are given a mild, sheltered site with free-draining soil where the temperature does not dip alarmingly below freezing. Plants include tall, thin spires with cup-shaped flowers and shorter kinds ('Bella Mixed'), that grow 40cm (16in) high. The more tender plants can be grown in pots for bringing under cover over winter, or be kept permanently in a conservatory. In early spring sow at 16–17°C (61–63°F); germinates in about three weeks, and flowers in two years. Also take spring or summer cuttings that quickly root.

ACER
Maple

There is a huge range of acers, including the medium-size, hardy, deciduous Japanese kind (*A. palmatum* and *A. japonicum*) with distinctive leaves and striking autumn colours. There are scores of *palmatum* cultivars, that will not get above 8m (25ft) high and 10m (30ft) wide, and it is worth visiting a specialist nursery to spot the one for you. Popular buys include the appositely named 'Crimson Queen', 'Osakazuki' that also turns bright red, and 'Sango-kaku' with its outstanding red winter shoots. If they can be grown by a pond, and given woodland-type shelter from cold winds, you will get a doubling of their colours when they reflect in the water. The slightly taller *A. japonicum* has slightly more rounded, not

so deeply lobed leaves. The sugar maple (*A. saccharum*), at 20m (70ft) high and 12m (40ft) wide, is famous for its New England autumn show, but you cannot replicate that in Europe. The deciduous paper bark maples (*A. davidii* and *A. griseum*) are also essential because of the coloured bark. The former grows to 9m (30ft) high and has green and white streaked bark, while the latter – at 12m (40ft) – makes a quirky sight in winter with its drapes of peeling bark, revealing patches of orange-brown. A good alternative with peeling bark is *Polylepis australis*. Acers are notoriously tricky to propagate, which is why most people leave it to the professionals, but layering should give good results when a low branch is bent down to the soil, and is pegged in place, enabling it to root.

Abelia x grandiflora

Abies grandis

Abutilon vitifolium

Acer palmatum

Actinidia kolomikta

ACTINIDIA
Chinese gooseberry

The best two choices are the deciduous *A. chinensis* and *A. kolomikta*, with the first being a frost-hardy, deciduous climber, reaching 10m (30ft). The leaves are huge, at 30cm (12in) wide, and there is a good show of early to midsummer white flowers followed by greenish-brown fruit on the females, which means you will also need to grow a nearby male. The hardier *A. kolomikta* grows half as high, and has young, heart-shaped, bronze-tinged leaves that are initially white and then pink at the tips. Both need a sheltered site, ideally being grown against a sunny wall, with good drainage. Propagate both by summer or autumn cuttings, or by layering when a long, straight, youngish, supple stem is bent down to the ground so that a leaf node can be buried where it is in contact with the soil.

AESCULUS
Horse chestnut

A. hippocastanum makes a massive deciduous tree reaching over 25m (80ft) high and nearly as wide. In late spring and early summer it produces large spikes (or 'candles') of white or pink flowers and they, in turn, produce spiny casings with brown conkers inside. When the conkers fall to the ground, carefully prise open the protective cover and remove the conker. Sow immediately at 13°C (55°F).

AILANTHUS
Ailanthus

The tree of heaven (*A. altissima*) gives one of the best garden displays. If left untouched it makes a spreading head of growth, easily clearing 18m (60ft), growing nearly as wide, with 60cm (2ft) long leaves, consisting of leaflets, and panicles

Aesculus hippocastanum

Ailanthus altissima

of small green summer flowers that give way to a show of reddish-brown fruit. But if you coppice the main stem each autumn, you will restrict its size the following year, and the tree puts all its energy into making huge leaves, twice as big as normal. For that reason make sure that it is being grown in a sheltered site or the large leaves will end up looking wind-battered and tatty. To propagate, either look for suckers, waiting for

them to develop roots before severing them where they join the parent, or take early winter cuttings. Alternatively, scrape back the soil to expose the roots and sever a length that has got a 12mm (½in) diameter. Slice this up into 5cm (2in) mini pieces, and plant them in pots of compost (soil mix). Make sure that the end that was furthest away from the plant's base is buried deepest. Just cover, water and keep in a cold frame.

TREES

Gardens don't just happen down in the soil; they also happen at head height and far higher. Trees provide the ultimate height, and though many grow to 30m (100ft), others are shorter and suitable for medium-sized gardens. They include …
Acers – especially the paper bark maples (*A. davidii* and *A. griseum*) and Japanese maples (*A. japonicum* and *A. palmatum*)
Amelanchier lamarckii
Arbutus unedo
Betula pendula and *B. utilis*
Cercis canadensis
Cornus alternifolia, C. kousa, C. mas
Cotinus coggygria
Crataegus laevigata
Cryptomeria japonica
Eucalyptus gunnii
Ficus carica
Ilex aquifolium
Juniperus communis 'Hibernica'
Laburnum x watereri
Liquidambar orientalis
Magnolia
Nyssa sinensis
Prunus serrula
Rhus typhina
Robinia pseudoacacia
Sorbus
Stewartia

Crataegus laevigata

Magnolia

Sorbus

Stewartia

CHOOSING THE RIGHT TREE

Trees add permanent structure (vital in winter) and shade, so before buying, check where your tree is going to be planted and which parts of the garden will be affected. Trees change the look of the garden, creating new vistas and blocking others. In addition, the scale of the garden will be radically altered, with tall plants now seeming relatively short. Trees change everything, so think very carefully before deciding which one to buy.

The best deciduous trees add flamboyant autumn colours as the green pigment (chlorophyll) fades, and yellows, orange and reds erupt just before the leaves drop. Some can be coppiced at ground level so that all the energy is channelled into a few new stems, giving large flagpole leaves; some have a great blast of spring blossom; some have coloured, peeling bark; and others have bright berries, coloured stems, and even richly scented flowers. In a small garden, try to choose a tree with several attractions.

Akebia quinata

Amelanchier lamarckii

Arbutus unedo

Argyranthemum

AKEBIA
Chocolate vine

A quirky, hardy, deciduous climber, *A quinata* produces scented brownish-purple early summer flowers, followed – given a long, hot summer – by fruit resembling a string of small purple sausages. To show it off, grow it against a sunny wall and carefully train the shoots along horizontal wires, spacing them out, approximately 23cm (9in) apart, and make sure that the ground is free draining. Alternatively, grow it up a pergola or into an old, stout tree. If the possible 10m (30ft) of growth exceeds the available space, cut it back. It can be propagated in two ways, by sowing seed the moment it is ripe in pots in a cold frame, or taking cuttings in spring or summer, for much quicker results.

AMELANCHIER
Juneberry

A. lamarckii doubles as a hardy, bushy, spreading, deciduous shrub or small tree, growing some 10m (30ft) high and even 12m (40ft) wide. The young foliage is copper-red, and there is a good autumn show of orange and red leaves, and in spring it is covered in white flowers. Grow in acid soil. Take early summer cuttings, or propagate by layering. 'Ballerina' has white spring flowers, then fruit which turns from red to black. If growing the suckering *A. canadensis* – at 6m (20ft) high and 3m (10ft) wide – scrape back the soil to look for a set of roots on a sucker, and sever it from the parent where the two join, but then remove the long length of sucker below the fibrous root system and discard.

ARBUTUS
Strawberry tree

The hardy 8m (25ft) high *A. unedo* makes a branching, shrubby tree and is grown for its peeling reddish-brown bark. The white flowers give way to the red fruit (hence the name) that actually take 12 months to grow and ripen. If you need a smaller form, go for 'Elfin King', which is just 1.8m (6ft) high by 1.5m (5ft) wide. While it can be propagated from the seed in the fruit (first getting rid of the pulp, then giving the cleaned seed a spell in the refrigerator), it is quickest to take late summer cuttings.

ARGYRANTHEMUM
Argyranthemum

Often thought of as a perennial, it is actually more of a tender shrub, with the most popular forms including *A. foeniculaceum* and *A. frutescens*, both from the Canary Islands. They make excellent bedding or pot plants, creating a mound 75cm (2½ft) high and wide. Free-draining soil and a sunny site are essential, as is a cool greenhouse for the winter. They're easy to propagate; just take spring or summer cuttings and they will quickly root. Take large numbers to create enough plants to line up at the front of a border. Worth taking precautionary cuttings in case pot plants get left out and get killed by a mixture of persistent heavy winter rains and freezing temperatures.

ARISTOLOCHIA
Dutchman's pipe

These frost-hardy and tender climbers generate a mass of leafy growth, with stems easily hitting 8m (25ft). For a sheltered, sunny site outdoors, grow *A. macrophylla* (the same height) with its amazing, mottled flowers that resemble a curved smoker's pipe with a bend in the middle. Grow it up a series of horizontal wires against a wall, and be prepared to undertake some judicious pruning to remove the clusters of leaves and reveal the summer flowers. The more tender kinds, including *A. grandiflora* – again, 8m (25ft) – from Mexico down to the West Indies, need to be grown in a conservatory with a large wall space. Propagate by taking spring or summer cuttings, but make sure that the outdoor kind are well-protected in the first winter, giving them a thick mulch to cover the roots.

TAKING ARGYRANTHEMUM CUTTINGS

1 Cut off a new vigorous length of stem in spring, removing it just below a node. It should be about 10cm (4in) long.

2 Using a scalpel or sharp knife, slice off the leaves, except for a small cluster right at the top. The new roots cannot support too many.

3 Dip the end in rooting powder, and tap off the excess. Then deeply insert in the cuttings compost (soil mix) and water.

TAKING AUCUBA CUTTINGS

1 Toward the end of summer remove a length of the current season's growth, removing it just above a node.

2 Carefully lay down the cutting and trim off the base, this time removing it just below a node. Discard the unwanted section.

3 Before planting it in cuttings compost (soil mix), cut off the top half of the large leaves to avoid excess transpiration.

Aronia melanocarpa

ARONIA
Chokeberry

The red and black chokeberries (*A. arbutifolia* and *A. melanocarpa*) make substantial, hardy, deciduous shrubs, the first growing 1.8m (6ft) high by 3m (10ft) wide, the second 3m (10ft) high by 2.5m (8ft) wide. Do not try packing them into a border; they need space to flourish. Both add plenty of high-voltage colour to the autumn garden, when their leaves turn orange-red-yellow and purple-red respectively in the autumn. They also produce plenty of small, white late spring flowers, sometimes with a hint of pink, in sun or light, dappled shade. The best way to propagate chokeberry shrubs is by using the suckers as new plant material. Scrape back the soil and look for roots, and provided they are well established sever the sucker where it joins the parent, cut off that part of the sucker beneath the roots and pot up. Alternatively, you can take early summer cuttings.

AUCUBA
Aucuba

The hardy, evergreen spotted laurel (*A. japonica*) makes a chunky 3m (10ft) high and wide shrub, with the female 'Variegata' having the familiar yellow-spotted leaves. (The species, despite its name, is plain green.) 'Golden King', with its large leaves and striking variegations, is a good alternative, as is 'Crotonifolia'. If you grow a male and female you will get bright red berries after the spring reddish-purple flowers. 'Nana Rotundifolia' produces a lot of berries. The variegated forms prefer light shade, while the all-green kind, such as 'Crassifolia', are not fussy, growing in sun or shade. The quickest way to propagate new plants is by late summer cuttings, raising them in a cold frame, or layering.

BERBERIS
Barberry

The huge range of evergreen and deciduous shrubs, most of which are hardy, include the miniature kinds for the rock garden that will not get much taller than 30cm (1ft) and giant, chunky specimens getting 3m (10ft) high, making good boundary and hedge plants. They typically have sharp prickles, sometimes alarmingly dangerous, bright flowers, autumn fruit and strong autumn leaf colour. For a mass of thick, impenetrable growth making a good feature plant to keep out intruders try the 3m (10ft) high and wide *Berberis julianae*. It is also excellent for birds; they nest in the tops, wedging their nests in the criss-crossing branches, safe from cats because of the spines. For a much more manageable size, *B. thunbergii* 'Atropurpurea Nana' gets just 60cm (2ft) high and 75cm (2½ft) wide. Propagate by taking midsummer or autumn heel cuttings, with a sliver of wood at the base to help a good set of roots to form, and raise them in a cold frame. The mound-forming kind can be divided.

BETULA
Birch

A group of hardy, deciduous shrubs and trees (many fast growing) that will thrive just about anywhere, even on chalk though growth will suffer, but wet ground is a non-starter except for *B. nigra*. The best have peeling bark (*B. albosinensis*), and bark that is bright white (for example *B. ermanii*, *B. pendula* and *B. utilis* var. *jacquemontii* and its different forms such as 'Grayswood Ghost'). All grow 18m (60ft) and more, and about 10.5m (35ft) wide, making thrilling individual features where they can be clearly seen. If the bark becomes muddy and discoloured lower down it can be easily cleaned with a brush and warm water. Before propagating, note that birches self-sow and it is worth looking for seedlings close by. Carefully dig them up, do not damage the roots, and pot up. Alternatively, take summer cuttings and give a mild feed to ensure good growth.

CHRISTMAS TREES

The Norway spruce (*Picea abies*) is the traditional Christmas tree, but you can use countless other conifers with more interesting shapes. The Serbian spruce (*P. omorika*) has a pyramidal form and bluish-green leaves, and the foliage of the Colorado spruce (*P. pungens*) is a similar colour. *Abies* are in some ways better than spruces, because they retain their leaves. Whatever you choose, buy something with good colour and shape, that you can later plant out in the garden.

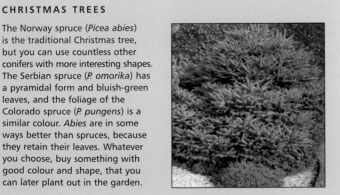

Berberis thunbergii

Betula pendula

Bougainvillea glabra

BOUGAINVILLEA
Bougainvillea

Unless you have a Mediterranean climate, it will have to be grown as a pot plant. In ideal conditions the evergreen bougainvilleas can easily make 9m (30ft) of growth, erupting in rich, flamboyant colours, covering great stretches of wall, growing up and over balconies, but with the restricted root run of a pot do not expect much more than 1.8m (6ft) of growth. If you can grow one in a conservatory border, you will get much better results. Give it a nitrogen-high feed when growth commences, generating plenty of leafy growth to support the flowers, switching to potash when it comes into bud to produce the best possible display. It can be stood outside over summer but it needs to be placed in a conservatory over winter, when it just needs the occasional drink. Propagate by taking cuttings in either spring or summer, or you can bend a new young stem down to the ground and layer, wounding it to promote roots, and burying it.

BUDDLEJA
Butterfly bush

All are hardy to some extent, either being evergreen or deciduous, and they will grow just about anywhere, by railway lines and on top of the roofs of old, derelict houses, provided they are not stuck in wet soil. The best place in the garden is at the back of a border, or against a sunny, protective wall where some of the floppy growth can be tied in, especially for those that are not completely hardy. The key to getting a lively show of the long flower panicles, in colours from white to dark purple, on the ubiquitous *B. davidii* – 3m (10ft) high by 5m (15ft) wide – and its many cultivars, is to cut it hard back in early spring. New shoots quickly extend, giving thick, bushy growth and a strong midsummer show of richly scented flowers. For a late spring burst of yellow-orange, there is *B. globosa* – 5m (15ft) high and wide – that makes more straggly growth with eye-catching flowers like golf balls. Take cuttings any time from spring to autumn, and make sure they are well protected the first winter, if it is cold and wet.

BUXUS
Box

This is one of the most invaluable garden plants, making evergreen hedges to well over head height, garden dividers, lengths of greenery for knot gardens and parterres, and specimens for topiary. Given how expensive ready-made topiary shapes can be, why not grow your own? Buy a small bushy plant, let it fatten and get bigger until it is the height you want, and then start snipping, creating a ball, a ball with a vertical stem poking out of the top for creating another ball on top, spirals, animals, you name it. Feed the plants well to build up strong growth, and site in partial shade. Trim in summer to keep it in shape, and it will quickly resprout, even when it is cut back hard. Use the trimmings – ideally 10cm (4in) long – to make new plants. Put them around the sides of pots, and pot them up individually the following spring. Keep nipping back the top growth to create bushy plants.

CALLUNA
Heather

The evergreen, hardy heathers consist of one species (*C. vulgaris*) with hundreds of different cultivars flowering over a long period from midsummer to autumn. All make low-growing plants, about 40–45cm (16–18in) high and 60cm (2ft) wide, though many are much shorter, for acid, free-draining, rich soil in full sun. The colours range from white to mauve and pink, while the leaves (in green, silver and bronze, etc.) gain a purple hue over winter. Provide an early spring trim, shearing over the tops, and grow in swirling batches for a strong effect. Plants are easily propagated, either by midsummer cuttings, layering (when long, supple stems are bent down to the ground and buried, where they root before being severed from the parent), or plants can be dropped to produce a large number of new plants.

Buddleja davidii

Buxus sempervirens

Calluna vulgaris

Camellia japonica 'Adolphe Audusson'

Ceanothus 'Julia Phelps'

Cercis canadensis

CAMELLIA
Camellia

Evergreen camellias (both shrubs and small trees) are slightly demanding, but provided you can give them acid soil and shelter from cold winds and late frosts, they are no problem. One of the best solutions to all three conditions is growing them in large tubs, guaranteeing ericaceous compost (soil mix) and a sheltered site, out of early morning sun. This also makes it easier to check that they are well watered during dry periods, which helps fatten the young buds. The tender types can be grown in conservatories. There is a huge range of plants with winter and spring flowers in white, pink, red and yellow. *C. japonica* – 9m (28ft) high and wide – has scores of excellent spring-flowering cultivars (look out for the red 'Adolphe Audusson', yellow 'Brushfield's Yellow', white 'Doctor Tinsley', white 'Hakurakuten',

white 'Masayoshi', white 'Nuccio's Gem' and red, pink and white 'Tricolor'). The same applies to *C.* × *williamsii*, approximately half as high (with the pink 'Windlesham Alex' very good for spring). Those growing in the ground can be propagated by layering, bending a youngish, flexible stem down to the soil, wounding it to promote roots, and then burying it in the ground until it forms an independent plant when it can be severed from the parent. Alternatively, take midsummer cuttings. Fresh seed can be sown in autumn (using ericaceous compost); stand the pots in a cold frame but germination can take six months.

CEANOTHUS
Californian lilac

The evergreen and deciduous, usually blue-flowering shrubs need protecting. Give them a sunny, sheltered position with excellent drainage. The deciduous

kind tend to be slightly hardier, but even they hate cold, exposed gardens where they get zapped by chilly winds. Get that right and the shrubs will put on prolific growth, making substantial blocks of blue when they flower, and the times vary from spring to summer to autumn, so in theory you could have one in flower through most of the growing season. One of the most impressive is the vigorous *C. arboreus* 'Trewithen Blue', a monster of a shrub with 6m (20ft) growth up and sideways, and spring to early summer flowers. Grow any of the bigger kind against a sunny wall and they will grow ever taller. To increase your supply of Californian lilacs, take heel cuttings from spring to autumn. The attached heel should help guarantee a good cluster of new roots.

CERCIS
Cercis

The hardy, deciduous eastern redwood tree (*C. canadensis*) is a mini tree or large shrub, just reaching 9m (30ft) high and wide. It compensates by usually being multi-stemmed, with a batch of pea-like flowers before the leaves open in spring. The flowers give way to long, bean-like pods. The leaves of 'Forest Pansy' make this a widely grown plant because they are dark red-purple-bronze all summer. It needs to be planted in the right position because it hates being transplanted. Provide moist soil in full sun, and coppice 'Forest Pansy' on a regular basis for even larger leaves. Propagate by taking late summer, semi-ripe cuttings for rooting in a cold frame. Alternatively, sow the seed at the same time in a cold frame.

PLANTING TREES

The best tree-planting time is during the dormant period, from autumn to late winter. This gives a tree time to settle in before the burst of spring growth. Make sure that the weather is decent, avoiding extreme conditions with freezing temperatures or sopping wet ground. Native trees are the easiest to plant, and you can simply thrust a spade into the ground, then lever it back to create a V-shape. Put the young tree in the hole, with the soil at the same level as in the pot, and close up the hole. Stamp down on the ground to make sure that the roots are in contact with the soil, and water in. Non-natives need a bit more help. Dig a shallow hole four times the width of the pot, and no more than 30cm (12in) deep. Stab at the bottom with a fork to loosen the soil and improve the drainage, then stand the young tree in the planting hole. Get a friend to

hold it vertically, and again check that the trunk is at the same soil level as when in the pot. Do not plant it any deeper. Finally, use a length of pipe angled down to the roots, with the top sticking out of the soil, so that when you give it a drink the water will go straight to the roots and will not run off the surface. Then back-fill and add a 7.5cm (3in) thick mulch, keeping it away from the trunk.

CHAENOMELES
Flowering quince

An essential deciduous, hardy shrub for the spring garden because it is completely unfussy about where it is grown. It thrives in average soil in sun or light shade, and can be easily trained against a wall or a system of posts and wires to create a hedge. The flowers appear before the leaves, which means they stand out strongly against the stiff, bare wood. C. × superba, at 1.5m (5ft) high by 1.8m (6ft) wide, has many attractive varieties including the dark red with yellow anthers 'Crimson and Gold', and the dark pink 'Pink Lady'. The slightly taller and much wider C. speciosa includes the white 'Nivalis' and pinkish-white 'Moerloosei'. The four ways to propagate are by taking cuttings (the easiest method) from spring to autumn, by layering (bending a supple stem down to the soil, and encouraging it to root in the ground before severing it from the parent), by removing rooted suckers, and collecting the ripe, yellow fruit. Extract the seed and sow it fresh, covering it with horticultural sand. Stand the pots in a cold frame and the seed should germinate in about five months.

CISTUS
Rock rose

The evergreen shrubby rock roses come from hot, dry areas, including North Africa and the Canary Islands, which means that none are reliably hardy. All need poor soil and excellent drainage, and a sunny hot spot where they can bake. Avoid cold, open sites and, if conditions are not ideal, add a thick winter mulch to protect the roots. Alternatively, dig them up and keep in pots over winter in a dry, mild place or in a frost-free greenhouse. All the species have thin, open petals that only last a day, but a succession of buds keeps up the flower supply over summer. The plants themselves are often short-lived, but spring and summer non-flowering cuttings (with young buds) quickly root and produce replacement plants that typically reach about 90cm (3ft) high and wide. If growing new plants from seed, sow the seed at 18°C (65°F) and shoots should appear within three weeks.

CLEMATIS
Clematis

It is almost perverse not to grow a clematis; if there is one particular group you dislike, there are other kinds that are completely different with huge attractions. The evergreen, 5m (15ft) high C. armandii is one of the first to flower in spring, and has two big plusses, the long, thin dark green leaves and the multiplicity of buds that produce pinkish-white flowers with a strong hint of vanilla in sunny, sheltered sites where the scent can hang in the air. There are scores for summer, including those with huge open flowers and the 1.8m (6ft) high texensis and 2–4m (6–12ft) high viticella kinds with exquisite, small, bell-shaped flowers, many flowering into autumn. The best of the latter include 'Bill Mackenzie', which can make a great mound over a sunny wall or shoot up into a tree, going 6m (20ft) high, erupting in small, yellow, downward-pointing flowers. The seedheads are even better, hanging on over winter as silvery spiders' legs. Grow all to thread through climbers, including roses, or up a pergola or over an arch. The pruning times vary according to when they flower. All like to have their heads in the

Chaenomeles japonica

Cistus x skanbergii

Clematis armandii

sun but their roots in cool shade, so when growing up a tree, for example, plant them on the shady side and train them round to get the sun. Propagate by layering a youngish, bendy stem, bending it down to the ground so that it can be buried and allowed to root, or by taking internodal cuttings. The top cut should be just above where the leaf stalk is attached to the stem, with strong shoots about to break out from the angle of stalk and stem. Large leaves will need cutting in half to reduce the amount of moisture loss.

CLIANTHUS
Clianthus

Glory pea (*C. puniceus*) is a frost-hardy climber from New Zealand, that will not get too rampant, with wonderfully strange, bright red flowers. It needs a sunny, sheltered wall where it can shoot to 4m (12ft) up a trellis or system of supporting wires, with its roots in free-draining soil because it hates standing in cold wet winter ground. If heavy soil is a problem, try growing it in a large container with free-draining compost (soil mix), but be prepared to protect the pot and the roots in icy weather by wrapping a protective cover around it. Alternatively grow in a conservatory bed. Sow seed at 16°C (61°F) in spring, though you can also take cuttings in summer.

COBAEA
Cathedral bell

Allow plenty of room for *C. scandens*, a massive, rampant, tender climber. Though an annual, it is quite capable of putting on prodigious summer growth, swarming 4.5m (15ft), and for this reason you must not plant it near other plants because they will quickly get swamped. Provide some form of support, a trellis or horizontal wires attached to stout posts to give it a leg up, and you will get a good view of the large, fleshy flowers that start off pale green and turn purple. In an excellent summer with high temperatures, the flowers may be followed by oval, egg-like fruit. A hot sunny position is vital.

Propagate by sowing seed in spring at 19°C (66°F). Germination is quick. Harden off young plants before planting out.

CORNUS
Dogwood

The best three trees for a medium-size garden are the hardy, deciduous pagoda dogwood (*C. alternifolia*), Chinese dogwood (*C. kousa*) and Cornelian cherry (*C. mas*), none of which exceeds 6m (20ft) high and wide. The first is highly ornamental, with a tiered arrangement of horizontal branches (making a good contrast against vertical shapes) and early summer white flowers. The second has a neat, compact shape with flaking bark, early summer white flowers, strawberry-like fruit and orange-red leaves in autumn. The third, more of a shrubby tree, is grown for its small, yellow, late winter flowers and plum red autumn leaves. For dogwoods with flashy winter stems, go for *C. alba*, *C. sanguinea* and *C. servicea* – all approximately 2.4m (8ft) high and wide – and their many forms. The new vertical growth spears out of the ground and comes in various colours, including dark purple, bright red, green, yellow-green and orange-yellow. If left, the brightly coloured new shoots will eventually darken, so you have to coppice them near ground level, say every other spring, to force up new, colourful replacement growth. You can dot these dogwoods around the garden where you have room for

large clumps about 1.8m (6ft) high and wide, or more, making sure that they will be picked up by the winter sun for maximum effect. Or, for a multicoloured look, grow two or three dogwoods with different colours right next to each other enabling their stems to intermingle. All like rich, moist soil, with *C. alternifolia* liking acid ground. To propagate, take hardwood autumn cuttings and raise in a cold frame.

CORYLUS
Hazel

The tallest of these hardy, deciduous trees can reach 20m (70ft) high and 7m (22ft) wide, but there are shrubbier forms, such as *C. avellana*, that just get above 3.6m (12ft) high and wide. All bear catkins at the end of winter on the bare branches, but 'Aurea' stands out with its young yellow leaves and 'Contorta' with its zig-zagging, corkscrewing-all-over-the-place unpredictable growth. Promptly remove any suckers on grafted plants, tugging them away where they join the parent. All are happy in sun or shade, and really thrive on chalk. They can be propagated by French layering or stooling, or by cuttings in spring or summer. Fresh seed can be promptly sown in autumn, but it needs to be scarified using sandpaper to help it germinate. Stand the pots in a cold frame for up to four months, when there should be a seedling. Side-veneer grafts can be made on to two-year-old *C. avellana*.

Clianthus puniceus

Cornus alba

Corylus avellana

Cotinus coggygria

Cotoneaster lacteus

COTINUS
Smoke bush

Hardy deciduous shrubs and trees, with *C. coggygria* making 5m (15ft) high and wide bushy growth for the back of the border. Excellent in summer when the tiny flowers produce a blurred, fuzzy look as if the plant were enveloped in an updraught of smoke. In autumn the leaves redden up and yellow before they fall. Happy in average soil, and at its best over a hot summer. There are several good forms including 'Notcutt's Variety' with wine red leaves, 'Royal Purple' with dark purple leaves, and 'Flame' with its punchy autumn colours. *C. obovatus*, from the south-eastern USA, is a more solid 10m (30ft) high and 8m (25ft) wide. Plants are easily grown by layering, by taking spring cuttings or by using fresh seed that has been separated from the seedheads by rubbing the latter between finger and thumb.

COTONEASTER
Cotoneaster

Reliable, robust deciduous and evergreen cotoneasters come in all sizes, from weenies to trees. You can use the midgets on rockeries, to edge paths, circular spaces and even beds and you will get, with the right choice, evergreen leaves, typically white or pink flowers (from mid-spring) and loads of fruit (often called berries) in red, yellow, orange, black, white, pink or even violet, which can hang on all winter, into the following spring. The smallest start with *C. procumbens*, which is practically flat on the ground. *C. astrophoros*

is fractionally higher at 45cm (18in) and spreads 60–90cm (2–3ft) in 30 years (it is that slow growing), and has crimson berries that hang on. Three top choices are the red-fruiting *C. glacialis* – set the plants close together, and 60cm (2ft) is about their maximum height; *C. turbinatus* with its shiny, shapely leaves that might reach 4.5m (15ft) high; and late-fruiting *C. lacteus* at 4m (12ft). If you want a high-performance tree that is deciduous, large-leaved and red-fruiting, then go for *C. frigidus* and not one of its cultivars, because they're simply not as good. It will hit 9m (30ft) or so high and wide. *C. shansiensis* can easily be trained as a small standard, stopping the single vertical stem when it is 1.3m (4½ft) high. 'Hybridus Pendulus' is also trained as a 1.8m (6ft) high standard or giant golfing umbrella that is amazingly thick with red fruit. In eastern Europe they go even further, grafting cotoneaster

on to crataegus and creating a tree like a fruiting lollipop. One that does not need improving is *C. hylmoei*, which grows about 2.5m (8ft) high and 4m (12ft) wide, with arching pendulous branches. Propagate by spring or summer cuttings, seed or layering.

CRYPTOMERIA
Japanese cedar

The hardy, evergreen conifer *C. japonica* 'Elegans' grows a good 15m (50ft) high and 7m (23ft) wide, and has wonderful, peeling, reddish-brown bark that is best when highlighted by the winter sun. It also makes a lovely winter show when the leaves on the windward side turn rust-reddish-brown when hit by cold winds, and the sunnier the site the better the colour. *Cryptomeria* is a rarity among conifers because it can be coppiced, and the new, low growth can be layered by bending it down to the ground for rooting.

X CUPRESSOCYPARIS LEYLANDII
Leyland cypress

It can be either grown as a freestanding tree that is capable of hitting 30m (100ft) and 5m (15ft) wide, making a thrilling sight, or as a hedge that is regularly cut (being given two or more trims a year), keeping it within socially acceptable (and, in some countries, legal) limits. There are several forms with non-green foliage, some golden-yellow, some bluish-grey. If you need more plants to make a hedge, then use the trimmings as cuttings, raising them in a cold frame.

CYTISUS
Broom

A mix of deciduous and evergreen shrubs, invariably hardy, for growing in poor acid soil in full sun. They flower prolifically in spring, being covered in small flowers, sometimes strongly scented, mostly yellow but some pink or red and yellow bicoloured, and are ideal in a wild or cottage garden. There is a wide choice, with *C.* × *praecox* 'Allgold' producing a dense, bushy block of 1.2m (4ft) growth (height and width). They perform best when given plenty of space. Cuttings take quickly, in mid- or late summer.

DAPHNE
Daphne

These deciduous and evergreen shrubs, both hardy and frost-hardy, can be tricky to grow, but if you can provide the right conditions you will get sumptuous scents in spring and summer. They need soil that is neither too dry, nor too moist, that is fertile and free draining. *D. mezereum* is an upright 1.2m (4ft) high by 90cm (3ft) wide shrub with pink scented flowers at the end of winter, and you will need a sunny sheltered site where the scent will not get blown away. *D. bholua* and *D. b.* 'Jacqueline Postill' grow to head height and more, by about 1.5m (5ft) wide, and flower at the same time, and deserve to be followed by the 90cm (3ft) high and wide *D. tangutica* that flowers in early summer with some repeat flowers later in the summer. Put them in the right position when planting, because they hate being moved.

Cryptomeria japonica

x *Cupressocyparis leylandii*

Cytisus scoparius

Daphne mezereum

Elaeagnus x ebbingei

If you do have to prune, note that the sap can be an irritant. To propagate there is a choice of seed, cuttings and layering. Sow the fresh seed, removed from the pulp, and cover with horticultural sand. Stand the pots in a cold frame to germinate within six months. Cuttings can be taken from spring to autumn, while layering can start at the end of spring. Bend stems down to the ground for wounding and burying in the soil, where they should take root.

DEUTZIA
Deutzia

Mainly deciduous shrubs needing average soil in full sun or light shade, they are very useful in modest gardens because they rarely grow above head height, and are covered with a mass of white or pink flowers in spring and early summer. *D. × elegantissima* 'Rosealind' is incredibly popular, getting no more than 1.2m (4ft) high and wide, making a rounded shrub with pink-tinted white flowers at the end of spring, into the start of summer. Either propagate by seed, sown in cold frames in autumn, or take summer cuttings.

ELAEAGNUS
Elaeagnus

A genus with hardy evergreen and deciduous shrubs and trees for full sun, with *E. × ebbingei* 'Gilt Edge' one of the best. It makes a substantial 4m (12ft) high and wide evergreen shrub, with green leaves edged yellow, which looks good at the back of a border, or a thick, chunky, colourful hedge. The small, white, scented flowers open in autumn. If there is an outbreak of all-green leaves, remove that stem or in time the whole plant might lose its variegation. The deciduous, suckering 'Quicksilver' gives a very different effect with yellow summer flowers set against the grey leaves. Propagate by taking cuttings in spring and summer, and they will root in pots in a cold frame. Suckering plants can either be divided, or wait until the sucker has started to root and then detach it from the parent.

ERICA
Heath

The winter heaths (*E. carnea*) provide a spread of low, hardy, evergreen growth, rarely getting above 15cm (6in) high, with the flowers ranging from white to pink and red. Choose wisely and you will have one in flower from mid-winter to the start of summer. The leaves are an added bonus because when the temperatures get chilly they turn reddish-orange. Grow them on acid soil, and shear over the tops after flowering. Space them correctly and you will not have a hint of bare soil where weeds can erupt. Plants are easily propagated, either by midsummer cuttings, layering (when long, supple stems are bent down to the ground and buried, where they root before being severed from the parent), or plants can be dropped to produce a large number of new plants. Make sure that the dropped plant is well watered during long, hot, dry spells to encourage the covered stems to produce a good set of roots.

Deutzia x elegantissima

Erica carnea

Escallonia rubra var. macrantha

Euonymus fortunei

FAGUS
Beech

The one everyone grows is the deciduous, hardy common beech (*F. sylvatica*), and for very good reasons. Grown as an individual tree, it will make 25m (80ft) high growth by 15m (50ft) wide, though some of its cultivars are under half that, with 'Dawyck Purple' producing a great dense spread of dark purple leaves that look best when contrasted with background bright greens and even yellow conifers. 'Purpurea Pendula' is also dark purple, but is just 3m (10ft) high and wide with dangling, weeping branches, being best grown in a lawn or an island bed surrounded by annuals and perennials. But the common beech comes into its own as a hedging, dividing or screening plant. Over winter most of the old leaves hang on (this only happens when the plants are clipped as a hedge), giving a near see-through look. In spring the new leaves break out, initially reddish before turning green. The growth can be cut back to whatever height you want, and you can even cut doors and windows in a beech hedge. If you do not like it, just let the growth fill back. Propagate by sowing the fresh nuts in pots outside, and growth will appear the following spring.

ESCALLONIA
Escallonia

Mostly evergreen, not reliably hardy shrubs, they make big, head-high hedges and windbreaks, being particularly useful in coastal gardens. Provided they get plenty of sun and good drainage, they will thrive, and if being grown in chilly regions try them against sunny walls to give them extra protection. The long show of summer flowers is in white, pink or red. 'Donard Radiance' gives very effective dense growth, 2.5m (8ft) high and wide, with pink flowers in the first half of summer set against the glossy green leaves. If you need to prune any for shape and size, then wait until after flowering. To raise more plants, take cuttings through summer and stand them out in a cold frame where they should root within about eight weeks.

EUCALYPTUS
Gum

Coming from regions around Australia and Indonesia, they are rarely fully hardy, but in the right conditions make spectacular evergreen trees and shrubs. The trees are prodigious growers, racing quickly to enormous heights, with long, lean main branches and, in the best cases, with beautiful patchwork bark. The snow gum (*E. pauciflora* subsp. *niphophila*) is relatively short at just 6m (20ft) high and wide, but the bark is a delightful mix of green, cream and grey, with more patches being exposed as the old bark flakes off. *E. gunnii*

is a favourite because its juvenile rounded leaves are greyish-blue, and the best way to perpetuate this show is by regularly coppicing the tree, when it has got a 5cm (2in) wide trunk, so keeping it short enough for a large border. If left to shoot up, it will produce long, narrow adult greyish-green leaves. Sow the ripe seed in spring, refrigerating it in a plastic bag with some damp vermiculite for a month. Then sow at 15°C (60°F) and raise the young plants in a cold frame.

EUONYMUS
Spindle tree

The deciduous and evergreen spindles come in various shapes and sizes, and varying degrees of hardiness. *E. fortunei* and its cultivars cannot decide whether they are low-growing shrubs or climbers for being trained into a tree or up a wall, when they put on much more vigorous growth.

'Silver Queen' gives both options. As a decent evergreen shrub, making 2.5m (8ft) high and 1.8m (6ft) wide growth, it fills large gaps at the back of the border and adds plenty of colour with its dark green leaves with a bright white edge. Grow in full sun in average soil, and if it threatens to break out of its allotted space then prune after flowering to rein it back. 'Emerald 'n' Gold' is a 90cm (3ft) high more manageable bushy evergreen with yellow variegations. If growing a non-variegated kind, then partial shade is fine. Propagate by taking summer cuttings, growing them in a cold frame where they should root within a month. Long stems can be layered, burying them in the soil to produce their own set of roots, and fresh seed can be sown in a cold frame, but note that the shoots will not appear until the following spring.

FATSIA
Fatsia

The frost-hardy, evergreen *F. japonica* is often grown as a houseplant because it is not completely hardy, but it also

Eucalyptus gunnii

Fagus sylvatica 'Dawyck Purple'

Fatsia japonica

Ficus carica

Forsythia

Fuchsia 'Swingtime'

makes an excellent show in the garden in a protected, sunny corner, where it produces huge, deeply cut leaves, up to 30cm (12in) wide, like a giant spread-eagled hand. Growth can easily get above 2.4m (8ft) and wide, and there is an abundance of cream-white autumn flowers. The taller it gets the smaller the leaves become, so it is worth occasionally cutting it right back to generate new, vigorous stems. 'Aurea' has gold variegations, and they will brighten up a semi-shady site, though it is not as vigorous as the species. While you can propagate by air layering and seed, summer cuttings give the quickest results.

FICUS
Fig
Deciduous common figs (*F. carica* and its many cultivars) can be grown for two reasons, because of their huge, architectural leaves – they can easily reach 24cm (10in) long – and their extremely tasty fruit. Make sure you choose

the right variety for your area because some, like 'Black Ischia', need long, hot summers to produce the fruit with deep red flesh, being ideally grown against a sunny wall, or in a greenhouse for cold-climate areas, while others, like 'Brown Turkey', are ideal for countries with cooler climates. To get fruit while the trees are still small, grow figs in large tubs or pits in the ground, about 60cm (2ft) wide and deep, with the sides lined by slabs of patio paving and broken bricks in the bottom to let the water sluice through. When growth gets out of hand the branches can be cut back, but wear rubber gloves, because the sticky sap sticks to the hand like glue. Pick off and discard the unripened fruit in early autumn (the easiest way is to rub a broom up and down the tree to knock them off). Fig trees can be pruned twice a year, in spring and summer. In mid-spring, when there are no more frosts, cut for shape and, in

summer, nip out the shoot tips when six leaves have formed to encourage embryo figs to form. The first crop is the one that ripens, with the tiny pea-like buds that hang on over winter needing a long summer to ripen. The midsummer crop will not have time to ripen in cold climates and gets removed. Propagate by spring cuttings, and let them root at just under 15°C (59°F).

FORSYTHIA
Forsythia
The hardy, mainly deciduous forsythias make lovely shrubs or hedges for cottage gardens with bare, vertical branches being covered in a mass of tiny, bright yellow flowers before the leaves open. Give them average soil in full sun or light, dappled shade. Heights vary from 1.8m (6ft) to twice that in the case of *F. giraldiana*. Cut back to strong buds after flowering, and tangled clumps can be thinned out. Any lengthy trimmings can be used

to prop up floppy perennials. Propagating is easy. You can layer stems, bending young, supple growth down to the ground, wounding them, burying them, and waiting for the roots to develop before severing the layers from the parent. Or take summer or autumn cuttings, letting them develop in a cold frame.

FUCHSIA
Fuchsia
There are many colours and sizes of fuchsia. Some are best grown in hanging baskets and containers, being brought indoors in winter because they are too tender to survive outside in the cold and wet, others being hardy enough to survive outside, though even they can get cut back by frosts, with new shoots emerging from lower down in the spring. To guarantee this happens, plant the outdoor kind slightly deeper and mulch around them in winter. Most flower relentlessly over summer, into autumn, given good conditions. Besides the flamboyantly showy kind, others make good flowering hedges. *F.* 'Riccartonii' can get over head high and over 1.2m (4ft) wide, a mass of twiggy growth with small red and purple flowers. Since it is not completely hardy, it can be dug up and kept in a pot in a protected site over winter, as can the even taller *F. magellanica* from Chile, hitting a maximum of 3m (10ft) high and wide. What it hates most is the winter wet, so if being left outside make sure it is in free-draining, light soil. All fuchsias can easily be propagated by taking spring or summer cuttings.

TAKING FORSYTHIA CUTTINGS

1 Find a vigorous shoot from the current season's growth. Remove it, leaving the bottom cut just below a node where the roots will appear.

2 Use a scalpel to slice away all the lower leaves, leaving a long clean stem. The total length should be about 10cm (4in).

3 When planted up hardwood cuttings go into a cold frame; those taken earlier need a propagating lid to increase the humidity.

GARRYA
Garrya

G. elliptica is a frost-tender evergreen shrub. It makes a tough, upright hedge, over 3m (10ft) high and wide, that comes to life over winter when it is liberally covered with dangling pale grey-green catkins, about 15cm (6in) long, 'James Roof' giving catkins up to twice as long. When the winter show is over, the shrubs can be trimmed for shape. They can look rather dull over summer and need a good show of perennials at the base to liven things up. They need good sun and free-draining ground, and a sheltered position away from cold winds. Take summer cuttings and they will quickly root, or bend supple youngish growth down to the ground, where it can be rooted and layered.

HAMAMELIS
Witch hazel

Deciduous hardy shrubs, the best being grown for their scented, spidery flowers in yellow, orange or red that open on the bare, stiff branches over winter. Worth cutting the flowers for the scent and bringing indoors. The second attraction is the autumn colour. The witch hazels are completely unfussy, and just need a sunny position (possibly with some shade), but space is the priority because they form sizeable shrubs, in the case of the Chinese witch hazel (*H. mollis*) and *H. × intermedia*

Garrya elliptica 'James Roof'

Hamamelis x intermedia

4m (12ft) high and wide. The Japanese witch hazel (*H. japonica*) is a similar size, with 'Sulphurea' giving a profusion of delicate flowers, while 'Zuccariniana' has good orange-yellow autumn foliage. Propagate by spring cuttings and help them root by providing about 16–18°C (61–64°F) of bottom heat, or layer the youngish stems by bending them down to the soil for rooting.

HEBE
Hebe

The evergreen hebes, most of which are frost-tender or hardy, are smallish, compact, manageable shrubs with small leaves. They are often used like bookends in sheltered, sunny borders with good drainage, or in borders against a sunny wall, though they are equally happy in large pots

Hebe

and rock gardens. They can easily be trimmed to a shapely oval. In mild gardens they can be grown as mini hedges or divisions, and stand out when flowering in white, pink, purple, red or blue. Choose wisely and you can have one in flower from late spring to autumn. If giving a prune in late spring or summer, use the 8cm (3in) long trimmings as cuttings. When overwintering, make sure that the cold frame is well ventilated, propping open the lid, to prevent outbreaks of mildew.

HEDERA
Ivy

There is a massive choice of evergreen climbers. You can train them into trees, over fences, and up walls, and even as topiary (over a frame) using one of the *canariensis* types or the American

Hedera helix 'Pittsburgh'

H. helix 'Pittsburgh' or 'Glacier'. Plant three stems around a vertical post and when they are, say, 1.2m (4ft) high, fix half a hanging basket frame on top of the post and weave the shoots through it, pinching them out, creating a bushy head. As leaves appear on top, strip off the leaves up the stem. The best thing about ivies is that they are multi-talented. For rockeries try the tiny 'Spetchley', 15–20cm (6–8in) high, with a leaf the size of a fingernail. The *colchica* and *canariensis* types have great big hand-size leaves. *H. helix* sprints 18m (60ft) and survives -15°C (5°F). Silvery *H. hibernica* 'Maculata' thrives in shade. 'Melanie' has a coppery red edging strip. 'Minty' has mottled shades of green, from lime to olive. To cover a hideous eyesore, you will

TAKING GARRYA CUTTINGS

1 Take a summer cutting, removing it with a clean cut just below a node. If there is too much of a snag left at the bottom, trim it off.

2 Then work up from the base, snipping off the leaves all the way up, but leave a decent cluster of leaves at the very top.

3 Finally, dab the end in rooting powder and give it a quick tap to dislodge the excess, and then plant in cuttings compost (soil mix).

need quick-growing, large-leaved *H. helix* 'Maple Leaf' or the bright green 'Parsley Crested'. Ivy sits quiet, goes rampant, does whatever you want. The flowers attract butterflies such as Red Admirals and Camberwell Beauties, Holly-Blues lay their eggs in it, birds nest in it, and if you've ever grown ivy near an open window, on a warm autumn day you will know about the zillions of wasps on the flowers as the days get shorter. A fast-growing plant, the cuttings (especially those taken early in the growing season) are also quick to take, but if you need a large batch of new plants to cover a wall, serpentine layering also gives very good results.

HYDRANGEA

There are two popular hardy, deciduous kinds, *H. anomola* subsp. *petiolaris* and the border hydrangeas, the lacecaps and mopheads. The first is a sturdy, woody climber that is capable of sprinting across and covering a 15m (50ft) high wall, though it can also be grown without any support as a shrubby bush. Grow it in sun or shade and you will get rich green leaves with large clusters of cream-white flowers for a short spell in summer. Excess growth can be pruned back. It is a very different plant from the summer-flowering *H. macrophylla*, which divides into the lacecaps (with flat heads of

flowers) and mopheads (spherical clusters) that can get up to 1.5m (5ft) high. Both have their colours affected by the soil; if it is acid the flowers will be blue, while on other soils they will be pink. The whites are unaffected by soil chemistry and stay white. Provide dappled shade to prevent any scorching, while pruning helps maintain a good show of flowers; if old clumps become overcrowded, prune them by one-third, and cut back the remaining stems to a strong pair of buds. The deciduous *H. paniculata* gets up to 6m (20ft) high and produces large clusters of late summer flowers up to 30cm (12in) long, being ideal for the back of the border. Give it plenty of space to flop, especially after heavy rain, or put supports in position. Propagate the climbing hydrangea by layering a young stem at the base of the plant, bending it down to the soil to let it root; cuttings can be tricky, but they're no problem with the rest. They quickly root, and the young plants need to have their tops pinched out to generate lots of bushy growth from lower down.

HYPERICUM
St. John's wort

A huge genus, with trees and shrubs (and even annuals), two of the most popular being the semi-evergreen shrubs 'Hidcote' and 'Rowallane'. They're happy in sun or light shade in average soil. The

Always check the likely eventual growth against the available space, and make sure that they tally. Also, check how much shade they will cast, and which sun-loving plants might need to be moved.

hardy 'Hidcote' produces plenty of thick, bushy growth, with an excellent covering of bright yellow set through the second half of summer against the dark green leaves. The more sheltered the site, the more it will hang on to its leaves over winter. It will fit into most borders, growing 1.2m (4ft) high and wide, while 'Rowallane' is taller and thinner at 1.8m (6ft) by 90cm (3ft), flowering slightly later in late summer and autumn. It is slightly more tender and needs a sheltered, sunny site. Do not leave it in an open exposed position where it will get killed by the cold. The best way to propagate is by seed or cuttings. Short cuttings, 7.5cm (3in) long, taken any time from the end of spring, through summer, give good results.

HYSSOPUS
Hyssop

A short shrub, just 60cm (2ft) high and 90cm (3ft) wide, *H. officinalis* is a terrific herb that comes into its own in the second half of summer with a mass of spikes of dark blue flowers. Both flowers and leaves can be used in the kitchen (but avoid if pregnant). Give it wall-to-wall sun and good drainage (for example in gravel or Mediterranean-type

gardens) and it will make miniature hedges to divide the different beds, with the added bonus that the flowers are a magnet to butterflies and bees. The growth can be easily kept in shape preventing it from becoming too shaggy by giving it a light spring clip with shears. The white form is *H. o.* f. *albus*, and *H. o.* 'Roseus' is pink. Use the chopped leaves in salads, soups and stews. Either collect seed and sow it fresh in autumn, standing the pots in a cold frame, or take cuttings in summer for quicker results.

Hydrangea macrophylla

Hypericum 'Hidcote'

Hyssopus officinalis

ILEX
Holly

Excellent evergreen and deciduous bushy shrubs or small trees, they're grown for hedging and topiary, as extremely effective windbreaks and tough, spiky boundary plants for keeping out intruders. Heights vary enormously from the giants at 15–25m (50–80ft) high to the miniatures at 60cm (2ft). The berry colours also vary from red to orange, black and yellow, or occasionally white. If growing a holly hedge, make sure you have a mix of male and female plants, unless you have a self-pollinator, to guarantee a good show of berries. The plant's name can be downright misleading because *I. aquifolium* 'Silver Queen', for example, is a male, while *I. altaclerensis* 'Golden King' is female. Always check before buying. *I. aquifolium* 'J.C. Van Tol' is a very good self-pollinator that sidesteps the issue and grows 5.4m (18ft) high with thick clusters of bright red berries. In all cases opt for young plants because large, well-established ones do not transplant well. They might look initially impressive, but a younger plant will soon overtake a taller one that will just waste time sulking. The variegated kind does best in sun (the moment you see a branch with any all-green leaves, cut it back before the whole plant reverts to all-green), while others can be grown in light shade. Sow fresh autumn berries, extracting the seed from the pith before sowing.

TAKING JASMINUM CUTTINGS

1 One long length of the growth of a new jasmine can be sliced up into several cuttings. Lay them down and plan where to make the cuts.

2 Take internodal cuts, meaning you do not cut off the bottom just below a node, but make the cut about half way between two nodes.

3 Treat the bottoms (given an angular cut to distinguish them from the top ends) with rooting powder, and plant up in a seed tray.

Cover with grit and stand pots in a cold frame, and be prepared to wait five months or so for germination. Alternatively, take cuttings when the leaves have darkened and lost their pale green look, especially at the tip of the cutting, to facilitate good rooting.

JASMINUM
Jasmine

From the wide selection of shrubs and climbers, two are essential, the hardy winter (*J. nudiflorum*) and frost-tender common jasmine (*J. officinale*). The first is an excellent wall shrub, growing 3m (10ft) high and wide, producing bright green arching stems that will need tying in to keep their heads up with their bright yellow winter flowers. It is very different from the summer-flowering, sweetly scented common jasmine that climbs and sprints up any kind of support. Use it to cover arches in full sun where it will twist and twine to the top, making 9m (30ft) of rampant growth, spurting out in all directions, though it can be easily cut back and controlled. Alternatively, grow it up a trellis (free-standing or attached to a wall), into tall, thin, twiggy, evergreen shrubs so that its flowering heads burst through them, or up and over pergolas. Make sure that it is growing in a sunny sheltered site so that the extraordinary scent hangs in the air. Either bend young, flexible stems down to the ground for layering, letting them root where they are buried, or take summer cuttings; if the cuttings are too long, opt for internodal ones.

JUNIPERUS
Juniper

The hardy, evergreen junipers come in all shapes and sizes, from the 30cm (1ft) high *J. horizontalis* to the 5m (15ft) tall, 30cm (1ft) wide spire of *J. communis* 'Hibernica'. It is a selection of a larger conifer (the species can reach 6m/20ft high), and is a garden designer's dream because it can be used to make exclamation marks, to delineate avenues, to flank vistas and features, and to contrast with rounder, blobbier shapes. Provide bright sun and average soil, including free-draining chalk. To propagate, take hardwood cuttings in autumn, and raise in a cold frame.

KALMIA
Kalmia

The hardy, evergreen *K. latifolia* and its many cultivars offer decent-sized shrubs – the species parent is 3m (10ft) high and wide, though others are just one-third of that – liberally covered with clusters of pink or white flowers. They make a big, showy attraction in the first half of summer, bursting with colour in full sun or light shade on acid soil, being a useful part of a mixed boundary hedge. In the second part of summer use the dark green leaves as a foil for white perennials in an adjacent border. The bendy, near-ground-level stems can be

Ilex aquifolium

Jasminum officinale

Juniperus communis

layered, bending them over so that they can develop a root system in the soil, though you can also take late spring and early summer cuttings.

KERRIA
Kerria

A one-species genus, there is just the deciduous *K. japonica* and its handful of forms that thrive in average soil in sun or light shade. 'Pleniflora' is the most popular, putting on vigorous 3m (10ft) of growth upwards and sideways; it makes an explosion of yellow through mid- and late spring. 'Picta' is the variegated form with white-edged leaves that is still sometimes sold as 'Variegata'. All need plenty of space, and not just for the mass of twiggy growth, because they are prolific suckering plants which means they are best planted as part of a boundary hedge, or in a wild or cottage garden. Take greenwood cuttings and let them grow in a cold frame, or scrape back a sucker and use that as a rooted cutting.

KOLKWITZIA
Beauty bush

A large, erupting mass of pink flowers, the hardy, deciduous and virtually indestructible *K. amabilis* makes a big impact in the second half of spring into early summer, with 'Pink Cloud' giving an even better show. The long, thin stems make a substantial shrub – easily reaching 3m (10ft) high and wide – that you can weave other climbers through, including clematis and jasmine, and if it

Kerria japonica

Kolkwitzia amabilis

Laburnum x watereri 'Vossii'

threatens to be too vigorous it can be easily cut back. No matter how hard you prune, it always responds with quick-growing new shoots. It thrives in full sun and average, quick-draining soil, and can be grown against a house wall, giving the climbers a leg up, or in a wild or cottage garden. Any suckers can be promptly removed or used to create new plants, scraping back the soil to check that they have rooted before severing them. Also take greenwood cuttings in early summer, though finding a non-flowering shoot might be difficult.

LABURNUM
Golden rain

Hardy, deciduous laburnums are quite modest trees until it comes to late spring when they erupt in a magical burst of yellow flowers. They can either be grown as stand-alone features in a lawn, or be trained to make tunnels and

arbours (with *L. × watereri* 'Vossii' being one of the best) so that you can walk beneath the long dangling bunches of yellow flowers. The tallest trees are about 8m (25ft) high, with a similar width, but if you want a smaller version try *L. alpinum* 'Pendulum' because it is just 1.8m (6ft) high and wide. All like average, free-draining soil. While you can propagate by seed and grafting, greenwood cuttings are easily taken and give good results.

LAVANDULA
Lavender

The shrubby, evergreen, not reliably hardy lavenders – about 60–90cm (2–3ft) high and wide – need a hot, sunny site and average soil that must be very free draining, making them ideal for gravel or Mediterranean-type gardens. The colours range from pink to pale blue and purple, and they work well in drifts or long

lines – for example running beside a path so that they half flop over it, obscuring any edges, while attracting butterflies and bees and releasing a delicious scent – and as mini hedges and garden dividers. *H. angustifolia* and its many forms, including the popular 'Hidcote' with dark purple flowers standing out against the grey leaves, make a reliable show, as does the much more striking (but less hardy) French lavender (*L. stoechas*), because its flowers have purple bracts that stick up like rabbits' ears. Individual plants can also be grown in containers for standing out in the summer sun, and moving to a sheltered site over winter if necessary. Give a light clip all over in spring but never cut back into the old wood. Take summer or hardwood autumn cuttings, using a heel from late summer on. Long, bendy, youngish stems can be used for layering.

Lavandula stoechas

TAKING LAVANDULA CUTTINGS

1 Remove the top 8cm (3in) of a new vigorous shoot in early summer, and then trim the base just below a node, where the roots will appear.

2 Dab the ends in rooting powder and plant up in free-draining cuttings compost (soil mix) with grit to facilitate good drainage.

3 When they are putting on good growth, plant them out. Use a long wooden board to create a straight row when planting a lavender hedge.

Lavatera thuringiaca

Leptospermum scoparium 'Lyndon'

Leycesteria formosa

Ligustrum lucidum

LAVATERA
Mallow

The evergreen, shrubby mallows (many frost-tender) have prolific displays of hollyhock-type summer flowers on generous, bushy growth that is ideal for cottage gardens. 'Burgundy Wine' is fairly typical, producing scores of dark pink flowers on bendy, arching growth, but if it ever gets walloped by heavy snow carefully brush it off quickly or the branches can easily get broken. Grow it in full sun where there is good drainage for a continuous show of summer flowers. There are also purple, pale pink and white shrubby lavateras. Many easily get 1.8m (6ft) and higher, and while they start to look like a permanent garden feature they can suddenly fail, being short-lived, and it is sensible to propagate new plants after their fifth year in case of a sudden calamity. Summer cuttings root quickly and easily, but keep them well protected in their first few winters; you can also layer by bending a low stem down to the ground.

LEPTOSPERMUM
Tea tree

The half-hardy, evergreen New Zealand tea tree (*L. scoparium*) is a shrub, not a tree, and has scores of forms (none of which are hardy) with the most widely available being the excellent 'Red Damask'. It needs a large space because it gets 3m (10ft) high and wide, and gets summer off to a lively start with its dark red flowers. Make sure it has a sunny,

sheltered position – for example in a sunny courtyard – because it is half-hardy and will not survive freezing temperatures. If growing one of the smaller forms, such as the 90cm (3ft) high and wide 'Kiwi' in a container, give it a light trim after flowering to generate more flowering growth. Take semi-ripe late summer cuttings, and make sure that the young plants are well protected in winter.

LESPEDEZA
Bush clover

The hardy, shrubby, deciduous *L. thunbergii* is one of the best autumn plants, giving sizeable, vigorous growth reaching a good 1.8m (6ft) high, with an even greater spread, that is covered with dark pink, pea-like flowers. It gets cut back over winter and is frustratingly slow into growth next spring, but then quickly produces a thicket of arching

stems with attractive, bluish-green leaves. It needs plenty of sun and free-draining soil that does not stay cold and wet over winter. Propagate by taking late spring softwood and early summer greenwood cuttings.

LEYCESTERIA
Leycesteria

The hardy, deciduous Himalayan honeysuckle (*L. formosa*) makes 1.8m (6ft) of cluttered, chunky growth, vertically and sideways, for a cottage or wild garden. It catches the eye through summer, into autumn, when the spikes of dark purple bracts and white petals appear in dangling clusters. In very mild winters or sheltered gardens it will hold on to its leaves, otherwise they will quickly drop, but the green stems do provide some attraction. Congested thickets can be easily thinned in spring by cutting back some of the stems to ground

level. Propagate either by using fresh seed in autumn, or more quickly by taking summer or hardwood autumn cuttings.

LIGUSTRUM
Privet

These plants might once have been over-used, but privets remain first-rate shrubs, many providing dense, thick evergreen growth that is ideal for a hedge. When given a smart trim it creates a bright green wall. *L. ovalifolium* is the most popular choice, and it will grow 4m (12ft) high and wide if left alone, but it can be easily cut back to give a head-high barrier. If not clipped, the midsummer burst of white flowers is followed by tiny black berries. Alternative forms have leaves variegated in white or yellow. Though it is sometimes grown in shade, it responds best to full sun and moderately fertile soil. If you just need a few new plants, then layer

TAKING LIGUSTRUM CUTTINGS

1 Take cuttings from early summer to mid-winter, nipping them off just below a node. If there is a long snag left at the base, slice it off.

2 If the tip of the cutting, which should be about 10cm (4in) long, is still on the soft side, slice it off with a sharp knife or pinch out.

3 Strip the lower leaves off the bottom of the stem, leaving a long, bare leg, and plant up. Hardwood cuttings go straight in a cold frame.

the low, bendy stems, pulling them down to root in the soil. If you need to create more plants, say for a hedge, then take 45cm (18in) long autumn hardwood cuttings and strip leaves up the bottom half. Then plant in weed-free rows, water well and make sure that the cuttings are given good drinks during dry spells the following summer. When they have taken, nip off their heads to promote bushy growth. Take extra cuttings in case of any failures. You may find that one or two cuttings lag behind and do not grow at the same rate as the rest, and they can be replaced with the best reserves.

LIQUIDAMBAR
Liquidambar

The large, maple-like leaves of liquidambars provide sensational autumn colour. They blowtorch rich reds, yellows and oranges, and their large size makes them quite unmissable. The hardy, deciduous sweet gum (*L. styraciflua*), a giant at 25m (80ft) high and 12m (40ft) wide, has many excellent forms, with 'Lane Roberts' and 'Worpledon' making an excellent show. The former stands out with dark red leaves verging on black in autumn, making a good contrast with the blast of orange-yellow on the latter. For a tall, thin liquidambar, try *L. orientalis*, which grows 6m (20ft) high and 4m (12ft) wide. Propagate by early summer greenwood cuttings, or if possible bend a young stem to the ground for layering in autumn.

LAYERING LONICERA

1 Layering does not have to be done in open ground. When dormant, nick the stem below a node, lift the bark, and dab on rooting powder.

2 Bend this wounded section down to a pot filled with compost (soil mix), and pin it in place under the soil, so that it cannot work free.

3 Insert a cane to train the end of the stem up. When the wounded part has finally rooted, it can be severed from the parent.

LIRIODENDRON
Tulip tree

A massive, deciduous, hardy tree, *L. tulipifera* can grow a whopping 30m (100ft) high in ideal conditions, with a spread of 15m (50ft). It gets its common name from the small, tulip-like, pale green flowers, though one of the best features is the autumn show when the leaves fizz yellow. Winter is not dull though, because the exposed bark is silver-grey. 'Aureomarginatum' is a good variation because the leaves have a gold edge, while 'Fastigiatum' provides a tall, thinnish shape, though you will still need room for its 18m (60ft) height and 6m (20ft) width. You can propagate by seed and grafting (essential in the case of 'Fastigiatum', which requires

a whip graft), but midsummer cuttings are the easiest, quickest option for the species.

LONICERA
Honeysuckle

This plant offers a terrific range of shrubs and climbers. The best shrubby kinds (for average soil in full sun) can be used for evergreen hedging and topiary, for divisions and knot gardens, with *L. nitida* 'Baggesen's Gold' – 1.5m (5ft) high and wide – being top of the list because of its tight, dense, bushy growth and small yellow leaves. If this or the species is left it can get very ragged, so give a regular summer trimming to keep them smart. The larger *L. fragrantissima* holds on to some leaves in a mild position, and is essential for the winter garden, when little else is out, because it has sweetly scented white flowers. Grow it against a sunny, sheltered wall where it should exceed head height, making a spread of 2.7m (9ft). For low-growing groundcover, *L. pileata* gets just 60cm (2ft) high while spreading 1.8m (6ft) and more, blocking out any weeds. It has late spring white flowers and violet berries. The best of the richly scented thornless climbers are easily trained into trees or against a trellis, or they can be allowed to flop. All need sun or partial shade and moist, rich, well-drained soil. The strongly scented early Dutch

honeysuckle (*L. periclymenum* 'Belgica') gets 6m (20ft) high, and is smothered in mid-spring red flowers. The mild daytime scent doubles in strength in the evening. Late Dutch honeysuckle (*L. p.* 'Serotina') starts flowering in early summer and has cream-white blooms with reddish streaks. Follow this up with the Japanese honeysuckle (*L. japonica* 'Halliana') with its pale cream summer flowers, turning darker yellow before they fade, while 'Horwood Gem' has young foliage stippled with cream. There are many more richly coloured honeysuckles, though not all are strongly scented. Propagate the shrubs and climbers by taking spring, summer or autumn cuttings, or by layering stems, bending them to the ground.

Liquidambar styraciflua

Liriodendron tulipifera

Lonicera periclymenum

LUPINUS
Tree lupin

A large, imposing American shrub, *L. arboreus* makes a good alternative to annual and perennial lupins, getting 1.8m (6ft) high and wide, with vigorous, semi-evergreen, but not reliably hardy growth. The spikes of blue flowers appear at the end of spring and summer, and it will thrive given a mild, sunny, well-protected site with free-draining soil. The better the winter conditions, the more likely it will hold on to its leaves. The only possible setback is that it will die out after four years, which means you need to take replacement cuttings in summer. However, you should find scores of young seedlings around the parent plant, in which case simply pot up those required, and grow them as possible replacements, making sure they are kept well protected in their first few winters.

MAGNOLIA
Magnolia

There is a huge range of first-rate hardy, deciduous and evergreen magnolias (trees and shrubs) to choose from, the most popular being those with thick, fleshy, spring flowers, many richly scented. You can grow them as feature plants, given a prominent place in a lawn where they can be underplanted with spreading bulbs, but they are extremely vulnerable to vicious spring weather when winds and rain can ruin their short burst of flowers. It is safer to provide a sunny, sheltered position, though if the

TAKING OSMANTHUS CUTTINGS

1 Take cuttings over summer, possibly with a heel. Make the cut using a sharp knife just below a node, where the roots appear.

2 Then strip off the lower leaves, leaving a bare leg at the base, and then slice the larger leaves in half to avoid excess transpiration.

3 Dip the cut edges in a fungicide, then dab the base of the cutting with rooting compound. Plant in free-draining compost (soil mix).

weather turns bad there is nothing much you can do. Alternatively grow the early summer flowering, richly scented deciduous *M. × wieseneri* that flowers slightly later in the first part of summer. It is a multi-stemmed large shrub or small tree, about 6m (20ft) high and 5m (15ft) wide. It will grow on light and heavy soil, and needs full sun. Propagate by taking early summer, greenwood cuttings (take semi-ripe cuttings of evergreens). Nip out the growing tip to induce quicker rooting. Alternatively layer low, bendy stems and check that they have rooted after 12 months, when they can be severed from the parent.

MAHONIA
Mahonia

The evergreen, sizeable, shrubby mahonias (many hardy, others requiring a well-protected, sheltered, sunny site) are essential winter shrubs getting about

1.8m (6ft) high and wide. They generate glossy green foliage, and in the case of *M. × media* have 40cm (16in) long incredibly striking composite leaves that really grab the eye. Bright yellow, strongly scented flower spikes 30cm (12in) long appear in winter. *M. × m.* 'Buckland' and 'Lionel Fortescue' are two of the best, adding plenty of presence to the cottage or wild garden, or for growing against a wall with perennials and bulbs in the foreground. Make sure that they are grown in full sun, so that the rich green leaves and bright yellow flowers stand out. They like rich, moist soil. Propagate the suckering kind by scraping back the soil to check when the suckers have rooted, and then sever from the parent. Otherwise take semi-ripe or hardwood cuttings. Raise in a cold frame until large enough to be planted out.

METASEQUOIA
Dawn redwood

If you really want to impress the neighbours, grow a hardy dawn redwood, though you will probably have to cut it down before it reaches its maximum height of 30m (100ft). A deciduous conifer, it shoots up, and is covered with beautiful soft, spongy, orange bark. Discovered in the 1940s, it is now an essential ingredient in botanic gardens. It is easily propagated using a spring cutting, but it will need some bottom heat in a propagator to ensure a decent batch of roots within about 10 weeks.

MYRTUS
Myrtle

The tenderish, evergreen common myrtle (*M. communis*) gives a bushy block of arching growth covered in glossy green leaves, which are quite aromatic when crushed. There is a good covering

Magnolia 'Iolanthe'

Mahonia x media 'Charity'

Metasequoia glyptostroboides

Myrtus communis

of white flowers at the end of summer, into autumn, followed by small blackish berries. Coming from the Mediterranean it needs a mild climate, with long, hot summers and winter protection keeping it away from icy winds, with very good drainage. If it stands in cold, sopping wet soil all winter it will die. At 2.4m (8ft) high and wide it needs a large space, but *M. c.* subsp. *tarentina* grows 1.5m (5ft) high and wide, with much smaller leaves, and has pinkish-cream flowers and white berries. 'Microphylla Variegata' has white-edged leaves. Propagate by taking late summer or autumn cuttings for rooting in a cold frame.

OLEARIA
Daisy bush
The most commonly grown form is *O.* × *haastii*, a hardy, evergreen shrub that makes a very chunky 1.8m (6ft) of vertical growth and

a spread of 3m (10ft). In summer it is liberally covered from head to toe in clusters of small, white, daisy-like flowers. One of its big advantages is that it tolerates salty coastal winds, which is why it is often grown as a seaside windbreak. It also has a two-tone leaf colour with the tops being dark green, and the undersides silver-grey, giving a good effect when ruffled by the wind. If it gets too big, or shoots beyond its allotted space, cut it back as much as you like and it will quickly regrow. To thrive, it needs endless sun and excellent drainage. Propagate by taking summer cuttings; pot them up and keep in a cold frame.

OSMANTHUS
Osmanthus
The hardy, evergreen *O.* × *burkwoodii* and *O. delavayi* make large attractive shapes for large borders, and also fine hedges. The former gets 3m (10ft) high and wide and stands out with its glossy green leaves liberally covered with clusters of scented white flowers through the second half of spring. It can even be topiarized, responding well to clipping and pruning, as does the latter. Potentially growing twice as tall, with a 4m (12ft) span, it too has glossy leaves and a prodigious show of scented white flowers. Both need a sunny position with some wind protection on exposed sites. When propagating, layer the lowest flexible stems, letting them root in the ground, or take summer cuttings.

Osmanthus delavayi

PAEONIA
Tree peony
Completely unlike the herbaceous perennial peonies, the multi-branching, shrubby, hardy, deciduous tree peonies (*P. delavayi* and *P. suffruticosa*) from China can grow a good 1.8m (6ft) tall, spreading 1.2m (4ft) or 2.2m (7ft) respectively. They are ideal for the back of the border, or for growing beside a path where you can get a good look at them. The late spring and early summer flowers of *P. delavayi* are bowls of dark red, while the cultivars of *P. suffruticosa* offer white, pink, red and reddish mauve. They need gentle pampering, requiring good sun in a sheltered position with rich, moist soil. If the plants are getting rather long, leggy and bare, they can be pruned for shape after flowering. Propagate by semi-ripe, late summer cuttings, keeping them well protected the first winter.

Passiflora caerulea

PASSIFLORA
Passion flower
The mostly evergreen climbing passifloras look incredibly exotic, and while some need to be grown in conservatories because they need a minimum temperature of 5°C (41°F), a few can be grown outdoors to produce great clusters of amazing flowers followed by egg-shaped fruits. *C. caerulea* is frost-tender and will thrive in a sunny site where there is plenty of support for its possible maximum 9m (30ft) of growth. Given protection from cold winds (without which it will lose its leaves) and excellent drainage, it can mound over a fence or pergola, piling up its 7.5cm (3in) wide white, blue and purple flowers. A thick winter mulch will help protect the roots in cold climates. Propagating by seed can be tricky; instead take spring or summer cuttings and they will quickly root.

Olearia x haastii

Paeonia delavayi

Paulownia tomentosa

Perovskia 'Blue Spire'

Philadelphus coronarius

PAULOWNIA
Foxglove tree
This type of tree includes a small group of species from East Asia. There are two good reasons for growing the hardy, deciduous *P. tomentosa*. The first is the flowers, and they do look like those on a foxglove, with a faint whiff of violets. The second is the chance to cut down the main stem, getting rid of all the potential top growth – and it is capable of making a large 12m (40ft) high specimen that gets 10m (30ft) wide – which will result in bigger leaves, up to 90cm (3ft) across. Full sun is essential, as is rich soil with good drinks in hot, dry spells. Give it a prominent position so it can be admired, among other large-leaved exotics, but make sure it is sheltered or whipping summer winds will ruin the effect, flaying the foliage. Take 5cm (2in) long root cuttings in the

first part of winter, and lay them in pots of cuttings compost (soil mix) to produce shoots in the spring.

PEROVSKIA
Perovskia
The hardy, shrubby, deciduous perovskia adds a soft, light, airy touch to late summer borders with its perky spikes of soft blue flowers and grey-green leaves. The popular choices are *P. atriplicifolia*, and *P.* 'Blue Spire', which has the added attraction of blue-grey leaves. They are remarkably adaptable, growing in average soil, though it must be free draining. To encourage plenty of flowering growth the following year, cut it back when the flowering has finished and vigorous new growth will fire up the following spring. The height rarely gets above 1.2m (4ft). Propagate by taking spring or summer cuttings, and they will quickly root.

PHILADELPHUS
Mock orange
Absolutely essential hardy, mainly deciduous shrubs, the best have a powerfully sweet scent when they flower in the first part of summer. Dot them around the garden and the scent should waft everywhere. If there is room for just one – and allow approximately 1.8m (6ft) of growth and width, though some can get much bigger – make sure it has got a sunny corner where the scent can hang in the air. Average soil is fine. By removing some of the stems each year, after flowering, you will help keep generating new flowering growth, thus making the plant constantly replace itself. You can also propagate new plants by taking cuttings, virtually any time from spring to autumn; the more you take, the higher the chances that you will get plenty of successes, and the more scent

you can pack into the garden. When sowing, collect fresh autumn seed and give it a two-month chilling in the refrigerator. Germination can take 10 weeks or longer.

PHLOMIS
Phlomis
From the long list of possibles, most nurseries stick to the hardy, evergreen *P. fruticosa* and *P. russeliana*. The latter is the hardier of the two (*P. fruticosa* only just qualifies), and has a concentrated burst in early summer (with more before and after) of pale yellow flowers at intermittent intervals up each vertical spike. The former, also called Jerusalem sage, has yellow flowers set against the grey-green leaves. Both are good ingredients in a gravel or Mediterranean-type garden where there is heat, shelter and good drainage, with average soil. If space is an issue, *P. russeliana*

TAKING PHILADELPHUS CUTTINGS

1 The 10cm (4in) long cuttings are easily taken from late spring to autumn; look for a vigorous shoot, and sever it just below a node.

2 Using a sharp knife, slice off the leaves flush with the main stem to leave a bare leg and a batch of leaves on the top quarter.

3 Finally, quickly dab the base of the leg in rooting powder, give a shake and then pot up. Hardwood cuttings go into a cold frame.

Phlomis fruticosa

is the more compact of the two growing 90cm (3ft) by 75cm (2½ft), while *P. fruticosa* reaches 90cm (3ft) by 1.3m (4½ft). Both can be propagated by taking summer cuttings, and letting them root in a cold frame. When sowing seed, let it germinate at 18°C (65°F), and growth should appear within three weeks.

PHOTINIA
Photinia

Only one photonia has hit the best-selling lists, and that is the not-quite-hardy evergreen *P. × fraseri* 'Red Robin', which became widely available only in the 1960s. It outscores other photinias because of its new spring leaves that are strikingly bright red. It also has small white summer flowers. Over summer the foliage quietens down and turns green, but to boost the burst of red next spring you can cut back some of the stems to generate extra, bushy growth. A good back-of-the-border plant at 5m (15ft) high and wide, or one for a wild garden; alternatively use as a hedge since it offers good privacy, but do not expose it to icy winds or the new foliage will get blasted. Alternatively, use it inside a windbreak, where the conditions are much gentler. Extra plants are easily raised from summer cuttings, but make sure they are rooted in free-draining compost (soil mix). If you want to try a different method, layering young, supple branches by pegging them down to the soil to root also has a high success rate.

Phygelius x rectus

PHYGELIUS
Phygelius

The top choices include the frost-hardy, evergreen, suckering *P. aequalis* 'Yellow Trumpet' and *P. × rectus* 'African Queen', both making growth about 90cm (3ft) high with a spread about 1.2m (4ft). The former has vertical stems and pale yellow flowers, while the latter has orange-red flowers. Both suffer in cold winters, dropping plenty of leaves, and if temperatures dive, then the top growth suffers. Cut it back to generate plenty of replacement growth the following spring. Ideally, provide free-draining soil and a sunny, sheltered site; avoid exposed areas with heavy clay that will quickly prove fatal. Propagate by taking cuttings from spring to autumn, though you can also sow spring seed at 18°C (64°F).

PIERIS
Pieris

The best of the pieris inject flashy leaf colours in spring, and for the rest of the year provide good evergreen cover on large shrubs, requiring virtually no attention. The frost-hardy 'Forest Flame' – a spacious 4m (12ft) by 1.8m (6ft) wide – has a startling covering of bright red spring foliage. Acid soil is *de rigueur*, as is a sheltered, sunny site to avoid attacks from icy winds. If flowers are more important than the spring foliage, then opt for *P. japonica* and its cultivars. They include the short, compact white 'Debutante', which will not get above waist height.

Pieris 'Forest Flame'

Again, acid soil is essential, as is a sheltered position to stop the new leaves getting frosted. To propagate it you can sow seed in spring, and provide a temperature of 17°C (63°F), or take cuttings at any time through the growing season. Layering also produces good results, bending a low flexible stem to the ground and getting it to root in the soil.

PITTOSPORUM
Pittosporum

The top choice is the tender New Zealand bushy shrub *P. tenuifolium* and its many cultivars. Heights are 90cm–3m (3–10ft) and more, but only grow it in mild regions where it makes a bushy evergreen, because it will not thrive in cold climate gardens. The species might flower at the end of spring, when it produces tiny dark red flowers, but for a better display opt for Japanese mock orange (*P. tobira*)

with its good display of scented white flowers. Good cultivars of *P. tenuifolium* include the variegated 'Abbotsbury Gold' and 'Margaret Turnbull'. Both 'Nigricans' and 'Tom Thumb' have bronze foliage, and all make good hedging plants. If they get straggly and need shaping, give them a spring trim. Summer cuttings quickly root in a cold frame, or low stems can be bent to the ground for layering.

PLATANUS
Plane

Deciduous plane trees are incredibly popular in inner cities because they tolerate pollution, and produce long, lean trunks and attractive mottled colours where the bark flakes, revealing patches of cream and grey. They will get very big though, with the hardy London plane (*P. × hispanica*) easily reaching 25m (80ft) high and more. It is very robust, as is the American sycamore (*P. occidentalis*), but that is not widely available and it is not hardy in all areas. The hardy oriental plane (*P. orientalis*) is easily pollarded at the end of winter, being cut back at about head high to send out a batch of thin stems like a magnified version of a porcupine's quills. Once you start pollarding a young tree (it cannot be done on old ones), you have to maintain the regime or the batch of young stems that fire out of the top of the stump will become too heavy. Take semi-ripe cuttings in late summer, and grow them in a cold frame.

Photinia x fraseri 'Red Robin'

Pittosporum tobira

Platanus x hispanica

Populus

COLLECTING PYRACANTHA SEED

1 Collect clusters of the ripe seed in autumn or winter. Only use those in pristine condition and which do not show any signs of rotting.

2 Start to squash each individual seed between finger and thumb, removing most of the flesh. Discard the unwanted husks.

3 Wash in warm water, after which the seed needs a period of three months in moist sand, stored in a refrigerator, to help it germinate.

POPULUS
Poplar

The large, quick-growing hardy poplars need a large garden, with many shooting up to 25m (80ft), and some well above that. Good choices include Lombardy poplar (*P. nigra* 'Italica'), the quaking and common aspens (*P. tremuloides* and *P. tremula*) and the Chinese necklace poplar (*P. lasiocarpa*). The Lombardy has a slender upright shape, with upright branches, but the quaking and common aspens give much better sound effects. The leaf stalks are so slender that the leaves shake and rattle in even the slightest breeze, and the effect is backed up when the foliage turns yellow in the autumn. The common aspen is the shortest of the trio, getting 15m (50ft) high – that is 6m (20ft) shorter than the quaking aspen and about 15m (50ft) shorter than the Lombardy. The Chinese necklace is equally striking, having the largest and thickest poplar leaves. It gets its common name from the long green seed capsules that open up in late summer, scattering the seed on the ground. Autumn hardwood cuttings give the best results, while the suckering kinds, including *P. tremula*, can be propagated by scraping back the soil around the sucker to check that it has rooted, before severing and planting up.

POTENTILLA
Cinquefoil

Besides the perennial potentillas, there are many shrubby ones, the hardy, deciduous *P. fruticosa* being the most popular. It grows a modest 90cm (3ft) high and 1.5m (5ft) wide, and is nicely covered in yellow flowers over a long summer period. There are countless cultivars offering a range of different colours in scarlet, red, pink, yellow, orange, and white, many only available from specialist nurseries. They can be grown to make a multi-coloured hedge, more than making up for the fact that in winter they're reduced to a mass of bare twigs. All like average to rich soil with free drainage in full sun. To bulk up the numbers of potentillas, take summer cuttings. They easily root and give quicker results than plants grown from seed.

PRUNUS
Ornamental cherry

Flowering, deciduous, hardy cherries are the highlight of the year, let alone spring, with the choice divided between the Japanese kind and the rest. There is a huge range of Japanese cherries, most with Japanese-sounding names, and many indistinguishable even to the experts. *P.* 'Amanogawa' is a good choice for most gardens because it is narrow, getting 8m (25ft) high by 4m (12ft) wide. It livens up the garden, having a massive covering of pink flowers on the bare spring branches, and in autumn the foliage turns yellow and red. 'Kiku-shidare-zakura' is even better for modest gardens because it grows just 3.6m (12ft) high and wide, and again has a rich show of pink flowers on its weeping branches. 'Shirotae' has a stronger presence with 6m (20ft) height and a spread of 8m (25ft), is packed with scented white flowers and also gives a lively autumn show when there is a mix of green, orange and red leaves. The Tibetan cherry (*P. serrula*) is not in the same league when it comes to spring blossom but it more than compensates with its extraordinary shiny brown peeling bark. All are fine on average, moist soil in full sun but avoid thin chalk. Propagate by taking early summer greenwood cuttings, providing gentle bottom heat to speed up the rooting process.

PYRACANTHA
Firethorn

The hardy, evergreen pyracanthas can be grown in three ways – as freestanding shrubs, as impenetrable hedges because of their vicious spines, and as wall cover – and all look sensational when covered in their brightly coloured autumn berries. The bright red berrying 'Mohave', 4m (12ft) high and 5m (15ft) wide, can be trained up and around windows when given strong horizontal wires for support, and they will give thick,

Potentilla fruticosa

Prunus 'Amanogawa'

Pyracantha watereri

extensive cover. Others provide bright yellow, orange, and orange-red berries, and when being trained can be easily cut back to maintain their shape. They can also be trained up a system of wires fixed to stout posts, arranged along the back of a border, to give flamboyant colour in autumn. You can propagate by using fresh seed from the berries that needs to be chilled in the refrigerator before sowing in a cold frame in the spring; summer cuttings give quicker results, but they will need some gentle bottom heat to speed up the growth of the roots.

QUERCUS
Oak
With over 100 species and forms, there is a massive choice, so try and visit a specialist nursery to spot the differences. You will need a huge space to accommodate one, with the hardy, deciduous common English oak (*Q. robur*) growing 36m (120ft) high with a 25m (80ft) spread. Smaller oaks are available, with *Q. ilicifolia*, a small tree verging on a shrub, ideal for filling a 6m (20ft) by 5m (15ft) space, with dark green leaves turning reddish-yellow in autumn, and a good show of acorns, but they are only available from a few specialist nurseries. Or try the frost-hardy holm oak (*Q. ilex*) in a sheltered spot — you can topiarize it to give a long bare trunk and a ball of green on top. Acorn-producing oaks do the propagating for you, so just look on the ground

beneath one and then carefully dig up a seedling. Do not damage its roots. Pot it up as often as necessary until it is the right size for planting out.

RHODOCHITON
Rhodochiton
The Mexican tender climber *R. atrosanguineus* is usually grown as an annual or a conservatory plant, and it quickly shoots up 3m (10ft) and fires out stems in all directions, needing a support to latch on to, anything from trellis to horizontal wire attached to stout posts. The small flowers, like upturned ruby red hats or lampshades, contain a long, dangling, rich velvet maroon tube. Provide a sheltered site with some midday shade and it will keep performing right to the end of autumn, until hit by the frosts. Conservatory plants can be cut back to generate more growth from the base. Sow the seed at 19°C (66°F) in spring indoors, and it will quickly shoot up; gradually harden off before planting out.

RHODODENDRON
Rhododendron
Evergreen rhodos come in all shapes and sizes, from miniature shrubs to 6m (20ft) high specimens, with flowering times ranging from mid-winter to midsummer. The hardy hybrids are the most popular, and it is just a case of what fits best in your garden, and which adds most to the colour scheme. 'Polar Bear' is a huge 5m (15ft) high and wide white, 'Blue Peter' is a 3m

Rhus verniciflua

(10ft) high and wide lavender-blue, while 'Ginny Gee' is a 90cm (3ft) high and wide purple-pink. All demand moist, rich, acid soil, and some woodland-like shade and shelter. Do not plant them too deeply because the roots stay close to the surface, which also means that you have to be careful when weeding to avoid causing damage. If you do not have acid soil then use a large container filled with ericaceous compost. The easiest way to propagate is by bending supple young branches down to the ground for layering. The problem with raising rhododendrons from seed is that the plants hybridize, and you will not know exactly what you have raised until it is old enough to flower.

RHUS
Sumach
The prime reason for growing sumachs is the startling autumn colour when the leaves turn

Robinia pseudoacacia

from green to high-voltage orange and red. The most popular is stag's horn sumach (*R. typhina*), a hardy, deciduous shrub or tree with an open network of velvety branches with multiple leaflets growing nearly 60cm (2ft) long. The summer spikes of yellow-green flowers are followed by clusters of hairy deep crimson-red spherical fruits. The whole plant is a modest 5m (15ft) high, with a similar spread, and makes an attractive shape, but you can cut it back if necessary. It suckers freely, but excess numbers can easily be sliced off with a spade and removed. To propagate, just scrape back the soil to check whether a sucker has rooted, and then separate it from the parent.

ROBINIA
False acacia
If you need a bright greenish-yellow shape, about 15m (50ft) high and 8m (25ft) wide, and do not want a conifer, this is the top choice. The leaves of the quick-growing, hardy, deciduous *R. pseudoacacia* 'Frisia' open bright yellow, before quietening down to yellow-green over summer, but come autumn there is a flashpoint of orange-yellow. Provide full sun and average soil. Since this is a suckering tree, propagate by scraping back the soil around a sucker, looking for roots, and then sever the sucker below that point so that it has both top growth and a good set of roots. Alternatively, you can take autumn hardwood cuttings.

Quercus ilex

Rhododendron 'Blue Peter'

Rubus cockburnianus

Sambucus nigra

Sarcococca hookeriana

Skimmia japonica

RUBUS
Ornamental bramble

One of the flashiest brambles, that really stands out in winter, is the hardy, deciduous *R. cockburnianus*. The packed tight, multiple young stems have a white coating, and they make a fun clump in the wild garden. Getting 1.8m (6ft) high and wide, they need a decent space where new shoots can fire out of the ground. To get a continuous supply of the white stems, cut back the old growth each spring leaving just a couple of buds at the base. In spring there is a covering of small purple flowers and inedible berries. Plants thrive in full sun, to pick up the white, and average soil. Propagate by cuttings at any time from spring to autumn. In the case of blackberries, layer plants, bending the low, supple new bendy growth to the ground, where it will quickly root.

SAMBUCUS
Elder

Hardy, deciduous elders belong in cottage or wild gardens where they shoot up and put out unmistakable flat heads of white flowers followed by sprays of tiny black berries. Good varieties include *S. nigra* 'Aurea' because of its yellowish leaves, which really stands out beside 'Guincho Purple' with its dark leaves. Both make a huge spread of 6m (20ft) in height and width, but they can be cut back in early spring to generate plenty of new vigorous growth with nicely coloured leaves. Incredibly unfussy, elder grows just about anywhere in sun or light shade, and in average soil. You can even include it in a wildlife hedge. The best way to propagate (with a high success rate) is by taking hardwood or greenwood cuttings, raising them in a cold frame.

SARCOCOCCA
Christmas box

Two hardy, evergreen shrubs with rich green leaves are *S. confusa* and *S. hookeriana*. The former grows 90cm (3ft) wide and twice as tall, and is high on most people's lists because of the clusters of small, white, scented winter flowers followed by black fruit. It makes a very effective, informal, bushy hedge in a carefree cottage or wildlife garden, and can be given a light trim after flowering to keep it in shape. The latter needs more space, growing 1.5m (5ft) high and 1.8m (6ft) wide, and it also sends up suckers. Again, it has a good covering of scented white winter flowers and berries. *S. hookeriana* is easily propagated by looking for suckers; check that they have rooted, and then sever them from the parent. *S. confusa* can be propagated by taking hardwood cuttings.

SKIMMIA
Skimmia

These hardy, evergreen shrubs, with glossy, rich green leaves, bear white or pink flowers, often opening from red buds, and later (if pollinated) red, black or white berries. To get a female (e.g. *S. japonica* 'Veitchii') to crop, you will need a male ('Rubella'), or instead opt for the bisexual *S. j.* subsp. *reevesiana*, which will pollinate itself. The latter is a sizeable 6m (20ft) high by 90cm (3ft) wide, while the two cultivars can reach 6m (20ft) high and wide. All are vigorous toughies, at their best on rich, acid soil in light shade. They also make good container plants for flanking a focal point, but need regular watering in hot, dry spells. While extra plants can be grown from seed, semi-ripe cuttings give good results, with some gentle bottom heat.

SORBUS
Sorbus

The hardy, deciduous sorbuses make excellent garden trees, with a good range of specimens under 10m (30ft) high, the mountain ashes having very attractive compound leaves consisting of small leaflets. The best sorbuses produce an abundance of small spring flowers followed by striking clusters of dangling, brightly coloured berries through summer and into autumn, adding plenty of panache on misty autumn days. *S. cashmiriana* and *S. hupehensis* – both 8m (25ft) high with a similar spread – have white berries, but if you want

TAKING SAMBUCUS CUTTINGS

1 From spring to winter, select a 10cm (4in) cutting from the new season's growth, nipping it off just below a node with a knife.

2 Strip off all leaves growing up two-thirds of the bottom of the leg, leaving a clean bare length. Remove the leaves flush to the main stem.

3 When planted up hardwood cuttings go into a cold frame; those taken earlier need a propagating lid to increase the humidity.

Sorbus cashmiriana

Stewartia sinensis

Syringa vulgaris

orange-red, go for the slightly taller *S. commixta* 'Joseph Rock', or try *S. sargentiana* in red. As a bonus, many sorbuses have flamboyant autumn leaf colours, especially 'Joseph Rock' – again at 10m (30ft) high, with a spread of 7m (22ft) – that burns purple, orange and red. None are remotely fussy, being happy in sun or light shade, though rich, moist soil gives the best results. Since cuttings can be problematic, remove the seed from the berries at the end of summer and chill it for eight weeks in the refrigerator before sowing at 15°C (60°F) in a propagator. Move seedlings into a cold frame in spring.

SPIRAEA
Spiraea
The hardy, deciduous, quick-growing shrubs make good hedges and border plants, with the smaller compact kind being great for rockeries. Popular forms, all

giving a terrific show of flowers, include cultivars of the chunky, mid- and late summer-flowering *S. japonica*, which grows 1.8m (6ft) high by 1.5m (5ft) wide, and *S. thunbergii* (the same size), for flowering in spring and the start of summer. The cultivars include the dark pink 'Anthony Waterer' and the miniature pink 'Goldflame', just 75cm (2½ft) high, with bronze-tinged young leaves that then go flashy yellow and finally green, while *S. thunbergii* has a prolific display of white flowers. All are happy in full sun or very light shade, and can easily be propagated by taking spring and summer cuttings. *S. thunbergii* can be divided in spring after it has been cut back.

STEWARTIA
Stewartia
The deciduous, hardy stewartias make large trees. *S. sinensis*, for example, can reach up to 20m (70ft) high and 7.5m (25ft) wide, and is widely grown because of its peeling bark (*S. pseudocamellia* is a good alternative). You cannot miss it in winter when the outer layer strips off to reveal red-brown patches of cream and grey. They are all woodland trees, and hate being exposed to cold blasts, so provide some shelter, growing them in dappled light or full sun. If grown on an open site the growth will slow down. Wherever grown, though, you will get a whoosh of bright red autumn leaves. When propagating, take cuttings throughout summer.

SYRINGA
Lilac
There should be at least one hardy, deciduous, richly scented, late spring-flowering lilac in every garden. The common lilac (*S. vulgaris*) is a modest 6m (20ft) high and wide shrub, verging on a small tree. The many excellent cultivars include the dark purple 'Charles Joly', white 'Madame Lemoine', and the purple-red 'Mrs Edward Harding'. Make sure they are given an open, sunny position and rich soil to get the maximum growth. To propagate, either take early summer cuttings, or layer using a low, bendy branch, angling it down to the ground to root in a patch of weed-free soil.

TAXUS
Yew
Capable of surviving for thousands of years, yews are typically grown not for their great height, with *T. baccata* capable of hitting 20m

(70ft) high and 10m (30ft) wide, an aerial thicket of tiny dark green leaves, but for hedging or topiary. Note that they do need full sun or they can get bare and leggy, and give a trim in summer and autumn to keep them smart. If you have an old shapeless specimen, cut it back as hard as you like and it will reshoot. Any soil is fine, including chalk, but avoid patches of wet ground. Most parts of the plant are highly poisonous if eaten, especially the seed, but not the red fleshy part of the fruit. When cutting back a yew hedge in early summer, save the cuttings for propagation. Use 13cm (5in) long vertical stems, and they should root in a cold frame. This is the cheapest way to create large numbers.

TIBOUCHINA
Brazilian spider flower
The common name might be completely over the top, but *T. urvilleana* is a beautiful, Brazilian, tender, evergreen shrub. It produces an open array of straggly branches with open, deep purple flowers nearly 8cm (3½in) wide. In cold climate areas it needs to be grown as a pot plant, though it does best in a conservatory border where the extra root space means it can get up to 2.5m (8ft) high and 1.5m (5ft) wide. Water well over summer, but just give the occasional moistener when dormant in winter. The best way to propagate is by taking cuttings at the end of spring, into the start of summer.

Spiraea thunbergii

Taxus baccata

Tibouchina urvilleana

Tilia oliveri

Ulmus x hollandica 'Dampieri Aurea'

Vaccinium corymbosum

TILIA
Lime

Hardy, deciduous lime trees can grow huge, many 30m (100ft) high and more, but a few grow half that height, two of the best being the small-leaved lime (*T. cordata* 'Greenspire') and *T. oliveri*. The former is the narrower of the two, being about 6m (20ft) wide, the latter being about 9m (30ft) wide, and both attract bees when the sweetly scented flowers open in midsummer. 'Greenspire' can be kept on the small side by regular coppicing. Cut it back about 30cm (12in) above ground and it will generate a batch of new, thin stems. They can be used to make fences or poles. If you need more trees, use one of these low branches, and bend it to the ground for layering. It will develop a root system where it is buried in the soil. Growing any lime from seed is tricky.

ULMUS
Elm

If you're lucky enough to live in an area that does not suffer from Dutch elm disease, try growing one. Hardy and deciduous, they include *U. × hollandica* 'Dampieri Aurea' and 'Jacqueline Hillier'. The first is a mini tree, growing just 3.6m (12ft) high and 2.5m (8ft) wide. It is narrowly conical with golden-yellow leaves, and is ideal for small spaces, while the latter is more of a 2.5m (8ft) high and 1.8m (6ft) wide bushy shrub with packed tight leaves, making it a good hedge plant. Look out for signs of disease

(yellowing and dying leaves in summer and autumn, and brown streaks if you raise the bark). All elms are potential targets, with flying elm beetles transmitting fungi to parts above 4m (13ft) high. The spores block the outer growth rings, stopping the uptake of water, causing gradual death. When infected, the whole tree has to be felled. Though elms sucker, producing new growth, this too will eventually be targeted by the beetles when the stems are high enough. To propagate, remove suckers, having checked that they have produced good roots, or take summer cuttings. There are still some regions where elms grow successfully.

VACCINIUM
Bilberry/whortleberry

Of the roughly 450 species of evergreen and deciduous shrubs, few are that popular, though they deserve to be more widely

grown in gardens with acid soil. *V. glaucoalbum* is an evergreen shrub, just 1.2m (4ft) high and 90cm (3ft) wide, with greyish-green leaves (distinctly bluish-white beneath). The pale pink flowers appear at the end of spring and the start of summer, being followed by a good show of black berries that persist into winter. It is not completely hardy and needs a mild, sheltered site. The 1.5m (5ft) high and wide bush blueberry (*V. corymbosum*) is much more robust and hardier, and makes a slightly larger size. In the USA and Canada it is grown for commercial fruit production, and is becoming increasingly popular elsewhere. The slightly shorter *V. glaucoalbum* freely suckers, and can be propagated by using severed, rooted growth. *V. corymbosum* can be propagated by layering, bending the low growth to the ground for rooting, or by taking summer cuttings.

VIBURNUM
Viburnum

The most popular viburnums are the heavily scented, winter-flowering kind, with the hardy, deciduous cultivars of *V. ×bodnantense* the pick of the bunch. 'Dawn' makes a decent shrub, 3m (10ft) high and 1.8m (6ft) wide, with packed tight clusters of dark pink flowers that gradually turn white. 'Charles Lamont' is also pink, and 'Deben' white. *V. × burkwoodii* 'Anne Russell' and 'Fulbrook', both about 2.4m (8ft) high and wide, carry on the show with more rich scents in spring. Other viburnums – including the twice as high guelder rose (*V. opulus*), and *V. davidii* at 1.2m (4ft) high and wide – give a good show of autumn colour with the guelder's leaves sharpening to red, and *davidii* producing blue berries. For a viburnum with a difference try the 4m (12ft) high and wide snowball tree (*V. opulus* 'Roseum'),

---

TAKING VIBURNUM CUTTINGS

1 If using standard late spring or summer cuttings for the deciduous and evergreen kinds respectively, nip off the end of a vigorous shoot.

2 Then trim it so that the base terminates in a node, and start removing any leaves up the bottom two-thirds, flush with the stem.

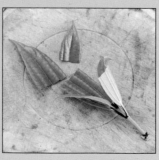

3 Finally, slice the large leaves in half to avoid overlapping and because they might transpire too much moisture, causing wilting.

Viburnum opulus 'Roseum'

Viscum album

Wisteria sinensis

which is liberally covered with rounded white blobs of flowers at the end of spring. The two simplest means of propagation are either taking cuttings from spring to autumn or, better still, layering by bending a supple low branch to the soil for rooting.

VINCA
Periwinkle
These two hardy, evergreen periwinkles make very good groundcover, and though they thrive in light shade they flower best in full sun. Greater periwinkle (*V. major*) is a prostrate shrub with dark green leaves, getting 45cm (18in) high with the ability to spread and spread as far as allowed. Excess growth is easily cut when it threatens to get out of hand. The summer flowers are dark violet, and if you want extra attractions there is a variegated kind with white edging around the leaves. Lesser

periwinkle (*V. minor*) is another spreader, though it will never get as high, being restricted to about 20cm (8in). The species has bluish-violet flowers, but there are several forms in slightly darker colours, with some ('Gertrude Jekyll') in white. Others have variegated leaves. If you have long stretches of wild or woodland garden needing cover, either dig up established clumps and replant elsewhere or propagate by taking divisions or semi-ripe cuttings. Success rates are high.

VISCUM
Mistletoe
Great aerial clumps of mistletoe are traditionally associated with apple trees, but other strains grow on ash, hawthorn, lime and oak. If you want mistletoe in your garden, here is what you do. In spring, insert fresh seed from mistletoe that is growing on the same kind of tree as the

one you want it to grow on. Apple trees are common hosts. Remove the seed coat and insert in a T-shaped cut in a branch with a diameter of 10cm (4in) or more, 1.5m (5ft) up so that it gets good light. Then fold the bark over and cover with hessian, and keep it in place with string. Do this several times on the same tree because you will need to get both a male and female to produce a crop of berries, and there is only a 10 per cent germination rate. In 20 months, with luck, there will be a shoot, and, three years later, flowers.

VITIS
Grape vine/ornamental vine
Some vines produce grapes, and the best selection is from a specialist nursery where you can taste the produce. Other vines are grown for their prodigious climbing energy and their ability to cover a wall, their leaves flashing extraordinary reds and yellow and orange in autumn, before falling. You can even grow them into mature trees so that their long whippy growths dangle out of the tops in autumn like red and yellow flags. The hardy, deciduous *V. coignetiae* is the one to cover a huge space, growing 15m (50ft) high. Its stems clamp on to any surface (but need to be kept away from roof tiles to avoid damage); look beneath the large leaves and you will find clusters of grapes but they are not worth bothering with, being completely inedible. The leaves give an amazing shock of primary colours

at the end of autumn. Smaller alternatives include the 6m (20ft) high *V. vinifera* 'Purpurea'.

WISTERIA
Wisteria
There is a basic choice between the hardy, deciduous *W. sinensis* and *W. floribunda*, the Chinese and Japanese twining climbers. Everything about the former is slightly bigger, with a taller height – 9m (30ft) – and larger scented flowers, but they appear at the end of spring and if your garden gets caught by late spring frosts, the flowers might be destroyed. The species is lavender with named varieties in white or violet. Japanese wisterias, in lavender, white and pink, flower slightly later, as summer gets under way. The white 'Alba' and pale blue 'Multijuga' are big sellers, the latter having 1m (3½ft) long flower clusters. All wisterias need a hot, sunny wall to climb up, initially with a system of supporting horizontal wires attached to stout posts, or a pergola. Provide average, free-draining soil. They need pruning twice a year, and you should check in a specialist reference source for the technique to ensure flowering. Even with the best treatment, they can be slow to establish. Large numbers of extra plants are easily raised by serpentine layering, using the lower, flexible stems. You can also take cuttings from spring to autumn.

Vinca minor

Vitis vinifera 'Purpurea'

Wet-loving, bog and water plants

ACORUS
Acorus

Sun-loving hardy perennials for the pond, with the taller kind making good, shapely plants and the shorter ones adding a graceful look. Good selections include the hardy 90cm (3ft) high deciduous sweet flag (*A. calamus* 'Variegatus'), which spreads by about 60cm (2ft) but is not invasive. It can easily be grown in an aquatic basket in water to a depth of 10cm (4in). The much smaller and more restrained Japanese rush (*A. gramineus*), 35cm (14in) high at most, does keep its leaves through winter but is not as hardy, and can be grown in very shallow water or boggy ground. There are many good selections including 'Hakuro-nishiki', and 'Ogon', which is the best choice for a lightly shaded position. The light green foliage has yellow stripes. Propagate by digging up the plants and dividing the rhizomes in spring. Each new section needs both a shoot for the top growth and roots to anchor it in the ground and feed. Replant in aquatic baskets, making sure that the

Acorus gramineus

Aponogeton distachyos

soil stays saturated, until ready for planting out. Discard the old exhausted rhizomes.

ALISMA
Water plantain

Hardy, robust marginal pond plants for full sun, flowering in summer, with the best-known being *A. plantago-aquatica*. It has tapering green leaves, grows to 75cm (2½ft), with a spread of 45cm (18in), and has pinkish-white or white summer flowers. Sink it in an aquatic basket from

15–45cm (6–18in) deep in the water, or let it spread around the edges of a large pond where it will rapidly self-seed in the muddy margins. Prise them out and replant where you want them to grow, discarding the rest (and cut off the fading flowers in future years to prevent even more seedlings appearing). For quicker results, divide the rhizomes at the end of spring, but carefully check that each 7.5cm (3in) long section has both roots and one or more shoots to provide a decent batch of top growth. Replant in an aquatic basket.

APONOGETON
Aponogeton

The frost-hardy, perennial South African water hawthorn (*A. distachyos*) is excellent for sending out a spread, up to 1.2m (4ft), of floating leaves that are evergreen in mild, protected, sunny sites. The small white flowers open in spring and autumn, sitting on the surface, and have a very distinctive scent of vanilla that is quite obvious on warm, still evenings. Grow plants in aquatic baskets at least 30cm (12in) wide, toward the centre of the pond at a depth of about 60cm (2ft). Propagation should not be necessary as it self-seeds prolifically, though you can also divide the rhizomes with a sharp knife in spring, ensuring that each 7.5cm (3in) length has both roots and shoots. *A. madagascariensis* has pretty, skeletonized, lace-like leaves, but needs a minimum temperature of 15°C (59°F).

ASTILBE
Astilbe

The *A.* × *arendsii* hybrids – about 90cm (3ft) high and 45cm (18in) wide – provide excellent hardy perennials for the sunny bog garden. 'Fanal' has fluffy plumes of dark red flowers in early summer poking above the clump of 23cm (9in) long, deeply cut leaves. The brown seedheads hang on over winter. Other good choices include the deep pink 'Bressingham Beauty' and white 'Irrlicht'. Add plenty of well-rotted compost to the soil every year. Plants are best propagated by dividing them every three years in early spring using two back-to-back forks to prise each clump apart. Each needs roots and shoots. Replant them immediately; if they are on the small side, pot them up and raise in a cold frame, keeping the soil moist, until well established.

Astilbe x arendsii 'Fanal'

DIVIDING ACORUS

1 In spring, lift the acorus in its aquatic basket from the pond, and carefully knock it out without damaging the roots or top growth.

2 Start separating the top growth, looking down to identify places where the rhizome can be cut into several decent chunks.

3 Now take a clean sharp knife and slice down through the rhizome, double checking that each section has roots and leafy top growth.

Azolla filiculoides

AZOLLA
Fairy moss

One of the commonest pond plants, *A. filiculoides* is a tiny, floating perennial fern that is a prolific spreader for a sunny position but it is not completely hardy. The mass of leaves turns red in full sun and in autumn. It is very useful, because this prodigious growth shades the water and halts the growth of algae. Keep it out of small ponds, though, because it can quickly cover the entire surface, and also out of any ponds with fish because it takes oxygen out of the water. To cut back the growth haul great lengths of it out of the water. If the water tends to ice over in winter then it will get cut back. Propagate by removing sections, and keep them in a large bucket of water and soil in a frost-free place over winter to ensure you have supplies for next summer.

BUTOMUS
Flowering rush

The 1.2m (4ft) high, 45cm (18in) wide rush (*B. umbellatus*) for growing at the sunny side of a pond, in the margins, is a hardy perennial with attractive bronze-coloured new growth that turns olive-green. The large numbers of rose-pink flowers are the main summer attraction. Though it can initially be grown in a container, it will soon become too cramped and need more space, especially if it is to flower well. Either grow in the boggy, muddy pond edges or in water to about 20cm (8in) deep. The best way to propagate is when dividing established clumps at the start of spring, every three years, to maintain vigorous growth and good flowering. Slice the rhizomes with a sharp knife into short sections, each with roots and a shoot for the top growth. Grow in moist soil in aquatic baskets until ready for planting out.

CALLA
Bog arum

C. palustris, a hardy perennial for full sun, is a showy pond-side and marginal plant, for growing in up to 10cm (4in) of water, that produces glossy, dark green, heart shaped leaves about 20cm (8in) long. It reaches 25cm (10in) tall by 60cm (2ft) wide. The white spathes in midsummer resemble those of an arum lily, except that they are much smaller. The tiny flowers are followed by a show of red or orange berries. The plants quickly multiply via the rhizomes

that snake through the mud. If you need even more plants, then slice up the rhizome in spring using a sharp knife into short sections, but each must have both a set of roots and shoots for the top growth. Replant.

CALLITRICHE
Autumn starwort

You will not see the hardy aquatic perennial *C. hermaphroditica* on the

surface because it stays submerged, but it produces lovely trailing growth of bright green foliage, in pairs up the stems, and is a very efficient oxygenator. It can be quite a vigorous spreader, and is best grown in baskets in up to 60cm (2ft) depth of water. Summer cuttings are easily taken using 15cm (6in) long shoots that are then rooted in soil in a basket. Topdress with shingle.

Butomus umbellatus

Calla palustris

Callitriche hermaphroditica

Caltha palustris

Canna 'Durban'

Cardamine pratensis

Carex pendula

CALTHA
Kingcup

A good choice for early spring flowers, the hardy, perennial *C. palustris* has a mass of bright yellow flowers set against the dark green foliage, and often has a second flush later in the summer, providing there isn't a heat wave. It is a good choice for the sunny, shallow edge of an informal pond, and for softening the outline of a more formal shape, though it will also grow in a bog garden. There is also a good white form (var. *alba*) and a double yellow ('Flore Pleno'). All grow about 25–30cm (10–12in) high by 25–45cm (10–18in) wide. For a taller, sturdier shape, go for the giant marsh marigold (*C. p.* var. *palustris*). All are best propagated by dividing the clumps with a sharp knife in spring. Each new section needs both roots and shoots. Replant in an aquatic basket topped with shingle.

CANNA
Canna

Many of the tender cannas can be grown in ponds, and they include *C. flaccida* and *C. glauca*, and those that tolerate the shallows at the edge of a pond (for example *C.* 'Durban' and 'Endeavour'). Like the border kind, they produce large, exotic leaves topped by relatively small gladiolus-like flowers. The 1.5m (5ft) high and 50cm (20in) wide 'Durban' is an excellent choice because the purple-maroon leaves are given a flashy twist thanks to the orange-pink stripes, with bright

orange flowers in the second half of summer through to autumn. 'Endeavour' is slightly shorter with bluish-green leaves topped by tomato-red flowers. Both need lifting in the autumn, like a border canna, with the tops being cut off and the straggly roots being trimmed. Leave them to dry, dust with a fungicide, and keep in a frost-free shed or garage over winter, covered in old potting compost or leaf mould. Give the occasional spray with water to stop them completely drying out. The following spring move to a greenhouse and provide some gentle warmth, and new shoots should soon appear. Gradually harden off in a cold frame before planting out or standing in a pond over summer. To propagate, divide the rhizomes and place the

7.5cm (3in) long sections with roots and buds in small pots filled with multi-purpose compost (soil mix) at 16°C (60°F).

CARDAMINE
Cuckoo flower

The hardy, perennial *C. pratensis* is an adaptable plant growing in sun or shade in the bog garden, where it makes rosettes of leaves topped by late spring white, purple or lilac flowers. It grows to 45cm (18in) high with a 30cm (12in) wide spread. 'Edith' is a pink form, with the flowers fading to white, and 'Flore Pleno' is lilac-pink. Make sure that the soil has plenty of well-rotted compost forked in, and propagate either by seed sown in pots in autumn or spring, kept in a cold frame, or divide after flowering.

CAREX
Sedge

Bowles golden sedge (*C. elata* 'Aurea') and weeping sedge (*C. pendula*) are hardy perennials that are ideal for growing in bog gardens or even the shallow edges of a pond. The former makes a tight, dense, deciduous clump – 45cm (18in) wide – of striking yellow leaves to 60cm (2ft) long, which gently arch over, being ideal for semi-shade. It makes good contrasts with dark greens and reds, and gives frogs and newts good hiding places in the shallows. The latter is even more impressive, making an evergreen cluster of glossy green leaves, about 1.2m (4ft) high and wide, that arch over and produce an excellent show of dark brown flower spikes, some 15cm (6in)

DIVIDING CAREX

1 To create extra numbers of carex, lift a plant in spring, forking it out of the ground keeping its root system intact.

2 If it is a large, hard clump insert two forks, back to back, to prise the clump into sections. If not, then make the separations by hand.

3 Plant up the different sections. Take this opportunity to improve the soil, digging larger holes than necessary and adding compost.

long. The quickest form of propagation is by dividing clumps in spring, using two forks back-to-back to prise them apart and create smaller, more vigorous sections each with roots and, in the case of *C. elata*, shoots. Replant in an aquatic basket.

CERATOPHYLLUM
Hornwort
C. demersum is one of the essential pond plants, used to both oxygenate and keep the water clear. All you need do is drop the hardy cuttings, with a weight tied to the bottom, in a sunny or shady pond, and it will sink and thrive. It does not have to root in mud. The stems are covered in short, dark green, whorled, bottle-brush-like foliage, and though it can spread indefinitely, it is easily controlled, with excess growth being hauled out of the water. In winter the plants sink to the bottom and survive as turions (swollen buds), and rise again the following spring as the water warms up. Propagate by snapping off 10cm (4in) lengths of stem, and pop them in the soil in an aquatic basket that is large enough to accommodate the mature plant. Alternatively, group a batch of cuttings and tie them together with a weight at the end, and lob them into the water so that they root in the mud at the bottom.

CYPERUS
Cyperus
These annual and perennial sedges are mainly from the tropics, with the American galingale (*C. eragrostis*)

Ceratophyllum

Cyperus involucratis

from the south-western USA being one of the more robust, though it is not completely hardy. It grows 60cm (2ft) high and 45cm (18in) wide, and has bright green leaves with pale green midsummer spikelets (good for drying) that last until autumn. If you live in an area where the water temperature can be kept above 10°C (50°F), you have the luxury of being able to grow *C. giganteus*, which comes from Mexico to South America and is capable of hitting 3.6m (12ft), though it will spread to 1.5m (5ft). The seed is best sown in spring by laying it on warm, moist soil, which must not dry out, but if this is not possible, divide plants in spring. Use two forks, back-to-back, inserted into the clump, and force them apart to give a few small sections, each with roots and shoots, for replanting.

DARMERA
Umbrella plant
D. peltata is a hardy perennial for part shade, where it makes excellent ground cover with its 35cm (14in) wide leaves – like an upturned umbrella – that create an extensive mound, 60cm (2ft) wide and 1.2m (4ft) high, of dark green, turning red and brown and yellow in autumn. It also produces a decent show of small pink flowers in the second half of spring. Grow it in large bog gardens where it has room to spread and by the side of streams, keeping it in cool shade and out of the sun. Do not try to pack it into a small area where a better

Darmera peltata

bet is the 35cm (14in) high 'Nana'. Propagate by seed sown in spring, keeping the pots in a cold frame, but making spring divisions – separating clumps into smaller sections using forks held back-to-back – is far quicker. Check that each portion has roots and shoots for the top growth, and promptly replant.

DIERAMA
Angel's fishing rod
The one to get is *D. pulcherrimum*. A South African frost-hardy perennial, it likes a sunny position in rich soil near water, making it ideal for a bog garden, where its long arching stems, reaching to near 1.5m (5ft) with a spread of 60cm (2ft), can angle over the pond water dangling clusters of pinkish-red flowers. Provide a thick winter mulch in cold areas to protect the roots. Young plants may take a few years to flower. When it is well established, you can propagate by dividing a clump

in spring, using two forks, back-to-back, to prise it apart. Replant the smaller sections immediately.

DROSERA
Sundew
The perennial Cape sundew (*D. capensis*) is an easily grown, 25cm (10in) high and 15cm (6in) wide carnivorous plant for planting in its pot, standing it in rainwater at the edge of a pond. The top of the leaves are covered in tiny red tentacles that are splattered with globules of sticky dew, making it very beautiful when held up to the light. They are remarkably efficient at catching passing small insects, which they soon chemically digest. If you suffer from mosquitoes indoors just stand one of these plants in a tray of rainwater, so that the soil is moist at all times, on a windowsill. Those kept outdoors in summer need to be moved to the protection of a cold frame in winter, where the soil needs to be damp rather than sopping wet. Those being grown on windowsills also need to be kept damp through winter. Propagate in spring by taking divisions, dividing up the clump, or sowing seed at 12°C (54°F).

EUPATORIUM
Hemp agrimony
E. purpureum (Joe Pye weed) is a big, lush plant for the sunny or partially shaded bog garden. Propagate by dividing the clumps in spring, but you will need help to manhandle such a clump, getting two forks into it, back-to-back.

Dierama pulcherrimum

Eupatorium purpureum

Filipendula rubra

FILIPENDULA
Filipendula

Meadowsweet (*F. ulmaria*) and queen of the prairies (*F. rubra*) grow in bog gardens. Both are hardy perennials for sun or shade, with fern-like leaves topped by small, colourful flowers. *F. ulmaria* makes strong growth to reach 90cm (3ft) high and 60cm (2ft) wide, a large clump with creamy white summer flowers. *F. u.* 'Aurea' is more striking because the leaves are golden-green, and if you promptly remove the flower buds you will get even more foliage. *F. rubra* grows even bigger, making 2.1m (7ft) by 1.2m (4ft) wide, with a good covering of pink flowers in the first half of summer. All need to be divided every few years to maintain a good show. Push two forks into the dug-up rootball, keeping them back-to-back, and force them apart to create small divisions, each with roots and buds, and promptly replant.

GLYCERIA
Glyceria

The hardy, perennial grass *G. maxima* var. *variegata*, with leaves about 30cm (12in) long and an indefinite spread, makes a strong show at the sunny edge of a pond, in shallow water, with its green leaves striped cream-white. In spring the stripes take on a pink tinge. If it is planted directly into the mud it can quickly spread, overwhelming neighbouring plants, and is best restrained in an aquatic basket. The leaves sometimes develop without the variegation, in which case cut off the part of the rhizome from which they emerged or the whole plant will soon revert to its all-green state. The best time to propagate is spring. Dig up the rhizomes and cut them into sections with a sharp knife, making sure that each one has both roots and shoots for the top growth, and replant in baskets topped by shingle.

GUNNERA
Gunnera

G. manicata is the big, essential, almost-hardy perennial for large bog gardens in sun or shade where there is a huge amount of space for its possible 2.5m (8ft) of vertical growth and maximum spread that is even greater. The thick, powerful, prickly stems burst up in spring and early summer, carrying gigantic, thick,

Glyceria maxima var. variegata

tough leathery leaves. Look underneath and you will see the highly impressive clusters of tiny flowers on a club- or cone-like structure. With room you can grow a small forest of these gunneras, creating long stretches of damp shade beneath. In autumn the plant dies back, and because it is not reliably hardy the leaves should be folded over the crown, which has been covered with straw, to provide protection. *G. tinctoria* is a smaller version, though it can still reach 1.5m (5ft) high by 2m (6ft) wide. To propagate, try dividing the crown in early spring, though this is near-impossible on established clumps because of the size.

HOSTA
Plantain lily

They might be thought of as border plants, but the hardy, perennial hostas demand damp soil and semi- to near permanent

Gunnera manicata

shade (the yellow-leaved kind like some midday sun to retain their colour), and bog gardens are ideal. The choice is massive with nearly 50 species and over 1,000 cultivars with mounds of different leaf shapes and colours and textures, the flashiest being strikingly variegated, others coming in beautiful shades of greyish-blue. All need rich soil that has been well composted. The one big problem they all face is slug damage that can reduce the leaves (the prime reason for growing them, though many have beautiful spikes of lilac, cream or white flowers) to tatters. Control them by whatever means works best for you – nightly patrols, beer traps, nematodes and copper barriers can all help. The best way to propagate is by dividing a clump in late summer or the start of spring, using two spades back-to-back to prise it apart, or simply slice down through it with a spade to create a few sections, each with roots and buds. Replant immediately.

HOTTONIA
Water violet

A very useful hardy perennial and flowering oxygenator, *H. palustris* spreads its leafy stems beneath the water, making quite extensive growth, with the flowers popping well above the surface. In winter the plant sinks to the bottom of the pond but starts lifting up again in spring, creating a mound of feathery greenery, and this is followed by the stalks bearing pale lavender flowers, like those of

Hosta nigrescens

a primula, held 30cm (12in) clear of the water. Propagate by dividing plants in spring, or take 10cm (4in) long cuttings, tie them together and weigh down the end and lob them into a pond where they will root in the mud at the bottom. Alternatively, root them in an aquatic basket.

HYDROCHARIS
Frogbit

There are just two species of frogbit, one being the popular, dainty *H. morsus-ranae*. It is a hardy floating perennial that spreads across the surface of the pond like a miniature water lily, with white summer flowers. Each individual is about 10cm (4in) wide but, with its many attached plantlets, it can reach 90cm (3ft) wide. However, they are easily controlled, being hauled out of the water, making this a good choice for a small, shallow pond where the plants root in the mud. In winter the growth sinks to the bottom where it stays dormant until it rises to the surface as the water warms up the following spring. If there is a danger that the shallow water might freeze to the bottom in winter, then remove the plants and keep in large buckets of soil and water over winter until the following spring. It naturally self-propagates by producing swollen buds on the ends of the roots. They sink to the bottom and produce new plants the next year. They can also be collected and grown in aquatic baskets top-dressed with pea shingle, being immersed in water, always keeping the shoot tips above the surface.

HYPERICUM
St. John's wort

H. elodes (marsh hypericum) is a hardy perennial for sun or shade that will pop just 23cm (9in) out of the water but spreads 45cm (18in). The attractions are the yellow midsummer flowers and the creeping stems that nose through the muddy shallows, in no more than 2.5cm (1in) of water. It makes an effective underplanting for taller vertical pond plants, and for hiding unattractive pond edges. Propagate by taking summer cuttings, about

Hypericum elodes

10cm (4in) long, and growing them in moist soil in aquatic baskets, or divide clumps into smaller sections, each having roots and shoots to produce top growth.

IRIS
Iris

A large group of hardy irises can be grown in water, including the Japanese iris (*I. ensata*), *I. laevigata*, *I. pseudacorus* (best for large ponds), and *I. versicolor*. The 90cm (3ft) high Japanese *I. laevigata* is one of the best. The purple-blue flowers, with yellow at the base, appear in the early part of summer. There are many excellent forms, as of the midsummer-flowering *I. ensata*, which is about the same height. The colours range from purple to white, and while it too tolerates up to 7.5cm (3in) of water over the crown in summer, it dislikes flooding when it gets swamped, and icy temperatures when the crown is locked in ice. The best solution is to dig it up and keep it in a damp border over winter with a thick mulch on top to provide some insulation. The slightly shorter *I. versicolor* (for an early summer show at the edge of a pond) generally comes in a range of blues from violet to lavender, with some nearer to reddish-purple ('Kermesina'). All three are best propagated by division, after flowering in colder climates, or in autumn in areas where the winters are mild. Dig up the rhizomes, clean off the mud, and slice into 7.5–10cm (3–4in) sections, making sure

that each one can survive on its own, having both roots and a fan of leaves. Trim the latter to 15cm (6in) long to reduce any stress or wind-rock and replant.

JUNCUS
Rush

The hardy, perennial corkscrew rush (*J. effusus*) needs to be grown at the edge of a large pond, where it grows to a modest 45cm (18in) high but does spread effectively to 60cm (2ft). The clumped, stiff, slender stems make good cover for tadpoles, newts and waterfowl, and a good contrast for other more rounded pond-side plants. 'Spiralis' is shorter with twisty-twirly corkscrew growth, and is often used in flower arrangements. The larger, bolder version – 'Unicorn' – can grow 60cm (2ft) high. If the growth of these rushes hangs on all winter, cut it right back every few years

Juncus effusus

to get rid of the older, tatty foliage and generate a batch of fresh new growth. The underground rhizomes can be divided in mid-spring, when they are cut into 7.5cm (3in) long sections, each having a combination of roots and fat, healthy shoots.

Iris versicolor

Ligularia 'The Rocket'

Lobelia cardinalis

LIGULARIA
Ligularia
The hardy, clump-forming perennial *L. przewalskii* is ideal for the back of a sunny bog garden where it sends up stems to 2m (6ft), with a 90cm (3ft) spread. The colour mix is green, black and yellow, with 23cm (9in) long, deeply cut green leaves, black flower stems and packed columns of tiny, flashy yellow flowers. *L.* 'The Rocket' is very similar. Try growing both in a sunny border and they will keep collapsing through lack of moisture, but in soil that never dries out they will put on a strong, impressive show all summer. They can be propagated from seed, but division in spring gives the quickest results. Separate clumps using back-to-back forks and prise them apart, checking that each new section has both roots and buds for the top growth. Replant immediately.

LOBELIA
Lobelia
The short-lived hardy, perennial *L. cardinalis* is traditionally grown in damp, sunny borders or bog gardens, but it also makes an excellent plant for the shallows. It produces scarlet flowers above dark bronze leaves, and at 90cm (3ft) high and 30cm (1ft) wide is incredibly striking. Since the stiff, upright stems are frequently chomped through by slugs and snails, it stands a greater chance of success in water, though disasters still occur. Propagate by taking an established plant out of the pot

in spring and separate the crown with a sharp knife, though you can also take 5cm (2in) long cuttings in early summer for flowering the following year. Keep well protected in a cold frame in the first winter.

LYSICHITON
Skunk cabbage
The two species, yellow skunk (*L. americanus*) – at 90cm (3ft) high and 1.2m (4ft) wide – and white skunk (*L. camtschatcensis*) – 75cm (2½ft) high and wide – make a flashy show in early spring on the muddy banks of a pond or river. What looks like the emerging flower is actually a huge spathe, or coloured bract, with the dozens of tiny flowers being clustered around the head of the central, poker-like spadix. Both appear before the large, glossy, veined leaves that can make an extraordinary sight when they reach 1.2m (4ft) long. While

they can be grown from seed, you will get quicker results by digging up a plant and dividing it into sections (check each has a set of roots) in spring after it has finished flowering. You can also take spring or summer cuttings.

LYSIMACHIA
Loosestrife
One of the showiest loosestrifes for the bog garden is the hardy, perennial *L. punctata*. It has a mix of horizontal leaves ranged up the flower stem, each one separating the flashy yellow flowers. Though it only grows 90cm (3ft) high and 60cm (2ft) wide, it is quite invasive and very capable of making a sizeable colony after several years in the bog garden, where it thrives in moist, rich ground in full sun or partial shade. If it does get out of hand, simply cull the excess growth using a spade to slice down into the marauding roots. It can either be raised from seed sown in spring, the pots being stood in a cold frame for up to four weeks, or divide plants in spring or autumn. Use a spade or two forks to separate the clumps into individual sections, each one having the means to feed and anchor (the roots), and put on top growth (buds).

LYTHRUM
Purple loosestrife
L. salicaria 'Feuerkerze' is a hardy perennial for a sunny site, where it puts out a mass of vertical flower spikes packed with bright rose-reddish-pink petals in summer.

Lythrum salicaria

At 90cm (3ft) high and 45cm (18in) wide, it is just the right size for most bog gardens, and makes a snappy show near a pond. If it threatens to colonize too large an area (and in parts of North America it is a major problem), simply slice through the expanding growth with a spade and cut it right back. Provided you have moist or wet soil, it will give a long flowering season and, being perfectly hardy, will survive a sudden freezing drop in the temperature. Good alternatives include the slightly shorter *L. virgatum*, or one of its named varieties such as the pink 'The Rocket'. Propagate either by sowing seed in the spring, leaving it uncovered on top of the compost, and leave in a cold frame for about six months or, far more quickly, by dividing plants in spring, when you can also take basal cuttings. The divisions need both roots and buds.

Lysichiton americanus

Lysimachia punctata

Mentha aquatica

Menyanthes trifoliata

Mimulus

Myosotis scorpioides

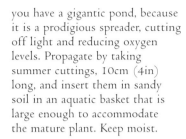

MENTHA
Mint

The hardy, aquatic perennial *M. aquatica* (watermint) thrives at the edge of most ponds, or in boggy soil, and has gentle, lilac summer flowers attracting plenty of butterflies on top of its 7.5–30cm (3–12in) high growth. Plants quickly spread, producing a mass of edible, aromatic leaves, and the best way of reining it back is by growing it in an aquatic basket. Should you need to produce even more plants, then either take stem cuttings or divide a clump in spring. Replant in aquatic baskets and cover the compost (soil mix) with shingle.

MENYANTHES
Bog bean

The bog bean is a one-species hardy perennial (*M. trifoliata*) that is ideal for growing around the sunny edges of a pond. The small leaflets are just 6cm (2½in) long, but the underground stems can creep along to a length of 1.2m (4ft) through the shallows, in up to 7.5cm (3in) of water. Because it is such a rapid spreader, make sure that your pond is big enough for it and waterlilies. The pink buds open to give white summer flowers, and if you can bend down to sniff them you will get a whiff of vanilla. Either grow in the muddy bottom or in an aquatic basket. Propagate by dividing clumps in spring, separating the rhizomes with a sharp knife. Divide into short sections, each with roots and buds, and raise in moist soil in aquatic baskets.

MIMULUS
Monkey flower

M. ringens is a hardy perennial with a profusion of spikes bearing small, soft lavender to white flowers poking out among the rich green leaves. The height is 90cm (3ft) and spread 30cm (1ft). Grow it in up to 15cm (6in) of water, while the yellow *M. luteus*, at 30cm (1ft) high and 60cm (2ft) wide, goes in shallower water, up to 5cm (2in) deep. The much more dramatic and eye-catching 90cm (3ft) high and 60cm (2ft) wide *M. cardinalis*, with scarlet flowers, needs to be grown in the bog garden. All can be grown from seed, sown in a cold frame in autumn to give quicker results, or the following spring, at 10°C (50°F). Alternatively, take summer cuttings, raising them in moist soil, or divide clumps in spring to create several new plants, each having roots and buds or shoots.

MYOSOTIS
Forget-me-not

The hardy, perennial *M. scorpioides* (water forget-me-not) needs boggy, marshy soil, or the shallows of a pond, in sun or part shade. The growth quickly juts out across the water producing branching stems, spreading 30cm (12in), and sprays of blue flowers in early summer. Given cool weather, it should periodically produce more flowers. The blue spring-flowering 'Mermaid' is sturdier and smaller, spreading by about 15cm (6in), creating more of a mound. 'Snowflakes' is the white form. All kinds help reduce algae. Propagate either by taking stem cuttings, by sowing seed directly in the muddy pond side in spring or, to keep a closer eye on the seedlings' development, in pots. Keep the containers in trays of water so that the compost does not dry out. Alternatively, plants can be divided into sections.

MYRIOPHYLLUM
Milfoil

Parrot's feather (*M. aquaticum*) and western milfoil (*M. hippuroides*) are two not-completely-hardy submerged perennials, with pretty leaves and spreading growth, that help oxygenate ponds and provide hiding places for young fish. Parrot's feather can easily cover 1.8m (6ft), and if grown in the shallows will start climbing up the banks. It has tiny yellow-green flowers, while western milfoil's are equally small and white. Whatever happens, avoid *M. spicatum* unless you have a gigantic pond, because it is a prodigious spreader, cutting off light and reducing oxygen levels. Propagate by taking summer cuttings, 10cm (4in) long, and insert them in sandy soil in an aquatic basket that is large enough to accommodate the mature plant. Keep moist.

NYMPHAEA
Water lily

When choosing a water lily, do make sure that you get the right kind for your garden because there are both hardy and tropical kinds, and because their spreads vary enormously with many being far too vigorous for smaller ponds. All have flat leaves that float on the surface, with day-blooming flowers in a huge range of colours from white to near black. The best way to buy is by ordering a catalogue from a specialist supplier. Most hardy water lilies need an open, sunny site, though some will take only four hours of direct sun a day. Do not try growing them with longer periods of shade, because they are unlikely to flower. Also avoid fountains and splashing water, sticking to the stillness of a pond and depths of about 45–75cm (18–30in), though the miniatures can grow in water that is just ankle deep. The easiest way to propagate is by division, lifting the plant at the end of spring. Slice up the storage organ, ensuring that each can survive on its own, having both roots and shoots for the abundant top growth.

Myriophyllum aquaticum

Nymphaea 'Rose Arey'

NYMPHOIDES
Water fringe
Also called the humble water lily, *N. peltata* is a fast-growing hardy perennial that can be planted to a depth of 60cm (2ft). It produces oval, bright green leaves that float on the surface and a profusion of bright yellow, star-shaped summer flowers rather like a buttercup. It is an incredible spreader, putting out lots of runners, and needs to be kept out of small ponds, though clusters can be hauled out of larger ones if it gets out of hand. Choose with care. The simplest way to propagate is by removing and separating the runners over summer.

ORONTIUM
Golden club
The hardy, perennial *O. aquaticum* – about 40cm (16in) long and 72cm (28in) wide – is grown for its clumps of hosta-like showy, dark greenish-blue leaves that grow about 25cm (10in) long, and superb white flower spikes in spring topped by scores of tiny yellow flowers. These curious, vertical, tentacle-like growths, stretching well above the leaves, are the prime attraction. It can be grown toward the sunny edge of an informal pond, or in water about 38cm (15in) deep, with the leaves floating on the surface. Easily grown and easily propagated by dividing the rhizome in spring (seed is possible, but takes a long time), slicing it with a sharp knife into short sections, each with roots and shoots for the top growth.

Orontium aquaticum

Osmunda regalis

OSMUNDA
Royal fern
At 1.2–1.8m (4–6ft) high and 3–4m (10–13ft) wide, the tropical-looking *O. regalis* is one of the most impressive hardy ferns for a semi-shady bog garden. Its lime-green fronds give a quick colour change in autumn, turning bronze, while the spore-bearing fronds are shorter and greenish-brown. There are many excellent selections, including 'Crispa', with wavy margins and a height of 60cm (2ft), the crested 'Cristata', which is 30cm (12in) higher, and 'Gracilis' with coppery new growth that also reaches 90cm (3ft) high. The best way to propagate all four is by dividing the crowns in spring, using back-to-back forks. Replant the new sections immediately.

PELTANDRA
Arrow arum
P. sagittifolia (white arrow arum) grows in the wild in North America, producing clumps of shiny, dark green leaves shaped like a large arrowhead on top of thin stalks that can reach 45cm (18in) long, with a spread of 45cm (18in). White spathes open in early summer, followed by red berries. Grow it at the sunny edge of a pond, or in a bog garden. It is a hardy perennial, like the green arrow arum (*P. virginica*), which is about 15cm (6in) smaller. The green spathes are followed by green berries. Both kinds can grow in deeper water but the performance will suffer. Propagate by digging up the plant in spring,

Phragmites australis

and dividing it with a sharp knife, slicing it vertically down through the root system, ensuring that both halves have a decent set of roots and shoots.

PHRAGMITES
Reed
P. australis (common reed/ Norfolk reed) is a giant of a spreading hardy perennial for large, sunny ponds with swampy ground at the edges, or in water to 60cm (2ft) deep, where it can easily top 3m (10ft) high, standing out with its swaying brownish summer plumes that gradually turn silver. If you are worried about it being too invasive, try it in large aquatic baskets, but that is not ideal because this spreads and spreads and it needs to be allowed to run, with occasional culls to rein it back. It provides good shelter for wildlife, including wildfowl, and has been used to make thatched roofs. *P. a.* 'Variegatus' has stripy leaves and is less invasive, and 'Towada' is a shorter version of *P. a.* that is not widely available. Should you need even more of this reed, divide the rhizomes of established plants in spring, slicing them into 10cm (4in) lengths, each having a root and shoots for the top growth.

PONTEDERIA
Pickerel weed
The hardy, perennial *P. cordata* – at 1.3m (3½–4ft) high and about 72cm (28in) wide – from North America makes large, thick, congested clumps of glossy, heart-

Pontederia cordata

shaped leaves that are offset in late summer by the spikes of blue flowers on top of 25cm (10in) long stalks. It gets its common name because pickerel fish were said to be attracted to such clumps growing in sunny shallows, but just about every kind of water-loving wildlife can be found among them, from fish to emerging dragonflies that climb up the leaves and shed their skin before drying their wings and flying away. Extremely good at keeping the water clean, it dislikes having its roots frozen, so if there is a chance that might happen, lift the plants and keep in moist soil over winter until it is safe to plant out again. The white form is 'Alba'. Propagate by making divisions in late spring, digging up the rhizome and slicing it with a sharp knife into 7.5–10cm (3–4in) long sections, each with roots and shoots.

POTAMOGETON
Pond weed
P. crispus is not a weed but an excellent submerged oxygenator, especially in moving and shady water, in the shallows or deep water. A hardy perennial, it has long, wavy, wiry stems with the leaves turning reddish or bronze in spring and winter, resembling slivers of seaweed. The minute pinkish-white flowers open in early summer. It is unlike most pond plants because it grows through the coldest months but goes dormant as the water warms up in midsummer. Do not use in small ponds, because the

DIVIDING PRIMULA

1 When the new growth appears in spring or after it has finished flowering, fork a clump of primulas out of the ground, roots and all.

2 Look for the point where the clump can be divided, and then start working up from the base, carefully teasing the roots apart.

3 Finally, start separating the top growth, and you should end up with two plants, both with a decent root system and lots of leaves on top.

creeping rhizomes inch their way through the muddy bottom, and the stems can grow to 1.8m (6ft) long. Propagation is easy, either by division or stem cuttings. Put them in the soil in an aquatic basket that is large enough to accommodate the mature plant, and keep moist.

PRIMULA
Primula
Of the scores of hardy, perennial primulas, many thrive in the moist, rich ground of a bog garden in cool shade. Some of the best include the drumstick primula (*P. denticulata*), which grows to 45cm (18in) high and wide with flowers in pink or purple from mid-spring to summer; the giant cowslip (*P. florindae*), which makes a much bolder clump, reaching 75cm (2½ft) high and 45cm (18in) wide, often growing right up to the water's edge, with several

heads of drooping yellow bells in summer on established plants; the Japanese primrose (*P. japonica*), which has several forms, including the deep red 'Miller's Crimson', and grows 30–60cm (1–2ft) high and wide, and flowers in late spring; *P. prolifera*, which is a vigorous plant with evergreen leaves and yellow flowers for early summer, getting 90cm (3ft) high and wide; and *P. pulverulenta*, which, at 60cm (2ft) high and wide, is an elegant candelabra primula with red flowers in late spring. All can be easily propagated from fresh seed, sowing it on the surface of the compost (soil mix) and covering it with vermiculite, then standing the pots in a cold frame. Germination should occur within four weeks. Clumps can also be divided in spring. Most will self-seed (including the short-lived *P. japonica*), in which case simply dig them up and replant where required.

RANUNCULUS
Buttercup
There are over 30 aquatic species, with one of the best being the hardy, perennial *R. aquatilis* (water crowfoot), which thrives in depths of up to 60cm (2ft), oxygenating the water. Its main attraction is the foliage that is more hair-like under the water, and clover-like on the surface. The yellow-centred white flowers resemble those of a buttercup. Growth is not so vigorous that it becomes completely impossible, but if it does threaten to spread too far, simply haul out great lengths

of it by hand. Propagate by seed, dividing plants in spring or by 10cm (4in) long stem cuttings in summer, growing them in moist soil in an aquatic basket.

RHEUM
Ornamental rhubarb
One of the best rheums for the bog garden is the hardy, perennial *R. palmatum* 'Atrosanguineum', with superb leaves that open dark red and gradually turn dark green. When fully grown they are some 90cm (3ft) wide, and the whole plant can reach 2m (6½ft) high and wide, even bigger in ideal conditions. The early summer flowers make huge plumes that reach high above the leaves. If you do not want the flowers to sap the plant's energy, so that the leaves provide the big display, then promptly cut off the flower stalks. Make sure you give it plenty of space to grow in a prominent position where it can be admired. Propagate by dividing the crowns in spring, replanting the sections – each with roots and buds for top growth – immediately. You can also raise plants from seed in a cold frame in spring, with new growth appearing within a couple of weeks.

Primula pulverulenta

Ranunculus aquatilis

Rheum palmatum

Rodgersia

Sarracenia

RODGERSIA
Rodgersia

The hardy Chinese perennial *R. podophylla* has huge leaves, growing up to 40cm (16in) long, and the whole plant can easily grow 1.2m (4ft) high and 1.5m (5ft) wide, making it a very good alternative to the huge *Gunnera manicata* where space is limited. The leaves are rich green but turn bronze in autumn, and there are panicles of whitish summer flowers. *R. aesculifolia* has leaves like those of a horse chestnut, and also makes a sizeable clump, about 1.6m (5½ft) high and 90cm (3ft) wide. Give both a sheltered spot in the bog garden where they like rich soil and sun or part shade. You can propagate by sowing seed in spring, putting a layer of moss on top of the compost and sowing directly into that, and then stand in a tray of water to keep constantly moist. Or divide plants in the spring, prising them apart to create different sections with roots and buds.

SAGITTARIA
Arrowhead

The hardy, perennial Japanese arrowhead (*S. sagittifolia*) is an ornamental leafy plant for the shallows of the pond or marshy areas, where it stands out with 25cm (10in) long leaves on thin, vertical stalks, getting 90cm (3ft) high. In summer there is an extra show, with white flowers opening well above the leaves. An extremely useful plant in large ponds, it is a prolific spreader and the underwater leaves help keep

the water clean and oxygenated. The plants die back in autumn, being replaced by new, small turions (or tubers) that start sprouting the following spring. If you need to propagate, separate clumps of plants in summer and divide them up, checking that each has both a good set of roots and shoots. This is much quicker than growing from seed that needs to be refrigerated for 30 days before sowing.

SALIX
Willow

This includes massive trees and small shrubs, but the best and most striking willow to put at the edge of a medium-size pond, in sunny, moist ground, is *Salix alba* var. *vitellina*, with 'Britzensis' the pick of the bunch. It has striking orange-scarlet new growth, poking out of the ground like the spikes of a gigantic porcupine. The best way to maintain this colourful

Sagittaria sagittifolia

effect is to coppice the plant, cutting it hard back in spring to generate the new reddish shoots. If left, they will gradually lose their smart colouring over the years, so cut them back, either taking out half each year, or all the growth every two years. The species parent has orange-yellow shoots, and you could plant the two right next to each other to get a mixture of the different colours, with the stems shooting up through each other. To double the effect, grow the plants on the banks of the pond where you can clearly see their reflection in the water. Willow is easily propagated by taking lengths of the current year's growth, about 25cm (10in) long. When cutting the end nearest the ground, make a horizontal cut, so you know which end is which. Then insert it into the ground, with half beneath the soil, which needs to have been prepared with plenty of well-rotted organic matter. Keep weeds well away.

SARRACENIA
Pitcher plant

A dramatic perennial carnivorous plant that devours flies and mosquitoes, with many species and cultivars (both fully and not completely hardy) offering different colours, patterning and shapes. One of the tallest is the frost-hardy *S. leucophylla*, which grows to about 80cm (2½ft) high and wide. When insects fly through the gap at the top of the tube, lured by nectar, they end up confused and fall to the bottom

of the pitcher where they are chemically digested. Look inside the tube over summer and you will see it is packed with dead insects. The extraordinary flowers are like upturned lanterns. Stand potted plants outside over summer in trays filled with rainwater, so the soil stays soaking wet, but over winter, in cold areas, it is best to bring them indoors and put them on a sunny windowsill, or in a cold or cool greenhouse. Clumps can easily be divided by slicing up the rhizomes with a sharp knife in spring, ensuring that each section has both roots and buds.

STRATIOTES
Water soldier

One of the best pond plants, because it both oxygenates and keeps the water clean. A depth of over 30cm (12in) is best for mature plants, though the young ones can be kept in the shallows until they get bigger. Each plant resembles a floating pineapple top. Just a few plants will soon produce plenty of plantlets on long stolons, like protruding umbilical cords, but keep an eye on small ponds because come midsummer you will find layers and layers of the plants, one above the other, and you will have to cull them so that you can see through the gaps between the plants to the bottom of the pond again. In winter, as the water gets colder, they sink to the bottom but float up again the following spring. Propagation is not necessary because the plants do it for you.

Stratiotes aloides

TIARELLA
Foam flower

A low-growing hardy perennial – at just 25cm (10in) high and 18cm (7in) wide – for the bog garden, *T. wherryi* makes small clumps of pale green leaves with a hint of maroon, especially in autumn. The white to pink flowers open through the end of spring, into early summer. Shear back the growth and you will get a second batch of fresh leaves and flowers. Grow it in cool, moist shade in the bog garden and it will spread by underground runners. Propagate by dividing the plants in spring, and replant immediately, carefully checking that each portion has both roots and shoots.

TROLLIUS
Globeflower

Three top choices for any sunny bog garden, especially the hardy, perennial common European globeflower (*T. europaeus*), *T. pumilis* and the cultivars of *T. × cultorum*. The first is a variable, compact plant, reaching some 60cm (2ft) high by 45cm (18in) wide, making a clump of lemon-yellow buttercup-like flowers in spring and the first half of summer. The second makes a smaller, slow-growing clump, with crinkled, divided leaves at the base topped by golden yellow flowers on erect stems, with red on the outside, again through spring and early summer. The cultivars of *T. × cultorum* give a slightly wider choice of colours, and all make decent clumps to about 75cm (2½ft)

Trollius europaeus

high and 45cm (18in) wide. 'Alabaster' is cream to pale yellow, though not impressively vigorous, 'Canary Bird' and 'Golden Queen' are both yellow, with many more yellows to choose from, and 'Feuertroll' makes a stronger show with orange-yellow. Two of the best include the strong-growing, deep orange-yellow 'Orange Princess' and the golden-yellow 'Superbus'. Propagate by division (especially the cultivars) when the new growth appears at the start of spring, or sow seed when newly ripe, or in spring, in containers in a cold frame – it may take 2 years to germinate.

TYPHA
Reedmace

T. latifolia makes a substantial hardy perennial that grows a good 1.8m (6ft) high and 60cm (2ft) wide, topped by dark brown seed heads. Do not be over-ambitious and grow it in unlikely

Typha latifolia

places. It needs plenty of space to spread and be seen, and when grown near muddy banks the seed will quickly germinate producing even more clumps, eventually creating a great spread of thickets. The best bet for a small pond is *T. minima* that grows just 30cm (12in) high and wide, with ginger brown seedheads. The latter can be propagated by dividing the rootstock in spring using a sharp knife. Pot up the new sections in aquatic baskets and keep the soil moist.

VERONICA
Speedwell

The hardy, perennial brooklime (*V. beccabunga*) likes sunny, shallow water or bog gardens, and grows just 10cm (4in) high. The blue flowers appear all summer. Should you need more, either divide clumps in spring or take summer cuttings and put them in sopping wet soil in trays or pots.

Veronica beccabunga

ZANTEDESCHIA
Arum lily

The hardy South African perennial *Z. aethiopica* 'Crowborough' – at 90cm (3ft) high and wide – gives the muddy margins or shallows of natural ponds an exotic touch, where it soon produces clumps of glossy, shiny green leaves up to 40cm (16in) long. The white spathes have a yellow spike. There are several other cultivars including 'Little Gem', 'White Giant', and 'Crowborough Variegated' with its yellow-splashed leaves. 'Crowborough' is slightly hardier than the parent species but, if it is being grown in areas prone to winter frosts, give it a thick, protective winter mulch or grow it in depths up to 30cm (12in) deep. To grow extra plants and create a lush, eye-catching display, propagate by dividing the tubers in spring. Each needs a set of roots and shoots.

DIVIDING TIARELLA

1 If not propagating by seed, dig up an established plant, and probe with your thumbs to separate the clump.

2 One large clump should provide several sections. Check that each has a good set of roots and a decent number of buds for the top growth.

3 The smallest new sections are planted in a container until they are big enough to be planted out. The large ones can go straight outside.

Zantedeschia aethiopica

Vegetables

ONION
Allium cepa
Onions can be grown from sets or seed, sets being the quickest option because they are small bulbs and that much more advanced. If growing seed, start in mid- or late winter at a temperature of 16°C (55°F) for hardening off in mid-spring, which gives an earlier crop than when sowing outdoors because warm soil is essential. The seedlings are spaced 10cm (4in) apart. When raising sets, they are planted out, at the same spacing, from early spring to harvest in midsummer. When the foliage starts yellowing and collapsing, fork up the onions and lie them in the sun to dry. Shake off the soil and store in a cool, dry shed.

LEEK
Allium porrum
A good crop of leeks can occupy a lot of ground all summer and winter, but they do stay in the ground (which should be average to heavy, and slightly moist) until you need them, and they do provide a good crop for soups and stews. Sow in seed trays in early spring at 19°C (66°F) for an autumn crop, and shoots should appear in 10 days (for a winter crop sow four to six weeks later in the open ground when the soil has warmed up). Scatter the seed thinly because germination rates

Leek

are high, and you will end up with a mini forest. Thin or prick them out about six weeks after sowing, leaving 5cm (2in) between each, and harden off in late spring. Plant out in early summer, when they are pencil thick, and use the end of a long broomstick like a giant dibber to make 15cm (6in) deep holes, 5cm (2in) wide, planting one seedling per hole (or more if you have spares), but do not then fill and firm in with soil. Instead give each leek a good drink. The soil will gradually slip back in over the following weeks, especially as you weed around the holes. If you want leeks with a long, white shaft then pile up soil around them in summer. Water well in dry spells.

Asparagus

ASPARAGUS
Asparagus officinalis
Before you start, note that this is a crop that can only be harvested for six weeks on the first occasion, but eight thereafter. Not long, but given how tasty they are, definitely worthwhile. It should be left alone for the first 2 years (3 years from seed), to let the plants build up. To help it germinate, at the end of winter soak the seed of a vigorous F1 (male) hybrid (which can crop for 20 years) for 12–24 hours in warm water, before planting in small pots at a depth of 12mm (½in). Keep at about 15°C (60°F), and harden off outside. Alternatively, buy young crowns for planting out in spring. Put them on top of a 10cm (4in) high ridge within a trench 30cm (12in) wide and 20cm (8in) deep, with well-rotted compost forked into the bottom. Arrange plants 30cm (12in) apart in rows 45cm (18in) apart. Spread out the roots and cover to leave the tips just visible. Thereafter, each spring, add a mulch to help suppress weeds, and also give an all-purpose feed, with a second one after the harvest. When harvesting, slice off the spear, when it is about 18cm (7in) tall, making the cut 2.5cm (1in) below the soil surface.

LAND CRESS
Barbarea verna
A hardy biennial, it produces two good crops a year, one sown in spring for a summer crop, and one in mid- or late summer to crop from autumn, over winter,

to the following spring. Grow it in sun or partial shade, ideally in moist, rich soil that does not dry out in summer. Sow at a depth of 12mm (½in), thinning to 15cm (6in). Always leave a few plants to flower and set seed to generate the next crop. It has a strong, watercress-type flavour.

BEETROOT
Beta vulgaris subsp. *vulgaris*
A multi-talented crop that can be picked for its roots, which keep well in the ground through winter, and its leaves, which can be added to salads. Provide full sun and rich, free-draining soil that has been beefed up with well-rotted compost. Then, about 10 days before planting out, fork an all-purpose fertilizer in the ground. Ideally sow F1 hybrid seed in early spring, first soaking it or rinsing it to wash off the natural inhibitor that can halt germination. Then sprinkle the seed on top of the compost (soil mix) at 15°C (60°F) but, because it needs plenty of light, only give it a light covering of perlite. If sowing outside, note that it will not germinate at temperatures under 7°C (45°F). After the first sowing, make more regular sowings (in summer you can do this straight in the ground) for a continuous supply of young, fresh, tasty roots. Give regular drinks in dry weather.

Beetroot

Onion

Kale

Cauliflower

Cabbage

KALE

Brassica oleracea **Acephala Group**

A good crop because it is just about the easiest brassica to care for, does not mind a bit of shade, is happy in poor soil (though it does much better in well prepared, enriched soil), does not suffer in the frost, can be used as a cut-and-come-again crop and is packed with vitamins. It also makes a dramatic show in the vegetable (or flower) garden, with some kinds having long, arching, dark green (even glaucous and bronze), smooth, crimped and even curled leaves. You need a slightly acid soil (if it is very acid, add lime) that is very firm — which is why you have to shuffle over it on your heels before planting — to provide good anchorage. Sow the seed at the start of spring 12mm (½in) deep, and when plants have developed six leaves (after about seven weeks) water before moving to their final position. Set each plant slightly deeper in the ground than previously, 45cm (18in) part, and immediately give one good drink after another. Subsequently mulch to lock the moisture in the ground. When the young, tasty leaves from the main stem have been harvested, the side shoots provide a further crop.

CAULIFLOWER

Brassica oleracea **Botrytis Group**

The trickiest of the brassicas, but by no means impossible to grow, cauliflower now comes in different colours with the heads in orange, white and purple. There is even a quick-grow summer kind, though the heads are on the small side. The soil needs to be slightly acid; if it is very acid, add lime. To provide good anchorage, walk over the soil on your heels before planting. The soil needs a pH of 6.5–7.5, and it is worth checking for the best results, with plenty of well-rotted compost having been added the previous autumn. Sow the seed from mid-spring to late spring, or earlier under glass at 13°C (55°F) for a summer crop. After several weeks (when about five or six leaves have developed), water the plants and then carefully move to their final position. Each plant then needs a good watering, and a planting distance of 60cm (2ft). Mulch and water well in dry periods. Never let them go thirsty. Start harvesting when the heads are quite small to generate even more. To help retain the colour of the heads, add lemon juice when cooking. Do not grow another crop on the same site for two years to avoid any problems with clubroot.

CABBAGE

Brassica oleracea **Capitata Group**

There is a wide range of cabbages, divided according to which season (spring, summer/autumn and winter) they are ready for harvesting. For a spring crop sow in the second half of summer, for a summer/autumn crop sow from late winter until late spring, and for a winter crop sow at the end of spring into early summer. All need transplanting about four weeks later to a site that has had plenty of well-rotted compost added several months before. You also need a slightly acid soil (add lime if it very acid), and it should be very firm, so shuffle over it on your heels before planting, in order to provide good anchorage. Sow the seed 12mm (½in) deep, and then thin out to leave gaps of 7.5cm (3in) between each. When the plants have developed six leaves, water and transplant to their final position, sinking them lower in the ground than previously to make sure the stems are firmly set in the ground, and give a good drink. Then another, and another (called 'puddling in'). Adding a mulch when the soil is wet helps lock moisture in the ground. Planting distances are 30–45cm (12–18in), depending on the size of the variety. Brassica collars are vital to keep off an attack of cabbage root fly, and a covering of fleece will deter cabbage white caterpillars and birds. After harvesting the spring and summer crop, cutting off the cabbage with a sharp knife, make a cross in the top of the stump and you will generate a second, smaller crop about six weeks later.

PLANTING CABBAGE SEEDLINGS

1 Summer cabbages are sown from late winter to late spring. To get them off to a decent start, sow in containers or modules.

2 When they make 10cm (4in) high seedlings, plant them out in full sun in soil that has had lots of well-rotted organic matter added to it.

3 Before planting add a general fertilizer at the recommended rate, and water in well. Always keep the site well weeded.

Brussels sprouts

Kohl rabi

BRUSSELS SPROUTS
Brassica oleracea **Gemmifera Group**
A good-value brassica crop that
stays fresh in the garden, waiting
to be picked over winter, with
a mix of green and red ('Red
Delicious') heads. Sow the seed
under glass in late winter for an
early crop, or outside from early
to late spring. Sow the seed just
12mm (½in) deep, and then thin
the seedlings to gaps of 7.5cm
(3in). When they have put on
13cm (5in) of growth, water and
move them to their final (ideally
wind-sheltered) positions, leaving
75cm (2½ft) between each plant.
Make sure that the ground had
plenty of well-rotted compost
added the previous autumn, and
that it has been well firmed down
before planting to lock the roots
in the ground and provide good
anchorage. Plants with weak stems

can be staked. Add a mulch after
a spell of heavy rain, and water
well in dry periods. Netting is a
good idea, warding off birds and
cabbage white caterpillars that can
create massive infestations, and
reduce the leaves to tatters. Crop
when required (with a sudden,
downward snap, working up from
the bottom of the plant), but
sprouts that have been frosted
are said to taste better.

KOHL RABI
Brassica oleracea **Gongylodes Group**
What might be thought of as
a slight novelty, it has a quick-
growing, edible swollen stem base,
with a nutty-celery flavour. Sow
the seed 12mm (½in) deep from
mid-spring *in situ* in rows 30cm
(12in) apart, but then thin as
soon as possible so that the
distance between each one

is 23cm (9in). Mulching is
important because the ground
needs to be constantly moist,
which means that adding well-
rotted compost the previous
autumn will certainly help. Keep
an eye on the plants and harvest
when the stem bases are smaller
than an apple, but bigger than a
squash ball. Do not let them sit
in the ground, waiting for them
to get bigger, because the flavour
will be impaired and they can
become quite bitter.

BROCCOLI, CALABRESE
Brassica oleracea **Italica Group**
A good choice brassica for its
high vitamin content, but you
have to decide whether you want
the hardy (white or purple)
sprouting types that are harvested
from mid-winter to spring, or
the fast-growing calabrese with
bluish-green heads for picking
from late summer into autumn,
or both. In both cases you need a
slightly acid soil (you should add
lime if it is very acid) that has
been enriched with well-rotted
compost the previous autumn.
It also needs to be very firm – so
you should walk over it on your
heels before planting – to provide
good anchorage. Sow the seed just
12mm (½in) deep in mid- or
late spring, and then thin out
the quickly emerging seedlings,
leaving gaps of 7.5cm (3in).
Slugs and snails are an immediate
problem, and they can devour an
emerging crop overnight. When
the plants have put on good

growth and are about 13cm (5in)
high, water and then transplant
to their final position, sinking
them lower in the ground than
previously to make sure that the
stems are firmly set in the ground,
and then give another good drink.
Leave 45cm (18in) gaps between
each plant because they dislike
being packed together, but for the
slightly smaller calabrese you can
reduce that by 15cm (6in). After a
night of heavy rain add a mulch,
and give regular drinks in dry
spells. A major problem is
marauding birds, and the crop
needs protecting by a net. The
best time for harvesting is just
before the flowers open, and this
also helps generate extra produce
on side shoots. Snap off or cut
the crop from the main stem first.

CHILLI
Capsicum annuum **Longum Group**
Chillies are becoming increasingly
popular, and there is a huge range
from specialist seed suppliers
offering everything from large,
sweet supermarket peppers in all
kinds of quirky shapes to chillies
for Asian recipes. The latter
include those that are relatively
mild and tasty to the ferociously
hot. Most chillies end up red,
but while maturing they can
go through a wide spectrum
including yellow and orange, with
some bright purple and others
near black. Again, shapes are
varied, from those like a short,
thin finger to the very long and
twisty. Keep picking and feeding
for a continuous supply through
summer. Sow seed in late winter
at 28°C (82°F) for 7–28 days,
and either grow well-established
plants in greenhouse pots – at
least 20cm (8in) wide – or
growbags, or to the front of a
sunny border. Cut back when
about 40–45cm (16–18in)
long to produce a bushier, more
productive plant. Some can be
overwintered indoors, being given
the occasional drink while dormant.

CUCUMBER
Cucumis sativus
You will get a longer season of
cucumbers if you can grow them
in the warmth of a greenhouse,
though you can get a perfectly

Broccoli

Chilli

Courgette (zucchini)

decent crop if you choose varieties specifically for the outdoors. Sow the seed of F1 female varieties at the end of winter or early spring for a heated greenhouse, or mid-spring for a cool one, or at the end of spring for growing outdoors. Lay the seed on its side in a pot and cover with perlite, providing a temperature of 21°C (70°F). When it shoots, pot on and give it a sunny place until it is ready for planting out. Those being grown outside need hardening off during the day, initially bringing them in at night, until ready. Plant out in the first few weeks of summer, when the temperature is consistently higher. The soil should be rich and moist, with plenty of well-rotted compost having been added the previous autumn. Water well in dry spells, and give a tomato liquid feed when the crop starts setting.

DESIGNING VEGETABLE BEDS

Planning the vegetable garden starts with getting the dimensions of the beds right. To avoid walking on, damaging and compacting the soil structure when you tend crops, measure how far you can reach with one arm, and almost double that to get the width of the bed. Double check the figure is right by trying to fork over soil in the middle of the proposed bed. The total should not exceed 1.3m (4½ft). Given that you will be walking around it, do not make it so long that you've got to keep walking long distances to get to the other side. You will benefit from having a series of smallish beds, separated by paths 45cm (18in) wide for a wheelbarrow, that can be easily tended.

Better still, especially where you have difficult soil, aim for a few raised beds. This simply means creating a large, open-top, open-bottom box made from materials such as railway sleepers (railroad ties), sawn logs, mortar-bonded frost-proof brick or stone, dry-stone walls, or pressure-treated gravel boards. Make sure you put it in the right position, because moving it will be a nightmare. If there is a chance you might also be growing ericaceous plants, you will need to

line the insides with polythene or plastic sheeting – nailing it in place – to prevent lime seeping out of the mortar and damaging the plants' roots.

What is the point of a raised bed? First, if you have a garden packed with heavy, poor-draining, hard-to-warm up (albeit fertile) clay soil, or soil with the wrong pH for your crop, a raised bed with made-to-measure, light, quick-draining, fertile, moisture-retentive soil is an excellent answer, facilitating good root development. It will not need extra feeding. Even better, raised beds warm up more quickly than those at ground level, getting you off to an

earlier start when it comes to sowing, and help reduce backache. However, on heavy ground you will first need to fork or dig up the base of the raised bed, especially when it is a low one, to guarantee good drainage, adding plenty of grit as well as well-rotted organic material. When you have finished, let the contents (a mixture of soil and organic matter) settle for several weeks before planting. Note: because raised beds warm up quite quickly, they do need extra watering in long, dry spells, especially at the sides.

When the stems reach the top of the climbing frame, pinch out the top and spreading laterals will take over. Pick regularly for a long crop.

COURGETTE, MARROW AND SQUASH
Cucurbita pepo
You need a lot of room for each courgette – 1m² (1sq yd), and twice that for marrows and squashes – and a site in full sun

or they really will not perform very well. The soil needs to be rich and moist, having had plenty of well-rotted compost forked in months before. Then add an all-purpose feed just before planting out. The seed is probably one of the quickest to shoot up; just pop a few in small pots on a sunny windowsill in mid-spring, and select the most vigorous. One plant will easily produce enough

courgettes for one family. Pot up and harden off in a cold frame before planting out in early summer, but look out for slugs which can demolish young plants (always grow a spare in case you need a replacement). Give good drinks in hot weather, and if powdery mildew strikes treat with sulphur dust. Pick when young and tender; the flowers can be stuffed and fried.

SOWING CUCUMBER SEED

1 Get plants off to an early spring start, sowing the seed in a container at 21°C (70°F). Plant two seeds per pot and remove the weaker seedling.

2 When the roots poke through the bottom, plant it up into a larger container, until the weather is mild enough for it to be planted out.

3 The climbing stems need to be woven through netting, or tied to supports, to stop them flopping across the ground.

Cucumber

GROWING CARROTS

1 The most essential task is before sowing. The soil needs to be fine and crumbly without any clods or large stones. Dig, rake and rake again.

2 Scatter the seed thinly, but you will still need to do some thinning, removing the seedlings, to give the others room to expand underground.

3 If the aim is to grow lots of tiny carrots, then such regimental thinning is not necessary. Keep picking and keep sowing.

Rocket

CARROT
Daucus carota

The key ingredient for growing long carrots is fine, crumbly soil that has not been freshly manured, and that is the same depth as the length of whichever carrot variety you are growing, or the root shape will be stunted. When growing on difficult, stony ground just choose the round or short-rooted varieties. Then choose between the different kinds (early and maincrop) for cropping from early summer to autumn, and sow at the appropriate times. However, note that carrot seed will not germinate at low temperatures, which should be above 7°C (45°F). Sow at a depth of 12mm (½in) in rows 15cm (6in) apart. Since carrot fly is a big potential problem, producing young that tunnel into the carrots, thin to 5–7.5cm (2–3in) apart, depending on the variety, in

the evening when the pest is less active. Immediately cover with horticultural fleece to keep the pest at bay or grow inside 60cm (2ft) barriers made of mesh or cardboard to keep out the low-flying, egg-laying females. Attempts at growing strongly scented nearby plants to confuse the fly are not the most reliable solution. The crop should be ready in three to four months.

ROCKET
Eruca vesicaria

An easy, quick-growing crop with a choice between the traditional leaf strain (*Eruca*) and the stronger taste of the wild kind (*Diplotaxis muralis*). Do not make the mistake of waiting for the leaves to grow to their maximum size before starting to crop for the kitchen because the more you cut, the more new leaves are produced, and just one packet of seed will provide a substantial

crop. You also need to start cropping before the leaves are ravaged by flea beatles (which attack various brassicas from mid-spring to late summer), when the foliage is riddled and lacerated with holes. Sowing the seed could not be easier. Sow in 12mm (½in) deep drills, thinning to gaps of 15cm (6in). Keep watering in hot, dry weather or rocket bolts, producing flowers, and the leaves turn bitter. If you see a mass of developing buds, shear off the tops immediately. Replacement crops quickly shoot up. Can be eaten raw in salads.

LETTUCE
Lactuca sativa

There are basically two different kinds of lettuce, the loose-leaf (non-hearting) kind that you can pick whole, or just a few leaves at a time, as required, leaving the whole plant to generate more growth, and the

more compact, denser (headed) kind, usually picked whole. Within the first category there is a wide choice from those with reddish leaves ('Lollo Rossa') and frilly edges ('Bergamo') and oak-like foliage ('Cocarde'), with the second offering everything from the upright, crunchy cos types to what are called crispheads ('Webb's Wonderful') and butterheads ('Tom Thumb') with soft leaves. Grow a wide mix, always growing the seed in the same way. Rake the ground to a fine, open tilth, so that it is very crumbly, and wait for the ground to warm up unless, for example, you want to sow individual seeds in root trainers under cover to get a few weeks start. When sowing directly outdoors, sow the seed in drills just 12mm (½in) deep, water in and wait for the seedlings to appear. They need thinning to approximately 23cm (9in) apart, depending on the variety. (Do not discard the unused thinnings because they can be scattered on a salad.) When young, lettuces are an easy target for birds, slugs and snails, and the whole crop can be demolished overnight. Keep sowing replacements to provide a continuous supply as more and more lettuces are picked (or wiped out) over summer, and water regularly or they bolt in hot, dry weather, when they suddenly and prematurely put all their energy into producing flowers and seed. This causes the leaves to taste very bitter. To get a near year-round crop you will need a large heated greenhouse.

SOWING LETTUCE SEED

1 Fill a number of small modules with seed compost (soil mix), tap down so that they are level, and water with a fine rose spray.

2 Sow one or two seeds in each module, 12mm (½in) deep, removing the feeblest seedling. Germination rates are normally very high.

Lettuce

Tomato

TOMATO

Lycopersicon esculentum

You can grow tiny or giant tomatoes (in purple, red, pink, yellow or orange) under glass or outside, as tall, thin stems (indeterminates or cordons) that fruit over a long season or as low-growing bushes with more of a sudden glut. There are also kinds specially for pots and hanging baskets that are not so prolific. There is now a wide range of tomato varieties available, with different seed companies competing for ever-sweeter kinds.

Positioning: before deciding which varieties you want, work out where you are going to grow them. If you have a greenhouse, that is the best option because it provides better warmth for a longer period, while outside tomatoes can suffer in a bad summer with poor temperatures and excessive rain. Greenhouses also enable you to train the cordons more easily up a vertical support, whether that is a tight piece of string anchored to the ground and tied to the roof, or a stout cane. If growing tomatoes outside, cordons benefit from a bed against a sunny wall where they get the extra benefit of the warm brickwork, and you can attach some support. Grow them in large pots to protect them from soil-borne diseases. Sun and shelter are essential. If providing support for the cordons is a problem, stick to bush tomatoes. They spread about 90cm (3ft) wide, and can be either left to themselves or better still, given a short support system.

To complicate matters, some tomatoes are semi-determinate, being part-bush and part-cordon. Also, note that some varieties really do benefit from being grown under glass, in the warmth. Check the back of the seed packet.

Sowing: sow seed in mid-spring, approximately eight weeks before planting out. When being grown in a cold greenhouse, sow in early spring, and in a heated greenhouse, late winter. The small seed rests on the surface of the compost (soil mix), being covered with perlite because it needs both warmth – 18°C (65°F) – and light to germinate. Pot up as required, and start hardening off the outside kind in late spring, standing plants out on warm days, but bringing them in at night because pre-summer nights can still get very cold. If the start of summer is cold, delay planting.

Soil: tomatoes being grown in the open ground need rich, fertile soil. Add well-rotted compost the previous autumn. In large pots they can be grown in grow-bag compost (soil mix) that has been broken up with a trowel.

Cultivation: good light is essential for all tomatoes, so plant them 45cm (18in) apart, which will also give you good access. Make sure the cordons are given strong support, which can hold up the weight of the stem and the tomatoes, and keep tying them in as they grow. Also, start removing the side shoots (only on cordons) the moment they appear. Water the pot and grow-bag tomatoes in dry weather, and start feeding all kinds with a liquid tomato feed when the first crop reaches pea size. From then on it is important that all kinds are kept evenly moist, because if the soil becomes dry followed by a sudden big drink, the tomatoes suddenly swell and the skins split. When greenhouse cordons have reached seven trusses, nip off the growing tip, or four in the case of the outdoor kind. That is because there will not be time for these top trusses to set, due to the onset of colder autumn weather and shorter days.

Harvesting: pick the fruit the moment it is ripe, while the unripened green tomatoes should be picked at the end of the season and put in a drawer with a banana to help them ripen.

PINCHING OUT TOMATOES

Identify shoots growing in the angle between the main stem and the leaves. Nip them out to save the plant's energy. Do not confuse them with the emerging trusses that will bear tomatoes.

Close care: tomatoes are quite time-consuming, especially if being grown in grow-bags, because they need regular watering and, in the case of cordons, pinching out. Outside crops also benefit from regular preventative sprayings every 10–14 days against blight, which can suddenly ruin a crop. The leaves and crop turn black, and the problem can spread with alarming speed. Everything must be discarded and destroyed. Provided you can keep on top of that, the rest is easy.

Tips for success: do not grow tomatoes in the same soil two years running. When having to grow them in exactly the same position outdoors, dig up the soil to a depth of 90cm (3ft) and replace with fresh soil from elsewhere. Also, use large pots because the weight of the soil will stop them from getting blown over.

METHODS FOR GROWING TOMATOES

Tomatoes can be grown in various ways. Greenhouse cordons are grown up a strong, stout support, tied in to stop them flopping over.

Grow bags are an excellent alternative method, but again you will need to insert a stout cane which should be tied securely to the backing fence.

To grow tomato plants in a hanging basket, choose a variety specifically bred for that purpose – these are mostly cherry tomatoes.

SOWING RUNNER BEAN SEED

1 You can plant runner beans outside in spring, but it is safer to start them off in containers, avoiding them getting eaten by slugs.

2 Plant the seed and stand the containers in a cold frame. Grow the beans as large as possible before planting them out.

Runner bean

RUNNER BEAN
Phaseolus coccineus

Incredibly easy to grow, with a huge crop just months after planting the seed. You will need a climbing frame or wigwam about 2.1m (7ft) high because beans are vigorous climbers and need support, though a few dwarf varieties are available. Note that a big block of runners will cast some shade, so be careful where you position it. You can plant the large, often colourful seeds *in situ* when the soil has warmed up in late spring or early summer, in rich, fertile soil that does not dry out too fast. Adding well-rotted compost two months before sowing helps, and then an all-purpose general fertilizer just weeks before sowing. Or, to get an earlier crop, sow the seed in root trainers under glass in mid-spring for planting out when there are no more frosts and the ground has warmed up. Give regular drinks in hot, dry weather; the more you pick, the bigger and more persistent your crop. If you leave the plants in the ground over winter, the roots improve the nitrogen levels in the soil.

PEA
Pisum sativum

Peas come in all sizes from rampant climbers – exceeding 2m (6½ft) – to the dwarf kind, with the former needing a batch of twiggy branches fixed firmly in the ground just after planting to climb up. Select carefully and you can have crops from early summer to mid-autumn. The soil needs to be rich and moist, having had plenty of well-rotted compost added, but do not start sowing until it has warmed up. To get an early crop (a way of avoiding attacks from the pea moth), sow the seed under cover in spring in lengths of guttering with added drainage holes. Alternatively, cover and warm the ground with polythene, to get an earlier crop from seed sown *in situ*. The seeds go into a flat-bottomed trench 5cm (2in) deep and 23cm (9in) wide, at gaps of about 8cm (3½in). Lightly backfill with soil. Keep watering during dry spells to maintain good growth, and add a mulch after a night of heavy rain. Keep picking to generate more produce.

POTATO
Solanum tuberosum

Select potatoes according to when they are planted and harvested, the main groups being first earlies (ready to be eaten in about 12 weeks), second earlies (about four weeks later) and maincrops (from the end of summer into autumn), with most people growing some of each to give a long season. The soil benefits from having had plenty of well-rotted compost added the previous autumn, with some all-purpose fertilizer added just before planting. Buy special virus-free seed potatoes (i.e. small tubers) in late winter, and start them into growth in a bright, cool shed. Stand them in egg boxes so that the dormant sprouts are facing up, and they will become small shoots in about six weeks. They can be planted out in spring. Dig a trench 10–15cm (4–6in) deep, and arrange the earlies at gaps of 30cm (12in) in rows 60cm (2ft) apart, with the maincrops being given gaps of 40cm (16in) in rows 75cm (2½ft) apart. Carefully cover the tubers with 2.5cm (1in) of soil so that you do not damage or snap off the shoots. As more shoots poke up through the soil keep piling more soil on top to avoid having a batch of green (toxic) potatoes and reduce the likelihood of an attack of blight (in warm, wet weather) on second earlies and maincrops, though they can be regularly sprayed every two weeks as a preventative measure. Alternatively, stick to cultivars showing good resistance to the problem (e.g. 'Cara', 'Markies' and 'Remarka'). To store, keep in hessian sacks in a cool, dry, dark place.

CORN SALAD
Valerianella locusta

A good salad choice, because lamb's lettuce, as it is also called, is hardy and unfussy when it comes to soil and situation. It can be sown twice a year – needing temperatures of just 8–10°C (46–50°F) to germinate – at the start of spring for a summer crop, and again at

Pea

Potato

EARTHING UP POTATOES

1 Earth up potatoes until the mound is 30cm (12in) high), to avoid blight and exclude light, which can turn them green and poisonous.

2 When the flowers open or the buds drop, start digging them up, checking that they really are big enough to harvest.

3 The crop can be stored in hessian sacks, but keep them in a cool, dark place; if exposed to light, they will soon turn green.

Sweet corn

the end of summer. Sow at a depth of 12mm (½ in), in rows 15cm (6in) apart, taking leaves as necessary. Since plants can reseed, leave several plants to flower.

SWEET CORN
Zea mays

Long, hot summers give the best results, on top of which you need a sheltered site in full sun. Sow the seed in spring, at 19°C (66°F), in root trainers to avoid root disturbance, and only plant out when the warm weather has picked up. Grow the taller varieties 45m (18in) apart in blocks of six by six plants to facilitate good wind pollination, and pile soil over the roots if they appear at the base of the stems. Water well when in flower, and as the kernels start swelling. Pick when ripe, when a squeezed or punctured, exposed segment (or kernel) bleeds a creamy liquid.

CROP ROTATION

The principle could not be simpler. If you grow the same groups of vegetables in the same plot of ground year after year, you will end up with a build-up of pests and diseases in the soil (this excludes the airborne kind, which are another matter) and the crops will suffer. Move the groups around, from one plot to the next, and you will help reduce (but not prevent, certainly not when the individual beds are close to each other) problems such as clubroot (affecting the cabbage family) and white rot (the onion family). Furthermore, some crops, such as potatoes, are good at smothering weeds and benefit each patch of ground on which they are grown. In reality, rotation of crops is not always possible, and if you do have to grow the same crop on the same site, year after year, at least dig up and replace the ground each year with fresh soil from other parts of the garden.

Ideally, divide the produce into the following five categories, the brassicas (cabbages and swedes), legumes (peas and beans), onions (including garlic and shallots), potato family (potatoes and tomatoes) and umbellifers (carrots, parsnips and Florence fennel), and each year move them around plots in the vegetable garden, according to your needs, so that each also benefits from the previous year's regime. So, the legumes that leave nitrogen in the soil are followed by the brassicas that thrive on it. Since most gardens will not have sufficient room for this five-bed system, the following three-group one is a good, traditional compromise.

Note: they are not strictly defined botanical groups, because the plants are partly organized by their growing needs. The main crops in each group are:
Root vegetables: beetroot, carrot, leek, lettuce, onion, potato.
Brassicas: broccoli, Brussels sprouts, cabbage, cauliflower, swedes, turnips.
Legumes and others: beans, courgette, cucumber, squash, sweet corn, tomato.

Corn salad

Herbs

GARLIC
Allium sativum
This is grown from individual cloves, not seed. In late autumn put them in 2.5cm (1in) deep holes in the ground, nose up, in rich, free-draining soil in full sun. Dig up and use next summer.

CHIVES
Allium schoenoprasum
They like a sunny site with rich, free-draining soil. Do not be afraid to massacre it, cutting clumps hard back to the ground over summer to generate a fresh batch of growth with its strong onion flavour. Water well. Grows easily from seed in spring at 19°C (66°F).

TARRAGON, FRENCH
Artemisia dracunculus
Has a very strong, highly distinctive flavour, so you will not need to grow much, but it cannot be grown from seed. Do not confuse with the less tasty Russian kind that can. Take tip cuttings in summer and raise in a misting unit, with gentle bottom heat, because the soil should be kept dryish while the leaves need to be moist.

FENNEL
Foeniculum vulgare
Both purple and green varieties are good self-seeders, and once in the garden will keep popping up. Fennel needs full sun in good, fertile, free-draining soil. Grow it to the front of a border so that you can easily pick the fronds,

Chives

Tarragon

Mint

which lose their strong sharp taste when roasted. Grow from seed in spring at 19°C (66°F). Shoots quickly appear within two weeks. The seeds make an aromatic tea.

BAY
Laurus nobilis
Thrives in warm, dry conditions, and if you can provide those you will not just be able to grow a couple of evergreen bay trees in pots outside your front door but a thick, dense bay hedge. It can be slightly tricky to propagate, with seed taking from two weeks to 12 months to germinate. Sow in early autumn at 19°C (66°F) or propagate by removing a sucker. Remove the soil to expose the join with the parent, and make

sure it has its own root system. If not, wait; if so, pull away and then trim back the main root below the fibrous roots. Pot up, and cut back the top-growth by 50 per cent. Keep it in a frost-free place until established.

MINT
Mentha
Will snake and spread all over the place, and is traditionally grown in a bottomless bucket sunk in the soil to restrain its stems. There is a huge variety available, with many different flavours to choose from. Seed can be sown in spring at 19°C (66°F), but you could equally take root cuttings from spring to late summer from an established clump. Remove a section with two growing nodes, trim to below a node, and grow in a seed tray with cuttings compost (soil mix). Plant at a depth of 18mm (¾in), water and a shoot might appear in two weeks.

BASIL
Ocimum basilicum
Likes long, hot summers, and given they do not always occur, it might be better growing it in containers in a greenhouse. The range of basils is now huge, though on a blind tasting you might not spot the difference, but it is well worth growing the large leaf kind ('Napolitano') as well as the small (Greek basil), those with curly edged leaves ('Green Ruffles') and coloured leaves

('Dark Opal'). Sow seed in early spring at 19°C (66°F), and keep pinching out the growth to get a bushy, productive plant. Do not let it flower or the taste of the leaves turns bitter. Grow huge amounts if making home-made pesto. Beware of slugs.

MARJORAM
Origanum
Best in hot, dry, quick-draining, alkaline (chalky) soil. Note plants make decent mounds so plant them out about 25cm (10in) apart. Sow the very fine seed mixed with sand, scattering it down the fold of a piece of paper to get a good spread and avoid getting congested clumps that make pricking out difficult. Leave the seed uncovered on top of the compost (soil mix) to germinate in spring at 19°C (66°F).

Fennel

Bay

PLANTING GARLIC

Insert the garlic bulbs with the woody base going into the soil, leaving the pointy top, where the new shoot emerges, just above the surface.

Basil

Marjoram

Parsley

Rosemary

PARSLEY (CURLY AND PLAIN-LEAF)
Petroselinum crispum

Needs rich, fertile soil and regular drinks when grown in hot sun. Keep picking to generate more growth. Grow a fresh batch each year in spring at 19°C (66°F), sowing the seed in pots or guttering to avoid root disturbance. Because the seed has a natural inhibitor, making it slow to germinate, wash it off in warm water. Or sow later, outside, in its final position, when the soil has warmed up. Beware of slugs.

ROSEMARY
Rosmarinus

Almost qualifies as an architectural plant because some kinds have (or can be given, with judicious pruning) a strong shape. Choose between the tall uprights ('Miss Jessopp's Upright') and the spreaders (Prostratus Group), growing individuals and hedges, and those with white and pinkish/bluish flowers. In spring sow seed at 21°C (70°F) or, more reliably, grow from cuttings.

THYME
Thymus

Loves a hot, dry site, and if you want a large collection of one particular herb, this is the best.

There are many different kinds producing an array of shapes and tastes, some with variegated leaves, all with a good covering of attractive summer flowers. Look out for *T. herba-barona*, which gets just 2.5cm (1in) high with a gentle spread of 20cm (8in) and tiny leaves with a strong caraway scent. It contrasts well with the upright kinds, such as common thyme (*T. vulgaris*) and its many cultivars (e.g. 'Silver Posie'). All need poor, free-draining soil, so they are often grown in gaps between paving, which also reflects back the heat. It is best grown from cuttings, though a few can be grown from the very fine seed. Germinate in spring at 20°C (68°F).

DESIGNING HERB GARDENS

When designing your herb garden, think first about which herbs you want, and in what quantities you are likely to use them. Many like full sun and poor soil, but some prefer more fertility and moisture. The area also needs to be accessible – ideally near the kitchen – and finally, it needs to look good.

Informality
The basic styles range from the informal to the smartly geometric, and the traditional to the modern. Informal designs work best in cottage gardens with a free-and-easy arrangement, but 'free-and-easy' can quickly turn into 'chaotic', with the vigorous herbs barging their quieter neighbours out the way, eventually smothering them, giving you minimal pickings. With all this mayhem, there is also a danger that weeds will start sprouting between the herbs, and gradually start taking over. So if you want an area that looks informal and relaxed while being highly productive, weed it regularly and keep the more vigorous herbs firmly under control.

Formality
The advantage of a well-organized herb garden is that it is immediately clear where everything is growing and when certain plants need to be cut back because they are outgrowing their allotted space, or need to be dug up and moved to give them more room. It is also clear when a new young plant starts floundering and does not grow that well. Either there is a problem with that plant, or it is growing in the wrong conditions. You can also immediately see which plants are being most regularly harvested, possibly to the point of needing extra numbers. But whichever design you use, make sure that the herbs are fronting paths or flower beds so that you can easily get close to them to check on their wellbeing and take cuttings, and that competing weeds are kept well away.

Thyme

Pests and diseases

The best way of growing problem-free plants is to start with healthy, vigorous forms, and to grow them well. That means starting with fresh compost (soil mix) and fresh seed, which will have a better germination rate than old seed, and using equipment (seed trays and pots, etc.) that has been freshly sterilized or scrubbed, even if it was thoroughly cleaned before being stored away.

Healthy young plants stand a much better chance of fighting off problems than poor, weak ones, and problems can pile up in the protected environment of a greenhouse. Beware the following.

• Poor ventilation – note that greenhouse doors and windows, and lids of cold frames, should be propped open whenever possible, even in winter.

• General clutter – put away all pots and containers etc., so that pests (including mice) will not have good access to hiding places, and fungal spores cannot build up. Keep on top of the mess.

• High temperatures – especially when they are with poor and high light levels.

• Poor-draining compost (soil mix) – you do not want seedlings and cuttings sitting (and rotting) in soggy conditions when they are dormant.

• Overfeeding – resulting in leggy, sappy growth that is a prime target for sap-sucking creatures and various diseases.

• Also note – biological controls cannot be used in conjunction with insecticides.

Blackbird

PESTS

Aphids Also called blackfly and greenfly – though they come in other colours, including pink, orange, yellow, brown and white – these are tiny sap-feeding insects, 1–6mm long. All suck the sap of a plant. Strongly growing plants will often shrug them off with only minor and temporary damage, but with small, delicate specimens the aphids can seriously weaken them and distort the shoot tips and new foliage. They can also spread viruses, so be extra careful with plants that are prone to viral disease. Look for the excreted sticky substance – called honeydew – on the upper leaf surface, that falls from the leaves above, attracting sooty mould. Badly infested plants should be destroyed. Control by picking off small numbers and crushing them, by applying a jet of water from a hose, and by using organic and chemical sprays. The parasitic wasp *Aphidias matricariae* works above temperatures of 18°C (64°F).

Bird and cats The former tuck into seedlings, basically a tasty salad, especially early in the morning when they strut round the garden hauling out what they like. Scarecrows do not scare crows, let alone anything else. Canes with string running from one to another with old CDs might help. Netting is the best bet, but make sure it is tightly pinned down at the sides because birds can get in and get trapped – and if a cat gets in, the seedlings will get shredded in the mayhem.

Caterpillar from vapourer moth

Aphids

Scale insects

Cats are more of a hindrance than a help at keeping birds out of the garden because the moment they spot a spare patch of bare soil (where you have sown annuals), they use it as a toilet, and all the seedlings go flying as they dig a hole and evacuate their bowels, then scatter soil in all directions in a hopeless attempt at burying it.

Caterpillars The larval stage of moths and butterflies feed on roots, stems, flowers, fruit and seedpods, with the cabbage white butterfly, elephant hawk moth and winter moth quickly shredding leaves. They also attack seedlings in autumn. They hide during the day under pots and in piles of dead leaves. Small numbers can easily be removed by hand, but use the biological control *Bacillus thuringiensis* or a systemic insecticide against large infestations.

Red spider mites Infestations occur in hot, dry conditions outside or more typically in the greenhouse or on a sunny windowsill. The mites are minuscule, eight-legged sap-suckers, initially yellowish-green but turning orange-red in autumn. They multiply at a fast rate, and can be seen with a magnifying glass moving from stem to leaf on fine webbing. Hang perforated envelopes containing the predatory mite *Phytoseiulus*

Red spider mites

Sciarid fly

persimilis that attacks the pest. Alternatively use a systemic insecticide and/or grow plants in a humid atmosphere, giving repeated sprayings of water.

Scale insects When you see a cluster of immobile brown bumps or flattish discs on stems and leaves, plants are being attacked by sap-sucking insects with a shell-like covering over their bodies. Some excrete a sticky substance called honeydew on the leaves, leading to sooty moulds. The problem can occur all year on indoor plants, or in midsummer outside. Heavy infestations limit plant growth and make the leaves turn yellow. Control by using the parasitic wasp *Metaphycus helvolus* in a greenhouse, or a systemic spray.

Sciarid fly Also called fungus gnats, these tiny black flies congregate on the surface of the compost (soil mix) in pots. The larvae live in the soil – and they are especially fond of peat – where they feed on roots and organic detritus, and consequently seedlings and cuttings put on poor, limited growth. Established plants rarely suffer, and the flies are more of an annoyance to humans than the plants. The best way to prevent an attack is to use free-draining, sterilized compost, and to make sure that it is never overwatered. Cover the compost surface with a 5mm (¼in) deep

Slug

Vine weevil

Snail

Whitefly

layer of grit. Once you see the flies running across the soil surface and around the rim of the pot, use an insecticide or hang up sticky yellow strips so that they are near soil level. The predatory mite *Hypoaspis miles* feeds on the maggots of various pests in the soil.

Slugs and snails It is rare to have a garden without slugs and snails, but you can try to limit their damage. They will quickly demolish stems and seedlings, attacking dahlias and lilies, for example. (All slugs were once snails but have lost their shells, replacing them with mucus, and the reason why one gaily slithers along in the wake of another's goo is that it does not have to make its own supply.) The best predators are hedgehogs, frogs and thrushes, so surround the garden with a wild area for the former, and site ponds among the more formal flowery areas. Keep going out at night to pick them off by hand (what happens next depends on how squeamish you are, with drowning a fairly quick death sentence). Also try any of the countless deterrents, from saucers of beer sunk in the ground (more drowning) to surrounding prize plants with sharp sand. Nematodes can be watered into beds and borders to seek out and destroy slugs (snails

being largely immune). Pots can be wrapped round with copper tape, and some toxic slug pellets are efficient killers, but check whether they are hazardous to other creatures, killing the very predators you want to encourage.

Vine weevils A potential killer of established pot plants (rarely those growing out in the open, and rarely seedlings and cuttings), with the adults being less of a pest than the larvae. But when you spot the adults (they cut semicircular sections out of the edges of leaves) act quickly. They are 9mm (³⁄₈in) long, dull black beetles usually seen at night (hiding during the day) scuttling about the foliage, which they feed on. They lay their tiny, almost impossible-to-see eggs in the soil (that is 1,500 eggs in a female's lifespan) and the emerging fat, white, legless, C-shaped grubs have beige heads. They devour a plant's roots and suddenly you've got a dead plant that was happy and thriving the day before. The grubs are also quite capable of boring into tubers. Check pot plants at night looking for the adults, and anywhere they might hide (e.g. in upturned pots), and use imidacloprid spray on the leaves. Water parasitic nematodes (*Heterorhabditis*) into the compost when the soil temperature is over 55°C (13°F) and the surface is

moist. Encourage ground beetles that prey on the larvae.

Whiteflies Keep checking under leaves for colonies of 2mm (¹⁄₈in)-long, white, winged insects on greenhouse plants, e.g. tomatoes and cucumbers. They take off and swarm at the slightest touch. The flies live just three weeks and breed quickly, with both young and adults sucking the sap. Like other insects they can also excrete sticky honeydew on the leaves. The upshot is that plants perform badly, and might be infected by a virus. Growing the strong-smelling French marigolds (*Tagetes patula*) nearby is a proven deterrent, but you can also use sticky yellow traps hanging on plants, the parasitic wasp *Encarsia formosa* – which will not eradicate a big infestation, but will severely reduce it provided night temperatures stay above 10°C (50°F) with the day ones above 18°C (64°F) – or a systemic insecticide.

DISEASES

Botrytis The commonest fungal problem, immediately recognized by the fuzzy, greyish mould appearing on flowers, stems and leaves. The spores rapidly spread. To discourage an attack, cut off any injured or dead parts of the plant and promptly discard.

Damping off A fungal disease that attacks germinating seeds and also rots seedlings at soil level. Avoid high humidity, and space out the seedlings, giving them room to grow uncluttered.

Mildew There are a wide range of mildews, most attacking a particular host plant, and all have the same symptoms. They include a dry coating of white powder on the flowers, shoot tips and/or leaves in summer, causing stunted growth and poor flowering. Dry soil and humid, stagnant air encourage the disease. Affected new foliage should be promptly removed or sprayed with a fungicide.

Rust Typically seen on roses, patches of bright orange appear on the underside of the foliage, with yellow on the top side, in bad cases resulting in heavy defoliation. It is absolutely vital that you promptly collect every last leaf because the spores can persist on fallen infected leaves on the ground over winter. Avoid by ensuring plants have an open centre, pruning to an outward-facing bud, and good air circulation. Spray with mancozeb.

Viruses The wide range of viruses are usually caused by aphids or infected tools, and can result in mottling and stunting. Sterilize tools and burn infected plants, and do not propagate from them.

Botrytis

Mildew

Rust

Cucumber mosaic virus

Glossary

Annual Plant that goes through its entire life cycle – germinating, flowering and setting seed – within a growing season.

Anther The part of the stamen where the pollen forms.

Basal cuttings Cuttings taken from the bottom of a plant.

Basal plate The bottom of a bulb from which new bulbs can grow.

Bedding plant An annual, biennial or perennial that is used to make a temporary display in a bed or border. The advantage is that new displays keep being created using a different mixture of plants.

Biennial plant Taking two years to complete their entire life cycle, with growth occurring in the first year, flowering and setting seed in the second.

Biological control Using living organisms – including the wasp (*Encarsia formosa*) and predatory mite (*Phytoseiulus persimilis*) – to control pests and diseases.

Bisexual Flowers with both male and female reproductive parts (hermaphrodite).

Bog garden Area of waterlogged soil – that does not dry out in summer – for plants that grow in the wild in such conditions. If the garden does not have such an area, it can be created by siting it next to a pond where the water is made to seep from the latter to the former, or using pond liner with holes pierced in it, buried under the ground.

Bolting Producing flowers and seed prematurely.

Bottom heat Artificial heat applied via electric cabling under the compost (soil mix)

Annual (*Dianthus* 'Mrs Sinkins')

Biennial (*Oenothera biennis*)

Ericaceous (*Rhododendron* 'Brilliant Blue')

to stimulate seed germination or rooting, in a greenhouse, to get quicker results than will occur in the colder conditions outside.

Bract A modified leaf that emerges at the base of a flower and, when large and brightly coloured, is often confused with the actual flower.

Budding The means of propagation in which the bud of one plant is grafted on to another plant.

Cold frame Outside glass-covered garden frame, without artificial heat, used for germinating seeds and getting seedlings and larger plants to acclimatize to outdoor conditions.

Compost Organic matter that has been gathered together and kept while it decomposes, being eventually used as a mulch.

Cotyledons The first set of leaves on a germinated seed, and which are invariably different from the second (true) set.

Crown That part of a plant that sits on, or just above, soil level, and from which new stems appear.

Cultivar A cultivated variety that first occurred naturally or through breeding.

Cutting That part of a plant – whether root, leaf, or shoot – that has been removed at various stages of growth and used to create a brand new plant.

Deciduous A plant that sheds or loses its foliage at the end of the growing season.

Dioecious Indicates that the male and female parts occur on separate plants. Usually mentioned when you need to buy a male and female to produce fruit.

Dormant The period when a plant rests before breaking into growth as more favourable growing conditions emerge.

Ericaceous Those plants requiring acid soil if they are to thrive. Typical examples include camellias, heathers and rhododendrons.

Etiolated Feeble, spindly, over-long, often bleached growth occurring in poor light.

Evergreen A plant that retains its leaves through more than one growing season. Most shed and replace their leaves throughout the year, rather than all in one season.

Frost hardy Plants that can survive temperatures to -5°C (41°F).

Frost tender Plants that should not be exposed to temperatures that dip below 5°C (41°F).

Fully hardy Plants that can stay outside all year because they can survive at -15°C (5°F).

Germination The process by which a seed evolves into a young plant, so that it has both roots and shoots.

Graft When the shoot of one plant is permanently attached and secured to the rootstock of another so that the two grow together and function as one.

Ground cover Typically low-growing plants that are valued because they spread across the soil surface and block out weeds.

Hardening off Plants that have been raised in a protected, artificial environment being exposed to conditions closer to those outdoors before going permanently outside.

Heel cutting A cutting with a sliver of bark or wood attached that minimizes the possibility of rot.

Insecticide Chemical used to kill unwanted insects.

Internode The length of stem lying between two nodes.

Frost hardy (*Alyssum spinosum* 'Roseum')

Frost tender (*Impatiens walleriana*)

Fully hardy (*Anemone blanda*)

John Innes This is not a brand name but a recipe for potting composts (soil mixes), with the different numbers (1 to 3) denoting the relative fertilizer strength with No. 3, the strongest, being used on long-term, greedy plants (shrubs). Seedlings can only take in small amounts of nutrients and would be damaged by higher concentrations.

Lateral Growing from the side.

Layering When a stem is used to create a new plant. It needs to be bent down to, and kept in contact with, the soil so that it has a chance to root. When the roots have formed the stem can be severed from the parent and used as an independent plant.

Leaf axil The angle between the stem and the leaf or its stalk.

Leaf cutting Using a leaf, or a portion of a leaf, to propagate new plants.

Leaf mould Extremely useful dark brown, friable, organic substance made from rotted, decayed leaves that is high in humus but low in nutrients. Used as a mulch and soil conditioner. It occurs naturally in woodlands where the ground is covered in fallen, rotting leaves – but note that it is illegal to collect it from the wild.

Microclimate The local climate within a specific area (or part of a garden) that is different from the conditions elsewhere, for example caused by sheltering walls providing greater protection than elsewhere in the landscape.

Monoecious Each individual plant has both male and female flowers.

Mulch

Offset (*Sempervivum tectorum*)

Pollination

Mound layering Piling earth up around an established plant so that when the stems are kept in contact with the soil (as in layering) they start to root. The rooted stems can be cut from the parent plant and used as new plants. Very useful technique where lots of new plants are required.

Mulch A layer of organic or inorganic material placed on the ground, typically around plants, for several reasons. It protects the roots in cold winters, it helps keep moisture locked in the ground so that it does not quickly evaporate, and organic types improve the soil structure and feed plants as worms drag it underground.

Node The point at which shoots or leaves emerge from a stem.

Offset A small, young plant that naturally (and vegetatively) occurs, being attached (and easily separated from) the parent. Most commonly seen on bulbs and other plants with rosettes of growth (such as *Sempervivums*).

Petiole A leaf stalk.

pH The measure of a soil's acidity or alkalinity.

Photosynthesis The essential process by which a plant absorbs the energy from sunlight using chlorophyll, with carbon dioxide and water being converted into sugars and oxygen.

Pinching out Removing the growing tip of a (usually) young plant, activating replacement buds further down, thereby giving a bushier and/or more floriferous plant.

Pollination When pollen is transferred by various means (including insects, animals, wind, etc.) from the male anther to the female stigma.

Potting on When a plant's root system is too large for its current container and it needs to be moved into a larger one, giving room for further growth.

Potting up Inserting a seedling or cutting into a pot filled with compost (soil mix).

Pricking out Transferring a seedling or young cutting from its first container into a slightly larger one, giving it more room to grow.

Rhizome An underground or soil-level, usually horizontal, fleshy storage organ producing both roots and top growth.

Rootstock A plant used in a graft to provide the roots.

Runner The colloquial name for a spreading, underground shoot that bears new growth.

Scion A plant used to provide the top growth to be joined to the rootstock.

Sport A shoot that shows a different characteristic (e.g. colour) from the rest of the plant. It can be propagated by taking cuttings.

Sucker A shoot that appears from the underground part of a plant, typically the roots. When it has rooted, it can be severed from the parent and used as a new plant unless it comes from the rootstock of a grafted plant, in which case it is best discarded because it will not resemble the attractive top growth, even though it might be extremely vigorous.

Tuber An underground storage organ formed from the roots or stem.

Union The point at which the rootstock and scion join together.

Variegation The often irregular arrangement of pigments on a leaf, usually caused by a mutation or even disease.

Rhizome (*Agapanthus* 'Loch Hope')

Scion (quince)

Tuber (*Dahlia* 'Fascination')

Index

Butomus umbellatus

Convallaria majalis

Eupatorium purpureum

Lilium longiflorum

Onopordum acanthium

Pelargonium 'Moon Maiden'

Petunia x *hybrida* 'Storm Lavender'

Tagates patula

AUTHOR'S
ACKNOWLEDGEMENTS
With thanks to the Dowager
E. de Pauley, Alexander, Barney,
the directors and staff at RBA
productions, and especially
the very talented, upbeat editor
Felicity Forster who knocked this
massive enterprise into shape and
skilfully made everything happen.

PUBLISHER'S
ACKNOWLEDGEMENTS
George Drye, estate manager,
kindly provided plant material
and allowed us to shoot in
the gardens and glasshouses
at Lamport Hall
(*www.lamporthall.co.uk*).

Thank you to Angus and Jo
Lock, Ian and Wendy Hall,
Tony and Anne White, and
Jim Butlin, who also provided
plants from their gardens.

Philippa Anderson of Haxnicks
(*www.haxnicks.co.uk*) supplied many
of the tools and equipment used
in the photographs.

The publisher would also like
to thank the following for
allowing their photographs
to be reproduced in the book
(t=top, b=bottom, l=left,
r=right, m=middle).
Alamy: 231tl. Felicity Forster:
54bl, 65bl, 65bm, 65br, 161tl,
209tmr. iStockphoto: 33bl,
33bm, 133tl. Photolibrary: 30tr,
31br, 33br, 41t, 47bm, 61b, 64t,
65m, 99b, 111bl, 115tr, 184t,
190br, 223br, 224tm, 225tm.

Verbena bonariensis